The Millennial Reign of the Messiah

CRAIG M WHITE

authorHOUSE®

AuthorHouse™
1663 Liberty Drive
Bloomington, IN 47403
www.authorhouse.com
Phone: 833-262-8899

Published by AuthorHouse 02/13/2024

ISBN: 979-8-8230-1937-8 (sc)
ISBN: 979-8-8230-1936-1 (e)

Library of Congress Control Number: 2023923863

TABLE OF CONTENTS

PART 1: THE EARLY YEARS OF THE KINGDOM ON EARTH

PART 2: THE MESSIAH AND HIS GLORIOUS KINGDOM

PART 5: APPENDICES

LIST OF TABLES AND CHARTS

LIST OF ILLUSTRATIONS

ACKNOWLEDGMENTS

The writing of this book has been an exercise in extensive Bible study, merging of old writings, reflection, receiving good advice, and patience.

My interest in the Millennium all began with conversations within the family and my grandmother in the late 1960s and early 1970s, who had a very rudimentary belief in this area of the Scriptures.

Reading the books by various authors and later by various Churches greatly expanded my understanding of the Millennium. My own studies delved ever more into the subject, and a series of studies were developed in which most Scriptures pertaining to the subject were analysed and explained.

My studies led to a desire to assemble a book on the subject. It has always been something I wanted to undertake for decades. Finally, in 2022, I felt the need to combine and integrate the many years of readings and studies.

God must always receive the glory, and so He is acknowledged as the One Who has opened our eyes to this wonderful truth.

My family comes next due to the religious upbringing and robust discussions around the dinner table or at family socials. This, and so many other aspects of the Scriptures, were discussed and debated.

Upon writing this book, a number of people were gracious and kind enough to provide advice or to examine particular chapters with feedback and corrections.

Rand Martens read through the entire draft from cover to cover, applying his skills to inform me of necessary changes. It was an immense task for anyone to slowly but surely pore through an entire manuscript of over 300 pages and over 130,000 words.

Susan Heming also waded through the manuscript, providing much-needed advice, suggestions, and corrections. Of particular value was her incredible effort at finding the Bible versions that are quoted throughout. This was a tedious but necessary task in helping to identify the particular version that is quoted.

Daniel Russo's contribution in wading through these pages and making suggestions for changes and contributing to the reviews is very much appreciated.

I thank Angelica Ponferrada for her enormous help with upgrading the website. This was done in a professional manner and was very helpful as expressed by so many.

The cover was designed by Nathan McClain. Someone with these abilities was most needed, and his skills in bringing this about were exceptional.

I would also like to express my appreciation for pastor Steve Buchanan for reviewing the book. As well as Michael Armstrong who also spent many hours poring over these hundreds of pages and finding grammatical errors that needed correcting.

Many others also read through specific chapters with input and advice: Chris Rowland, Dan Love, Don Hooser, Jeff Perkins, John Guenther, John Van der Have, Leonie Peers, Michael Evans, and Rose Difley.

Each and every one of them contributed or provided input that helped to bring this book to fruition. Their time and effort spent in this project can only be described as "awesome."

And last, but not least, I acknowledge the publishing team for their efforts in expediting this book's publication.

To all of you (and any others I may have missed), a big thank you from my heart!

PREFACE

This author will normally not write much on a subject unless he is value adding and enlarging upon it, providing new and unique information and insights, or filling in gaps in a subject, doctrine. You will find that this book fulfills each of these criteria.

This book concerns the 1,000-year reign referred to in Revelation 20:1-6 and many other Scriptures.

We need to make this topic come alive and relevant for our times. To make it interesting and engaging. To explore deeply God's Word; to examine and teach all that is possible on the subject instead of a limited approach to this essential doctrine.

As such before you is the book *The Millennial Reign of the Messiah*, the basis of which is a table that incorporates most Scriptures on this period and assembles them into categories such as the new temple, the economy and role of Israel and so forth (refer to chapter seven). By breaking down the Millennium into its component parts, we will have a better understanding of it and the reader may find that aspects of it may differ from one's expectations. Prepare for a few surprises.

Integrating a number of previous articles and studies into a single document was difficult due to the nature and content of each, but this extensive work has helped me to produce a single volume with the most comprehensive study I am able to produce.

Finally, I would like to thank all those that provided encouragement in getting this task completed and the various discussions with friends around the subject of the Millennium that have occurred over time. All this has provided motivation and energy to complete the book.

INTRODUCTION

The aim of this book is to present the most thorough presentation possible of the future Kingdom of God on earth (sometimes termed *World Tomorrow* throughout), to explore it in detail and to uncover every Scripture one is able to. The purpose is to present a complete picture and understanding of the Messiah's reign as possible, thereby directing worship and glory to Him.

To enable this to be accomplished in this book, I need to restrain its length and to do this, what could be lengthy and tedious explanations of this or that aspect of the Kingdom, I have incorporated a number of tables, charts and Bible studies to this end.

This may be a bit unusual, but the aim is to get the message across to the reader without burdening them with a tome that they may not read from cover to cover.

In writing this book, I found that my research and previous writings naturally fell into four areas which in turn became the overall structure for this book:

- The Early Years of the Kingdom on Earth
- The Messiah and His Glorious Kingdom
- The Religious System Established
- The Nations in the World Tomorrow

In fact, my hope is that due to the set-out of the book, the reader can read and study parts of it that initially interests them and come back and read the rest at his or her leisure. In such a case, I would recommend studying the following tables in the first instance to gain an overview for this wonderful 1,000-reign:

- The Sequence of Events During the Millennium (table 2 refers)
- Analysing the Kingdom on Earth (table 9 refers)

From the above one could be forgiven in thinking that this is more of a study manual and guide to this doctrine. After all it is designed to make you think, cross-reference and look deeply into this critical doctrine.

The Wonderful World Tomorrow has been a central theme to the message of the Churches of God and other groups. It is an essential aspect of God's Plan and covered in regard to national salvation in Part Four, *The Nations in the World Tomorrow*.

It is the time that the Messiah returns to this planet to rescue humanity and to establish His reign on earth. In other words, it is the essence of the true Gospel message – the Good News of God's Kingdom established upon the earth.

Yet outside of the Church of God there are many others that have written books and articles on the subject or made contributions to commentaries discussing or mentioning the subject.

These include many conservative scholars and commentators, Jehovah's Witnesses, Sunday Adventists and Christadelphians. Some Protestant scholars who hold similar views on His reign include: John Nelson Darby, John Walvoord, Charles Ryrie, Norman Geisler, Chuck Missler, Walter Martin, Rousas Rushdoony, Greg Bahnsen, Gary North, John Bright, Herman Ridderbos, George Beasley-Murray and Gregory Beale.

They understood much about the Millennium, but not necessarily all the details. In other aspects they have insights that we should take note of.

Given the comprehensive nature of this work, it is unavoidable that there might be details of the Millennium the reader might not be aware of and even shocked about - it will not be a period that is a bed of roses and yet it will be immeasurably better than man's world under the influence of Satan and his minions.

It is now up to the reader to find out more about God's future Kingdom on earth – beginning by reading this book and looking up the many Scriptures quoted to support explanations throughout and to continue exploring this essential subject.

NB: this book presupposes that the reader has some knowledge of the modern identity of the Israelitish peoples, given Israel's role during the Millennium. In short, the northwest Europeans (Anglo-Saxons, Kelts and Nordics) descend from the sons of Jacob, whose name was changed to Israel.

PART ONE

THE EARLY YEARS OF THE KINGDOM ON EARTH

THE RETURN OF THE MESSIAH

Aт the outset we should have an overview of the events leading up to His return. The section below provides that outline at a high level, devoid of much detail.

An outline in effect acts as a large framework of overview for the subject. One the overall plan is grasped, infill can be provided to 'flesh out' the subject into topics and detail. In other words, we approach the subject step-by-step instead of rushing into it with preconceived ideas.

OUTLINE OF EVENTS LEADING TO CHRIST'S RETURN

Table 1 Sequence of Events in the End-Times

Order	Event	Supporting Scriptures
1	Great Tribulation (also known as Jacob's Trouble. The focus of these times is to punish and 'break' Israel).	Matt 24:4-8; Rev 6:1-8.
2	Signs in the Heavens (these herald or warn of the coming Day of the Lord; Israel also 'wakes up' with hope that their Redeemer is coming to rescue them).	Matt 24:29-30; Luke 21:25; Joel 2:30-32; Rev 6:12-17; Hos 6:1-2.
3	Day of the Lord (this punishes those nations that had invaded and enslaved Israel and humbles mankind. It is the time of God's intervention in human affairs and Christ's return as Messiah at the end of that one year period).	Joel 2:1; Rev 6:15-17; 11:18; 14:19; 15:1; Ob 1:15.

The Messiah's rule will be a time of tremendous revitalisation and renewal of everything: people, animals, plant life, soil, the environment, together with a new economic and financial system and a religion that is true and pure.

For example, when the Messiah returns, He will restore all of the nations and peoples outlined in Genesis 10 to their original condition with each enjoying incredible blessings, developing their own cultures and lifestyles, economies and so on within the bounds of His Law and Truth. He will establish a New Order under His Law – an Order unlike man has ever seen and utterly different to man's attempts at World Order. All nations will even have that great means of cultural transmission – their own national language (Is 19:18; Dan 7:14; Zech 8:23), but there shall also be a single universal tongue, enabling the nations to communicate and develop commercial relations (Zeph 3:9) devoid of tensions and wars.

The nations will eventually be at peace and will dwell in perfect harmony – but not necessarily overnight. No more will they fear invasion by hostile armies; or captivity; nor will they fear globalisation destroying their beautiful and unique identities which God has bestowed upon all peoples.

There is coming instead, a time of national self-determination within the context of God's New Order and His Law - self-determination under His Government and in harmony and cooperation between all the nations.

A wonderful world tomorrow that is MUCH better than today's does not mean it will be perfect because humans will not be sinless spirits and because they will be subject to choice and human nature. A link to a good sermon on the subject is found in the footnotes.[1]

Yet, overall, it will be much better than today's world.

SEQUENCE OF MAJOR EVENTS DURING THE MILLENNIUM

Prior to getting into the details of the Millennium, let us gain additional insights based on the previous table overview and thereby develop a quick understanding of the steps involved with the setting up of His Kingdom across the earth. The table below provides this overview and it is important to look up some of the Scriptures as part of a personal study of this 1,000 year period.

Table 2 Sequence of Events During the Millennium

Order	Event	Supporting Scriptures
1.	The Messiah returns to Israel and the world, setting foot on the Mount of Olives. He is the Melchizedek Priest-King with the accompanying saints composing the Royal Priesthood (i.e. kings and priests) under Him.	Zech 14:4; Acts 1:9-12; Matt 2:6; 15:24; John 1:49; Rev 5:10; IPet 2:9.
2.	Beast and False Prophet cast into the lake of fire which will be burning for 1,000 years.	Rev 19:20; 20:10; Is 30:33; 66:24.
3.	Satan exiled into a pit. Does this commence a new Jubilee cycle?	Rev 20:1-6.

---

[1] Here is a sermon from 1976 and is worthwhile listening to. Go to www.friendsofsabbath.org/ABC/Lectures%20&%20Sermons/HL%20Hoeh%20sermons/

What was pleasing to me, was how it gelled with this author's articles over the years and my presentation on the early years of the Millennium – that those years will not be a 'bed of roses' – in fact, right through the Millennium there will be tests on peoples and issues to resolve to enhance character development.

Order	Event	Supporting Scriptures
4.	Close by is Mount Zion where He will rule from (will there will be separate political and religious centres?).	Ps 2:6; 76:2; 135:21; Joel 3:16.
5.	Scattered and enslaved Israelites begin to repent and are brought into proximity to the Holy Land where rebels are purged in the wilderness (Is 30:18; Jer 50:20; Ezek 20:38, 42-44) thus reviving the nation (Ezekiel 36).	Ezek 20:38, 42-44; Matt 19:28.
1.	After the purging, the righteous Israelites enter the Promised Land in the Second Exodus (typed by the First Exodus and later some Judahites returning from Babylonian captivity).	1). Deut 4:26-29 (cp Is 55:1; Hos 6:1-3; Lam 3:23-24; Deut 30:1-5), 30-31; 30:4 (cp Matt 24:31); Is 10:20-22; Zeph 3:18-20. 2). Is 1:11-16; 27:12-13 (it would appear that this may begin at the 7th Trump of Revelation). See also Zech 9:14; Is 10:20-22; Jer 16:14-15; 23:3, 7-8; 31:8-9; 43:1-6; 50:3-5; Ezek 20:42-43.
2.	His rule extends throughout Jerusalem and the Promised Land from the Euphrates to the Nile. The desert flowers!	Ezek 36:35; Is 51:3.
3.	Christ completes His ministry to Israel (Dan 9:24-27).	Is 59:20-21; Jer 31:31-34; Heb 8:8; Ezek 16:59-60; 36:26-28; Hos 2:16-19.
4.	Israel and Judah are re-united and a New Covenant established between them (Ezekiel 37) and their Messiah after 3 ½ years of His ministry. The Marriage Covenant with the Church is made at the resurrection prior to this).	Jer 31:1, 7-9; 50:4-5; Ezek 11:17; 34:12-13; 37:19-22. Other related Scriptures include: Jer 12: 14-15; 16:15; 23:3-4, 7-8; 24:6-7; 30:3, 8-10; 33:6-9; 50:4-5, 19-20; Ps 14:7; 53:6; 68:6; 30:4; Lev 26: 42-46; Jer 3:17-19; Zech 12:10-14; Rom 11:26; Acts 15:16-17; Hos 1:11; 2:14; Mic 2:12; 5:4-7; Zech 8:7-8; 10:9-12.
5.	Israel assigned tribal allocations (does this occur before or after the attack by the forces of Ezek 39 & 39?)	Ezek 48.

6.	Gog and Magog et al attempt to invade the Holy Land and will be brought to heel. This may occur, prior to the completion of the Temple.
	    The above nations defeated and repent. Meschech is probably the leading Japhetic nation as Mizraim is the leading Hamite nation.
	    A great earthquake shakes the region.
		Ezekiel 38 and 39.
		
		Ezek 38:19-20.

7.	The New Temple is built and inaugurated (presumably it is being built during the 3 ½ years of Christ's ministry to Israel). God's glory fills the Temple (i.e. Christ as the Messiah enters the Temple).	Ezek 40-48 (Cp Acts 2:2; Is 44:28; Zech 6:13. Ezek 43:5.

Order	Event	Supporting Scriptures
8.	Israel is trained for world leadership and becomes His battle-axe.	Ps 47:1-9; Deut 28:12-13; Is 61;1-9; Zech 8:23; Is 41:15-16; 42;1-6, 10-12; 49:1-10, 22-24; 54:3-7; 55:4-5; 60:1-16; 66:19-20; Mic 4:13.
9.	Israel set up as leading nation of the world – reigns under Christ and the saints for 1,000 years – to be a light to the world by re-colonising parts of the world.	Acts 1:6-7; Gen 13:16; Deut 32:9; Is 54:2-3; 61:4; 26:15; 27:6; 49:8; Ezek 28:25-26; Ezek 19:10; (cp Gen 49:22); Amos 9:14-15; Ob 17.
10.	Israel swoops upon some nations to take them under the control of the Messiah's government.	Jer 51:20; Is 14:1-2; 60:5-16; 19:17; 61:4-9; 66:19-21; Ezek 25:13-17; Ob 1:17-21; Zech 9:11-14; 10:3-10; 12:7-8; 14:14; Amos 9:11-12; Zeph 2:7-13.
11.	The Messiah's rule through the saints and Israel is gradually extended throughout the world until all are brought under His rule. Rebellions are dealt with sternly.	Ps 149:1-9; Is 47:1-9.
12.	Assyria repents (leading Shemite nation).	Is 19:21-25.
13.	Egypt (Mizraim) repents (leading Hamitic nation).	Is 19:1-25; Zech 14:18-19.
14.	Rebellions and national sins decrease during the Millennium as peoples and individuals are converted until there is world peace and prosperity National sins gradually decline over decades and possibly centuries.	Typology of Numbers 29:12-38 applies.
15.	The restoration of all things[1]: a new economy, nature of animals, new language etc gradually unfold across the world in tandem with or alongside the above – the Wonderful World Tomorrow achieved!	Act 3:20-22.

With the basic overview under our belt, let us now detail a most significant event in God's Plan to restore or reconcile all mankind to Himself.

It entails finalising the blessings given to Abraham and the tribes of Israel (Gen 12:1-3; 28:2-4; 48:4-6; 49:1-33) – because it is through the saints and Israel that God will rule the earth. But, because the Millennium will not be a 'bed of roses' nor an overnight event, it will take some time to expand His rule over the entire earth and to bring peace and prosperity for all nations. This will become apparent as we delve deeper into this period.

---

[2] "In Matthew 19:28 Jesus declared that 'the regeneration' would take place 'when the Son of man shall sit on the throne of his glory.' His terminology is significant. It indicates that when Christ, as the Son of man (as a human, a kinsman of mankind) rules the earth, there will be a return to the original state that existed when the earth was born, which is recorded in Genesis and involved mankind's tenant possession or administration of the earth as God's representative. Christ taught that He will begin to exercise that rule when He returns in glory with His holy angels (Mtt. 25:31) ... Peter declared that 'the times of refreshing' and 'the times of the restitution of all things' will come when God sends Christ back to be personally present on the earth ... F. F. Bruce wrote that **'the restitution' to which Peter referred in Acts 3:21 'appears to be identical with' 'the regeneration' to which Jesus referred in Mat. 19:28, and that the restoration involved will include 'a renovation of all nature**.'" (Renald E. Showers, *Maranatha, Our Lord Come*, pp. 86-87) [emphasis mine]

ISRAEL'S SECOND EXODUS

INTRODUCTION

IN THIS CHAPTER (WHICH IS more a Bible study than anything else) I attempt to answer questions that have come to mind based on obvious applications of so many Scriptures. Also, this chapter concentrates on an issue which has been neglected or forgotten due to a number of reasons, not least political correctness/wokeness and its impact upon theology – Israel's importance as a tool of God in gentile conversions during the coming Word Tomorrow.

While a fine study could be presented on how many Old Testament prophecies are typological or will be fulfilled by the Church in a dual sense, with Israel, the concentration of this chapter is on Israel for the aforementioned reasons. Let us not forget what we have learned from our spiritual forebears, but rather let us go deeper and deeper into these truths as never before, with more information and proof for our long-held and cherished beliefs.

The Church does not replace Israel as we shall see – it works alongside Israel and both are integral to God's plan.[3]

We can find much support in this belief by a number of conservative commentators and researchers such as John Whitcomb, Walter Kaiser et al. For example:

> "God will fulfill His covenant promises to Abraham, Isaac and Jacob. God's "chosen people" **will enjoy their "promised land" some day, after they have experienced national regeneration** (Jer. 31:31-34; Rom. 11:25-26). Not just for the Church, but also for Israel, "the gifts and the calling of God are irrevocable" (Rom. 11:29, ESV)." (John Whitcomb, "The Millennial Temple of Ezekiel 40-48," *The Diligent Workman Journal*, May 1994, p. 21). [emphasis mine]

---

[3] A good work on this is by Michael J. Vlach, *The Church as a Replacement of Israel: An Analysis of Supersessionism*, *EDIS Israelogie*, (Peter Lang, Frankfurt am Main, Germany, 2009).

"... the NT, including the book of Hebrews, **does not teach that Israel has been forever set aside**. It *does* teach the end of the Old Covenant given by God to Israel through Moses. Yet it does *not* reject the Abrahamic Covenant (which the New Covenant of Jeremiah 31 further elaborates ..."

"Israel will indeed be under a New Covenant program, not the Old Covenant given to Moses which was not designed to guarantee salvation." (John Whitcomb, "Christ's Atonement and Animal Sacrifices in Israel," *Grace Theological Journal*, Vol. 6, No. 2, 1985, pp. 203, 216) [emphasis mine]

"**There are just too many historical events and too many explicit texts** (some well beyond the Babylonian Exile, e.g., Zech. 10:8-12; Rom. 9-11) **to shut the door on a revived Israelite nation** thesis." (Walter Kaiser, "The Old Promise and the New Covenant: Jeremiah 31:31-34," *Journal of the Evangelical Theological Society*, Vol. 15, No. 1, 1972, p. 15) [emphasis mine]

"Thus in the OT and literature of the Second Temple period there exists an interplay in expectation: Yahweh as **God will judge and restore his people**, and his agents will carry out that ministry of judgment and restoration." (Robert L. Webb, *John the Baptizer and Prophet: A Socio-Political Study*, p. 258)[4] [emphasis mine]

Why adopt watering-down of this supremely important doctrine? Why not simply accept the plain truth? Another author's views agrees with the above:

"Here not only giving the millennial nations 'cleansed' or 'purified' lips, as regenerated peoples, but apparently also in the sense that 'lip' signifies 'language' (Gen. 11:1, Gen. 11:6-7, Gen. 11:9) ... That would be not all that surprising, since **Israel will be the chief nation in that economy (Deu. 28:13) and Jerusalem in that day will be the religious and governmental capital of the millennial earth** (Isa. 2:2-3; Zec. 8:20-23). Moreover, it is all the more probable since the judgment of the nations at the second advent will eventuate in the destruction of the satanic world system ... That system had its beginning in ancient Babylon with its pride, idolatry, and rebellion (Gen. 10:8-10; Gen. 11:1-6). The gift of a pure speech will remove the curse of Babel, and it will anticipate the great millennial outpouring of the Spirit (Joel 2:28-32), of which Pentecost (Acts 2:1-11) was an illustration." (Merrill Unger, *Unger's Commentary on the Old Testament*. Note on Zeph 3:9) [emphasis mine]

---

[4] Cohen in *Israel and the Arab World*, for instance, states that "according to Commodianus when Christ returns it will be at the head not of an angelic host but **of the descendants of the ten lost tribes of Israel, which have survived in hidden places, unknown to the rest of the world**" (p. 28). [emphasis mine. We would agree partially with Commodianus who lived in the 3rd century that Christ will head up the revived tribes of Israel but we would disagree with his point about angelic forces, for Christ will come with the angels and also resurrected saints].

"The LORD doth build up Jerusalem: he gathereth together the outcasts of Israel.

He healeth the broken in heart, and bindeth up their wounds.

He sheweth his word unto Jacob, his statutes and his judgments unto Israel.

He hath not dealt so with any nation: and *as for his* judgments, they have not known them.

Praise ye the LORD." (Ps 147:2-3, 19-20, KJV)

"But he that knew not, and did commit things worthy of stripes, shall be beaten with few *stripes*. For unto whomsoever much is given [e.g. Israel], of him shall be much required: and to whom men have committed much, of him they will ask the more." (Luke 12:48, KJV)

What is the significance of Shem – forefather of Israel?

Shem was to be the carrier of God's way of life: "And he said, Blessed be Jehovah, the God of Shem" (Gen 9:26, MKJV). His name means Name! That is, he was famous, honourable, righteous, noted, man of renown and noble. His descendants were known as the Noble Ones.

In verse 27 Moses wrote that "God shall enlarge Japheth, and he shall dwell in the tents of Shem and Canaan shall be his servant." (KJV) While this may mean that Shem shall dominate Japheth, there is another meaning which should be explored.[5]

The clear inference is that God shall dwell with Shem as in a tabernacle which God did indeed do in ancient Israel and He also dwells in spiritual Israelites through the holy spirit. Similar wording is used in relation to Israel in Isaiah 54:

> "Enlarge the place of your tent, and let the curtains of your habitations be stretched out; do not hold back; lengthen your cords and strengthen your stakes.
>   For you will spread abroad to the right and to the left, and your offspring will possess the nations and will people the desolate cities." (Is 54:2-3, ESV)

Shem fathered Arphaxad, the light-bringer. From Arphaxad we have Salah, followed by Eber, Peleg, Reu, Serug, Nahor, Terah and then Abram. This is the line that God has worked with both spiritually/religiously and physically/nationally.[6] He has remained faithful to Israel ever since.

---

[5] Take a look at Ex 25:8; Num 9:15; IISam 7:6; IChron 15:1; Ps 78:59-60; Is 40:22; Jer 10:20; Rev 21:3.

[6] An old booklet explains this succinctly: "**QUESTION: I understand you teach that God's promises to Abraham were two-fold-race and grace. Would you explain what these promises mean?**

ANSWER: Many fail to comprehend the **underlying dual nature of God's promise**. Abraham and his seed were promised not only great material blessings, but ultimately salvation as well. Unfortunately, the latter promise-which is by far more important-is misunderstood by many. After Abraham proved that he would obey God unconditionally, even to the point of being willing to sacrifice his beloved son, Isaac, God promised "That

Here we have what commentators so long ago described as 'the righteous line' or as we would say today, the lineage which God was working with.

ISRAEL'S ORIGIN

Protestant commentators in the mid-nineteenth century through to the early twentieth, wrote of a 'righteous line' from Noah, Shem, Arphaxad, down to Abraham, Isaac, and Jacob (Israel). God chose to work through these people.

God started His plan in a small way, like the grain of a mustard seed. Prior to Noah's Flood, there were just a handful of people He worked with. After the Flood, through Noah, Shem, Arphaxad and others, this number gradually grew through Israel's descendants who were called to a physical salvation and blessings. Amongst them were people with the spirit of God within them. Later, this spiritual dimension grew when the New Testament Church was raised up and continues to this day. More people will be called during the Millennium and the Last Great Day periods – so God is starting His Plan with a small number of people and gradually expanding calling more and more of mankind until during the reign of the Messiah He will call all of mankind, through Israel and the saints.

One only has to look at the British Empire with its expansion and religious teachers as a forerunner. And how the Church operated out of Israel in these last days, to spread the True Gospel and the Israel Message because it is only the prosperity and freedoms that the 'lost' tribes of Israel provides which offers the Church the capacity to spread the Gospel. Israel and spiritual Israel operate in tandem (see Rom 9:3-8; Luke 22:28-30).

Have a read of Scriptures such as Is 42:1; 45:4; 52:1-2, 13; 65:9 and many more to find out how important Israel is to God's Plan – here Israel is called His "elect" (it should be remembered, though that some of these scriptures are obviously dual, referring also to Christ Himself). In the New Testament we are told that "unless those days should be shortened, no flesh would be saved. But for the elect's sake, those days shall be shortened." (Matt 24:22, MKJV) And this was prior to the formation of the Church. While the Church is spiritual Israel and is also called the elect in places such as Col 3:12 etc, this does not mean that Israel is no longer His elect - which replacement theology attempts to teach. Therefore, because of the elect (both physical and spiritual Israel), God will intervene in world affairs to ensure that life is not wiped off the face of this planet – reminiscent of ancient Egypt where He destroyed the firstborn (and thus an entire generation), though others survived.

---

in blessing I will bless thee, and in multiplying I will multiply thy seed as the stars of the heaven, and as the sand which is upon the sea shore; and thy seed shall possess the gate of his enemies; And in thy seed shall all the nations of the earth be blessed; because thou hast obeyed my voice" (Gen. 22:17-18). **The physical, material, national (RACE) blessings are included in what the Bible terms as "the birthright."**

... **The promise of salvation-of GRACE-was handed down through Judah but it comes, not as a birthright, but by GRACE.** It is an unmerited gift, God's pardon of sins through Jesus Christ the Messiah, who was of the tribe of Judah." (*In the Beginning. Answers to Questions from Genesis*, p. 11)

IN WHAT WAY IS ISRAEL A SPECIAL PEOPLE?

Nationally and religiously, Israel was to be a special people before God and to thereby bring light, truth and righteousness to the world. In Ex 19:5-6; Deut 28:1; Is 42:6; 43:1, 10-12, 21; 60:3; 61:6; 62:1-7 they are portrayed as God's witness.

From the aforementioned scriptures the Israelites were to function as God's representatives on earth, to administer it under Him. Below are a number of Scriptures proving the point:

> "And now if you will obey My voice indeed, and keep My covenant, then you shall be **a peculiar treasure to Me above all the nations**; for all the earth *is* Mine.
>
> And you shall be to Me a **kingdom of priests and a holy nation**. These *are* the words which you shall speak to the sons of Israel." (Ex 19:5-6, MKJV)[7]

> "And it shall be, because you listen to these judgments and keep and do them, Jehovah your God shall keep to you the covenant and the mercy which He swore to your fathers.
>
> And He will love you and bless you and multiply you. He will also bless the fruit of your womb, and the fruit of your land, your grain, and your wine, and your oil, the increase of your cattle, and the flocks of your sheep, in the land which He swore to your fathers to give you.
>
> You shall be blessed above all people. There shall not be male or female barren among you or among your cattle.
>
> And Jehovah will take away from you all sickness, and will put none of the evil diseases of Egypt which you know upon you. But He will lay them upon all who hate you.
>
> And you shall destroy all the people which Jehovah your God shall deliver you. Your eye shall have no pity upon them, neither shall you serve their gods, for *they will be* a snare to you." (Deut 7:12-16, MKJV)

> "And it will be, if you shall listen carefully to the voice of Jehovah your God, to observe *and* to do all His commandments which I command you today, Jehovah your **God will set you on high above all nations of the earth**." (Deut 28:1, MKJV)

> "For Jehovah's portion *is* His people. Jacob *is* the lot of **His inheritance**.
>
> He found him in a desert land, and in the deserted, howling wilderness. He led him about, He cared for him, He kept him as **the pupil of His eye**." (Deut 32:9-10, MKJV)

---

[7] "… the priestly calling has a missionary dimension insofar as the Israelites as a kingdom of priests would intercede on behalf of the other nations and be an example of the essence of living a life of sacrifice" (X. DeBroeck, *Becoming a Priestly People: A Biblical Theology of Liturgical Sacrifice as Spiritual Formation*, p. 48).

"In all likelihood, the expression 'a kingdom of priests' implies that God intends every Israelite to have a royal and priestly status… The Israelites shall enjoy the status that Adam and Eve had prior to their betrayal of God in the Garden of Eden…" (T. Desmond Alexander, *Exodus. Apollos Old Testament Commentary*, p. 369).

"I Jehovah have called You in righteousness, and will hold Your hand, and will keep You, and give You for a covenant of the people, for **a Light of the nations**." (Is 42:6, MKJV)

"The beasts of the field shall honor Me, the jackals and the ostriches; because I give waters in the wilderness, rivers in the desert, to give drink to **My people, My chosen.**
   This people *that* **I formed for Myself**; they shall declare My praise." (Is 43:20-21, MKJV)

"So says Jehovah, the Holy One of Israel, and the One who formed him, Do you ask Me of things to come? Do you give command to Me about My sons, and about the **work of My hands**?" (Is 45:11, MKJV)

"… and said to Me, You *are* **My servant, O Israel**, in whom I will be glorified." (Is 49:3, MKJV)

"But you will be named the priests of Jehovah; it will be said of you, **Ministers of our God**; you will eat the riches of the nations, and you will revel in their glory.
   For Zion's sake I will not be silent, and for Jerusalem's sake I will not rest, until its righteousness goes out as brightness, and her salvation as a burning lamp.
   And the **nations will see your righteousness**, and all kings your glory; and you will be called by a new name, which the mouth of Jehovah will name.
   You also will be a crown of glory in the hand of Jehovah, and a royal diadem in the hand of your God.
   You will no more be called Forsaken; nor will your land any more be called Desolate; but you will be called **My Delight** *is* in her, and your land, Married; for Jehovah delights in you, and your land is married.
   For *as* a young man marries a virgin, so will your sons marry you; and *as* the bridegroom rejoices over the bride, *so* will **your God rejoice over you**.
   I have set watchmen on your walls, O Jerusalem, who will not always be silent all the day nor all the night; you who remember Jehovah, do not be silent.
   And give Him no rest until He establishes and **makes Jerusalem a praise in the earth**." (Is 62:1-7, MKJV)

"The Portion of Jacob *is* not like them; for He *is* the Former of all things, and *Israel is* the rod of His inheritance. Jehovah of Hosts *is* His name.
   You *are* **My war-club** *and* **weapons of war; for with you I will shatter nations; and with you I will destroy kingdoms.**
   And with you I will shatter the horse and his rider; and with you I will shatter the chariot and his rider." (Jer 51:19-21, MKJV)

Notice that Israel was the apple or pupil of God's eye. Bullinger in the *Companion Bible* explains: "First occurrence of Heb. 'ishon, used of the small round dark pupil of the eye. Heb. = hole, gate, or door of the eye … called 'pupil' [in English] = a little girl." See also Ps 17:8 and Zech 2:8.

Israel was also God's bride and wife and He, the Husband, according to Ex 19; 20; Jer 3:14; Ex 16; Jer 31:32. For God to court and choose as wife one of the nations, tells us something about His choice.[8]

From the above we see that Israel currently has the primacy over all nations and will also have the primacy again in the Millennium as we shall see.

Finally, some consider Israel to have been an inferior people. Look at the following Scriptures that some use to 'prove' this:

> "Jehovah did not set His love upon you, nor choose you, because you were more in number than any people, for you *were* the fewest of all people.
>
> But because Jehovah loved you, and because He would keep the oath which He had sworn to your fathers, Jehovah has brought you out with a mighty hand and redeemed you out of the house of slaves, from the hand of Pharaoh king of Egypt.
>
> Therefore, know that Jehovah your God, He *is* God, the faithful God who keeps covenant and mercy with them that love Him and keep His commandments, to a thousand generations." (Deut 7:7-9, MKJV)

God was using a nation which was small in number, yet with qualities, to confound the other nations. There is nothing here to suggest that they were inferior. Rather, they possessed natural attributes which gave them a capacity to rule in service to the world - attributes that were inherited from their forefathers. Yet it was to little avail without the indwelling of the holy spirit and God's direction.

ISRAEL'S REWARDS FOR RIGHTEOUSNESS

Almost unbelievable blessings were offered Israel in Gen 29; 30; 49, Num 23; 24; Deut 7; 8; 33; Jud 5.

The letter to the Hebrews may be of some assistance with regard to the blessings in physical and spiritual aspects. Spiritual Israel is offered even "better" blessings – better than what? Let us now explore what the word "better" means in the book of Hebrews in association with *national* blessings and rewards for obedience.

- **Chapter 1:4** Christ Who is the image of the Father (Greek means to be an exact replica or impression as when metal is pressed into a die) is made **better than the angels** "for unto which of the angels said He at any time, "Thou art My Son, this day have I begotten you"?" Bullinger notes: "begotten, &c. = brought Thee to the birth. I.e. at resurrection, when the Son became the glorified federal Head of a new order of beings ... Quoted from Ps. 2:7, which, with Acts 13:33, tells us that this day was the day of His resurrection".[9]

---

[8] Other scriptures include: Deut 9:5; 4:33, 37; Ps 44:1-3; 47:4; IChron 17:20-21.

[9] See further information on this in my paper on the born again doctrine.

- **Chapter 6:9** speaking of the second death, Paul writes "But beloved, we are persuaded **better** things of you, and things that accompany salvation, though we thus speak". In other words, Paul was saying that their future is eternal life, not eternal death.
- **Chapter 7:7** in discussing Abraham and Melchizedek, "And without all contradiction, the less (Abraham) is blessed of the **better** (Melchizedek)". The discussion continues about the superiority of the Melchizedek priesthood over the Levitical priesthood. The discussion is not over whether the law or tithing is abolished, but concerning the better Melchizedek priesthood.
- **Chapter 7:19** Christians today have a **better hope** than the Israelites who did not have God's Spirit to keep the Law (cp Rom 8:3; Heb 8:8, 10)
- **Chapter 7:22** in addition we have a **better covenant** than the old
- **Chapter 8:6** here Paul emphasises again how we have a **better covenant and better promises** than given to Israel
- **Chapter 9:23 Christ's sacrifice was (infinitely) better** than those found in the book of Moses
- **Chapter 10:34** we have **better possessions** kept in heaven for us
- **Chapter 11:16** we also have a **better country** promised us, than the land of Canaan given to Israel
- **Chapter 11:40** God has promised us **better things** so that the Old Testament people of God could not be perfected without us
- **Chapter 12:24** Christ and the new covenant speak **better things** than that of Abel
- **Chapter 11:35** Christians are destined for a **better resurrection**. But what exactly is it better than?

What can we deduce from the above? What resurrection is the Christian promised, and which is it better than?

Upon examination of the above references to 'better', it is apparent that most of the comparisons that Paul uses are between the old covenant and the new; between physical and spiritual Israel. Logically, given this theme, it would likely follow that the old covenant Israelites will be resurrected to temporary, physical life (to be offered eternal life). While spiritual Israelites will be resurrected to eternal, immortal, spirit life. But by and large, the promises to Israel were futuristic only insofar as they applied to the well-being of their descendants and promises to those righteous amongst Israel generally related to the present. Other promises refer to the future reward or restoration of the nation, while the promises to spiritual Israelites were for spiritual blessings.

Eternal life was not promised to everyone under the old covenant, but neither were they to be denied a chance for eternal life under the new (or refreshed) covenant. During their life on earth, they were promised immense physical blessings which would last even to many generations extending to the return of the Messiah. At the completion of their physical life upon the earth, they go the way of all men with inevitable death and burial – their physical being disintegrating and their very molecules and atoms disappearing into the earth from whence we all originate.

They would have been aware of the possibility of eternal life, as it is clear that the saints of the Old Testament knew that this was God's purpose for man (cp Gen 3:22; Heb 11:8-11). It is also clear from several Old Testament scriptures that a future resurrection was commonly known (ISam 2:6; Job 14:14-15; 19:25-27; Ps 16:10; Is 26:19; Dan 12:2-3).

The Bible also speaks of a future restoration as a type of a 'physical resurrection' of Israel. Hos 6:1-2 and Ezekiel 37:1-14 are clear: a physical resurrection of Israel will occur. Will this be at the return of Christ when the saints will be resurrected to spirit life; during the Millennium; or at the Last Great Day? Do Dan 12:1-3 and Is 26:19-16; 27:6 reveal a resurrection of physical Israelites at the time of the first resurrection? The Bible gives us some clues.

Ezekiel 37 compares resurrected Israel to a great army (verse 10); similarly in the famous resurrection chapter, Paul states:

"For as in Adam all die, even so in Christ shall all be made alive,
   But every man in his own order [Gr for 'order' means army or body of soldiers
in succession]:
   Christ the firstfruit [hence reference to Him as the firstborn in Col 1:18];
   Afterward they that are Christ's, at His coming,
   Then cometh the end when He shall have delivered up the kingdom to God, even
the Father; when He shall have put down all rule and authority and power.
   For He must reign, till He hath put all enemies under His feet.
   The last enemy that shall be destroyed is death" (ICor 15:22-26, KJV).

From the above one gets the impression that there will be successive resurrections or successive parts to resurrections. For instance, in IThess 4:16-17 two parts to the resurrection of the saints are revealed: first those that are dead and a little later, those that are alive at His coming. Whether this be in a matter of seconds, minutes or hours of each other is not known. Similarly, at the resurrection of Christ to spirit, eternal life, there was also a resurrection to physical life of certain saints (Matt 27:51-53). These saints may have either had a premature death and were given some years to finish their natural lives; or they lived out their normal lives and God raised them to a short life as a witness to His might and glory which will be demonstrated again at the time of Christ's return and the resurrection of the saints.

So, Israel was promised a resurrection to physical life (Ezek 37) after which they will be offered eternal life.[10]

---

[10] Take a look at Matt 12:41-42 (also 10:12-15). Here we are told about what appears to be one successive generation rising up after another at the Last Great Day. If this be so, then it may be that the second resurrection may consist of successive generations rising up, overlapping with each other, over a period of time. Could this be for 1,000 years (an eighth day, so to speak) after the millennium? The 100 years mentioned in Is 65:20 refers to the life span of humans, not only to a 100-year period. In fact, looking at the context of that scripture through to verse 25, it appears millennial and thus could be a reference to persons living for 100 years either during the millennium or during the Last Great Day period. When we take into account that perhaps up to 40 billion or more humans have been on this earth since Adam and Eve, it is obvious that they cannot all be resurrected at the same time. An orderly approach of "every man in his own order" in overlapping generations starting with Adam, would seem to be a sensible approach.

DOES THE CHURCH REPLACE ISRAEL?

Some turn to Romans 9, claiming that the Church replaces Israel (that is they believe and teach replacement theology). This is not Biblical and denies God's intent and plan for the physical descendants of Israel and the birthright promises made to Abraham. In effect it is a counterfeit doctrine that undermines large portions of the Bible and prophecy.

Unfortunately, there are those who teach that Israel will be just another of the nations in the Millennium. However, Scripture indicates that God and His children (the saints) will rule the world *through* Israel (similarly, Satan rules the world through his physical agents, as a means of mirroring God's rule, but in a negative way).

Rather, the Church is spiritual Israel – the Israel of God (Gal 6:16; IPet 2:10; Eph 2:10), continuing the righteous line of men from Noah, Shem, Abraham through to Christ. This righteous line contained both physical and spiritual elements. The genetic line continues as a special people (the 'holy seed') He has and will use again for His purpose and rule over the earth.

Note the words of a specialist on the subject:

> "… the NT calls Gentile believers "the seed of Abraham" because of their union with Jesus Christ, "the Seed of Abraham" (Gal 3:6-29). Jesus as the Christ is the "Seed" who brings the blessings of the Abrahamic Covenant to Israel and the Gentiles (Gal 3:16; cf. Gen 22:17b-18). **The church today experiences in Christ some spiritual benefits that Israel and the nations will experience (with physical results) in the future when Jesus implements fully the blessings of the Abrahamic Covenant.** The NT, like the Old, views the complete fulfillment of the Lord's promises to Abraham as a future event (Matt 8:11; Acts 3:19-26; Rom 11:25-32". (Keith Essex, "The Abrahamic Covenant," *The Master's Seminary Journal*, Vol. 10, No. 2, 1999, p. 212) [emphasis mine]

The completion of these promises is indeed future and thus Millennial as we shall soon discover.

The righteous men in ancient Israel (e.g. Moses, certain judges, prophets and kings) comprised the spiritual order or component within Israel for their day. In that sense they were *spiritual* Israel among *physical* Israel. The Church is the continuation or perhaps in a way the successor organisation to them, paralleling Israel. Physical Israel is not called to eternal life yet, but spiritual Israel of both the Old and New Testament periods was. The Church in the New Testament period included gentiles who are spiritually (but not physically) grafted into Israel by entering into the same Covenant as Israelites with God.

That is why so many prophecies in the Old Testament which refer to Israel also refer to spiritual Israel in a dual sense (e.g. where we read *daughter of Zion, Thy People, My People* etc). The two go together and work in tandem.

It is with the New Testament Church that the New Covenant is emphasised, but it is already contained in the Old Testament, but now inclusive of gentiles that are being called.

"**If revelation is to recommence in the millennial kingdom, converted Israel must head humanity**. Jews and Gentiles stand on an equal footing, as both alike needing mercy; but **as regards God's instrumentalities for establishing His kingdom on earth, Israel is His chosen people**. The Israelite priest-kings on earth are what the transfigured priest-kings are in heaven... Earthly and heavenly glories shall be united in the twofold election. Elect Israel in the flesh shall stand at the head of the earthly; the elect spiritual church, the Bride, in the heavenly. These elections are not merely for the good of the elect, but for whom they minister. The heavenly Church is elected, not merely to salvation, but to rule in love, and minister blessings over the earth, as king-priests" (Fausset et al, "The Revelation of St. John the Divine," in *A Commentary, Critical and Explanatory, on the Old and New Testaments*, p. 722). [emphasis mine]

As we have seen, one conservative scholar, John Whitcomb, truly understands that Israel is to have a major role in the *Age to Come* and is one of a small percentage that do so – purely based on a plain reading of the promises and prophecies:

"Does this mean, then, that Israel, the chosen theocratic nation, with its unconditional Abrahamic Covenant guarantee of a land (Gen 12:1; 13:14-17; 15:18-21; Deut 30:5) and divine blessing (Gen 12:2-3) has been forever set aside nationally in favor of the Church? This has indeed been the conclusion of many Christian theologians from the days of the church fathers down to modern times. Israel as a national entity is seen as apostate and therefore broken off forever as a distinct nation in the program of God... **However, the NT, including the book of Hebrews, does not teach that Israel has been forever set aside** ... it does *not* reject the Abrahamic Covenant (which the New Covenant of Jeremiah 31 further elaborates)." ("Christ's Atonement and Animal Sacrifices in Israel," *Grace =Theological Journal*, Vol. 6, No. 2, 1985, pp. 202-03) [emphasis mine]

In footnote 6 (p. 204) he quotes C. Cranfield from his *Critical and Exegetical Commentary on the Epistle to the Romans* "and so entertains the ugly and unscriptural notion that God has cast off His people Israel and simply replaced it with the Christian Church. These three chapters emphatically forbid us to speak of the Church as having once and for all taken the place of the Jewish people [i.e., Israel]".

Whitcomb has so many excellent points, but I shall restrain from quoting them and provide one further quote below:

"The Abrahamic/New Covenant and the Mosaic Covenant are not in contradiction with each other. God promised, "I will put My law within them, and on their heart I will write it" (Jer 31 :33; Rom 2:25-29; 8:3-4: Heb 7:18-19). The reappearance of *some aspects* of the Mosaic ritual during the Millennium will not necessarily, therefore, be a contradiction to the dynamics of the New Covenant." (footnote 2, p. 202)

DOESN'T THE NEW TESTAMENT VIRTUALLY IGNORE ISRAEL?

Here are just some verses proving otherwise:

"And you, Bethlehem, *in* the land of Judah, are not the least among the governors of Judah. For **out of you shall come a Governor who shall rule My people Israel**." (Matt 2:6, MKJV)

"But when they persecute you in this city, flee into another; for truly I say to you, In no way shall you have finished the cities of Israel until the Son of Man comes." (Matt 10:23, MKJV)

"But He answered and said, **I am not sent except to the lost sheep of *the* house of Israel.**" (Matt 15:24, MKJV)

"And Jesus said to them, Truly I say to you that you who have followed Me, in the regeneration, when the Son of Man shall sit in the throne of His glory, **you also shall sit on twelve thrones, judging the twelve tribes of Israel**." (Matt 19:28, MKJV)

"And behold, there was a man in Jerusalem whose name *was* Simeon. **And this man *was* just and devout, waiting for *the* Consolation of Israel.** And *the* Holy Spirit was on him…

"a light for revelation *to the* nations, and the glory of Your people Israel…

"And Simeon blessed them and said to Mary His mother, Behold, **this One is set for *the* fall and rising again of many in Israel**, and for a sign spoken against." (Luke 2:25, 32, 34, MKJV)

"And I appoint a **kingdom** to you, as My Father has appointed to Me,

that you may eat and drink at My table in **My kingdom, and sit on thrones judging the twelve tribes of Israel**." (Luke 22:29-30, MKJV)

"Nathanael answered and said to Him, Rabbi, **You are the Son of God. You are the King of Israel!**" (John 1:49, MKJV)

"Then, indeed, these coming together, they asked Him, saying, Lord, do You at this time **restore the kingdom to Israel**?"

"After this I will return and will build again the tabernacle of David *which* has fallen down; and I will build again its ruins, and I will set it up." (Acts 1:6; 15:16, MKJV)

"And He said, What is the **kingdom of God** like? And to what shall I compare it?

It is like a grain of mustard seed which a man took and threw into his garden. And it grew and became a great tree, and the birds of the air lodged in its branches." (Luke 13:18-19, MKJV)

"They therefore, when they were come together, asked him, saying, **Lord, dost thou at this time restore the kingdom to Israel?**...

and that he may send the Christ who hath been appointed for you, *even* Jesus:

whom the heaven must receive until the times of **restoration of all things [including Israel restored to glory]**, whereof God spake by the mouth of His holy prophets that have been from of old...

This One God *has* exalted *to be* a Ruler and Savior to His right *hand* **in order to give repentance and remission of sins to Israel**...

You know the Word which *God* sent to the sons of Israel, preaching the gospel of peace by Jesus Christ (He is Lord of all!) ...

For this cause therefore did I entreat you to see and to speak with *me*: for because of the **hope of Israel** I am bound with this chain." (Acts 1:6, KJV; 3:20-21, ASV; 5:31, MKJV; 10:36, MKJV; 28:20, KJV)

"Brothers, truly my heart's desire and **prayer to God for Israel** is for *it* to be saved." (Rom 10:1, MKJV)

In fact, Israel is referred to in scores of places – just pick up a *Strong's Concordance* and see for yourself. Israel is also referred to in Matt 10:6; James 1:1; Rev 7; 12; 21 and her tribulation is referred to in Matt 24; Mark 13; Luke 21; Rev 18.

Now what if Israel was not mentioned at all in the New Testament? Would it make any difference to God's Plan? Not at all! Israel is not mentioned or seldom is in some Old Testament books. Mentioning or not mentioning and the extent of mention has no bearing on the Plan of God. After all, the New Testament enriches the Old and builds upon its foundation, it does not replace the Old Testament. Notice the importance of Israel in the New Testament"

"Jesus sent out these twelve, commanding them, saying, Do not go into the way of the nations, and do not enter into *any* city of *the* Samaritans.

But rather **go to the lost sheep of *the* house of Israel**." (Matt 10:5-6, MKJV)

"James, a servant of God and of *the* Lord Jesus Christ, **to the twelve tribes** in the Dispersion, greeting." (James 1:1, MKJV)

Various scriptures indicate the great blessings that the House of Israel would enjoy in the last days, before the Tribulation (e.g. Gen 49, which Israel typologically fulfills today).[11]

Israel's growing dominance in the last days, prior to punishment in Tribulation, in many ways pictures her Millennial role. The Tribulation interrupts this natural progression, under the guidance of God. Like a mustard seed growing into a great tree, so Israel is expanding its

---

[11] As a tiny mustard seed which grows into a large tree, the Kingdom of God, ruled by Christ and His bride, through Israel, will dominate the world. Commencing with the first British Empire under Elizabeth I and later through the second British Empire and now the American Empire, Israel has been growing in dominance. It has also given place for spiritual Israel to grow. While physical Israel has found place for spiritual Israel to survive, so spiritual Israel is loyal to Israel, unlike this world's establishment and its media.

power and influences across the globe. This does not mean that everything it does is perfect of course, but that it does a much better job at global leadership than gentile powers.

> "They therefore, when they were come together, asked him, saying, **Lord, dost thou at this time restore the kingdom to Israel?**" (Acts 1:6, KJV)

The answer is that the restoration of the kingdom of Israel, which is destined to rule the world, is yet future.

WILL THERE BE A SECOND EXODUS?

The Great Tribulation will be the single major means used by the Almighty to teach the Houses of Israel and Judah their biggest lessons for all time. It will be a thrashing of massive proportions.

But since the early 1960s with the advent of political correctness and Woke radicalism which can only be described as evil, end-time Israel resident in the Anglo-Keltic and Northwest European nations has misled the world. Its leadership has been tainted with a mixture of good and bad when they were meant to lead the world in the ways of God and to be a light.

Therefore, God will teach Israel lessons – to become strong, righteous leaders – through humiliation and cleansing. This will be via the greatest trials ever to come upon any nation, but which will bear the fruits of repentance, righteousness and character.

Many conservative commentators and scholars agree that there are a large number of Scriptures on a future, Millennial Exodus of Israel (whom they restrict to the Jews only).[12]

> "Most of the themes in Isaiah 24-27 are found throughout the entire book: the judgment of the nations, the restoration of Israel, the rule of the Lord in Jerusalem … these eschatological themes are concentrated in Isaiah 24-27 … **He has promised that … the sinful nation, after its conversion, will eventually prosper and become the center of universal worship.** The "new world order" has been introduced: God is King. He must punish sinners and bless the faithful." (Neil Skjoldal, "The Function of Isaiah 24-27," *Journal of the Evangelical Society*, Vol. 36, No. 2, pp. 171-72) [emphasis mine]

Many scriptures refer to the coming Exodus from future slavery are:

1. Deut 4:26-29 (cp Is 55:1; Hos 6:1-3; Lam 3:23-24; Deut 30:1-5), 30-31; 30:4 (cp Matt 24:31); Is 10:20-22; Zeph 3:18-20 (the enslaved remnants of the Israelitish nations of North America, NW Europe, British Isles, Australasia and South Africa will be brought into the Holy Land).
2. Is 11:11-12, 16; 27:12-13 (it would appear that this will begin at the 7th Trump of Revelation). See also Zech 9:14; Is 10:20-22; Jer 16:14-15; 23:3, 7-8; 31:8-9; 43:1-6; 50:3-5; Ezek 20:42-43.

---

[12] Unfortunately most evangelicals and Pentecostals believe that the various prophecies of blessings concerning Israel in the last days (Ezekiel 38 and 39 etc) are pre-Millennial.

Figure 1 Israel's Second Exodus in Stages

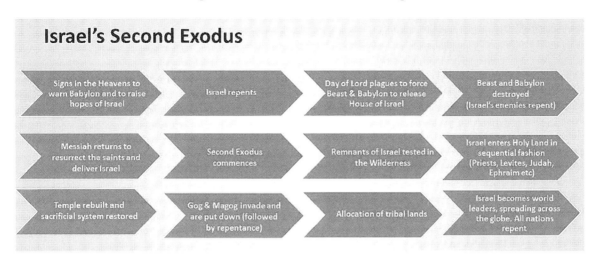

Below are several key Scriptures supporting this view:

"And it shall be in that day, the Lord shall again set His hand, **the second time**, to recover the remnant of His people that remains, from Assyria and from Egypt, and from Pathros, and from Ethiopia, and from Persia, and from Shinar, and from Hamath, and from the coasts of the sea.

And He shall lift up a banner for the nations, and shall gather the outcasts of Israel and gather together the scattered ones of Judah from the four corners of the earth.

And the envy of **Ephraim** shall depart, and the foes of **Judah** shall be cut off; Ephraim shall not envy Judah, and Judah shall not trouble Ephraim. [English and Scots will stop their fighting]

But they shall fly on the shoulders of the Philistines to the west; they shall spoil the sons of the east together; they shall lay their hand on Edom and Moab; and the sons of Ammon shall obey them. [God will use them to conquer various nations]

And Jehovah shall utterly destroy the tongue of the Egyptian sea; and with His scorching wind He shall shake His hand over the River, and shall strike it into seven streams, and make one tread *it* with shoes.

And there shall be a highway for the remnant of His people, **those left from Assyria; as it was to Israel in the day that he came up out of the land of Egypt**." (Is 11:11-16, MKJV) [the future Exodus will include fleeing from Germany! This is just another proof that the Assyrians are the enemies of Israel in the latter days]

"And it shall be, in that day the great ram's horn shall be blown [the 7th Trumpet – symbolised by the Feast of Trumpets], **and those perishing in the land of Assyria shall come**, and the outcasts in the land of Egypt shall come and shall worship Jehovah in the holy mountain at Jerusalem." (Is 27:13, MKJV)

"But now so says **Jehovah who created you, O Jacob, and He who formed you, O Israel**; Fear not, for I have redeemed you; I have called *you* by your name; you *are* Mine.

When you pass through the waters, I *will be* with you; and through the rivers, they shall not overflow you [i.e. disasters will not totally destroy them]. When you walk through the fire, you shall not be burned; nor shall the flame kindle on you.

For I *am* Jehovah your God, the Holy One of Israel, your Savior; I gave Egypt *for* your ransom, Ethiopia and Seba for you [these peoples will be ruled by Israel].

Since **you were precious in My sight**, you have been honored, and I have loved you; therefore I will give men for you, and people for your life.

Fear not; for I *am* with you. **I will bring your seed from the east, and gather you from the west.**

I will say to the north, Give up; and to the south, Do not keep back; bring My sons from far and My daughters from the ends of the earth;

everyone who is called by My name; for I have created him for My glory, I have formed him; yea, *I have* made him.

Bring out the blind people who have eyes, and the deaf who have ears." (Is 43:1-8, MKJV) [physical and spiritual blind and deaf]

During this time, Israel and Judah will, at last, be united! The major scriptures on this subject are: Jer 31:1, 7-9; 50:4-5; Ezek 11:17; 34:12-13; 37:19-22.[13]

"For there shall be a day *that* the watchmen on Mount Ephraim shall cry, Arise and let us go up to Zion to Jehovah our God!

For so says Jehovah, Sing with gladness for Jacob, and shout among the chief of the nations. Cry out, give praise and say, O Jehovah, save Your people, the remnant of Israel.

Behold, I will bring them from the north country and gather them from the corners of the earth, and with *them* the blind and the lame, the woman with child and she who is in labor with child, together; a great company shall return there.

They shall come with weeping, and with prayers I will lead them. I will cause them to walk by the rivers of waters in a straight way; they shall not stumble in it, for **I am a father to Israel**, and **Ephraim** *is* **My firstborn**.

Hear the Word of Jehovah, O nations, and declare *it* in the coastlands afar off. And say, He who scattered Israel will gather him and keep him, as a shepherd *keeps* his flock." (Jer 31:1-10, MKJV)

And that Scripture sums it all up.

A casual reading of the accomplishments of Joshua and his comparison to Christ evokes the realisation that there is clear typology at work: Joshua is a type of Christ in various ways. The crossing of the River Jordan (second phase of the Exodus) pictures spiritual Israel dispossessing the leaders of this world and taking over the world under Christ (Dan 7:17-18). This is outlined in the chart below.

---

[13] Other related scriptures are: Jer 12: 14-15; 16:15; 23:3-4, 7-8; 24:6-7; 30:3, 8-10; 33:6-9; 50:4-5, 19-20; Ps 14:7; 53:6; 68:6; 30:4; Lev 26: 42-46.

Other scriptures on the reunion of Israel and Judah include: Jer 3:17-19; Zech 12:10-14; Rom 11:26; Acts 15:16-17; Hos 1:11; 2:14; Mic 2:12; 5:4-7; Zech 8:7-8; 10:9-12.

Table 3 Joshua and Jesus: Conquest of the Promised Land Compared

Joshua	Jesus	Comments
Joshua.	Jesus = Greek form of Joshua.	= God is my salvation.
2 spies (Joshua 2:1-24).	2 witnesses (Rev 11).	
The spies look over the land and return with their report/witness (Joshua 2:23).	The 2 witnesses would proclaim God's Kingdom and what it will be like. In effect they spy out the land and report to the world what is on offer.	Presaged by Moses and Aaron.
Joshua was responsible for circumcision (Joshua 5:2) which was performed in preparation of the first Passover to be observed in the Promised Land (a prerequisite for observing the Passover was circumcision) – making Israel ready to take the Promised Land.	Christ is responsible for our spiritual circumcision (Col 2:10-11; Rom 2:28-29) in preparation for Passover and forgiveness – making us ready to take the spiritual Promised Land.	Circumcision = outward willingness to obey God. Thus is was a sign of a covenant between an Israelite and God.
The ark had 7 priests with 7 trumpets preceding it (Joshua 6:6).	7 angels with 7 trumpets sound prior to the ark being revealed in heaven (Rev 11:19).	
The enemy is defeated by the 7 trumpets (Joshua 6). Seven aspects of judgment?	The seven trumpets destroy the enemy (Rev 8-11). Seven aspects of judgment (Rev 8; 16).	= completeness of warning or destruction.
Signs in the heavens (moon and sun) (Joshua 10:12).	Signs in the heavens (Matt 24:29-30; Rev 8:12).	
Kings of Canaan flee and hide in the caves (Josh 10:16).	Kings of the earth flee and hide in the caves (Rev 6:15-16).	
Chs 4-6, 11-12 – Seven Canaanite tribes defeated over seven years (Joshua 4-6, 11-12). Joshua dispossesses the kings of Canaan (Joshua 11:3).	Armies invade the Holy land after the Messiah returns and defeated (Ezek 38; 39). Christ dispossesses the kings of the earth (Rev 11:15; 19).	
After resting from war, Israel inherits the Promised Land (Joshua 11:23).	After resting from war, spiritual Israel inherits the spiritual promised land (Rev 20).	The ultimate rest is found in Rev 21; 22.
Land at peace (Joshua 11).	Peace reigns (Ezek 39:21-29).	Post millennial period including second resurrection -peace reigns (Rev 21:10-15).
The area that is called Jerusalem becomes capital.	Jerusalem becomes capital of the world.	The New Jerusalem becomes capital of the universe and inheritance of spiritual Israel (21:12; 22).

Joshua	Jesus	Comments
Tabernacle relocated to Shiloh (Joshua 18). David later plans to build a Temple in Jerusalem which was fulfilled by Solomon. Tribal allotments/inheritance (chs 18-19, 21). Seven years of settlement.	Millennial temple (Ezek 40-48) and tribal allotments/inheritance (Ezek 48).	Will spiritual Israel be allocated parts of the solar system and even the universe?

The Bible speaks of several sorts of Exoduses and these are captured in the table below.

Table 4 Comparison of the Various Biblical Exoduses

Exodus	Pre-Exodus	Departure	Wilderness tests	Promised Land	Putting down of enemies
Abraham (from Ur)	Famine Time in Egypt Plagues upon the Pharaoh (Gen 12).	To Canaan (Gen 13).	Gen 13.	Jordan Valley Bethel.	Battle with 5 kings (Gen 14).
Israel (from Egypt)	In tribulation under the heel of Egypt. Plagues upon Egypt.	Spiritual baptism (ICor 10:1-5).	Deut 8:2.	Conquest of the land (Josh 3 and 4).	Josh 7-11.
Judah (from Babylon)	In captivity (Ps 137:1-9).	Repentance (Neh 1).	Route from Babylon (most never returned) via the wilderness (Ezra 2).	Entry into the Promised Land by a part of Judah (Ezra 2).	Ezra 4.
Israel (from end-time enemies)	In tribulation and captivity. Plagues.	Repentance Brought from four corners of the earth (Rev 18:4).	Tested in the wilderness.	Entry into the Promised Land (Is 61; Ps 47; Is 14:1-2; Zech 10:3-10).	Ezek 38 and 39.
Christians (from spiritual Babylon}	Spiritual trials.	Repentance Baptism (Rev 18:4).	Sojourners in this world (IPet 2:11).	Pulling down spiritual strong-holds (ICor 10:4-5) Spiritual birth into the Kingdom.	Christians encounter opposition within and without.

These various forms of exodus inform us of what it entails and even the Christian's spiritual exodus from this world's ways and into His light.

ISRAEL'S ROLE AFTER THE SECOND EXODUS

In Daniel 9:27 it indicates that Christ has 3 ½ years of His ministry to complete. As He was sent to the lost sheep of the House of Israel, it figures that He will complete His ministry to them. Why? Because it is through Israel that Christ and the spirit-born children of God will rule and reign.

First, the rebels must be purged out (Ezek 20:35-38; Joel 3:20-21):

> "*As* I live, says the Lord Jehovah, surely with a mighty hand, and with a stretched out arm, and with fury poured out, I will reign over you.
>
> And I will bring you out from the people [second Exodus], and I will gather you out of the lands in which you are scattered among them [captivity in foreign lands], with a mighty hand and with a stretched out arm and **with fury poured out** [i.e. the 7 last plagues poured upon those that took Israel captive, to force their release].
>
> And I will bring you into the wilderness of the people, and there I will enter into judgment with you face to face.
>
> Just as I entered into judgment with your fathers in the wilderness of the land of Egypt, so I will enter into judgment with you, says the Lord Jehovah. [this seems to be referring to a purging process during the Tribulation and/or soon thereafter]
>
> And I will cause you to pass under the rod [Amos 5:3; Lev 27:32 – this refers to the 'Lord's tithe' or 1/10th of people set aside by Him], and **I will bring you into the bond of the covenant**.
>
> **And I will purge out from among you the rebels and those who sin against Me.** I will bring them out from the land where they reside, and they shall not enter into the land of Israel [rebels will be liberated but will not enter the Holy Land – they will be purged – possibly with the aid of the Priests and Levites]. And you shall know that I *am* Jehovah." (Ezek 20:33-38, MKJV)

In Jer 31:2 and Hos 2:14 we are told that God (presumably assisted by the resurrected saints) will work with and cleanse Israel in the wilderness – somewhere close to the Holy Land (see also Zech 13:9; Amos 5:3; Lev 27:32; Ezek 20:37). The prophecies show that only 1/3 of

Israel will be left alive after drought, famine and disease epidemics and only one 10th of that figure will be alive after the cleansing, to make it into the Holy Land (Is 6:11-13; Amos 5:3; Ezek 20:35-38. See Hos 1:4-11; 2:14; Is 40:2. Cp Lev 27:32).

In the Bible, when God set something back on track, He first cleansed the Priests followed by the Levites (see Malachi 3:2-6). Due to its senior leadership position of the Israelite tribes, Judah would have to be cleaned up at the outset as well:

"Then shall the offering of Judah and Jerusalem be pleasant unto the LORD, as in the days of old, and as in former years" (Mal 3:4, NKJV). See too Ezek 44:10-12; 48:11. Levi then, will be the tribe carrying out religious duties such as acting as the religious teachers, ministers, executers of the Law as well as probably functioning as many or most of the judges.

After her cleansing, Israel will be led into the Holy Land to complete her training to be guided by the Messiah and the saints, to colonise parts of the world and to rule it under Him and the saints (Hos 2:23; Zech 10:9). If the above analysis of Scripture is correct, then we will find the following occurring at the outset of the Millennium, after the Day of the Lord:

1. Second Exodus from captivity in foreign lands after repentance
2. cleansing of the princes, Priests, Levites and Judah (in accordance with the principles of the Old Testament that there is an order with such events. See IIChron 29:1-5, 15-16, 34; 30:1)
3. cleansing then probably follows on to Ephraim and Manasseh as the leading nations under Judah (30:1-3)
4. the rest of Israel will then be cleansed
5. the New Covenant will be made after this cleansing (possibly including water baptism)
6. as we shall see, Israel will take certain gentile nations into servitude, at least for a while and re-colonise their former lands around the world. Gradually, Christ will bring the rest of the world under Him through the children of God and Israel.

THE MAKING OF THE NEW COVENANT WITH ISRAEL

Israel broke the Covenant with God – an agreement to observe His perfect Law. This proved that man, without the spirit of God, cannot keep the Law to the heights required. Because of the hardness of their hearts certain allowances were made for ancient Israel. For example: "He said to them, Because of your hard-heartedness Moses allowed you to put away your wives; but from the beginning it was not so." (Matt 19:8, MKJV) So, the Law remains as the central agreeing point of the Covenant – it is not abolished.

After separating or divorcing from Israel and sending her away (Jer 3:1, 7-8; 4:1; IIKings 17:18-24; Jer 11:10; Hos 2:2; Is 59:1-2), God will again make an agreement or covenant with Israel.

Following are the key Scriptures on this New Covenant:

"And the Redeemer shall come to Zion, and **to those who turn from transgression in Jacob**, says Jehovah.

As for Me, this *is* My covenant with them, says Jehovah; My Spirit that is on you, and My Words which I have put in your mouth, shall not depart out of your mouth, nor out of the mouth of your seed, nor out of the mouth of your seed's seed, says Jehovah, from now on and forever." (Is 59:20-21, MKJV)

"Behold, the days come, says Jehovah, that **I will cut a new covenant** with the house of Israel, and with the house of Judah,

not according to the covenant that I cut with their fathers in the day I took them by the hand to bring them out of the land of Egypt; which covenant of Mine they broke, although I was a husband to them, says Jehovah;

but this *shall be* the covenant that I will cut with the house of Israel: After those days, says Jehovah, **I will put My Law in their inward parts, and write it in their hearts**; and I will be their God, and they shall be My people.

And they shall no more teach each man his neighbor and each man his brother, saying, Know Jehovah; for they shall all know Me, from the least of them to the greatest of them, says Jehovah. For I will forgive their iniquity, and I will remember their sins no more." (Jer 31:31-34, MKJV)

"For so says the Lord Jehovah: I will even deal with you as you have done, who have despised the oath in breaking the covenant.

But I will remember My covenant with you in the days of your youth, and I will establish to you an everlasting covenant.

And you shall remember your ways and be ashamed, when you shall receive your sisters, your older and your younger. And I will give them to you for daughters, but not by *your* covenant.

And I will establish My covenant with you; and you shall know that I *am* Jehovah." (Ezek 16:59-62, MKJV)

"For I will take you from among the nations and gather you out of all lands, and will gather you into your own land.

And I will sprinkle clean waters on you, and you shall be clean. I will cleanse you from all your filthiness and from your idols.

And I will give you a new heart, and I will put a new spirit within you. And I will take away the stony heart out of your flesh, and I will give you a heart of flesh.

And I will put My Spirit within you and cause you to walk in My statutes, and you shall keep My judgments and do *them*.

And you shall dwell in the land that I gave to your fathers. And you shall be My people, and I will be your God.

I will also save you from all your defilements, and I will call for the grain, and will increase it, and will lay no famine on you.

And I will multiply the fruits of the tree and the increase of the field, so that you shall never again receive the curse of famine among the nations.

And you shall remember your own evil ways, and your doings that *were* not good, and shall despise yourselves in your own sight for your iniquities and for your abominations." (Ezek 36:24-31, MKJV)

Other Scriptures on this important subject are listed in the footnotes.[14]

At the commencement of the chapter it was stated that in Dan 9:27 there is indication that Christ would be cut off after 3 ½ years of His ministry confirming the Covenant with Israel:

"And after sixty-two weeks Messiah shall be cut off, but not *for* Himself. And the people of the ruler who shall come shall destroy the city and the sanctuary. And the end of it *shall be* with the flood, and ruins are determined, until *the* end *shall be* war.

And he shall confirm a covenant with many *for* one week. And in the midst of the week he shall cause the sacrifice and the offering to cease, and on a corner *of the altar* desolating abominations, even until *the* end. And that which was decreed shall be poured on the desolator." (Dan 9:26-27, MKJV)

This tells us that Christ will continue for another 3 ½ years confirming the Covenant with Israel, after the second Exodus and after the purging out of rebels. What will this New Covenant be like?

Paul quoted Jeremiah in Heb 8:8: "For finding fault with them [the nation Israel], he saith, Behold, the days come, saith the Lord, when I will make a **new covenant** with the house of Israel and with the house of Judah." (KJV) Refer also to Heb 12:24. This covenant is being made with the New Testament Church (which consists of those that are spiritual in Israel plus those gentiles who are called and grafted into Israel by entering into that covenant) but will be completed with Israel upon His return and later with gentile nations.

According to *Strong's Concordance*, the Greek word in 12:24 "3501 neos, including the comparative neoteros neh-o'-ter-os; a primary word; "new", i.e. (of persons) youthful, or (of things) fresh; figuratively, regenerate:--new, young" which implies the 'renewing covenant'. The same laws comprise the Old and New Covenants. But instead of writing them on stone, they are written into one's mind or heart through the indwelling of the holy spirit – this

---

[14] Other scriptures include: Ezek 34:25; Is 55:3; 59:20-21; 62:4-5.

"And it shall be at that day, says Jehovah, **you shall call Me, My Husband**, and shall no more call Me, My Baal.

For I will take away the names of the Baals out of her mouth, and they will no more be remembered by their name.

And in that day **I will cut a covenant for them**, with the beasts of the field, and with the birds of the heavens, and *with* the creeping things of the ground. And I will break the bow and the sword and the battle out of the earth, and will make them to lie down safely.

And **I will betroth you to Me forever**. Yea, I will betroth you to Me in righteousness, and in judgment, and in loving-kindness, and in mercies.

I will even betroth you to Me in faithfulness. And you shall know Jehovah.

And it will be, in that day I will answer, says Jehovah. I will answer the heavens, and they shall answer the earth, and the earth shall hear the grain and the wine and the oil. And they shall hear Jezreel.

And I will sow her to Me in the earth. And I will have mercy on No-mercy. And I will say to Not-my-people, You are My people. And they shall say, My God." (Hos 2:16-23)

actually was the case already during Old Testament times for anyone with the holy spirit such as the patriarchs and prophets. But now it is extended to more people including gentiles.

A prominent scholar and specialist on the covenants, Walter Kaiser, has written about this:

> "Jeremiah 32:31-34 … was also the largest piece of text to be quoted *in extenso* in the NT, viz., Hebrews 8:8-12 … When items of continuity found in the New Covenant are tabulated in this passage [i.e. Jer 31:31-34] they are: (1) the same covenant-making God, "My covenant"; (2) **the same law, My torah (note, not a different one than Sinai)**; the same divine fellowship promised in the ancient tripartite formula, "I will be your God" (4) the same "seed" and "people," "You shall be my people" and (5) the same forgiveness, "I will forgive their iniquities."
>
> "Even the features of inwardness, fellowship, individualism, and forgiveness had been either hinted at or fully known in the covenant made with the fathers…
>
> **"Thus the word "new" in this context would mean the "renewed" or "restored" covenant (cf. Akkadian *edesu* "to restore" ruined temples, altars, or cities; Hebrew *hds* connected with the new moon and Ugaritic *hdt*, "to renew the moon"). We conclude that this covenant was the old Abrahamic-Davidic promise renewed and enlarged** … Thus the new is more comprehensive, more effective, more spiritual, and more glorious than the old - in fact, so much so that *in comparison* it would appear as if it were totally unlike the old at all. Yet, **in truth, it was nothing less than the progress of revelation**" (Walter Kaiser, *Towards an Old Testament Theology*, pp. 232-34). [emphasis mine]

Most Protestants would not know about this and that is a real pity because, amongst other things, it shows that the Laws of God are not abolished or sidelined. However, there is a growing school of thought on the truth about the New Covenant and its relationship to the continuing observance of God's Law.

ISRAEL'S DESTINY TO COLONISE PARTS OF THE WORLD

In Gen 28:14, God promised Israel the world. Later, there were probably worldwide colonies at the time of Solomon. Later we had what became known as the first British Empire starting with Elizabeth I, followed by the second British Empire reaching its zenith under Queen Victoria.[15]

Is 60:9-17 and 49:20 reveal that the Holy Land will become too small for Israel due to its population explosion during that time, that she would have to set out to colonise implying that the old colonial territories will be repopulated.

---

[15] Why are they a colonising people? What is God trying to teach us? Like a colony of bees, the English (Ephraim) under the aristocracy and with the Scots (part of Judah), were set up as ruling classes around the world with government pointing to the British Royalty, seated (so to speak) on the Stone of Scone (Jacob's pillar stone, which Christ may sit on upon His return). This teaches us the lesson that the Kingdom of God through Israel, will be a colonising empire, typed by the British Empire at its best moments.

Note Gen 13:16; Is 54:2-3; 66:19-20; 61:4 where we have indication of these Millennial colonies and it is clear that they rule over the gentiles for their own good, in love and respect, under God and His saints (see also Gen 9:27; Is 49:21-23; 61:5-6, 9) and especially to bring the Gospel message to them.

Also, in Ezek 36:10-11 we are told that Israel will inhabit the former places (where they were taken captive from. See also Ps 80:8-11; Gen 49:22; Hos 14:5-8) and in Deut 4:5-8 we see that Israel will rule over the nations again – how can she do so unless she returns to her former lands of North America (as a light to the central and south Americans), northwest Europe (to be a light to the Europeans), South Africa (to be a light to the Africans) and Australia and New Zealand (to be a light to the Asiatics and Pacific Islanders)?[16]

Further, in Deut 32:9 we are told that "For Jehovah's portion *is* His people. Jacob *is* the lot of His inheritance." (MKJV) The "lot" given to Israel has an expanded meaning when the Hebrew is examined – it can include the concept of a country, coast, region, girdle, cord, belt, measuring line, outside circle, indicating colonies outside of the Holy Land (see also Is 49:8b; Hos 14:5). It is through Israel that Christ and the saints will rule the world – in other words they continue to be a special people to serve the world in this capacity:

> "*To the Chief Musician. A Psalm for the sons of Korah.* Clap your hand, all you peoples; shout to God with the voice of triumph.
>> For Jehovah Most High *is* awesome, a great king over all the earth.
>> **He shall humble the peoples under us, and nations under our feet.**
>> **He shall choose our inheritance for us, the majesty of Jacob** whom He loved. Selah.
>> God has gone up with a shout, Jehovah with the sound of a trumpet.
>> Sing praise to God, sing praise; sing praise to our King, sing praise.
>> For God *is* King of all the earth; sing praises with understanding.
>> God reigns over the nations, God sits on the throne of His holiness.
>> The rulers of the peoples are gathered together, **the people of the God of Abraham**;
> for the shields of the earth *are* God's; He is lifted up on high." (Ps 47:1-9, MKJV)

In the end, Israel will inherit the whole world under the Messiah (a part of the promised blessings and their reward for repentance and obedience), during the Millennium, preparing the way for the next phase of God's plan (Is 61: 5-6, 9; 54:2).

Notice what several commentators have to say about this period:

> "... Israel definitely had a sense of mission, not in the sense of *going* somewhere but of *being* something. They were to be the holy people of the living God YHWH. They were to know him for who he is, to preserve the true and exclusive worship [of] YHWH, and **to live according to his ways and laws within loyal commitment to their covenantal relationship with him. In all these respects they would *be* a light and witness to the nations...**

---

[16] Is 26:15; 27:6; 49:8 speak of Israel's colonies as do Ezek 28:25-26; Amos 9:14-15; Ezek 19:10; (cp Gen 49:22); Ob 17 (Israel "shall possess their possessions" – ie the Holy Land, colonies and treasures).

"... the nations were portrayed in the Old Testament as witness of all that God was doing in, for or to Israel... the expectation of Israel's faith and worship (if not always the outcome of their practice) was that the nations would come to benefit from that salvation and give thanks for it. This meant that the nations would eventually acknowledge and worship Israel's God, YHWH, with all the concomitant responsibilities and blessings of such worship." (Christopher Wright, *The Mission of God*, pp. 455, 504) [emphasis mine]

Walter Kaiser devotes an entire book to the subject, *Mission in the Old Testament*:

"Once it is admitted that Israel also functioned and was designated as the "Servant of the Lord," it is difficult to limit her involvement in the spread of the gospel simply to a passive role of centripetally calling the nations of the world to herself. **She must bring the religious teaching, usually translated "bring justice," to the nations**. The instruction as to what is right must come from those who have been entrusted with the oracles of God.

"... They [the covenants] were initially given to Israel so that Israel could share them with all the peoples of the earth.

"If any doubts remain as how far Israel was to go with this message, that too is abundantly clear in this text of Isaiah: it was "to the ends of the earth."

"Such a witness must not be carried out of Israel's own power, but the Holy Spirit would come on this remnant like rain on a dry and thirsty land. So Israel must witness on behalf of the Lord... **All their speaking up as servant-messengers must reach out to beckon the Gentiles until all humanity was a chance to know the at the Lord is the only Savior**, Redeemer, and Mighty One over all." (Walter Kaiser, *Mission in the Old Testament*, pp. 62-63) [emphasis mine]

"**The entrance of the heathen into the kingdom of God is depicted under the figure of the festal journeys to the sanctuary of Jehovah**, which had to be repeated year by year. Of the feasts which they will keep there every year, **the feast of tabernacles** is mentioned, not because it occurred in the autumn, and the autumn was the best time for travelling..., or because it was the greatest feast of rejoicing kept by the Jews, or for any other outward reason, but simply on account of its internal significance ... in its historical allusion as a feast of thanksgiving for the gracious protection of Israel in its wanderings through the desert, and its introduction into the promised land with its abundance of glorious blessings, whereby it foreshadowed the blessedness to be enjoyed in the kingdom of God... **This feast will be kept by the heathen who have come to believe in the living God**, to thank the Lord for His grace, that He has brought them out of the wanderings of this life into the blessedness of His kingdom of peace." (Keil & Deilitsch, *Minor Prophets*, p. 625)[17] [emphasis mine]

---

[17] Keil and Deilitsch also state: "With this view of the significance of the feast of tabernacles, it is also possible to harmonize the punishment threatened in v. 17 for neglecting to keep this feast, - namely, that the rain will not be (come) upon the families of the nations which absent themselves from this feast. For rain is an individualizing expression denoting the blessing of God generally, and is mentioned here with reference to the fact, that without rain the fruits of the land, on the enjoyment of which our happiness depends, will not flourish. The meaning of

"The heathen, regarded as tributary to Israel, they believed would also live again, in accordance with the promises of restoration they had received; but **it was to be only as the subjects of the chosen race**, who as kings in the kingdom of God were to rule over them." (Henry Dunn, *The Kingdom of God. Or What is the Gospel*, p. 11.)

"What he [the Judahite] looked for and anticipated was … distinction, high service, rule over the nations, the possession of a boundless kingdom, in which every Israelite should be a kingly priest. So he read the word of the Lord to Moses on the mount, 'Ye shall be unto me a kingdom of priests.' (Exodus 19:6) **All other nations were, he supposed, to be governed and taught by Israel. This privilege, with all that it involved, he believed would be his simply as a child of Abraham.** For the Messiah that was to introduce this kingdom he watched and waited with an unwavering faith from infancy to old age." (ibid, p. 15)[18] [emphasis mine]

During the Millennium, there will be

"… Israel's own enjoyment of God as well as their mission from God to the nations … in the sense of being set apart to YHWH God for the sake of the nations; Israel was to be a mediator between God and the nations …

without one to incarnate God's reign, Israel would persistently all away into apostasy. **Israel needed to be subdued before they could be a light to the Gentiles**" (L. Michael Morales, *Who Shall Ascend the Mountain of the Lord?* pp. 210, 234).[19]

This subjugation will occur during the coming Great Tribulation and subsequent Second Exodus.

---

the threat is, therefore, that those families which do not come to worship the Lord, will be punished by Him with the withdrawal of the blessings of His grace. The Egyptians are mentioned again, by way of example, as those upon whom the punishment will fall… It (the fact that the rain does not come) will be the plague, etc. The prophet mentions Egypt especially … as the nation which showed the greatest hostility to Jehovah and His people in the olden time, and for the purpose of showing that this nation was also to attain to a full participation in the blessings of salvation bestowed upon Israel (cf. Isa 19:19.) … Moreover, we must not infer from the way in which this is carried out in 17-19, that at the time of the completion of the kingdom of God there will still be heathen, who will abstain from the worship of the true God; but the thought is simply this: there will then be no more room for heathenism within the sphere of the kingdom of God. To this there is appended the thought, in vv. 20 and 21, that everything unholy will then be removed from that kingdom." (p. 625)

[18] "They did not even contemplate anything like a 'new testament,' the result of their national perversity, and of the calling of the Gentiles. … Ezekiel had distinctly told them that when Jehovah should gather Israel, he would put a new spirit within them; would 'take the stony heart out of their flesh, and will give them a heart of flesh' (Ezekiel 11:19). Jeremiah, in almost the same words, had similarly characterized the day of restoration (Jeremiah 31:33). Isaiah had said that then all their children should be taught of God (Isaiah 54:13); and Micah had enforced the same truth in connection with the period when the nations should come and go up to the house of the God of Jacob (4:2)." (Henry Dunn, *The Kingdom of God*, p. 20)

[19] On page 252 he provides a number events that will occur and the restoration of Israel will look like.

Will Israel rule over or deal with gentile nations?

J Richard Middleton writing in the Journal for Christian Theological Research *maintains that:*

> "God sends his son, Jesus the Christ, as a helper or agent to restore Israel to their purpose and task. It is important to note that, in terms of the plot structure of the Bible, **Jesus did not come initially to save the world from sin, but to restore Israel—and this is confirmed by looking at the actual ministry and message of Jesus in the Gospels. Not only do we have Jesus' famous comments to a Canaanite woman about his mission to "the "lost sheep," of the house of Israel,"** (Matthew 15:21-28), but he also commissions the Twelve (symbolizing the core of a restored remnant) to aid him in this mission (Matthew 10:1-16). In this first commissioning of "apostles" (meaning "sent ones"), Jesus explicitly enjoins them not to go to the Gentiles or the Samaritans, but only to the towns of Israel.

> "Plot Level 2: The Gentile Mission
> Of course, by the end of Matthew, after the death and resurrection of Jesus, when a sufficiently large body of (Jewish) disciples have been gathered, the risen Jesus finally commissions **the apostles to take up the Abrahamic task, namely to go to the nations/Gentiles** with the message of the Gospel. The story of the Gentile mission then takes up much of the book of Acts and is the background to the Pauline and general epistles." (p. 84)

> "… (1 Peter 2:9) … **This is a continuation of the Abrahamic calling. God's redeemed people are called to mediate blessing to the world** …
> The Gentile mission that was inaugurated with the call of Abraham/Israel is here portrayed as complete—the nations have received the blessing of salvation … the redeemed human race will once again utilize their God-given power and agency to rule the earth as God intended." (p. 85) [emphasis mine]

Middleton is correct and has a good grasp of the continuation of the Abrahamic Covenant with its ultimate fruition during the time of the Messiah's rule.

In a pronouncement in the book of Deuteronomy, God says that if Israel hears His voice, they will be the head and not the tail:

> "Jehovah shall open to you His good treasure, the heaven to give the rain to your land in its season, and to bless all the work of your hand. And you shall loan to many nations, and you shall not borrow.
> And Jehovah **shall make you the head**, and not the tail. And you shall be always above, and you shall not be beneath, **if** you listen to the commandments of Jehovah your God, which I command you today, to observe and to do them." [and they *will* listen to the commandments after the Tribulation] (Deut 28:12-13, MKJV)

And they **will** hear His voice and obey Him during the coming Exodus.

As we have seen, the prophecies are clear that Israel will take captive certain gentile nations – especially those that had previously taken Israel captive during the Great Tribulation, or who have caused Israel nothing but trouble by being constant thorns in their side. Take a look at Is 14:1-2 in this regard:

> "For Jehovah will have mercy on Jacob, and will yet choose Israel and set them in their own land; and the stranger shall be joined with them, and they shall cling to the house of Jacob.
>
> And **the peoples shall take them and bring them to their place**; and the house of Israel shall possess them in the land of Jehovah for slaves and slave girls. And **they shall be captives of their captors; and they shall rule over their oppressors**." (Is 14:1-2, MKJV)

Here we see certain gentile nations, repentant, bringing Israel to the Holy Land and Israel taking them captive for a season. The logic is that the servitude of these peoples will be in accordance with Old Testament's laws on the subject and Biblical principles (Ex 21:1-6; Deut 15:1-5; 31:10) and will be for seven years. This servitude represents their repentance, at least in part. During this season of servitude, they will learn about God, learn new skills and come to understand that God's plan for mankind includes rulership through Judah and Israel.

Isaiah contains a number of prophecies concerning this:

> "The Spirit of the Lord Jehovah *is* on Me; because Jehovah has anointed Me to preach the Gospel to the poor; He has sent Me to bind up the broken-hearted, to **proclaim liberty to the captives**, and the opening of the prison to those who are bound; [liberation of physical Israel; spiritually liberating the world also]
>
> to preach the acceptable year of Jehovah and the day of vengeance of our God; to comfort all who mourn;
>
> to appoint to those who mourn in Zion, to give to them beauty for ashes, the oil of joy for mourning, the mantle of praise for the spirit of heaviness; so that they might be called trees of righteousness, the planting of Jehovah, that He might be glorified.
>
> **And they will build the old wastes** [this must be the colonies], they will raise up the ruins of former times. And they will repair the waste cities, the ruins of many generations [colonies, not only cities in the land of Israel].
>
> **And strangers will stand and feed your flocks, and the sons of the stranger** *will be* **your plowmen and your vinedressers**. [Israel will bring into servitude certain nations to teach them humility]
>
> But you will be named the priests of Jehovah; it will be said of you, Ministers of our God; **you will eat the riches of the nations**, and you will revel in their glory. [how like the British Empire]
>
> For your shame *you will have* double; and for disgrace they will rejoice in their portion; therefore in their own land they will possess double; everlasting joy will be theirs.
>
> For I Jehovah love judgment, I hate robbery for burnt offering; and I will direct their work in truth, and I will make an everlasting covenant with them.

And their seed will be known among the nations, and their offspring among the peoples; all who see them will acknowledge them, that they *are* the seed Jehovah has blessed." (Is 61:1-9, MKJV)

"So says Jehovah of Hosts: In those days ten men, out of all languages of the nations, shall take hold, and will seize the skirt of a man, a Jew [Judah], saying, We will go with you, for we have heard that God is with you." (Zech 8:23, MKJV)

Dare we water-down the above truth of God or ignore it? Or do we humbly accept the Word of God and thank God for His supreme wisdom? Let us simply accept what the Scriptures say and not wrestle with it!

"Behold, I have given Him *for* a witness to the people [gentiles], a Leader and Commander of peoples.

Behold, You shall call a nation that You do not know; a nation *that* did not know You shall run to You because of Jehovah Your God, and for the Holy One of Israel; for He has glorified You." (Is 55:4-5, MKJV)

"And He said, It is but a little *thing* that You should be My servant to raise up the tribes of Jacob, and to **bring back the preserved ones of Israel**; I will also give You for a light to the nations, to be My salvation to the end of the earth.

So says Jehovah, the Redeemer of Israel, His Holy One, *to Him* whom man despises, *to Him* whom the nation hates, the servant of rulers: Kings shall see and arise, rulers also shall worship, because of Jehovah who is faithful, the Holy One of Israel, and He shall choose You.

So says Jehovah, in a favorable time I replied to You, and in a day of salvation I have helped You; and I will preserve You, and **give You for a covenant of the people, to establish the earth, to cause them to inherit the wasted inheritances**;

that You may say to the prisoners, Go out! To those who *are* in darkness, Show yourselves! They shall feed in the ways, and their pastures shall be in all high places.

They shall not hunger nor thirst; nor shall the heat nor sun strike them; for He who has mercy on them shall lead them; even by the springs of water He shall guide them." (Is 49:6-10, MKJV)

The above Scriptures, in context, are dual, referring to both Christ and Israel. Indeed, Christ will be working through Israel to reach the world.

Here are some further scriptures on the subject concerning Israel's and Judah's operations during His reign:

"**And the land of Judah shall be a terror** to Egypt [Mizraim]; everyone who mentions it shall be afraid toward it, because of the purpose of Jehovah of Hosts, which He has purposed against it." (Is 19:17, MKJV)

"And He shall judge among the nations, and shall rebuke many people; and they shall beat their swords into plowshares, and their spears into pruning-hooks. Nation shall not lift up sword against nation, neither shall they learn war any more." [how will He do this? Through Israel] (Is 2:4, MKJV)

"My anger was kindled against the shepherds, and I will punish the he-goats; for Jehovah of Hosts has visited **His flock the house of Judah, and has made them as His beautiful horse in battle.**

Out of Him came the cornerstone; out of Him the nail; out of Him the battle bow; out of Him every oppressor together.

And they shall be like mighty ones who trample the mud of the streets in the battle. And they shall fight because Jehovah *is* **with them**, and they shall make the riders on horses ashamed.

And I will strengthen the house of Judah, and I will save the house of Joseph, and **I will return to save them; for I have pity on them. And they shall be as though I had not cast them off**; for I *am* Jehovah their God, and I will answer them.

And Ephraim shall be like a mighty one, and their heart shall rejoice as *by* wine. And their sons shall see and be glad; their heart shall rejoice in Jehovah.

I will hiss for them and gather them; for I have redeemed them. And they shall be many as they were many.

And I will sow them among the peoples, and they shall remember Me in the distances; and they shall live with their sons and return.

I will return them out of the land of Egypt, and I will gather them out of Assyria; and I will bring them into the land of Gilead and Lebanon; **for** *room* **shall not be found for them**." [this population explosion will necessitate them to become colonisers again] (Zech 10:3-10, MKJV)

"Jehovah also shall save the tents of Judah first, so that the glory of the house of David and the glory of the people of Jerusalem may not be magnified above Judah.

In that day Jehovah shall defend around the people of Jerusalem. And it will be, he who is feeble among them at that day *shall be* like David; and the house of David *shall be* like God, like the Angel of Jehovah before them." (Zech 12:7-8, MKJV)

"And Judah also shall fight at Jerusalem; and the wealth of all the nations all around shall be gathered, gold, and silver, and clothing in great abundance." [those nations who stole Israel's wealth in the Tribulation, will have that wealth confiscated] (Zech 14:14, MKJV).

"Do not fear, worm of Jacob *and* men of Israel; I will help you, says Jehovah, and your Redeemer, the Holy One of Israel.

Behold, I make you a new sharp threshing instrument, a master of teeth; you shall thresh the mountains [nations] and beat *them* small, and shall make the hills like chaff.

You shall winnow them, and the wind shall carry them away, and a tempest shall scatter them. And you shall rejoice in Jehovah *and* shall glory in the Holy One of Israel." (Zech 41:14-16, MKJV)

"So says Jehovah, The labor of Egypt, and merchandise of Ethiopia, and of the Sabeans, men of stature, shall come to you, and they shall be yours [many African nations]. They shall come after you in chains; and they shall cross in chains and they shall fall down to you. They shall plead to you, *saying*, Surely God *is* in you; and none else, no *other* God.

Truly You *are* a God who hides Yourself, O God of Israel, the Savior.

They shall be ashamed, and also confounded, all of them; they *who are* makers of idols shall go into disgrace together.

But Israel shall be saved in Jehovah *with* an everlasting salvation. You shall not be ashamed nor blush to the forevers of eternity." (Is 45:14-17, MKJV)

"Listen, O coastlands, to Me; and listen, *lend your ear*, peoples from afar; Jehovah has called Me from the womb; He has made mention of My name from My mother's bowels.

And He has made My mouth like a sharp sword; in the shadow of His hand He has hidden Me, and made Me a polished shaft. He has hidden Me in His quiver,

and said to Me, **You *are* My servant, O Israel**, in whom I will be glorified.

Then I said, I have labored in vain; I have spent My strength for nothing, and in vain; *yet* surely My judgment is with Jehovah, and My work with My God.

And now, says Jehovah who **formed Me from the womb *to be* His servant**, to bring Jacob again to Him, Though Israel is not gathered, yet I shall be glorious in the eyes of Jehovah, and My God shall be My strength.

And He said, It is but a little *thing* that You should be My servant to raise up the tribes of Jacob, and to bring back the preserved ones of Israel; I will also give You for a light to the nations, to be My salvation to the end of the earth.

So says the Lord Jehovah, Behold, I will lift up My hand to the nations, and have set up My banner to the people; and **they shall bring your sons in *their* bosom, and your daughters shall be carried on *their* shoulders**.

And kings shall be your nursing fathers, and their queens your nurses. **They shall bow to you, faces to the earth, and lick up the dust of your feet**; and you shall know that I *am* Jehovah; by whom they shall not be ashamed who wait for Me.

Shall the prey be taken from the mighty, or the lawful captive delivered?" (Is 49:1-6, 22-24, MKJV)

"… for you shall break out *on* the right hand and on the left. And **your seed shall inherit the nations, and people will inhabit ruined cities**.

Do not fear; for you shall not be ashamed, nor shall you blush; for you shall not be put to shame; for you shall forget the shame of your youth, and shall not remember the reproach of your widowhood any more.

For **your Maker *is* your husband**; Jehovah of Hosts is His name; and your Redeemer *is* the Holy One of Israel; the God of the whole earth shall He be called.

For Jehovah has called you as a woman forsaken and grieved in spirit, and a wife of youth, when you were rejected, says your God.

For a little moment [3 ½ year Tribulation] I have left you; but with great mercies I will gather you." (Is 54:3-7, MKJV)

"Then you shall fear and become bright, and your heart shall throb and swell for joy; because the abundance of the sea shall turn to you, **the wealth of the nations will come to you**.

A host of camels shall cover you, **the camels of Midian and Ephah. All of them from Sheba [east Africa, southern India] shall come**; they shall bring gold and incense; and they shall proclaim the praises of Jehovah.

All the flocks of Kedar shall be gathered together to you; the rams of Nebaioth shall minister to you. They shall come up on My altar pleasing Me, and I will glorify the house of My glory.

Who *are* these *who* fly like a cloud, and as the doves to their windows?

Surely the coastlands shall wait for Me, and the **ships of Tarshish first, to bring your sons from far [the Japanese returning the Israelite slaves]**, their silver and their gold with them, to the name of Jehovah your God, and to the Holy One of Israel, because He has glorified you.

And the sons of strangers will build up your walls, and their kings will serve you; for in My wrath I struck you, but in My favor I had mercy on you.

Therefore your gates will always be open; they will not be shut day nor night, **to bring to you the wealth of the nations**, and their kings may be led.

For the nation and kingdom that will not serve you will perish. Yes, *those* nations will be completely wasted. [cp Ezek 25:12-14, MKJV]

The glory of Lebanon will come to you, the fir tree, the pine tree, and the box tree together, to beautify the place of My sanctuary; and I will make the place of My feet glorious.

Also the sons of your afflicters shall come bowing to you; and all your despisers will bow down at the soles of your feet. And they will call you, The city of Jehovah, The Zion of the Holy One of Israel.

Instead of being forsaken and hated, so that no one passes through, I will make you for everlasting majesty, a joy of many generations.

You will also suck the milk of nations, and suck the breast of kings; and you will know that I Jehovah *am* your Savior and your Redeemer, the mighty One of Jacob." (Is 60:5-16, MKJV) [as kings don't have milk producing breasts, this must mean that certain gentile kings will produce sustenance for Israel]

Moss and Baden (like some other authors) maintain that this refers to the future Exodus of Israel:

"… Isa 60.8: 'Who are these who fly like a cloud, like doves to their cotes?' According to the usual scholarly understanding of this verse, the white clouds and doves are likened to the white sails of **the ships bringing the far-flung Israelites back from the diaspora** (Isa 60.9). Although part of a larger prophetic unit that is clearly eschatological, this verse in its original context is no more than a metaphor and a simile, with little import: no one was actually imagined to be flying … for the rabbis 'flying as a cloud' from Isa 60.8 was connected not just with **the restoration of the Temple**, but with the entire concept of **the world to come, the eschatological era that will follow the Day of Yahweh**." (Candida Moss & Joel Baden, "1 Thessalonians

4.13-18 in Rabbinic Perspective," *New Testament Studies*, Vol. 58, Issue 2, p. 206). [emphasis mine]

Further prophecies may be found in the following chapter:

"And they will build the old wastes, they will raise up the ruins of former times [the colonies]. And they will repair the waste cities, the ruins of many generations.

And **strangers will stand and feed your flocks, and the sons of the stranger *will be* your plowmen and your vinedressers**.

But you will be named the priests of Jehovah; it will be said of you, Ministers of our God; **you will eat the riches of the nations**, and you will revel in their glory.

For your shame *you will have* double; and for disgrace they will rejoice in their portion; therefore in their own land they will possess double; everlasting joy will be theirs.

For I Jehovah love judgment, I hate robbery for burnt offering; and I will direct their work in truth, and I will make an everlasting covenant with them.

And their seed will be known among the nations, and their offspring among the peoples; all who see them will acknowledge them, that they *are* the seed Jehovah has blessed." (Is 61:4-9, MKJV See Is 65:9)

"And I will set a sign among them, and I will send those who escape [presumably escaped death in the Great Tribulation] from them to the nations, *to* Tarshish [Japan], Pul [Poles], and Lud [Albanian], drawers of the bow; *to* Tubal [Great Russians], and Javan [some descendants in southern Europe and others in east Asia], *to* the far away coasts that have not heard My fame, nor have seen My glory. **And they will declare My glory among the nations**.

And they will bring all your brothers *for* an offering to Jehovah out of all nations on horses [the gentiles will bring the Israelite slaves to the Holy Land], and in chariots, and in litters, and on mules, and on camels, to My holy mountain Jerusalem, says Jehovah, as the sons of Israel bring an offering in a clean vessel *into* the house of Jehovah.

And I will also take some of them for priests *and* for Levites, says Jehovah." (Is 66:19-21, MKJV)

"But upon Mount Zion shall be those who escaped [presumably escaped the Tribulation]; and it shall be holy. And the house of Jacob shall possess their own possessions.

And the house of Jacob shall be a fire, and the house of Joseph a flame. And the house of Esau *shall be* for stubble. And they shall kindle in them and burn them up. And no survivor shall be to the house of Esau; for Jehovah has spoken it.

And *those of* the south shall possess the mountain of Esau and the low country of the Philistines. And they shall possess the fields of Ephraim and the fields of Samaria; and Benjamin *shall possess* Gilead.

And the exiles of this army *shall go* to the sons of Israel who shall possess *the land* of the Canaanites to Zarephath; even the exiles of Jerusalem who *are* in Sepharad shall possess the cities of the south.

And deliverers shall go up into the mountain of Zion to judge the mountain of Esau; and the kingdom shall be to Jehovah." (Ob 1:17-21, MKJV)

"… therefore so says the Lord Jehovah: I will also stretch out My hand on Edom, and will cut man and beast off from it; and I will make it a waste from Teman, even to Dedan they shall fall by the sword.

And I will lay My vengeance on Edom by the hand of My people Israel. And they shall do in Edom according to My anger and according to My fury. And they shall know My vengeance, says the Lord Jehovah.

So says the Lord Jehovah: Because the Philistines have taken vengeance; yes, have taken vengeance with spite in *their* soul, to destroy *with* never-ending enmity,

So the Lord Jehovah says this: Behold, I will stretch out My hand on the Philistines, and I will cut off the Cherethites, and will destroy the rest of the sea coast.

And I will execute great vengeance on them with rebukes; and they shall know that I *am* Jehovah, when I shall lay My vengeance on them." (Ezek 25:13-17, MKJV) [how will God do this – via the might of revived Israel!]

"In that day I will raise up the booth of David that has fallen, and close up its breaks; and I will raise up its ruins, and I will build it as in the days of old;

so that they may possess the remnant of Edom, and of all the nations *on* whom My name is called, says Jehovah who is doing this." (Amos 9:11-12, MKJV) (see Num 24:17-19)

"Moab *is* my washpot; over Edom will I cast out my shoe; over Philistia will I triumph.

Who will bring me into the strong city? who will lead me into Edom?

Wilt not *thou*, O God, *who* hast cast us off? **and wilt not thou, O God, go forth with our hosts?**

Give us help from trouble: for vain *is* the help of man.

Through God we shall do valiantly: for he *it is that* shall tread down our enemies." (Ps 108:9-13, MKJV)

"And the coast shall be for the remnant of the house of Judah; they shall feed on them. In the houses of Ashkelon they shall lie down in the evening, for Jehovah their God shall visit them and turn away their captivity.

I have heard the reproach of Moab, and the curses of the sons of Ammon, *with* which they have cursed My people and have magnified *themselves* on their border.

Therefore, *as* I live, says Jehovah of Hosts, the God of Israel, Surely Moab shall be like Sodom, and the sons of Ammon like Gomorrah; a possession of nettles, and salt pits, and a ruin forever. **The remnant of My people shall plunder them, and the remnant of My people shall possess them**.

They shall have this for their pride, because they have cursed and magnified themselves against the people of Jehovah of Hosts." (Zeph 2:7-10, MKJV)

Jehovah *will be* frightening to them; for He will make all the gods of the earth lean; *each* man from his place and all the coastlands of the nations shall bow to Him.

You Ethiopians also *shall be* slain by My sword.

And He will stretch out His hand against the north and destroy Assyria, and will make Nineveh a desert and dry like a desert." (Zeph 2:11-13, MKJV) [God will use Israel to bring Edom, Assyrian, Moab, Ammon and Ashkelon (Philistines) into His realm]

"For I have bent Judah for me *as* a bow; I filled it with Ephraim, and I will stir up your sons, O Zion, against your sons, O Greece, and make you as the sword of a mighty man.

And Jehovah shall be seen over them, and His arrow shall go forth like the lightning [how? Via the Ephraimites, led by Judah]; and the Lord Jehovah shall blow the ram's horn [Day of Trumpets – symbolising war?], and shall go out with the windstorms of the south [Judah].

Jehovah of Hosts shall defend them; and they shall devour and trample the slingstones. And they shall drink and be boisterous, as through wine. And they shall be filled like a bowl, and like the corners of the altar." (Zech 9:13-15, MKJV)

"Arise and thresh, O daughter of Zion [this refers to both end-time Israel and the Church]; for I will make your horn iron, and I will make your hoofs bronze; and **you shall crush many peoples**. And I will give their gain to Jehovah, and their wealth to the Lord of the all the earth." (Mic 4:13, MKJV)

From the above, we logically come to the following conclusions:

1. After the liberation of Judah and Israel from captivity, they (under the direction of God and His saints) will subdue and admit into God's realm, many gentile nations
2. They shall inherit enormous physical blessings, bringing into final fulfillment, the blessings pronounced in the Pentateuch
3. Many gentile nations will be servants of Israel, at least for a season (probably 7 years)
4. Israel has the primacy.

Many of these scriptures speak also of the Church because of the dual nature of the Bible and spiritual Israel's spiritual blessings. But how will spiritual Israel inherit the earth? How will she conquer nations, convert peoples and receive homage?

The Bible is clear: in part *through* physical Israel.

The concepts of Christ, His body the Church and physical Israel are inextricably intertwined very closely in Scripture – possibly more than we have often realised.

WHERE DOES EZEKIEL 38 AND 39 FIT IN?

It is of interest that Ezekiel 38:18-39:16 is read in many synagogues during the Feast of Tabernacles which should provide us with a clue.

Perhaps after the first seven years or so of Israelites being settled back in the Holy Land, after Israel has swooped upon certain gentiles, many from these forces, yet to be converted, will rise up in an attempt to attack the returned Israelites.

Just as God gives us enough time to repent or show our true colours; just as He allowed Lucifer plenty of time to foment rebellion; so He will allow these forces to develop.

It would appear that these are remnants of the forces of the Second Woe (Rev 9:13-21) which God would have used to conquer and punish the countries of the Beast power.[20] The picture we get is that these peoples are led by the forces that previously attacked the nations comprising the Beast power in Europe. As such, they comprise the remnants of the 200 million army pictured in Rev 9:16.

They shall see the great blessings and wealth of Israel returned to them and want it for themselves (see Rev 18:11-13; Hag 2:7-9; Is 23:17-18; Ex 12:35-36; Jos 6:18-19). Their bitterness and jealousy toward restored Israel will well-up into a lust for war leading God to bring about circumstances which will result in their humbling.

> "Wrath *is* cruel, and anger *is* overwhelming; but who *is* able to stand before envy?" (Prov 27:4, MKJV)

Ezekiel reveals the following:

> "So says the Lord Jehovah: And it shall be in that day that things shall come into your heart, and you shall devise an evil plan.
>
> And you shall say, I will go up to the land of open spaces. I will go *to* **those at ease** [cp Lam 1:3], who **dwell securely**, all of them dwelling **without walls**, and there are no bars nor gates to them,
>
> **in order to take a spoil**, and to steal a prize; to turn your hand on the inhabited waste places, and **on the people gathered out of the nations, who have gotten cattle and goods**, who dwell in the midst of the land." (Ezek 38:10-12, MKJV)

Notice: this rebellion is against the Israelites who have returned from captivity and who now have gathered much wealth as we have seen. They are also dwelling in peace.

And why does this war occur?

> "And I will set My glory among the nations, and all the nations shall see My judgments which I have done, and My hand that I have laid on them.

---

[20] So much of scripture is dual that these chapters, whilst primarily refer to a time near the beginning of the Millennium, they may also refer to the Gog and Magog referred to in Rev 20:7-9. They may also refer in some way to the forces of the north and east which fights the Beast power.

So the house of Israel shall know that I *am* Jehovah their God from that day and forward. [there will be no more doubting Thomas's]

And the nations shall know that the house of Israel was exiled [i.e. prior to this Gog and Magog invasion] for their iniquity. Because they sinned against Me, therefore I hid My face from them and gave them into the hand of their enemies. So they all fell by the sword." (Ezek 39:21-23, MKJV) [it follows on therefore that these gentile nations will now be called to repent and allow God to rule over them through Israel]

There may be parallel passages in Zechariah. Chapter 12 has a Trumpets theme and is read in synagogues on the Day of Trumpets; chapter 13 has an Atonement theme and read on the Day of Atonement; while chapter 14 is read during the Feast of Tabernacles.

Chapter 14:1-11 refers to the first few years of the Millennium and specifically states that Jerusalem (and by extension the land of Israel) will be safely inhabited (cp Ezek 38:11,14). Then we are told:

"And this shall be the plague with which Jehovah will strike all the peoples who have fought against Jerusalem [both before and after the return of Christ]. Their flesh shall rot while they stand on their feet, and their eyes shall rot in their sockets. And their tongue shall rot in their mouth.

And it shall be in that day a great panic of Jehovah shall be among them **And they shall each one lay hold of his neighbor,** and his hand shall rise up against the hand of his neighbor.

And Judah also shall fight at Jerusalem; and the wealth of all the nations all around shall be gathered, gold, and silver, and clothing in great abundance.

And so shall be the **plague** of the horse, the mule, the camel, and the ass, and of all the beasts which shall be in these tents, like this plague.

And it shall be, everyone who is left of all the nations which came up against Jerusalem shall go up from year to year to worship the King, Jehovah of Hosts, and to keep the Feast of Tabernacles.

Yea, every pot in Jerusalem and in Judah shall be holy to Jehovah of Hosts. And all those who sacrifice shall come and take of them, and boil in them. And in that day there shall no longer be a trader [i.e. Canaanite] in the house of Jehovah of Hosts." (Zech 14:12-21, MKJV)

Compare the above with Ezekiel:

"And I will call for a sword against him on all My mountains, says the Lord Jehovah. *Each* **man's sword shall be against his brother.** [cp Hag 2:22]

And I will judge him with a **plague** and with blood. And I will rain on him, and on his bands, and on the many peoples with him, an overflowing shower, and great hailstones, fire and brimstone.

So I will magnify Myself and sanctify Myself. And I will be known in the eyes of many nations, and they shall know that I *am* Jehovah." (Ezek 38:21-23, MKJV) [and they know God by loving Him and obeying Him e.g. by observing the Feast of Tabernacles]

What of those nations that, prior to the liberation of Israel by Christ, would have enslaved Israel, but by now have repented and even assisted in the transporting of liberated Israelitish captives to the Holy Land?:

> "Sheba and Dedan, and the merchants of Tarshish, with all their young lions [**Assyria or Germany – See the proof in Nah 2:8-12; Hos 5:13-14; Jer 2:14-15, 18; 4:7; 50:17; Zech 11:3; Joel 1:6**], shall say to you, Have you come to take a spoil? Have you gathered your company to steal a prize, to carry away silver and gold, to take away cattle and goods, to take a great spoil?" (Ezek 38:13, MKJV)

Here we are told that the intent is to take from Israel what she has gathered from other nations. The nations speaking up and warning them are Sheba (Schwabians), Dedan (Prussians), Tarshish (Spain and the eastern Tarshish residing in Japan) and the young lions (Assyria which is Germany today. See the proof in Nah 2:8-12; Hos 5:13-14; Jer 2:14-15, 18; 4:7; 50:17; Zech 11:3; Joel 1:6). These are nations which had formerly comprised part of the Beast power (and their allies). But now they are repentant and warn the enemies of Israel not to attack Israel, God's people! Why? Because they would be very well aware of the consequences of such action!

WILL THE TRIBES OF ISRAEL HAVE SPECIFIC ROLES?

From the descriptions of the tribes, the way they acted in the Bible and from their modern histories, it would appear that they have definitive pre-determined, organised roles. See Gen 29; 30; 49; Num 23; 24; Deut 33; Jud 5.

Judah -

> "Judah, may your brothers praise you. May your hand *be* in the neck of your enemies. May your father's sons bow before you.
> Judah *is* **a lion's whelp**. My son, you have gone up from the prey. He stooped, he crouched like a **lion**; and like a **lioness**, who shall rouse him? [a warrior people]
> The **scepter** [the royal line] shall not depart from Judah, nor a **Lawgiver** from between his feet, until Shiloh come. And the obedience of the peoples to him." (Gen 49:8-10, MKJV) [cf IIChron 9:8; IChron 29:23; Jer 33:14, 17]

> "And the sons of Israel rose and went up to the house of God and asked counsel of God, and said, Which of us *shall go up* first to the battle against the sons of Benjamin? **And Jehovah said, Judah first**." (Judges 20:18, MKJV) [see Deut 33:7]

> "For **Judah prevailed among his brothers, and from him** *came* **the chief ruler** [the royal line of David which includes the Messiah], but the birthright *was* Joseph's." (IChron 5:2, MKJV)

"And He refused the tabernacle of Joseph, and chose not the tribe of Ephraim;
but chose the tribe of Judah, the mount Zion which He loved." (Ps 78:67-68, MKJV) [see IKings 11:36; Zech 8:15]

"Gilead *is* Mine, and Manasseh *is* Mine; and Ephraim *is* the strength of My head, **Judah *is* My lawgiver**." (Ps 60:7, MKJV) [see Ps 108:8; 114:2]

"Ephraim *circles* around Me with lying, and the house of Israel with deceit. **But Judah still rules with God, and is faithful with the saints**." (Hos 11:12, MKJV)

"**For I have bent Judah for me *as* a bow**; I filled it with Ephraim, and I will stir up your sons, O Zion, against your sons, O Greece, and make you as the sword of a mighty man." (Zech 9:13, MKJV) [see 10:3-7]

"And the governors of Judah shall say in their heart, The people of Jerusalem *shall be* my strength in Jehovah of Hosts their God.

In that day **I will make the governors of Judah like a hearth of fire among the wood, and like a torch of fire among cut grain. And they shall devour all the peoples all around**, on the right hand and on the left hand. And Jerusalem shall be inhabited again in her place, in Jerusalem.

Jehovah also shall save the tents of Judah first, so that the glory of the house of David and the glory of the people of Jerusalem may not be magnified above Judah.

In that day Jehovah shall defend around the people of Jerusalem. And it will be, he who is feeble among them at that day *shall be* like David; and **the house of David *shall be* like God**, like the Angel of Jehovah before them." (Zech 12:5-8, MKJV)

"And it shall be, in that day the mountains shall drop down new wine, and the hills shall flow *with* milk, and all the rivers of Judah shall flow *with* waters; and a fountain shall come forth from the house of Jehovah, and shall water the valley of Shittim.

Egypt shall be a ruin, and Edom shall be a desolate wilderness, from violence *done* to the sons of Judah, whose innocent blood they poured out in their land.

But Judah will dwell forever, and Jerusalem to generation and generation." (Jer 3:18-20, MKJV) [just as the Scots were the pioneers leading the way so often in the colonies, in bringing tribes and peoples to heel under Israel, so they shall fulfill this function again].

Judah produced the royal line, a warrior class and lawmakers. In other words they were to be the political leaders. It is interesting that the Scots have produced inventors, military leaders and political leaders well above their numbers in the America, Australia and South Africa. In ancient Israel they led the other tribes in the camp. In America they were in the forefront of the colonising people, leading the way. They are a very brave people who are willing to take on anything no matter how large or foreboding:

"The wicked flee *when* no man pursues; but the righteous are bold as a lion." (Prov 28:1, MKJV)

Throughout Bible times Judah dwelt within and in proximity to Jerusalem, the capital city of Jerusalem as the leading tribe. And as fierce defenders of God's way and the Temple and all that goes with leadership, the Levites are nearby:

Levi -

"But the Levites who have gone far away from Me, when Israel went astray; those who went astray from Me after their idols; they shall even bear their iniquity.

Yet **they shall be ministers in My sanctuary, overseers at the gates of the house and ministering to the house**. They shall kill the burnt offering and the sacrifice for the people, and they shall stand before them to minister to them.

Because they ministered to them before their idols, and caused the house of Israel to fall into iniquity, therefore I have lifted up My hand against them, says the Lord Jehovah, and they shall bear their iniquity.

And they shall not come near Me, to do the office of a priest to Me, nor to come near any of My holy things, in the most holy place; but they shall bear their shame and their abominations which they have committed.

But I will make them keepers of the charge of the house for all its service, and for all that shall be done in it." (Ezek 44:10-14, MKJV)

"Behold, the days come, saith the LORD, that I will perform that good thing which I have promised unto the house of Israel and to the house of Judah…

Neither shall the priests the Levites want a man before me to offer burnt offerings, and to kindle meat offerings, and to do sacrifice continually." [this seems to imply that ministers would emanate from Levi for all generations and many of them are found in the Church] (Jer 33:14, 18, MKJV)

Here it is self-evident that the tribe of Levi shall occupy their traditional roles again during the Millennium.

Ephraim -

"Again you shall plant vineyards on the mountains of Samaria; the planters shall plant and shall enjoy the fruit.

For there shall be a day *that* the watchmen on Mount **Ephraim shall cry, Arise and let us go up to Zion** to Jehovah our God!

For so says Jehovah, Sing with gladness for Jacob, and shout among **the chief of the nations**. Cry out, give praise and say, O Jehovah, save Your people, the remnant of Israel…

Is **Ephraim My dear son?** *Is he* **a delightful child?** For as often as I spoke against him, I earnestly remember him still. Therefore My heart is troubled for him; I will surely have mercy on him, says Jehovah." (Jer 31:5-7, 20, MKJV)

"How shall I give you up, Ephraim? How shall I deliver you, Israel? How shall I make you like Admah? How shall I set you as Zeboim? My heart is turned within Me; My compassions are kindled together.

I will not carry out the heat of My anger; **I will not return to destroy Ephraim**. For I *am* God and not man, the Holy One in your midst; and I will not enter into the city." [God has special feelings toward Ephraim] (Hos 11:8-9, MKJV)

"And I will strengthen the house of **Judah**, and I will save the house of Joseph, and I will return to save them; for I have pity on them. And they shall be as though I had not cast them off; for I *am* Jehovah their God, and I will answer them.

And Ephraim shall be like a mighty one, and their heart shall rejoice as *by* wine. And their sons shall see and be glad; their heart shall rejoice in Jehovah." [Judah and Ephraim mentioned together once again, working together] (Zech 10:6-7, MKJV)

Refer also to Is 7:9; Jer 31:5-6, 20; 10:6-7; Ps 78:67-68.

As we have seen in so many Scriptures, Ephraim and Judah are sometimes mentioned together. Therefore, like the Scots and English, they must be in unison to some degree to assist in bringing about God's Kingdom on earth.

These people are very innovative and suitable for colonising due to their attributes. They shall continue to supply the majority of inhabitants to the colonies.

Manasseh -

The Bible doesn't specify, but given the attributes of Anglo-Americans, they think big, mass produce goods and services which has resulted in improvements to the world's economy and standard of living for many millions. It would seem that they would have a similar role in the Millennium.

Some have speculated that the inventive genius of these peoples will be guided by God to provide technological breakthroughs for the benefit of man in various fields, just as they have today, in many ways.

Similarly, the other tribes' contributions will be based on national talents and blessings.

From all the Scriptures, how could one believe in replacement theology? For Israel obviously has the primacy, even throughout the Millennium.

What will the land allotment be for Israel in the Millennium?

As we have seen in this study, Israel will be a light to the nations and rule the world under the Messiah. To achieve this, they will reclaim their former territories, which were stripped from them during the Tribulation. Through the Priests and Levites, they will help convert the world, leading all peoples to submit to the Messiah.

As will be demonstrated below, they will be allocated land within the Holy Land but it doesn't end there. Their territory will expand to the river of Egypt and Euphrates (Gen 15:18) before extending to the entire globe.

Dr Gromacki in his article *The Fulfillment of the Abrahamic Covenant* explains:

"This covenant with Abraham ... is a promissory oath made by God alone ... the nearest parallel to this form is the royal land grant made by kings to loyal servants. These grants of land were typically made to a man and his descendants in perpetuity. In form and content they thus run in parallel to the patriarchal promises." (p. 87)

A large number of detailed studies have been undertaken of the allocation of the tribes of Israel during the Millennium of which a handful are referred to herein.

Note Israel will not be restricted to that area for too long and will once again become a colonising people as explained in the section *Israel's Destiny to Colonise parts of the World*.

Here is one map for this period drafted by one scholar, followed by important quotes about those allotments:

Figure 2 Land Allotment in the Millennium

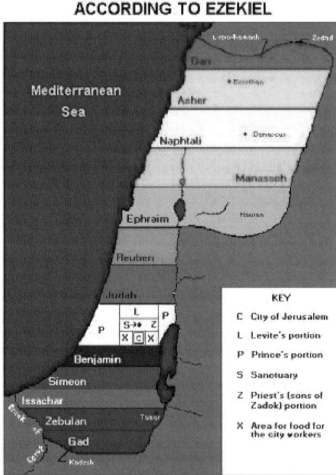

Adapted from map prepared by Lambert Dolphin © 1996

"After the land is enlarged and given its new and promised borders, it would seem logical that Jesus will next order the redistribution of the land. Ezekiel 48:1-29 gives us the outline of how it will look (see map above).

The land will be divided into three portions. In the northern section the land will be allotted to the tribes of Dan, Asher, Naphtali, Manasseh, Ephraim, Reuben, and Judah, in that order from north to south (Ezek. 48:1-7). In the southern section the land will be allotted to Benjamin, Simeon, Issachar, Zebulun and Gad, in that order (Ezek. 48:23-27).

The section in the middle will be known as the holy district. As you see on the map below" (Stephen Nielsen, *The Redistribution of the Land of Israel in the Millennial Kingdom*, 17 Aug 2014)

(Map below from https://studyingbibleprophecy.wordpress.com/2014/08/17/the-redistribution-of-the-land-of-israel-in-the-millennial-kingdom/)

Figure 3 Millennial Land Borders and Allotment

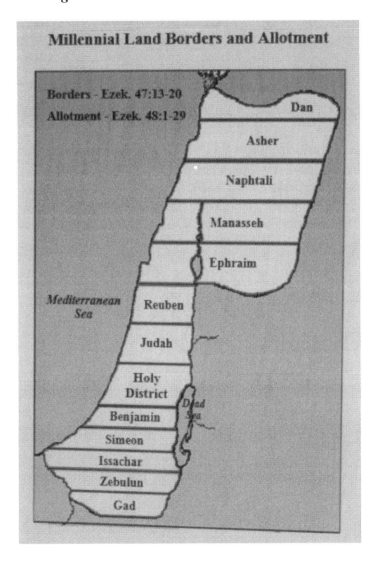

"In the center of this area will be a square shaped parcel of land, 25,000 cubits square (or 8 1/3 miles square). This area, as you see, is divided into three sections. In the northern sector, an area 8 1/2 miles by 3 1/3 miles is where the Levites will live.

Below this area an area of the same dimension is where the Zadokian priest will dwell. **This area is most holy because it is where the temple will be—the place of worship, and where Christ (or possibly where David),** will sit on the throne. The sector of land farthest to the south is where the city of Jerusalem is located. The enlarged city (about 1 1/2 miles square) will sit in the middle of this sector, with city land on either side of it. This land will be designated for farmland, in which the workers of the city out of all the tribes of Israel will cultivate and produce food for themselves (Ezek. 48:18-19).

Now on the east and the west sides of this square area, these areas are designated for the Prince. There isn't any indication in Ezekiel who this one will be, but we have already suggested that it will either be Christ of David." (ibid) [emphasis mine]

Figure 4 The Holy District

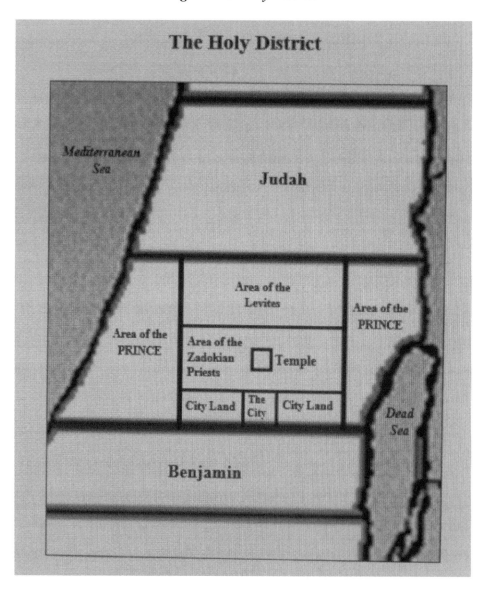

(ibid)

As LaHaye and Hindson note:

"The 12 tribes of Israel, after they are regathered, reidentified, reunited, and restored to the Lord and to the land, will be redistributed within the boundaries of the land according to their tribal allotments. The seven northern tribes will be separated from the five southern tribes by the holy portion on the mountain on which the temple rests ...

"At the beginning of the millennium, topographical changes will occur in and around the city of Jerusalem. These changes will create the millennial mountain, which will be elevated above the hills (Isaiah 2:2), while all the surrounding land will be flattened into a vast plan (Zechariah 14:10). This will be done so that the site of the Lord's residence occupies the highest location in the region ...

"The symbolic school of biblical interpretation finds the immense dimensions ascribed to the millennial mountain and its holy portion (temple and city) proof that Ezekiel 40-48 cannot be interpreted literally. However, given the extensive topographical expansion described by Ezekiel, the new boundaries and dimensions are quite realistic." (*Exploring Bible Prophecy from Genesis to Revelation*, pp. 217-218)

Blenkinsopp explains:

"Judah and Levi are on the north side and therefore closest to the sacred area together with Reuben, the firstborn. All three are Leah tribes. Opposite them, on the south side, are Simeon, Issachar, and Zebulun, the other three Leah tribes. **Three concubine tribes – Gad, Asher, and Naphtali – are grouped together on the west**, while the Rachel tribes, Joseph and Benjamin, with **the son [Dan] of Rachel's concubine Bilhah, are opposite them on the east**. The entire arrangement is reminiscent of the sanctuary in the wilderness surrounded by the tribal camps, three on each of the four sides (Num. 2)." (*Ezekiel*, pp. 238-39) [emphasis mine]

Keil & Delitzsch:

"The division of the land, like the definition of the boundaries (Eze 47:15), commences in the north, and enumerates the tribes in the order in which they were to receive their inheritances from north to south: first, seven tribes from the northern boundary to the centre of the land (Eze 48:1-7), where the heave for the sanctuary, with the land of the priests and Levites and the city domain, together with the prince's land on the two sides, was to be set apart (Eze 48:8-22; and secondly, the other five tribes from this to the southern boundary (Eze 48:23-29) ...

"**The new division of the land differs from the former one effected in the time of Joshua, in the first place, in the fact that all the tribe-portions were to extend uniformly across the entire breadth of the land from the eastern boundary to the Mediterranean Sea on the west, so that they were to form parallel tracts of country; whereas in the distribution made in the time of Joshua, several of the tribe-territories covered only half the breadth of the land.** For example, Dan received his inheritance on the west of Benjamin; and the territories of half Manasseh and Asher ran up from the northern boundary of Ephraim to the northern boundary of Canaan; while Issachar,

Naphtali, and Zebulon received their portions on the east of these; and lastly, Simeon received his possession within the boundaries of the tribe of Judah. And secondly, it also differs from the former, in the fact that not only are all the twelve tribes located in Canaan proper, between the Jordan and the Mediterranean Sea; whereas previously two tribes and a half had received from Moses, at their own request, the conquered land of Bashan and Gilead on the eastern side of the Jordan, so that the land of Canaan could be divided among the remaining nine tribes and a half. But besides this, the central tract of land, about the fifth part of the whole, was separated for the holy heave, the city domain, and the prince's land, so that only the northern and southern portions, about four-fifths of the whole, remained for distribution among the twelve tribes, seven tribes receiving their hereditary portions to the north of the heave and five to the south, because the heave was so selected that the city with its territory lay near the ancient Jerusalem. - In Eze 48:1-7 the seven tribes which were to dwell on the north of the heave are enumerated. The principal points of the northern boundary, viz., the way to Chetlon and Hazar-Enon, the boundary of Damascus, are repeated in Eze 48:1 from Eze 47:15, Eze 47:17, as the starting and terminal points of the northern boundary running from west to east." (*Commentary on the Old Testament, Ezekiel, Zechariah*) [emphasis mine]

John Taylor in *Ezekiel. Tyndale Old Testament Commentaries* (chapter 8) wrote:

"**The northern tribes** (beginning from the north) are Dan, Asher, Naphtali, Manasseh, Ephraim, Reuben and Judah. **Of these it is worth noting that the three which are farthest from the sanctuary are tribes descended from sons of Jacob's concubines, Dan and Naphtali having been born to Rachel's maid Bilhah, and Asher to Leah's maid Zilpah (Gen. 30:5-13). The fourth son by concubinage, Gad, is the farthest away from the sanctuary among the southern group of tribes.** Judah has pride of place immediately to the north of the central portion, as being the inheritor of the Messianic promise through the blessing of Jacob (Gen. 49:8-12), and he supersedes Reuben, the first-born, who is in the next position away on the north side. The other two places are held by the two grandsons of Rachel, the children of Joseph...

"**To the south** of the holy portion are the allotted areas for the remaining five tribes. Benjamin has the privileged position nearest to the sanctuary, as his father's youngest son by Rachel; Simeon, Issachar and Zebulun come next, all born of Leah; **and finally, as we have already noticed, Gad, the child of the concubine, Zilpah.** It needs little imagination to realize that, apart from Judah and Benjamin, which adjoin the holy portion and which always had the closest geographical interest in Jerusalem, **the other ten tribes are allotted without any regard to their original position in the land of Israel at the time of the conquest...**

"On the north side, the side facing towards the sanctuary, the gates are named after Reuben the first-born, Judah the Davidic ancestor, and Levi the founder of the priesthood. To the south are Simeon, Issachar and Zebulun, and this pattern corresponds with their southerly geographical placing. To the west are three concubine tribes, Gad, Asher and Naphtali. Perhaps the least consistence trio are those on the east side, where Joseph and Benjamin, the two children of Rachel, are linked with Dan, a child of Rachel's maid." [emphasis mine]

Note also the explanation from the *Jewish Bible Quarterly*:

"Lands outside a ritually defined Israel are considered unclean (cf. Josh. 22:19; Amos 7:17; Hos. 9:3; Ezek. 4:13). Thus on issues related to purity "a clearly observable distinction between clean and unclean land" is required. In addition, this boundary description "is patterned after a royal grant." It probably suggested to the exiles of Israel a supremely royal or Divine grant of territories to Israel from which future offerings will be acceptable at a restored Temple." ("The Utopian Map in Ezekiel (48:1-35)," *Jewish Bible Quarterly*, Vol. 34, No. 1, p. 21)

Harold Brodsky (p. 20) also explains:

Figure 5 Tribal Arrangement

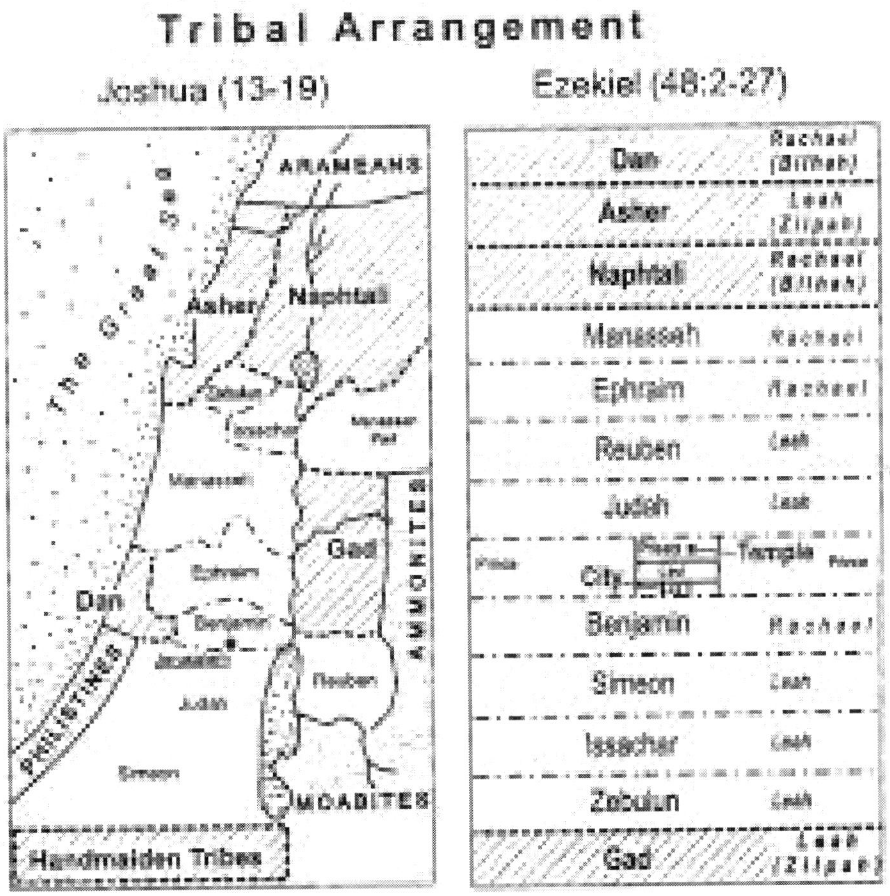

"Tribal ancestry: Asher – Leah/Zilpah; Naphtali – Rachel/Bilhah; Zebulon & Issachar – Leah; Gad – Leah/Zilpah; Menasseh & Ephraim (sometimes Joseph alone) – Rachel; Benjamin – Rachel; Dan – Rachel/Bilhah; Judah – Leah; Reuben – Leah; Simeon – Leah. (Levi – under Joshua, distributed in various cities; Ezekiel locates this tribe between the Temple and the city)"

The map above and the one below are from Harold Brodsky's article (p. 22):

Figure 6 Ezekiel Land Allotment

Ezekiel
Land Allotment
with
Boundaries
(Ezek 45:1-8;
47:13 - 48:35)

The Great Sea

Dan
Asher
Naphtali
Manasseh
Ephraim
The Jordan
Reuben
Judah
Temple
City
Levi
Benjamin
Dead Sea
Simeon
Issachar
Zebulun
Gad
Brook of Egypt
Handmaiden Tribes

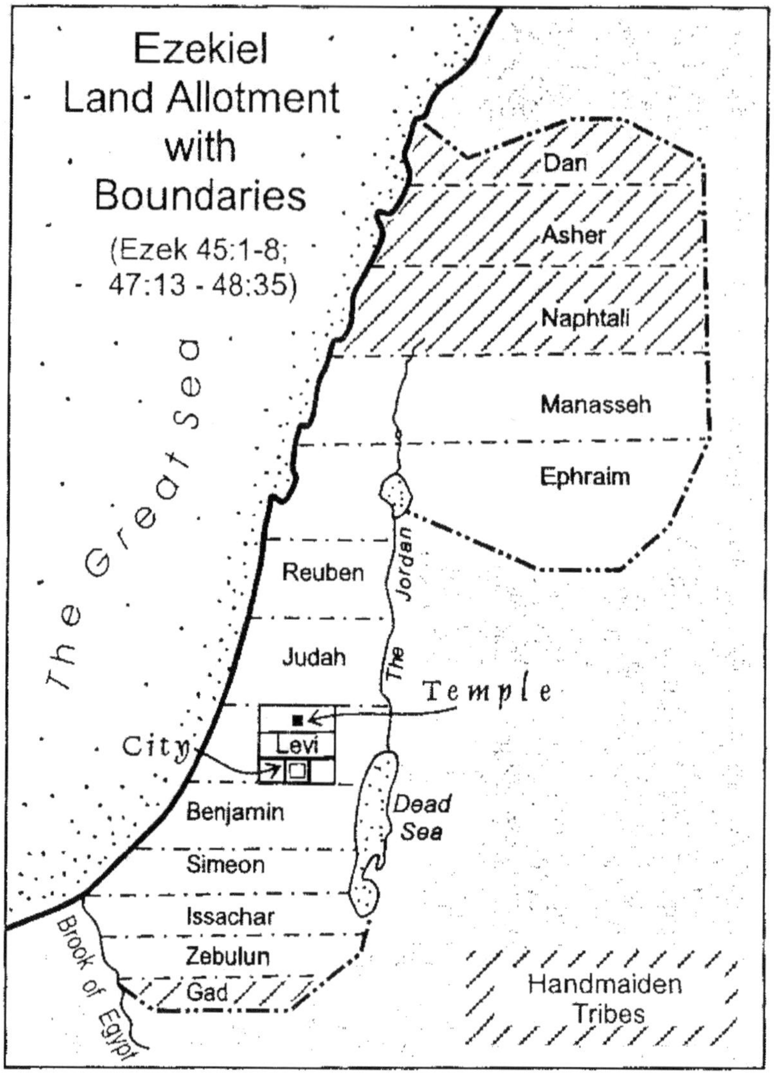

"… in contrast to the past, Judah is placed in the northern region with former rivals Ephraim and Manasseh. Perhaps a principle of political accommodation is implied in a tribal arrangement that uses a merger to avoid rivalry. Royal lineage is represented in both regions with the Davidic line of Judah in the north and that of King Saul of Benjamin in the south." (p. 23)

"Ezekiel places the "handmaiden tribes" toward the frontier, seemingly at a disadvantaged distance from the restored Temple." (p. 25)

And why are the handmaiden/concubine tribes located at the periphery? Stevenson explains:

"What is most significant is that Duguid has used vertical language to describe the social change while the book uses horizontal language. **It is not a matter of being *up or down* a social ladder as it is a matter of being *near or far* from sacred space.**

It is a subtle point, but it is significant to grasping the worldview of the book. In our time, we tend to use vertical metaphors to expose social status. In the worldview of Ezekiel, the metaphorical language is horizontal, based on the degree of access to sacred space" (Kalinda Stevenson, *The Vision of Transformation*, pp. xxiii-iv).

So, tribal locations appear to be related to social status, related to marriage versus concubinage.

The above represents some of the materials available on this complex Millennial subject, often overlooked by the Churches for some reason.

Note especially that the handmaiden's descendants/sons are allocated the outer areas. And Judah is near the Temple territory.

Will Israel and the nations be extant in the eternal Kingdom of God?

So far we have discussed Israel during the Millennial reign of the Messiah. But what of the spirit world?

Because the physical world is typological of the spirit realm, there may be spirit nations in God's Family. The New Earth will have non-Israelite nations (Rev 21:24-26) and as such, there must also be a spirit Israel. Indeed, the 12 gates to the New Jerusalem will have the names of the tribes of Israel. This indicates that there will be spirit tribes of Israel.

So, the nations of Genesis 10 and the 12 tribes of Israel, which are extremely important aspects of God's Plan, will still be extant in the Kingdom. This particular means of rule and service, will continue into the eternal Kingdom!

Now we can see why Israel and the role of the gentile nations are so important that they are referred to so very often throughout the Bible. It is not some little thing that can be ignored, but critical to God's Plan – it is how God works and will continue to work.

Starting with Adam, then through to Noah, Shem, Arphaxad down to Abraham, Isaac, Jacob and the tribes of Israel (especially Judah, Levi and Ephraim), God is working with and through a particular line. That does not end with the Church at all. Instead, the concepts of Church and Israel are closely intertwined and fit together.

Allow this author to iterate: Israel has the primacy, it is a Biblical principle.

Summary

From the aforementioned we find the following:

- In certain ways, the British Empire was typological of the coming reign of Israel over the world
- So much more is said of Israel ruling in the Millennium than what is said of the Church

- Israel is to return to her former (colonial) lands
- Israel will take gentile nations into servitude for a period, probably seven years
- Under the Messiah, Israel will be ruling over all gentile nations as a blessing
- Huge physical blessings will flow to Israel
- The Church does not replace Israel, but will rule through her

What then, can we make of the above? What will Israel be doing in the World Tomorrow? In effect, there will be an Israelite union bringing about the fulfilment the dreams of certain men in Britain and the USA in the early decades of the twentieth century. Later some led a movement called 'Union Now' – an Anglo-Saxon-Keltic hegemony to rule the world – the British Empire and America were to join forces to do so. The Rhodes scholars were to be trained to be rulers for this honour. Churchill and other British leaders had similar hopes for British ruling classes to be set up all over the world. The time for this was premature, but certainly the British Empire was typological of the Millennial rule of Israel - presaging what the scriptures obviously demonstrate shall be.

Israel is in serious decline today. She will be enslaved and punished terribly during the Great Tribulation. After being rescued by her God and Messiah, she will renew her covenant and rule the world for 1,000 years under Christ and the children of God.

Table 5 Stages in Israel's Coming Exodus

1. Day of the Lord intervention with nations that came against Israel during the Tribulation brutally punished.
2. The Messiah returns to the earth to rescue Israel and the world, setting foot on the Mount of Olives.
3. Scattered and enslaved Israelites begin to repent and are brought into proximity to the Holy Land where rebels are purged out in the wilderness (Is 30:18; Jer 50:20; Ezek 20:38, 42-44) thus re-assembling and reviving the nation (Ezek 36).
4. The righteous Israelites enter the Holy Land in the Second Exodus (typed by the First Exodus and Judahites returning from Babylonian captivity) (Is 27:13; 10:20-22; 11:11-12; Jer 16:14-15; 23:3, 7-8; 31:8-9; 50:3-5). The entry will likely be in a planned sequence (i.e. Priests, Levites, Judah, Ephraim etc).
5. Israel and Judah are re-united, Christ completes His 3½ year ministry with Israel (Dan 9:27) and a New Covenant made with them (Ezekiel 37) (the Covenant with the Church is made at the resurrection prior to this).
6. Close by is Mount Zion where He will rule from. His place of residence and love affair with Mount Zion is extant throughout the Scriptures and is easy to read over.
7. His rule extends throughout Jerusalem and the Promised Land from the Euphrates to the Nile.
8. Either before or after the Temple inauguration, Israel is assigned tribal allocations (Ezek 48).

9. God entices Gog and Magog et al to attempt to invade the Holy Land in order to bring them to heel (Ezekiel 38 and 39).
10. An earthquake shakes the land (Ezek 38:19-20).
11. The New Temple is built and inaugurated (Ezekiel 40-48).
12. Christ enters the New Temple after its completion (Ezek 42:3-7).
13. Israel is trained for world leadership and becomes His battle-axe to put down rebellious nations (Is 60:1-16).
14. Israel swoops upon many nations to take them under the control of the Messiah's government.
15. The Messiah's rule through the saints and Israel is gradually extended throughout the world until all are brought under His rule which this study concentrates upon. All rebellions are dealt with sternly.
16. Rebellions and nations sins decrease during the Millennium as peoples and individuals are converted until there is world peace and prosperity – the Wonderful World Tomorrow achieved!

THE MILLENNIAL CONCEPT

THE AGE TO COME

Most groups and authors do not use the term *World Tomorrow*, but a few do to promote the future Millennium and Kingdom of God on earth.[21]

Where does the term originate?

Essentially it is a modern English variation of the English term *world to come* found in Heb 6:5; Matt 12:32; Mark 10:30; Luke 18:30; Eph 1:21. It is the time that the Messiah rules the earth; Israel is revived; and the restoration of all things under God (Acts 1:6; 3:21; Matt 2:6; 10:23; 19:28; John 1:41).

According to Nathaniel West in *The Thousand Years* (1889), the Messianic Kingdom:

> "is called "*Olam Habba*," or "the world to come." The New Testament employs these divisions of time, and they are ever in the mouth of our Lord and His Apostles, as "*Aion ho houtos*," "this present world," and "*Aion ho mellon*," "the world to come," *i.e.*, "this age," and the "coming age." (pp. 12-13)

It is "ever in the mouth of our Lord and His Apostles" because that is the emphasis of the Gospel – the future Kingdom on earth.

Albert Barnes' Notes on the Whole Bible on Heb 6:5:

> "And the powers of the world to come - Or of the "**coming age.**" "**The age to come**" **was a phrase in common use among the Hebrews, to denote the future dispensation, the times of the Messiah.** The same idea was expressed by the phrases "the last times," "the end of the world," etc. which are of so frequent occurrence in the Scriptures. They all denoted an age which was to succeed the old dispensation; the time of the Messiah; or the period in which the affairs of the world would be wound up; see the notes on Isaiah 2:2." [Emphasis mine. Refer also to Heb 2:5]

---

[21] It is chiefly the Church of God and its offshoots that utilise this term to express the millennial reign of the Messiah.

Figure 7 Warm, cosy homes

Others make similar note of this such as McNeile's *The Problem of the Future Life*:

> "*Aonios* (eternal, "ayonios"), for all practical purposes, when applied to things of the New Age means 'belonging, or proper to **the New Age**'" (p. 48). [emphasis mine]

Another is C Kingsley Barratt in *The Gospel According to St. John*:

> "The meaning of 'the life of eternity' (Dan. 12:2) was expressed by the rabbis as 'the life of **the coming age**'" (p. 179). [emphasis mine]

The Gospel According to Mark by Vincent Taylor explains this similarly:

> "In origin the conception [eternal life] is eschatological: eternal life is '**Life in the coming age**'" (p. 426). [emphasis mine]

Thayer in his *Lexicon* throws further light upon this

> "As the Jews distinguished 'this age,' the time before the Messiah, and **the 'coming age,' the time after the advent of the Messiah**, so most of the New Testament writers

distinguish 'this age' (or simply 'the age -- Matt. 13:22; Mark 4:19; 'the present age' -- Gal. 1:4; 1 Tim. 6:17; 2 Tim. 4:10; Titus 2:12), the time *before* the appointed return or truly Messianic advent of Christ -- and the *future age* (or 'that age' -- Luke 20:35), 'the coming age' (Luke 18:30; Matt. 12:32), i.e., the age *after* the return of Christ in majesty, the period of the establishment of the Divine Kingdom with all its blessings" (p. 19). [emphasis mine]

Or as we are told in the book of Acts:

"Therefore repent and convert so that your sins may be blotted out, when the **times of refreshing shall come** from *the* presence of the Lord.

And He shall send Jesus Christ, who before was proclaimed to you, whom Heaven truly needs to receive until the times of **restoration of all things** [i.e. Eden is coming back!], which God has spoken by *the* mouth of His holy prophets since the world began." (Acts 3:19-21, MKJV)

The word *apokatastasis* (restoration) means to restore, to set back to the correct position. Thayer's *Lexicon* says that it is "the restoration not only of the true theocracy but also of that more perfect state of (even physical) things that existed before the fall."

Figure 8 Edenic Conditions

In other words, it is the restoration of the Garden of Eden concept.[22]

---

[22] Renald Showers in *Maranatha, Our Lord Come* indulges in further explanatory detail:

"In Matthew 36 Jesus declared that 'the regeneration' would take place 'when the Son of man shall sit on the throne of his glory.' His terminology is significant. It indicates that when Christ, as the Son of man (as a

There will be a return to Edenic conditions across the world – gradual as that may be (see Is 51:3; Ezek 36:35-36). Mankind – one with God, each other and nature. The beauty of the world will be beyond compare when He brings it about because "Yahweh is the 'Lord of the end of things.'" (Christopher North, *The Old Testament Interpretation of History*, p. 126).

COMPARING EDEN WITH THE MILLENNIUM AND FEAST OF TABERNACLES

A number of Scriptures make reference to the time of the Messiah to be the restoration of conditions similar to that of the Garden of Eden.

The following table has been prepared below to demonstrate this similarity and which, I believe, provides further proof that this Feast is a type of the Edenic Millennial reign of the Messiah.

Table 6 Chart comparing the Garden of Eden with the Millennium and Feast of Tabernacles

Garden of Eden	Millennium and Feast of Tabernacles
Gen 2:8-9 - God in the garden and the tree of life in the midst	The Messiah will be in the midst, granting life. Cf Ezek 37:27; 43:4-5.
Gen 2:8; Ezek 31:8 – it is the Lord's Garden	Tabernacles is the Lord's Feast typological of when He will return the world to Edenic qualities. The Millennium is the sabbath Lord's Day. See Acts 3:19-21; Is 51:3; Ezek 36:35-36.
Gen 2:9 - Magnificent and edible fruits	A time of super-abundance and agricultural blessings. Cp Deut 11:10; IKings 21:2 – herbs and spices.
Gen 2:6,10; Is 58:11 - Well watered	The deserts will bloom and the earth will be well-watered. Is 32:15; 35:1-2, 7-8; 41:19.

---

human, a kinsman of mankind) rules the earth, **there will be a return to the original state that existed** when the earth was born, which is recorded in Genesis and involved mankind's tenant possession or administration of the earth as God's representative. Christ taught that He will begin to exercise that rule when He returns in glory with His holy angels (Mtt. 25:31) … Peter declared that 'the times of refreshing' and 'the times of the restitution of all things' will come when God sends Christ back to be personally present on the earth … F. F. Bruce wrote that 'the restitution' to which Peter referred in Acts 3:21 'appears to be identical with' 'the regeneration' to which Jesus referred in Mat. 19:28, and that **the restoration involved will include 'a renovation of all nature.'"** (pp. 86-87) [emphasis mine]

Garden of Eden	Millennium and Feast of Tabernacles
Ezek 31:6, 9 – large trees with large boughs and a place for the birds to nest and brood. Three of the trees were mentioned – cedar, fir, chestnut	Lev 23:40 – booths made from palms, boughs of large trees, willows. Neh 8:15 – booths made from olive, pine, myrtle, palm branches and from large trees. Refer to the Scriptures re palm trees in Ex 15:27; Ps 11:7; 92:12. And willows Ps 1:3.
Is 51:3 - There was joy and happiness in Eden	Lev 23:40 – the Feast was to be a time of rejoicing as will be the Millennium. See Is 25:9; 35:1-2; Jer 31:11-14.
Gen 2:2-3 - The Sabbath rest was instituted in Eden	Tabernacles – the 7th festival in the 7th month lasted 7 days – pictured the Millennial rest and ingathering of the nations. See Is 32:17-19.

Of further interest is that the Garden of Eden contains temple or sanctuary typology. For evidence of this, please refer to Peter Beckman's, *The Garden of Eden an Archetypal Sanctuary*. MA Thesis, Dallas Theological Seminary (2017); Tony Reinke's *The Temple of Eden* article (you can read it in the appendix **The Temple of Eden**); and Ernest Martin's article *The Temple Symbolism in Genesis* available on the internet.[23]

A GOLDEN AGE IS COMING

Bible prophecy predicts a time when there will be a time of global peace and security which is evidently during the Millennium.

> "Also the wolf shall dwell with the lamb, and the leopard shall lie down with the kid; and the calf and the cub lion and the fatling together; and a little child shall lead them.
> And the cow and the bear shall feed; their young ones shall lie down together; and the lion shall eat straw like the ox.
> And the suckling child shall play on the hole of the asp, and the weaned child shall put his hand on the adder's den.
> They shall not hurt nor destroy in all My holy mountain; for the earth shall be full of the knowledge of Jehovah, as the waters cover the sea." (Is 11:6-9, MKJV) (compare Job 5:22-23; Hos 2:18)

In other words Eden will be restored and expanded over time to include the entire earth. But it is not only the Bible that shows that a golden age was once extant in the days of old.

The concept of a Golden Age of peace and abundance is found throughout the art, architecture and religion of early civilisations. All over the ancient Middle East this has

---

[23] "History is and remains eschatologically oriented. At the end of history is the Kingdom of God." (John Bright, "Faith and Destiny. The meaning of history in Deutero-Isaiah," *Interpretation. A Journal of Bible and Theology*, Vol. 5, Issue 1, p. 11).

been chronicled and recalled in various texts. The Greeks called it *the age of Kronos* and was described as follows:

> "They lived like gods, and their souls knew neither sorrow nor toil. Neither were they subject to age, but ever the same in hand and foot, they spent their time in leisure apart from evil ... The bounteous earth bear fruit for them of her own will, in plenty and without stint. They lived in peace and quiet in their lands with many good things, rich in flocks and dear to the blessed gods" (*Work and Days*, lines 108-130).

Figure 9 Homes, people and nature all at one

Homes, people and nature – all at one

Later, the Latin tradition of the Golden Age was recorded by Ovid:

> "The first millennium was the age of gold;
> Then living creatures trusted one another;
> People did dwell without the thought of ill; ...
> Nor helmets marched the streets, country and town
> Had never heard of war: and seasons travelled
> Through the years of peace. The innocent earth
> Learned neither spade nor plough" (*The Metamorphoses*, pp. 33-34).

Even in ancient China, the historian Kwang Tze (c400BC) also wrote of an idyllic age:

> "In the age of perfect virtue ... They were upright and correct ... they loved one another ... they were honest and leal-hearted" (*Myths of China and Japan*, p. 276)
> [NB leal = faithful, loyal or true].

Finally, in the sacred literature of the Hindis, the *Mahabharata*, it explains that man needed nothing, was without disease and

> "there was no lessening with the years; there was no hatred, or vanity, or evil thought whatsoever; no sorrow, no fear" (*Indian Myth and Legend*, pp. 107-108).

Ancient sources record this wonderful time though their religions are corrupted.

The Bible predicts that another golden age is in front of us – the Messiah shall reign over the entire earth, bringing peace and justice for all peoples and even for the animals. There will be no more fear, tension or stress. All will enjoy harmony and a full, abundant life. No more hatred of other peoples on the one hand nor globalism which is resulting in the end of diversity, on the other.

For the Messiah will reign with justice and overpowering authority – to enforce peace and prosperity for all!

I trust that the following pages and chapters will assist the reader with understanding what the World Tomorrow will actually be like and what will happen during its term because not enough depth and detail is provided for in most literature. The Word of God has a lot more to say about this 1,000-year period than many realise. Although the overwhelming majority of Scriptures detailing this period are found in the Old Testament, there are plenty of references to it in the New as well. In particular references to Christ's Lordship and of course, the context that the book of Revelation provides.

As George Peters put it in his book published in 1884:

> "The Old Test is not superseded by the New ... and we are urged to observe the intimate and enduring connection existing between them. Both form the Word of God, and therefore it is our duty on a subject like this to consult both, and ascertain what God has been pleased to reveal." (George Peters, *The Theocratic Kingdom of our Lord Jesus, the Christ, as Covenanted in the Old Testament and Revealed in the New*, p. 64).

FURTHER READING

* Armstrong, H. W. (1979), *The Wonderful World Tomorrow*. Pasadena, CA.
* Davidson, R. M. (2000), "The Eschatological Literary Structure of the Old Testament," in *Creation, Life, and Hope: Essays in Honor of Jacques B. Doukhan*, ed. Jiri Moskala, Berrien Springs: Old Testament Department, SDA Theological Seminary, Andrews University, pp. 349–366.
* Grandin, T. & Johnson, C. (2009), *Animals Make Us Human. Creating the best life for Animals*. Houghton Mifflin Harcourt, Boston, MA.
* Kaiser, W. C. (1973), "The Promise Theme and the Theology of Rest," *Bibliotheca Sacra*, Vol. 130, Dallas Theological Seminary, April, pp. 135-150.
* Kaiser, W. C. (1972), "The Old Promise and the New Covenant: Jeremiah 31:31-34," *Journal of the Evangelical Theological Society*, Vol. 15, No. 1, pp. 11-23.

PART TWO

THE MESSIAH AND HIS GLORIOUS KINGDOM

"KISS THE SON" – THE MESSIAH'S AWESOME POWER

INTRODUCTORY COMMENTS

Psalm 2 stands as one of this author's favourites alongside Psalms 23, 51, 55, 110. This particular Psalm grips me because of its intensity, throws light on the Messiah's reign and is easily cross-referenced with other Scriptures to expand our understanding of what really will be going on during His glorious reign.

Firstly, let the reader know that this chapter is not a lengthy commentary or a technical, in-depth study. Rather it is a short Bible study cross-referencing with other Scriptures on the Messiah's rule to assist with understanding that rulership.

Nor will this author be covering the various interpretations of this chapter whether it be multi-layered, dual or historical. Although intriguing parallels can be drawn referring to King David followed by Solomon as a type of Christ in His Priest-King (Melchizedekian role) and the prophesied Millennium,[24] the focus will be on this Psalm informing us of one aspect of the Messiah's reign.

This chapter provides a simple reading of the pertinent Scriptural references with short commentary. Let the Bible interpret and speak for itself.

Prophetic drivers can be difficult to discern especially with respect to the following inquiries:

- Is the prophecy generically reinforcing the Messiah's domination and rule over the nations?

---

[24] "Based upon this brief historical-contextual analysis, the speaker of the psalm is most likely King David speaking at King Solomon's coronation. "YHWH says to my lord (Solomon), 'sit at my right hand...'" (Ps 110:1). The speaker (David) is therefore viewing Solomon as the heir to the promises of the Davidic Covenant, glorified to sit at God's right hand as God punishes all of Israel's enemies, and subdues them under Solomon's feet. This idealized metaphor fits the time of the monarchy through the prophetic covenant in 2 Sam 7, as well as the court writings of surrounding nations, especially Egyptian texts and iconography." (Bryan Babcock, "Who is "My Lord" in Psalm 110?" *Crucible*, November 2017, p. 10)

- Are there specific references to rebellions during His reign?
- What leads to the Meshech, Tubal, Gog and Magog invasion and destruction detailed in Ezekiel chapters 38 and 39?

Sometimes we focus on the fundamental aspects of the Millennium such as peace and prosperity that we seem not to notice a number of verses that attach His fierce wrath toward rebellious gentile nations during that period (and not only during the Day of the Lord). Missing this aspect robs us of a fuller understanding of His reign. As we shall see, He will not only be putting down nations upon His arrival at the end of the Day of the Lord – but that this work will continue throughout the Millennium until all nations come under His rule through the saints and Israel.

Christopher Wright remarks on Israel's rule in his book *Old Testament Ethics for the People of God:*

> "God created and called Israel to fulfil his purpose of blessing the nations. The covenant with Abram in Genesis 12:1-3 has this as its climax … as God's priesthood, Israel was to be teacher, model and mediator *for* the nations." (p. 319)

There can be no doubt that the Messiah's rule *gradually* extends across the world. It does not occur over night, but instead Israel will eventually rule the world under Him; and peace will come to all of humanity. But peace will not come without a fight and the Messiah's demonstration of immense power and authority to bring the nations to heel. The following Scriptures confirm this:

> "Come, observe the mighty works of the LORD, who causes desolation in the earth.
>
> He causes wars to cease all over the earth, he causes the bow to break, the spear to snap, the chariots to ignite and burn.
>
> Be in awe and know that I am God. **I will be exalted among the nations.** I will be exalted throughout the earth." (Ps 46:8-10, ISV)

> "The word that Isaiah the son of Amoz saw concerning Judah and Jerusalem.
>
> It shall come to pass in the latter days that the mountain of the house of the LORD shall be established as the highest of the mountains, and shall be lifted up above the hills; and all the nations shall flow to it,
>
> And many peoples shall come, and say: "Come, let us go up to the mountain of the LORD, to the house of the God of Jacob, that he may teach us his ways and that we may walk in his paths." For out of Zion shall go forth the law, and the word of the LORD from Jerusalem.
>
> **He shall judge between the nations, and shall decide disputes for many peoples**; and they shall beat their swords into plowshares, and their spears into pruning hooks; nation shall not lift up sword against nation, neither shall they learn war anymore." (Is 4:1-4, ESV. Cp Is 60:18. Cp Ezek 38:8, 11; Mic 4:1-3)

"Speak to Zerubbabel, governor of Judah, saying, I am about to shake the heavens
and the earth,

and **to overthrow the throne of kingdoms. I am about to destroy the strength
of the kingdoms of the nations**, and overthrow the chariots and their riders. And
the horses and their riders shall go down, every one by the sword of his brother."
(Hag 2:21-22, ESV)

**Finally, a few scholarly works are referenced at the rear. In the appendices Keil &
Delitzsch Commentary on the Old Testament – Psalm 2; E.W. Bullinger's** *Companion
Bible* **Notes – Psalm 2; Treasury of Scripture Knowledge – Psalm 2 lengthy quotes are
employed. The information provided in these throws additional light on this Psalm and
augment our understanding.**

The appendix *Zion in Prophecy and Typology* lists the many prophecies and typology
concerning Zion demonstrating God's great love for the mount and all it represents and typifies.

PSALM 2 AS A PROPHECY

We should understand the historical context of this Psalm and its prophetic meaning. A
number of commentaries demonstrate that Psalm 2 was David writing about his experiences
about nine years into his reign

Werner Bible Commentary states:

"In the book of Acts (4:25), this psalm is attributed to David. After he had made
Zion his royal residence, the Philistines made two attempts to unseat him as king.
Both times they suffered humiliating defeat. (2 Samuel 5:17-25; 1 Chronicles 14:8-
17) It appears that their futile efforts to overthrow David provided the historical
background for this psalm, which first-century Christians came to recognize as being
fulfilled in the plotting against Jesus Christ, the one greater than King David. (Acts
4:23-30) The psalm itself is, in fact, framed in such exalted language as to suggest
developments of greater significance than those in David's life."

"**One of the most neglected applications of Psalm 2 within the church is its
eschatological implications. Psalm 2 envisions an eschatology of victory wherein
the Christ-King rules the nations** with comprehensive dominion and inherits the
earth and its inhabitants (v. 8; cf. Dan. 7:14). The most common eschatological
outlook among American evangelicals is one wherein the church is defeated and
the vast majority of the world is lost (i.e., dispensational premillennialism). **Instead,
Psalm 2 depicts a triumphant Messiah whose prize is all the inhabitants of the
earth**." (Michael Burgos, "An Exposition of the Second Psalm, *Academia Letters*,
Oct, p. 5) [emphasis mine]

This Psalm's historical context may be during the rebellion by the vassal nations of Syria
and Ammon described in IISamuel 10 but also prophetically of Millennial discontent leading
to subterfuge. With that background, let us reveal the insights of Psalm 2:

"Why are the nations in an uproar, and their people involved in a vain plot?

As the kings of the earth take their stand and the rulers conspire together against the LORD and his anointed one, they say,

"Let us tear off their shackles from us, and cast off their chains."

He who sits in the heavens laughs; the Lord scoffs at them.

In his anger he rebukes them, and in his wrath he terrifies them:

"I have set my king on Zion, my holy mountain."

Let me announce the decree of the LORD that he told me: "You are my son, today I have become your father.

Ask of me, and I will give you the nations as your inheritance, the ends of the earth as your possession.

You will break them with an iron rod, you will shatter them like pottery."

Therefore, kings, act wisely! Earthly rulers, be warned!

Serve the LORD with fear, and rejoice with trembling.

Kiss the son before he becomes angry, and you die where you stand. Indeed, his wrath can flare up quickly. How blessed are those who take refuge in him."
(Ps 2:1-12, ISV)

Think deeply on this Psalm. Notice its intensity, fierceness, and Godly justice – as the lion of the tribe of Judah, He roars! In particular, notice its Millennial setting. That time will not be a proverbial 'bed of roses' will it?

Steven Mittwede laments the naïveté of many commentators:

"Sadly, even many seminary-trained clergy seem unable or unwilling to look at the Old Testament as anything other than a collection of moralistic stories, or as a stockpile of character studies that provide fodder for sermon series focusing on good and bad examples of faith, courage, wisdom and the like …

we want our students to appreciate the unity of Scripture—that it reveals, beginning to end, the promise-plan of God, and that the unifying element in that plan is the Messiah. Only this interpretive approach properly comprehends the coherency and cogency of the biblical message." ("Will you rage with the Nations, or Will you kiss the Son?" *Old Roads*, May 2014, pp. 13-15)

Unfortunately, this pathetic watering-down affects the called and chosen - those who should know so much better than the mainstream. Therefore, let us study all of God's Word and free ourselves from the milk of superficiality thereby honouring Him and growing in grace and knowledge as He inspires all of the Word (2Tim 3:16).

This chapter reveals an important dimension of the Messiah's reign – severe and swift treatment of any disobedience by the nations and their leaders. Further, we find linkages with the true Gospel message of the Wonderful World Tomorrow, a period ruled by the Messiah - the prophesied blessing to all mankind.

We find this universal blessing mentioned in Genesis 12:3:

"Now the LORD said to Abram, "Go from your country and your kindred and your father's house to the land that I will show you.

And I will make of you a great nation, and I will bless you and make your name great, so that you will be a blessing.

I will bless those who bless you, and him who dishonors you I will curse, and **in you all the families of the earth shall be blessed**."" (Gen 12:1-3, ESV)

Two chapters previously, Genesis 10 forecasts those blessed families and nations that will be extant throughout the plan of God (and they will continue to approximate their original form per Genesis 10). As the massive worldwide destruction of the Great Tribulation and Day of the Lord unfolds, these various peoples will survive and be rescued from utter destruction (Matt 24:22).

So, God has formed and preserved the nation for His honour and glory demonstrating His creative capacity that endows gifts and talents to all peoples.

These prophecies referenced in this study and in the chapter on *Judging of the Nations* establishes that the Millennial rule of the Messiah will be a time that He tests and tries the various nations listed in Genesis 10. He seeks their voluntary obedience and love from them and not individuals only. He desires their heart and devotion to Himself as supreme universal Ruler and Creator. Their Redeemer and Saviour.

He works with individuals, families, clans, tribes and sub-nations which constitute nations. Each individual has a national or 'corporate' consciousness for righteous acts. And so He does within the Church. – it must work as a community.

It should now be clear that He is coming to judge the nations. Any negative consequences must be eschewed collectively; while good attributes must be maintained and enhanced. Everyone within a nation has a responsibility to realise that outcome. Starting with the individual and consequently through families, clans, tribes, sub-nations until the nation bears the fruits of Godliness.

So with the Church as Revelation 2 and 3 as well as IPeter 4:17 demonstrate both corporate and collective responsibility. God wants an entire people or in this case, church, to produce fruit meet for Him.

Walter Kaiser explains:

> "the scope of the seventy nations listed in Genesis 10, when taken with the promise of Gen 12:3 that in Abraham's seed "all the nations of the earth [viz, those just listed in Genesis 10] shall be blessed," constitutes the original missionary mandate itself. The redemptive plan of God from the beginning, then, was to provide a salvation as universal in scope as was the number of the families on the earth.
>
> … This promise spoke of one people—a "people of God," a "people for his possession." It also spoke of a single purpose—the "blessing" of God for the "kingdom of God." **The "seed" of God was always collective, never plural; yet it embraced a physical and spiritual seed for Abraham under the one seed, Christ himself**. Likewise, its program was one—a veritable "charter for humanity"

... "Edom" along with the other nations would be brought under that reign of the Davidic King who is to come—the Messiah. This "remnant" must also share in the covenant promise to David.

... Isaiah's contemporary, Amos, had briefly but comprehensively referred to the same prospect: nations being called or owned by the name of the Lord. This was to dramatically increase "in that day," a characteristic phrase used of the messianic era—i. e., of both the first coming (e.g., cf. Heb 1:1 and Acts 2:17) and the second coming." (Walter Kaiser, "The Davidic Promise and the Inclusion of the Gentiles (Amos 9:9-15 And Acts 15:13-18): A Test Passage For Theological Systems," *Journal of the Evangelical Theological Society*, Vol. 20, No. 2 (June 1977), pp. 98, 100, 102, 109) [emphasis mine]

Kaiser's entire article explains that from the earliest times, God had a plan to incorporate the Gentiles. His plan is staged and gradual in its expansion (Matt 13:31) so that it eventually becomes a blessing to *all* the nations.

Abraham's seed which is used for this great blessing is as follows:

- Christ as Messiah offering eternal life to all;
- Christ as Messiah rescuing the world from oblivion when He returns to the earth;
- During His reign on earth He brings salvation to all the gentile nations; and
- The "seed' includes both physical and spiritual Israel – the two inseparable and interconnected promises as one does not replace the other. During the Millennium the work of the Messiah and those assisting Him will become manifest, when salvation is offered to all.

Considering Genesis 12:3, let us explore this Psalm verse-by-verse.

"Why are the nations in an uproar, and their people involved in a vain plot?" (v 1, ISV. Cp Rev 11:18)

Answer:

"Righteousness exalts a nation, but sin is a reproach to any people." (Prov 14:34, ESV)

"Let no one say when he is tempted, "I am being tempted by God," for God cannot be tempted with evil, and he himself tempts no one.
    But each person is tempted when he is lured and enticed by his own desire.
    Then desire when it has conceived gives birth to sin, and sin when it is fully grown brings forth death." (James 1:13-15, ESV)

The following verse refers to the smashing of nations at a later stage, not Christ's coming at the Day of the Lord when some will be attempting to initially prevent His rule from being established (as in Dan 7:24-25; 11:36; Rev 19:19). Instead the timing occurs in the Millennium, mirrored by David's experiences during his rule.

"As the kings of the earth take their stand and the rulers conspire together against the LORD and his anointed one, they say," (v 2, ISV)

Christ, as the world ruler, reveals their conspiracy against and deals with it swiftly, destroying its impact, lest the insurrection spreads.

WHAT OF THE "ANOINTED ONE"?

The practice of anointing kings is revealed in Judges 9:8; ISam 1:10; 9:16; 10:1; 16:12-15.[25]

"Let us tear off their shackles from us, and cast off their chains." (v 3, ISV)

In a time prior to the Tribulation, Israel similarly rebelled against God:

> "I will go to the great and will speak to them, for they know the way of the LORD, the justice of their God." But they all alike had broken the yoke; they had burst the bonds." (Jer 5:5, ESV)

Adam Clarke's *Commentary* explains:

> "These have altogether broken the yoke - **These have cast aside all restraint, have acted above law, and have trampled all moral obligations under their feet,** and into their vortex the lower classes of the people have been swept away. Solon said, "The laws are like cobwebs; they entangle the small fry, but the great ones go through them, and carry all away with them."" [emphasis mine]

The *Expositor's Bible Commentary* on Psalms arrives at a similar conclusion:

> "The goal of the rebellious is lordship (v.3). In the ancient Near East there were lords (suzerains) and servants (vassals). The poet, in hyperbolic language, portrays the kings of earth as breaking away from their required allegiance to the King of Kings ... Thus the yoke of God's kingship is not merely rejected; it is insolently thrown off (cf. Jer 2:20)." (p. 67)

In a footnote, the *Commentary* adds:

> "The variety of terms for the nations (v.1) and their rulers (v.2, 10) brings out the comprehensiveness of the rebellion: all kinds of nations and rulers rebel against the Lord. How dare they!" (p. 68)

Psalm 149 informs us further on the punishment of the nation's leaders:

---

[25] Priests are also anointed into their office according to Lev 8:12; Num 3:3. Cp Ps 83:6.

"Let the high praises of God be in their throats and two-edged swords in their hands,
**to execute vengeance on the nations and punishments on the peoples,
to bind their kings with chains and their nobles with fetters of iron.
to execute on them the judgment written!** This is honor for all his godly ones. Praise the LORD!" (Ps 149:6-9, ESV; Cp Is 24:21-13; 45:14)

So, the saints carry out the judgment upon the nations on behalf of and under the Messiah – for He rules both through them and Israel.

"I beheld, and the same horn made war with the saints, and prevailed against them;
Until the Ancient of days came, and judgment was given to the saints of the most High; and **the time came that the saints possessed the kingdom.**
And the kingdom and dominion, and the greatness of the kingdom under the whole heaven, shall be given to the people of the saints of the most High, whose kingdom *is* an everlasting kingdom, and all dominions shall serve and obey him." (Dan 7:21-22, 27, KJV)

Keil and Delitzsch explain in the Commentary:

"The glance is here directed to the future. The people of the present have again, in their God, attained to a lofty self-consciousness, the consciousness of their destiny, viz., **to subjugate the whole world of nations to the God of Israel.** In the presence of the re-exaltation which they have experienced their throat is full of words and songs exalting Jahve (רוממות, plural of רומם, or, according to another reading, רומם, Psalm 56:1-13:17), and as servants of this God, the rightful Lord of all the heathen (Psalm 82:8), they hold in their hand a many-mouthed, i.e., many edged sword (vid., *supra*, p. 580), in order to take the field on behalf of the true religion, as the Maccabees actually did, not long after: ταῖς μὲν χερσὶν ἀγωνιζόμενοι ταῖς δὲ καρδίαις πρὸς τὸν Θεόν εὐχόμενοι (2 Macc. 15:27). ... **all kingdoms shall become God's and His Christ's. Subjugation (and certainly not without bloodshed) is the scriptural מִשׁפָּט for the execution of which Jahve makes use of His own nation.** Because the God who thus vindicates Himself is Israel's God, this subjugation of the world is הדר, splendour and glory, to all who are in love devoted to Him. **The glorifying of Jahve is also the glorifying of Israel.**" (Vol. 5, pp. 856-57). [emphasis mine]

A similar Scripture is found in Isaiah 63:

"I have trodden the winepress alone, and **from the peoples [gentile nations] no one was with me; I trod them in my anger** and trampled them in my wrath; their lifeblood spattered on my garments, and stained all my apparel. [cp Rev 19:11-16]
For the day of vengeance was in my heart, and my year of redemption had come.
I looked, but there was no one to help; I was appalled, but there was no one to uphold; so my own arm brought me salvation, and my wrath upheld me.
I trampled down the peoples in my anger; I made them drunk in my wrath, and I poured out their lifeblood on the earth." (Is 63:3-6, ESV)

This Scripture may refer to the Day of the Lord or a time shortly thereafter. Note the reflective undertones of various Psalms demonstrate that despite its timing, God will severely shatter all national uprisings. Unfortunately blood is shed.

> "Anointed—Hebrew, *Messiah*, for which the Greek is *Christ*, (see note Matthew 1:1,) here referring historically to the Hebrew king whom God had anointed with holy oil, (1 Samuel 16:13,) but prophetically to Christ, the royal Son of David, to whom it is directly applied Acts 4:24-27, and who was consecrated, not with oil, but by the fulness of the Holy Ghost at his baptism. Matthew 3:13-17"
>
> 3. Their bands … their cords—The plural suffix *their* refers to Jehovah and his Messiah. **The result of these hostile deliberations is the mutual exhortation to break asunder and cast away the bands of Messiah's government. "Bands" and "cords "are the restraints and authority of law, and its moral rebuke of sin. The enemies will neither submit to law and obligation nor accept pardon through Christ. Their language implies that they already felt the restraining and reproving power of the Law and Gospel, and were partly under that power, but were bent on freedom in sin and hostility to God**. This was the course of the Pharisees and rulers against Christ. (*Whedon's Commentary*)" [emphasis mine]

This *Commentary'* interpretation seems correct as this event is not the time of the conquest of nations at the Messiah's return; nor the Gog and Magog attack outlined in Ezekiel 38 and 39; nor that referred to in Isaiah 45:14. Rather, it appears to be a rebellion against His government at some point during the Millennium. This rebellion is a spiritual rejection of His Laws rather than physical release from shackles and chains. Refer to the examples in Rom 1:1; 6:18; ICor 7:22.

Notice:

> "As the Millennium, therefore, although a vast advance … upon this present time, will not be a perfect state to the inhabitants of the earth because they will still be in the flesh; **it will be necessary … that there should be … a test of their obedience … in the Millennium**." (Robert Brown, *Outlines of Prophetic Truth*)[26]

---

[26] Robert Brown's work contains further insights:

"And that some of the nations will at some time or other, neglect or refuse to do this, we have the express authority of the Divine Word, which details also the punishment, which the Lord Himself will summarily inflict upon them in consequence: for He Himself has prophetically told us, that "the sons of the strangers," i.e., the Gentile nations, will, in the first instance, " yield" but a " feigned obedience to Him ; of which this instance is a clear and most convincing proof. **The second test is absolute submission to Israel, as God's vicegerent in the earth**: for " thou, O Tower of the flock, the stronghold of the daughter of Zion unto thee shall it come, even the first dominion; the kingdom shall come to the daughter of Jerusalem " — which will also be resisted by some in the first instance, as we have seen." (*Outlines of Prophetic Truth*, Vol. 2, p. 527) [emphasis mine]

Other researchers agree with this position:

"It is vital that we realize, however, that **the fulfilment in Christ does not obliterate the special place of Israel in God purposes, it brings it to perfect realization**. Only by bowing the knee to the true seed of

Similarly the *NIV Application Commentary (Ezekiel)* reveals:

> "God had made a perfect world for Adam and Eve to live in and placed them in the most perfect spot within it, a paradise. Their area of personal freedom was large; the restrictions minuscule. **Yet being deceived into reading the minuscule restrictions as bondage, they gave in to Satan's temptation, only to discover too late what true bondage was.**" (p. 267)

This is what Christ Himself tells us:

> "Come to me, all who labor and are heavy laden, and I will give you rest.
>   Take my yoke upon you, and learn from me, for I am gentle and lowly in heart, and you will find rest for your souls.
>   **For my yoke is easy, and my burden is light.**" (Matt 11:28-30, ESV)

Another author asserts:

> "Gog and Magog refer to the tribes of the outer rim of civilization mentioned in Ezekiel 38 and 39. **There is no hint that all the earthly enemies of Christ are exterminated at His return; in fact, only the doom of the leaders is stated. Even under the universal reign of righteousness there could still be a smoldering discontent of evil which would burst into flame if opportunity were provided.** The integration of these factors indicates that the thousand years are an era in which the righteous dead will be resurrected; in which the former martyrs shall reign with Christ; in which the powers of evil shall be repressed and dormant; and during which the earth shall be governed by righteousness." ("The Importance and Exegesis of Revelation 20:1-8," Merrill Tenney, *Bibliotheca Sacra*, April 1954, pp. 144-45) [emphasis mine]

The perfect way of God holds light 'burdens' but rebels regard His government and laws as shackles. Why? Because their 'freedom' anchors to the tree of knowledge of good and evil that shuns His revelation and way of life: The way of GET (selfishness) versus the way of GIVE (outgoing concern for others) – the Tree of Good and Evil vs the Tree of Life.

"He who sits in the heavens laughs; the Lord scoffs at them." (Ps 2:4, ISV)

Abraham, the one perfect Israelite, can one be saved. There is no Saviour but Israel's Messiah, and no God but Israel's God..." (Barry Webb, *The Message of Zechariah. Bible Speaks Today*, pp. 82-83).

"The purpose of God blessing *this* people is ultimately so that God can bless **all the peoples on earth**" (Christopher Wright, *Deuteronomy. New International Bible Commentary*, p. 281).

"... according to the prophet's meaning, **to be ruled by the people of God is the true happiness of the nations,** and to allow themselves to be so ruled is their true liberty" (Keil & Delitizsch, *Isaiah. Commentary on the Old Testament*, p. 199). [emphasis mine]

Other Scriptures reveal His humorous views of puny men:

"The wicked plots against the righteous and gnashes his teeth at him,
    but the Lord laughs at the wicked, for he sees that his day is coming." (Ps 37:12-13, ESV. Cp 2Thess 1:5-6)

"You, Lord God of hosts, are God of Israel. **Rouse Yourself to punish all the nations; spare none of those who treacherously plot evil.** Selah [cp 60:12]
    Each evening they come back, howling like dogs and prowling about the city.
    There they are, bellowing with their mouths with swords in their lips— for "Who," they think, "will hear us?"
    But you, O Lord, laugh at them; you hold all the nations in derision." (Ps 59:5-8, ESV)

"The Call of Wisdom
    Wisdom cries aloud in the street, in the markets she raises her voice; at the head of the noisy streets she cries out; at the entrance of the city gates she speaks:
    How long, O simple ones, will you love being simple? How long will scoffers delight in their scoffing and fools hate knowledge?
    If you turn at my reproof, behold, I will pour out my spirit to you; I will make my words known to you.
    Because I have called and you refused to listen, have stretched out my hand and no one has heeded, **because you have ignored all my counsel and would have none of my reproof,**
    I also will laugh at your calamity; I will mock when terror strikes you,
    when terror strikes you like a storm and your calamity comes like a whirlwind, when distress and anguish come upon you." (Prov 1:20-27, ESV)

God derides the plans of nations and individuals – for their tyranny and defiance.

"In his anger he rebukes them, and in his wrath he terrifies them" (v 5, ISV)

Other Scriptures expose His further vehemence against rebellion:

"For the nation and kingdom that will not serve you shall perish; those nations shall be utterly laid waste." (Is 60:12, ESV) [cp Ps 59:5]

"Behold, the nations are like a drop from a bucket, and are accounted as the dust on the scales; behold, he takes up the coastlands like fine dust.
    All the nations are as nothing before him, they are accounted by him as less than nothing and emptiness." (Is 40:15, 17, ESV)

"He shall judge between many peoples, and shall decide for strong nations far away; and they shall beat their swords into plowshares, and their spears into pruning hooks; nation shall not lift up sword against nation, neither shall they learn war anymore" (Micah 4:3, ESV)

HOW LONG WILL IT TAKE TO UNLEARN WAR?

No doubt it will take some nations longer than others to unlearn war and to strive for peace (see Is 34:14; 1Pet 3:11).

But what happens when nations do not learn the ways of God, especially peace? He pronounces:

> "O house of Israel, can I not do with you as this potter has done? declares the LORD. Behold, like the clay in the potter's hand, so are you in my hand, O house of Israel.
>
> If at any time I declare concerning a nation or a kingdom, that I will pluck up and break down and destroy it, **and if that nation, concerning which I have spoken, turns from its evil, I will relent of the disaster that I intended to do to it.**
>
> **And if at any time I declare concerning a nation or a kingdom that I will build and plant it, and if it does evil in my sight, not listening to my voice, then I will relent of the good that I had intended to do to it.**" (Jer 18:6-10, ESV. Cp Ps 33:12; 47:7-9)

> "Therefore wait for me," declares the LORD, "for the day when I rise up to seize the prey. **For my decision is to gather nations, to assemble kingdoms, to pour out upon them my indignation,** all my burning anger; for in the fire of my jealousy all the earth shall be consumed."
>
> "For at that time I will change the speech of the peoples to a pure speech, that all of them may call upon the name of the LORD and serve him with one accord." (Zeph 3:8-9, ESV)

> "Then everyone who survives of all the nations that have come against Jerusalem shall go up year after year to worship the King, the LORD of hosts, and to keep the Feast of Booths.
>
> And if any of the families of the earth do not go up to Jerusalem to worship the King, the LORD of hosts, there will be no rain on them.
>
> And if the family of Egypt does not go up and present themselves, then on them there shall be no rain; there shall be the plague with which the LORD afflicts the nations that do not go up to keep the Feast of Booths.
>
> **This shall be the punishment to Egypt and the punishment to all the nations that do not go up to keep the Feast of Booths**." (Zech 14:16-19, ESV)

From the above it seems the putting down of nations will not be just at the time of Christ's return (Day of the Lord) – that would be merely the first stage by dealing with those nations comprising Babylon (the captors of Israel). A few years later the invasion outlined so graphically in Ezekiel 38 & 39 will be dealt with; and as Israel gradually extends the rule of the Messiah across the earth, other nations will be encountered and many will be forcefully brought to heel. Some will repent quickly; others will take time to repent; while there would possibly also be those nations that would repent and then decide God's way was not for them – these must be taught a lesson they will never forget – for it is for their own good.

In turn some individuals within rebellious nations will probably remain faithful to the Messiah; contrariwise there would likely be individual rebels within a submissive nation. All will be dealt with to ensure that the Messiah's mission to bring peace and prosperity to the entire world succeeds.

One wonders how far into the Millennium these rebellions will extend.

There can be no doubt about God's resolve – all nations will bow down to Him and obey Him. They WILL have to learn the way of peace and outgoing concern for others. They will HAVE to obey His Laws, learn to inculcate the beatitudes, fruit of the spirit and aspects of His character to be acceptable to Him.

> **"I have set my king on Zion, my holy mountain."** (v 6, ISV. Cp Joel 3:16-17; Heb 12:18-24)

You can read more about Mount Zion and its importance to God in Mic 4:1-2; Ps 78:68; 87:1-7; 132:13. The appendix *Zion in Prophecy and Typology* provides a listing of relevant prophecies.

A number of other Scriptures refer to a time that God will be exalted above all in a literal and prophetic (and not just generic or spiritual) sense:

> "And **the LORD will be king over all the earth**. On that day the LORD will be one and his name one." (Zech 14:9, ESV)

> "**The LORD is high above all nations**, and his glory above the heavens!" (Ps 113:4, ESV)

The Lord's son is then mentioned:

> **"Let me announce the decree of the LORD that he told me: "You are my son, today I have become your father.""** (v 7, ISV. Cp Ps 89:27; 110:2-3; Is 49:2-3)

Why is He called a 'son'? What does this mean? According to *Whedon's Commentary*:

> "Thou art my Son—The "my" denotes the promulgator of the "decree;" the "Son" is he in whose favour the decree is proclaimed—David's royal descendant and yet David's Lord—the Christ. He is "Son," not by adoption, as are all the true Israel of God, but by being the "only begotten of the Father."
> This day have I begotten thee—The expression, "this day," does not mark the origin of Christ's Sonship, but the period of the promulgation of this decree, be that when it might. The open manifestation of its fulfilment was, when "Christ was declared to be the Son of God with power by his resurrection from the dead.""[27]

---

[27] *Albert Barnes' Notes on the Whole Bible* similarly explains:

"Have I begotten thee - That is, in the matter referred to, so that it would be proper to apply to him the phrase "my Son," and to constitute him "King" in Zion. The meaning is, that he had so constituted the relationship of Father and Son in the case, that it was proper that the appellation "Son" should be given him,

Continuing in Psalm 2:

"Ask of me, and I will give you the nations as your inheritance, the ends of the earth as your possession." (v8, ISV)

What I find of interest is that Satan tempted Christ by offering him the nations which, it seems, he was 'entitled' to do, given that he is "god of this world" (IICor 4:4; Rev 12:9):

"Once more the devil took him to a very high mountain and showed him all the kingdoms of the world, along with their splendor.

He told Jesus, "I will give you all these things if you will bow down and worship me!"

Then Jesus told him, "Go away, Satan! Because it is written, 'You must worship the Lord your God and serve only him.'" (Matt 4:8-10, ISV)

---

and that he should be regarded and addressed as such. So Prof. Alexander: "The essential meaning of the phrase "I have begotten thee" is simply this, "I am thy Father." This is, of course, to be understood in accordance with the nature of God, and we are not to bring to the interpretation the ideas which enter into that human relationship. It means that in some proper sense - some sense appropriate to the Deity - such a relation was constituted as would justify this reference to the most tender and important of all human relationships. In what sense that is, is a fair subject of inquiry, but it is not proper to assume that it is in anything like a literal sense, or that there can be no other sense of the passage than that which is implied in the above-named doctrine, for it cannot be literal, and there are other ideas that may be conveyed by the phrase than that of "eternal generation." The word rendered "begotten" (ילד *yâlad*) determines nothing certainly as to the mode in which this relationship was formed. It means properly:

(1) to bear, to bring forth as a mother, Genesis 4:1;
(2) to beget, as a father, Genesis 4:18; and then
(3) as applied to God it is used in the sense of creating - or of so creating or forming as that the result would be that a relation would exist which might be compared with that of a father and a son.
… The result of the exposition of this passage may therefore be thus stated:

(a) The term "Son," as used here, is a special appellation of the Messiah - a term applicable to him in a sense in which it can be given to no other being.
(b) As used here, and as elsewhere used, it supposes his existence before the incarnation.
(c) Its use here, and the purpose formed, imply that he had an existence before this purpose was formed, so that he could be personally addressed, and so that a promise could be made to him.
(d) The term "Son" is not used here in reference to that anterior relation, and determines nothing as to the mode of his previous being - whether from eternity essentially in the nature of God; or whether in some mysterious sense begotten; or whether as an emanation of the Deity; or whether created.
(e) The term, as Calvin suggests, and as maintained by Prof. Alexander, refers here only to his being constituted King - to the act of coronation - whenever that occurred.
(f) This, in fact, occurred when he was raised from the dead, and when he was exalted to the right hand of God in heaven Acts 13:33, so that the application of the passage by Paul in the Acts accords with the result to which we are led by the fair interpretation of the passage.
(g) The passage, therefore, determines nothing, one way or the other, respecting the doctrine of eternal generation, and cannot, therefore, be used in proof of that doctrine."

Christ did not accept this offer as it would have made Him subject to Satan. He knew that the Father had already offered Him the entire world and that, in due time, all nations would eventually come under His leadership.

> "For by him all things were created, in heaven and on earth, visible and invisible, whether thrones or dominions or rulers or authorities—all things were created through him and for him.
>
> And he is before all things, and in him all things hold together." (Col 1:16-17, ESV)

> "I saw in the night visions, and behold, with the clouds of heaven there came one like a son of man, and he came to the Ancient of Days and was presented before him.
>
> And to him was given dominion and glory and a kingdom, that all peoples, nations, and languages should serve him; his dominion is an everlasting dominion, which shall not pass away, and his kingdom one that shall not be destroyed." (Dan 7:13-14, ESV)

A number of other Scriptures demonstrate clearly that His rule will encompass the entire world. Cf Ps 22:27-31; 47:2,7; 67:1-7; 89:19-29; Dan 7:18,27; and Zech 9:10; 14:1-9.

> **"You will break them [the nations] with an iron rod, you will shatter them like pottery.""** (Ps 2:9, ISV)

There are many other verses that discuss this aspect of the Messiah, sometimes overlooked:

> "He is clothed in a robe dipped in blood, and the name by which he is called is The Word of God.
>
> And the armies of heaven, arrayed in fine linen, white and pure, were following him on white horses.
>
> **From his mouth comes a sharp sword with which to strike down the nations, and he will rule them with a rod of iron.** He will tread the winepress of the fury of the wrath of God the Almighty." (Rev 19:13-15, ESV. Cp Rev 2:26-27; 12:5; Dan 2:44; Jer 19:11; Matt 21:43-44)

> "Your hand will find out all your enemies; your right hand will find out those who hate you.
>
> **You will make them as a blazing oven when you appear. The LORD will swallow them up in his wrath, and fire will consume them.**
>
> **You will destroy their descendants from the earth, and their offspring from among the children of man.**
>
> Though they plan evil against you, though they devise mischief, they will not succeed.
>
> For you will put them to flight; you will aim at their faces with your bows." (Ps 21:8-12, ESV. Cp Ps 89:20-23; 110:5-6)

Then certain national leaders are warned and better heed:

> "**Therefore, kings, act wisely! Earthly rulers, be warned!**
>   **Serve the LORD with fear, and rejoice with trembling.**" (Ps 2:10-11, ESV)
> [Cp Ps 34:9-10; 146:5]

> "On that day the LORD will punish the host of heaven, in heaven [demons], **and the kings of the earth, on the earth.**
>   **They will be gathered together as prisoners in a pit; they will be shut up in a prison, and after many days they will be punished.**
>   Then the moon will be confounded and the sun ashamed, for the LORD of hosts reigns on Mount Zion and in Jerusalem, and his glory will be before his elders." (Is 24:21-23, ESV)[28]

But should the nations repent, they will be considered like Israel:

> "Blessed is the nation whose God is the LORD, the people whom he has chosen as his heritage!" (Ps 33:12, ESV. Cp Ps 47:7-9; Jer 18:6-10)

> "**All the ends of the earth shall remember and turn to the LORD, and all the families of the nations shall worship before you.**
>   For kingship belongs to the LORD, and he rules over the nations." (Ps 22:27-28, ESV)

'KISS THE SON' OR ELSE!

Because of all of the aforementioned, the nations and their leaders better learn to 'kiss the Son' – and quickly. Make haste! For the ruler of the world is loving, kind and merciful and fierce and yet will not tolerate any opposition to His reign.

> "**Kiss the son before he becomes angry, and you die where you stand.** Indeed, his wrath can flare up quickly. How blessed are those who take refuge in him." (Ps 2::12, ISV)

---

[28] "**A king's wrath is a messenger of death, and a wise man will appease it.**
In the light of a king's face there is life, and his favor is like the clouds that bring the spring rain.
How much better to get wisdom than gold! To get understanding is to be chosen rather than silver.
The highway of the upright turns aside from evil; whoever guards his way preserves his life.
Pride goes before destruction, and a haughty spirit before a fall." (Prov 16:16-18 *ESV*)
"For **the day of the LORD is near upon all the nations.** As you have done [to Israel], it shall be done to you; your deeds shall return on your own head.
For as you have drunk on my holy mountain, so all the nations shall drink continually; they shall drink and swallow, and shall be as though they had never been." (Ob 1:15-16 *ESV*)
"And his delight shall be in the fear of the LORD. He shall not judge by what his eyes see, or decide disputes by what his ears hear, but with righteousness he shall judge the poor, and decide with equity for the meek of the earth; **and he shall strike the earth with the rod of his mouth, and with the breath of his lips he shall kill the wicked.**" (Is 11:3-4 *ESV*)

The following supports this verse:

> "The Father judges no one, but has given all judgment to the Son,
>
> that all may honor the Son, just as they honor the Father. Whoever does not honor the Son does not honor the Father who sent him." (John 5:22-23, ESV)

> "But as for these enemies of mine, who did not want me to reign over them, bring them here and slaughter them before me." (Luke 19:27, ESV. Cp Rev 19:11-16; Ps 110:4-6)

> "I came to cast fire on the earth, and would that it were already kindled!
>
> I have a baptism to be baptized with, and how great is my distress until it is accomplished!" (Luke 12:49-50, ESV)

The New Testament interprets Psalm 2 as a prophecy about Christ. The proof Scriptures are: Acts 4:25–27; 13:33; Heb 1:5.

WHAT COMMENTARIES REVEAL

It seems that this "kiss" or embrace is so that the representative of the particular nation literally bows down before Him (probably during the Feast of Tabernacles, as this represents the ingathering of the nations under the Messiah) and humbly offers Him a gift on behalf of the nation, demonstrating submission to Him and His authority.

A collection of these gifts (i.e. an estimate of 70 nations x 1,000 years = approximately 70,000 gifts but not all nations will bring gifts within the first few years or even decades of His reign) they would fill a large museum! Perhaps these gifts will be on display in a museum in Jerusalem as a witness for all to view and be in awe of.

Notice the requirements:

> "They that dwell in the wilderness shall bow before him; and his enemies shall lick the dust.
>
> **The kings of Tarshish and of the isles shall bring presents: the kings of Sheba and Seba shall offer gifts**." (Ps 72:9-10, KJV)

> **"And the Gentiles shall come to thy light, and kings to the brightness of thy rising.**
>
> Lift up thine eyes round about, and see: all they gather themselves together, they come to thee: thy sons shall come from far, and thy daughters shall be nursed at *thy* side …
>
> **The multitude of camels shall cover thee, the dromedaries of Midian and Ephah; all they from Sheba shall come: they shall bring gold and incense; and they shall shew forth the praises of the LORD.**" (Is 60:3-6, KJV)

> "Thus saith the LORD, **The labour of Egypt, and merchandise of Ethiopia and of the Sabeans, men of stature, shall come over unto thee,** and they shall be thine: they shall come after thee; in chains they shall come over, and they shall fall down

unto thee, they shall make supplication unto thee, saying, Surely God is in thee; and there is none else, there is no God." (Is 45:14-17, KJV)

The gifts from the Magi to the baby Christ – future King of the world – may be considered a forerunner - a type of acknowledgement and submission of the world's leaders to the Messiah during His reign (Matt 2:10-11; Luke 2:28-32).

It is interesting to see how the national leaders will be presented to the Messiah and how they come with a pure heart, and probably presenting a report on national conduct and submission to His government. Will they come before Him in fear? Will they literally bow on their knees or bellies?

The Messiah's reign embodies 'tough love' as no rebellion or treachery will be tolerated.

Let us continue with insight from the commentaries. *The Psalms Translated and Explained* by Joseph Alexander assists our understanding:

"A SUBLIME vision of the nations in revolt against Jehovah and his Anointed, with a declaration of the divine purpose to maintain his King's authority, and a warning to the world that it must bow to him or perish.

… The imagery of the scene presented is evidently borrowed from the warlike and eventful times of David. He cannot, however, be himself the subject of the composition, the terms of which are wholly inappropriate to any king but the Messiah, to whom they are applied by the oldest Jewish writers, and again and again in the New Testament.

… 3. Having described the conduct of the disaffected nations and their chiefs, he now introduces them as speaking. In the preceding verse they were seen, as it were, at a distance, taking counsel. Here they are brought so near to us, or we to them, that we can overhear their consultations. **Let us break their bands, i. e. the bands of the Lord and his Anointed, the restraints imposed by their authority.**

… And we will cast, or let us cast away from us their cords, twisted ropes, a stronger term than bands. The verb, too, while it really implies the act of breaking, suggests the additional idea of contemptuous facility, as if they had said, Let us fling away from us with scorn these feeble bands by which we have been hitherto confined. The application of this passage to the revolt of the Ammonites and other conquered nations against David, or to any similar rebellion against any of the later Jewish kings, as the principal subject of this grand description, makes it quite ridiculous, if not profane, and cannot therefore be consistent with the principles of sound interpretation. **The utmost that can be conceded is that David borrowed the scenery of this dramatic exhibition** from the wars and insurrections of his own eventful reign. The language of the rebels in the verse before us is a genuine expression of the feelings entertained, not only in the hearts of individual sinners, but by the masses of mankind, so far as they have been brought into collision with the sovereignty of God and Christ, **not only at the time of his appearance upon earth, but in the ages both before and after that event, in which the prophecy,** as we have seen, attained its height, but was not finally exhausted or fulfilled, since the same rash and hopeless opposition to the Lord and his anointed still continues, and is likely to continue until the kingdoms of this world are become the kingdoms of our Lord and of his Christ (Rev. xi. 15), an expression borrowed from this very passage." [emphasis mine]

The Expositor's Bible. The Psalms, Vol. 1 similarly explains:

"The transition from the representative of Jehovah to Jehovah Himself, which takes place in the next clause, is in accordance with the close union between them which has marked the whole psalm. It is henceforth Jehovah only who appears till the close. But the anger which is destructive, and which may easily flash out like flames from a furnace mouth, is excited by opposition to Messiah's kingdom, and the exclusive mention of Jehovah in these closing clauses makes the picture of the anger the more terrible."

Adam Clarke's *Bible Commentary*

""*Thou art my Son*" - Made man, born of a woman by the creative energy of the Holy Ghost, that thou mightest feel and suffer for man, and be the first-born of many brethren. **"*This day have I begotten thee.*" - By thy resurrection thou art declared to be the Son of God, en dunamei, by miraculous power, being raised from the dead.** Thus by thy wondrous and supernatural nativity, most extraordinary death, and miraculous resurrection, thou art declared to be the Son of God. And as in that Son dwelt all the fullness of the Godhead bodily, all the sufferings and the death of that huma nature were stamped with an infinitely meritorious efficacy.. **We have St. Paul's authority for applying to the resurrection of our Lord these words, "Thou art my Son; this day have I begotten thee; " – see Acts xiii. 33; see also Heb. v. 6; - and the man must indeed be a bold interpreter of the Scriptures who would give a different gloss to that of the apostle**. It is well known that the words, "Thou art my Son; this day have I begotten thee," have been produced by many as a proof of the eternal generation of the Son of God.

Verse 12. *"Kiss the Son, lest he be angry "* - It is remarkable that the word son (rb bar, a Chaldee word) is not found in any of the versions except the Syriac, nor indeed any thing equivalent to it.

The Chaldee, Vulgate, Septuagint, Arabic, and AEthiopic, have a term which signifies doctrine or discipline: "Embrace discipline, lest the Lord be angry with you," &c. This is a remarkable case, and especially that in so pure a piece of Hebrew as this poem is, a Chaldee word should have been found; rb bar, instead of b ben, which adds nothing to the strength of the expression or the elegance of the poetry. I know it is supposed that rb bar is also pure Hebrew, as well as Chaldee; but as it is taken in the former language in the sense of purifying, the versions probably understood it so here. Embrace that which is pure; namely, the doctrine of God." [emphasis mine]

Calvin's Commentary:

"The term kiss refers to the solemn token or sign of honor which subjects were wont to yield to their sovereigns. The sum is, that God is defrauded of his honor if he is not served in Christ. The Hebrew word בר Bar, signifies both a son and an elect person; but in whatever way you take it, the meaning will remain the same. Christ was truly chosen of the Father, who has given him all power, that he alone should stand pre-eminent above both men and angels. On which account also he is said to be "sealed" by God, (Joh 6:27) because a peculiar dignity was, conferred upon him, which removes him to a distance from all creatures. Some interpreters expound it, *kiss or embrace what is pure*, which is a strange and rather forced interpretation. For my part, I willingly retain the name of son, which answers well to a former sentence, where it was said, "Thou art my Son, this day have I begotten thee."

Albert Barnes' *Notes on the Whole Bible* explains the kiss and its dual nature (i.e. prophetic/political and spiritual):

"Kiss the Son - Him whom God hath declared to be his Son Psalm 2:7, and whom, as such, he has resolved to set as King on his holy hill Psalm 2:6. The word "kiss" here is used in accordance with Oriental usages, for it was in this way that respect was indicated for one of superior rank. This was the ancient mode of doing homage or allegiance to a king, 1 Samuel 10:1. It was also the mode of rendering homage to an idol, 1 Kings 19:18; Hosea 13:2; Job 31:27. **The mode of rendering homage to a king by a kiss was sometimes to kiss his hand, or his dress, or his feet, as among the Persians**. DeWette. The practice of kissing the hand of a monarch is not uncommon in European courts as a token of allegiance. **The meaning here is that they should express their allegiance to the Son of God, or recognize him as the authorized King, with suitable expressions of submission and allegiance; that they should receive him as King, and submit to his reign. Applied to others, it means that they should embrace him as their Saviour.**"[29]

---

[29] Other experts add to our knowledge:

"What was new was that Yahweh should now treat David's son in a manner clearly reminiscent of the patriarchal and Mosaic promises. This was more than the Near Eastern titulary of divine sonship: "son of god-x"; it was a divine gift, not a proud human boast. It was also a particularization of the old word given to Israel (viz., His "firstborn") which is now addressed to David's seed (Ps 89:27). In a totally unique way David could now call Him "my Father" (v.26), for each Davidite stood in this relation of son to his God. **Yet it is not said that any single Davidite would ever realize purely or perfectly this lofty concept of divine sonship. But should any person qualify for this relationship, he would also be need to be a son of David**" (Walter Kaiser, *Towards an Old Testament Theology*, p. 152).

"Divine sonship (2:7) is a characteristic ... often associated with Jesus, and through him we can claim it for ourselves (John 1:12-13). **Yet almost a thousand years before Christ (e.g., 2 Sam. 7:14; Ps. 2:7), the Davidic kings of Israel were already claiming to be sons of Yahweh** ..." (Gerald H. Wilson, *Psalms Vol. 1, NIV Application Commentary*, p. 107).

"The background of this relationship is clearly the Davidic covenant described in 2 Samuel 7:4-16. There, as here, Yahweh describes his relationship to the Davidic kings in terms of sonship (2 Sam 7:14). Such sonship with God would have imparted to the kings special powers and privilege as well as the responsibility to mediate justice and equity to all God's people and to lead them in the way of true faith ...

"The idea of world domination expressed in 2:8 is not derived directly from 2 Samuel 7, which focuses primarily on an enduring, just rule over God's people of Israel and Judah. The submission of the kings of the earth to the Davidic monarch also appears in Psalm 72:8-11 - another royal psalm that reflects the official ideology of the Jerusalem monarchy... **the "official line" of these Davidic kings was their right to rule all the earth by Yahweh's authorization and support...**" (ibid, p. 111-12).

"To make plain that Jerusalem's king is (merely) Yahwah's agent, the king now speaks, publishing **the decree of the LORD. By themselves the phrases, you are my son and "today I have begotten you" (Hb. ... NIV I have become your Father), might imply a genetic relationship between the Israelite king and God, especially in the ancient Near East. Within the horizon of the OT, however, this language points to**

The Lion of the Tribe of Judah

As we reflect on His dominion, we grasp why He is referred to as the "lion of the tribe of Judah." In the book of Revelation:

> "And one of the elders said to me, "Weep no more; behold, **the Lion of the tribe of Judah**, the Root of David, has conquered, so that he can open the scroll and its seven seals." (Rev 5:5, ESV)

Figure 10 Christ, fiercely protecting His people

Why a lion? Lions, ferocious when under pressure, exhibit impressive power; sterling courage, and royal authority.

> "Judah, your brothers shall praise you; your hand shall be on the neck of your enemies; your father's sons shall bow down before you.
>
> **Judah is a lion's cub; from the prey, my son, you have gone up. He stooped down; he crouched as a lion and as a lioness; who dares rouse him?**
>
> **The scepter shall not depart from Judah, nor the ruler's staff from between his feet, until tribute comes to him; and to him shall be the obedience of the peoples.**

adoption. **First, these phrases issue from a legal decree. Second, they have become a reality only today,** that is, the day of the king's enthronement. Third, this decree echos the Davidic covenant: "I will become to him a father and he will become to me a son" (2 Sam. 7:14; more clearly than the NIV, this literal translation ["today I have begotten you"] shows that language is metaphoric). The point of this metaphor is to show that Yahweh would punish disobedient Davidic kings, not disown them as he had removed Saul. The king certainly enjoyed a privileged position with Yahweh (though note Exod. 4:22; Deut. 14:1) but he is not deified. The remarkable revelation in the NT, however, is that the fulfillment of 2:7 exceeds the original expectation. **What was originally a figure of speech has become a literal historical reality**" (Craig Broyles, *Psalms. New International Biblical Commentary*, p. 46)

Binding his foal to the vine and his donkey's colt to the choice vine, he has washed his garments in wine and his vesture in the blood of grapes.

His eyes are darker than wine, and his teeth whiter than milk." (Gen 49:8-12, ESV)

The peoples of Judah are brave and combative. For so is Christ as shown in this prophecy Who descends from Judah. While He was a lamb led to the slaughter during His time on the earth, He was indeed assertive with the moral imperative. However, the next time He comes, He roars and devours the defiant nations!

"For thus the LORD said to me, **"As a lion or a young lion growls over his prey, and when a band of shepherds is called out against him he is not terrified by their shouting or daunted at their noise, so the LORD of hosts will come down to fight on Mount Zion** and on its hill.

Like birds hovering, so the LORD of hosts will protect Jerusalem; he will protect and deliver it; he will spare and rescue it." (Is 31:4-5, ESV)

"The LORD roars from Zion, and utters his voice from Jerusalem, and the heavens and the earth quake. But the LORD is a refuge to his people, a stronghold to the people of Israel.

So you shall know that I am the LORD your God, who dwells in Zion, my holy mountain. And Jerusalem shall be holy, and strangers shall never again pass through it." (Joel 3:16-17, ESV)

"And he said: **"The LORD roars from Zion** and utters his voice from Jerusalem; the pastures of the shepherds mourn, and the top of Carmel withers." (Amos 1:2, ESV)

But not only do the gentiles become devoured by Christ the lion – so does Israel:

"They shall go after **the LORD; he will roar like a lion**; when he roars, his children shall come trembling from the west; they shall come trembling like birds from Egypt, and like doves from the land of Assyria, and I will return them to their homes, declares the LORD.

Ephraim has surrounded me with lies, and the house of Israel with deceit, but Judah still walks with God and is faithful to the Holy One." (Hos 11:10-12, ESV)

"But I am the LORD your God from the land of Egypt; you know no God but me, and besides me there is no savior.

It was I who knew you in the wilderness, in the land of drought; but when they had grazed, they became full, they were filled, and their heart was lifted up; therefore they forgot me.

So I am to them like a lion; like a leopard I will lurk beside the way.

I will fall upon them like a bear robbed of her cubs; I will tear open their breast, **and there I will devour them like a lion, as a wild beast would rip them open**.

He destroys you, O Israel, for you are against me, against your helper." (Hos 13:4-9, ESV)

REBELLIONS AND JUDGMENTS DURING THE MILLENNIUM

In summary, we see that there will be Millennial rebellions.

How can this be? Why would entire nations rebel against the Messiah's government when they can see the good fruits that it produces?

Because human nature lingers from the pre-Millennial period. In certain cases some nations would not have been reached and been taught the ways of God. Or they are in the beginning phase of learning and thus probably resenting Christ's Government, His saints and Israel. Reaching these distant peoples to bring them into submission may take a number of years.

"And he that overcometh, and keepeth my works unto the end, **to him will I give power over the nations**:

And he shall rule them with a rod of iron; as the vessels of a potter shall they be broken to shivers: even as I received of my Father." (Rev 2:26-27, KJV)

"But in the last days it shall come to pass, *that* the mountain of the house of the LORD shall be established in the top of the mountains, and it shall be exalted above the hills; and people shall flow unto it.

And **many nations** [though not all initially] shall come, and say, Come, and let us go up to the mountain of the LORD, and to the house of the God of Jacob; and he will teach us of his ways, and we will walk in his paths: for the law shall go forth of Zion, and the word of the LORD from Jerusalem.

And he shall judge among many people, and rebuke strong nations afar off; and they shall beat their swords into plowshares, and their spears into pruninghooks: nation shall not lift up a sword against nation, neither shall they learn war any more." (Mic 4:1-3, KJV)

Notice, He adjudicates between nations and resolves conflicts during the Millennium. He administers justice within certain distant and powerful nations.

Figure 11 All rebellions will be forcefully put down!

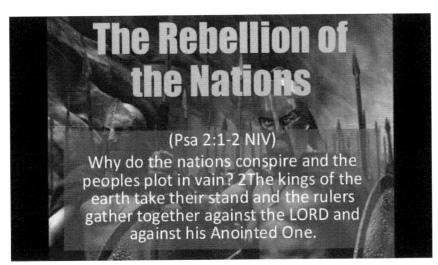

He "rebukes strong nations afar off" from His place of rulership in Jerusalem. How does He rebuke? And who are the "strong" nations? Something to ponder as we explore His rule in this book.

The timing of these national rebukes appears to be after He establishes Himself in Jerusalem.

> "For the LORD taketh pleasure in his people: he will beautify the meek with salvation. [Israel will be exalted, a type of Christians]
>> Let the saints be joyful in glory: let them sing aloud upon their beds.
>> *Let* the high *praises* of God *be* in their mouth, and a **twoedged sword** in their hand;
>> **To execute vengeance upon the heathen, *and* punishments upon the people;**
>> **To bind their kings with chains, and their nobles with fetters of iron;**
>> To execute upon them the judgment written: this honour have all his saints.
> Praise ye the LORD." (Ps 149:4-9, KJV; Cp Is 24:21-23; 45:14)

All knees must bow before the great King of the Earth – the Messiah. Bow, kneel, submit and serve – or face the horrific consequences.

> "Your hand will find all Your enemies; Your right hand will find those who hate You. You shall make them as a fiery oven in the time of Your anger; **The LORD shall swallow them up in His wrath**, And the fire shall devour them. Their offspring You shall destroy from the earth, And their descendants from among the sons of men." (Ps 21:8-10, NKJV)

> "And they will be afraid. Pangs and sorrows will take hold of them; They will be in pain as a woman in childbirth; They will be amazed at one another; Their faces will be like flames. **Behold, the day of the LORD comes, Cruel, with both wrath and fierce anger, To lay the land desolate**; And He will destroy its sinners from it. For the stars of heaven and their constellations Will not give their light; The sun will be darkened in its going forth, And the moon will not cause its light to shine." (Is 13:8-10, NKJV)

> **"The LORD roars from Zion, and utters his voice from Jerusalem, and the heavens and the earthquake**. But the LORD is a refuge to his people, a stronghold to the people of Israel.
> "So you shall know that I am the LORD your God, **who dwells in Zion, my holy mountain**. And Jerusalem shall be holy, and strangers shall never again pass through it." (Joel 3:16-17, ESV)

During the Millennium, rebellious national leaders will be dealt with. Although the Lord is merciful (Prov 20:28), uprisings against the King, in particular, are very serious crimes and will not be tolerated. Psalm 110 echoes:

> "A Psalm of David. The LORD said unto my Lord, Sit thou at my right hand, until I make thine enemies thy footstool.

The LORD shall send the rod of thy strength **out of Zion: rule thou in the midst of thine enemies.** [cp Rev 2:26-27; 19:15][30]

Thy people *shall be* willing in the day of thy power, in the beauties of holiness from the womb of the morning: thou hast the dew of thy youth.

The LORD hath sworn, and will not repent, Thou *art* a priest for ever after the order of Melchizedek.

The Lord at thy right hand shall strike through kings in the day of his wrath.

He shall judge among the heathen, he shall fill *the places* **with the dead bodies; he shall wound the heads over many countries.**

He shall drink of the brook in the way: therefore shall he lift up the head." (Ps 110:1-7, KJV)

He is the Melchizedek Priest-King with the accompanying saints composing the Royal Priesthood (kings and priests within the Order of Melchizedek) under Him (Rev 5:10; IPet 2:9).

"Therefore thy gates shall be open continually; they shall not be shut day nor night; that *men* may bring unto thee the forces of the Gentiles, and *that* their kings *may be* brought.

For the nation and kingdom that will not serve thee shall perish; yea, *those* **nations shall be utterly wasted.** [this is during the Millennium]

The glory of Lebanon shall come unto thee, the fir tree, the pine tree, and the box together, to beautify the place of my sanctuary; and I will make the place of my feet glorious.

The sons also of them that afflicted thee shall come bending unto thee; and all they that despised thee shall bow themselves down at the soles of thy feet; and they shall call thee, The city of the LORD, **The Zion** of the Holy One of Israel.

Whereas thou hast been forsaken and hated, so that no man went through *thee*, I will make thee an eternal excellency, a joy of many generations.

Thou shalt also suck the milk of the Gentiles, and shalt suck the breast of kings: and thou shalt know that I the LORD *am* thy Saviour and thy Redeemer, the mighty One of Jacob." (Is 60:11-16, KJV)

Israel will gather the 'nutrients' or blessings to serve and assist other nations and peoples:

The LORD shall judge the people: judge me, O LORD, according to my righteousness, and according to mine integrity that is in me." (Ps 7:8, KJV)

---

[30] "The verb poimanei ("will rule") in 19:15 is future active indicative and reveals that Jesus' rule over the nations is future at the time of His second coming from heaven. Jesus is not coming to consummate an already kingdom reign. His second coming brings His rule over the nations. This truth is consistent with Jesus' words in Matthew 19:28 and 25:31-32 where He stated that His Davidic throne reign awaits His second coming to earth." (Michael Vlach, *Revelation 19:15 and the Coming Reign of Jesus over the Nations*, https://sharperiron. org/ 30 Sept 2020) Note that we will be reigning with Christ (Matt 19:28; Rev 3:21) but note Ephesians 2:6 as if we are already reigning with Him – a figure of speech known as a *prolepsis*.

"He shall subdue the people under us, and the nations under our feet! For God is the King of all the Earth: sing ye praises with understanding! God reigneth over the heathen: God sitteth upon the throne of His Holiness." (Ps.47:2,3,7,8, KJV)

"The LORD has sworn And will not relent, "You are a priest forever According to the order of Melchizedek." The Lord is at Your right hand; **He shall execute kings in the day of His wrath. He shall judge among the nations, He shall fill the places with dead bodies, He shall execute the heads of many countries**." (Psalm 110:4-6, NKJV. Cp Luke 19:27)

Terror and fear strikes the hearts of rebels (Heb 10:31).

This prophecy does not refer to the Day of the Lord when nations and leaders are destroyed nor is it a reference to the Beast and False Prophet who are thrown into the lake of fire. Instead, these are rebels who show their true colours later in the Millennium.

"Arise, O God, **judge the earth: for thou shalt inherit all nations**." (Ps 82:8, KJV)

"Yea, all kings shall fall down before Him: **all nations shall serve Him**. And blessed be His glorious Name for ever: **and let the whole Earth be filled with His glory**; Amen, and Amen!" (Ps.72:11,19, KJV)

"But the LORD shall endure for ever: he hath prepared his throne for judgment. And **he shall judge the world in righteousness, he shall minister judgment to the people in uprightness**." (Ps 9:7-8, KJV)

"Behold, the days come, saith the LORD, that I will raise unto David a righteous Branch, and a King shall reign and prosper, and **shall execute judgment and justice** in the earth." (Jer 23:5, KJV)

"But with righteousness shall he judge the poor, and reprove with equity for the meek of the earth: and he shall smite the earth with the rod of his mouth, and **with the breath of his lips shall he slay the wicked**." (Is 11:4, KJV)

He judges individuals and nations with justice and fairness. How will they be judged? By testing the nations and their leaders – by allowing them to err and even to temporarily gather strength to oppose the King. In other words they will be either given time to repent or 'enough rope to hang themselves.' They must learn to appreciate and praise Him!

How will Christ judge and measure the nations? According to prophecies this judgment will be applied through His saints and Israel.

"Say among the heathen that the LORD reigneth: the world also shall be established that it shall not be moved: **he shall judge the people righteously**. Let the heavens rejoice, and let the earth be glad; let the sea roar, and the fullness thereof. Let the field be joyful, and all that is therein: then shall all the trees of the wood rejoice.

Before the LORD: for he cometh, **for he cometh to judge the earth: he shall judge the world with righteousness, and the people with his truth**." (Ps 96:10-13, KJV) [He will judge righteously and justly]

"That thy way may be known upon earth, thy saving health among all nations.

Let the people praise thee, O God; let all the people praise thee.

O let the nations be glad and sing for joy: **for thou shalt judge the people righteously**, and govern the nations upon earth. Selah.

Let the people praise thee, O God; **let all the people praise thee**.

Then shall the earth yield her increase; *and* God, *even* our own God, shall bless us.

God shall bless us; and all the ends of the earth shall fear him." (Ps 67:2-4, KJV)

"Before the LORD: for he cometh, **for he cometh to judge the earth: he shall judge the world with righteousness, and the people with his truth**." (Ps 96:13, KJV)

"Before the LORD; for **he cometh to judge the earth**: with righteousness shall he judge the world, and the people with equity." (Ps 98:9, KJV)

"Of the increase of his government and peace there shall be no end, upon the throne of David, and upon his kingdom, to order it, and **to establish it with judgment and with justice** from henceforth even for ever. The zeal of the LORD of hosts will perform this." (Is 9:7, KJV)

"And in mercy shall the throne be established: and he shall sit upon it in truth in the tabernacle of David, **judging, and seeking judgment, and hasting righteousness**." (Is 16:5, KJV)

"And many people shall go and say, Come ye, and let us go up to the mountain of the LORD, to the house of the God of Jacob; and he will teach us of his ways, and we will walk in his paths: for out of Zion shall go forth the law, and the word of the LORD from Jerusalem. **And he shall judge among the nations, and shall rebuke many people**: and they shall beat their swords into plowshares, and their spears into pruninghooks: nation shall not lift up sword against nation, neither shall they learn war any more." (Is 2:3-4, KJV)

"And **he shall judge among many people, and rebuke strong nations afar off**; and they shall beat their swords into plowshares, and their spears into pruninghooks: nation shall not lift up a sword against nation, neither shall they learn war any more." (Mic 4:3, KJV)

"Until the Ancient of days came, **and judgment was given to the saints of the most High**; and the time came that the saints possessed the kingdom." (Dan 7:22, KJV. See ICor 6:3)

Figure 12 The Messiah must be respected and served

Christopher Wright, writing in *The Mission of God* explains:

"Psalm 22 puts the worship of the nations in a very universal frame: it will be offered by the poor and the rich (i.e., every segment of society [Ps 22:26, 29]), and it will be offered by generations who have already died and as yet unborn (Ps 22:29, 31). Whether vertically throughout human society or horizontally throughout human history, the praise of YHWH as sovereign ruler will be universally offered …

Psalm 2 sees the rule of YHWH as a severe warning to the nations not to continue their rebellion against him but rather to take the wiser course of worshiping him in humility …

The nations ought to adopt this stance toward YHWH because he has installed his anointed king on Zion." (p. 481)

The Judgment of the Nations occurs during the Millennial reign of Christ. This is not the Great White Throne Judgment that occurs after the Millennium, though this judgment will extend into that period.

Eventually, over a period of time all nations will be subjected to His rule:

"To the choirmaster. A Psalm of the Sons of Korah. Clap your hands, all peoples! Shout to God with loud songs of joy!
For the LORD, **the Most High, is to be feared, a great king over all the earth.**
He subdued peoples under us, and nations under our [Israel's] feet.
He chose our heritage for us, the pride of Jacob whom he loves. Selah.
God has gone up with a shout, the LORD with the sound of a trumpet.
Sing praises to God, sing praises! Sing praises to our King, sing praises!
For God is the King of all the earth; sing praises with a psalm!
God reigns over the nations; God sits on his holy throne.

The princes of the peoples gather as the people of the God of Abraham. For the shields of the earth belong to God; he is highly exalted!" (Ps 47:1-9, ESV) [cp Ps 33:12; Ezek 25:14; Is 11:14; 19:24-25; Gen 27:29]

If the gentiles are considered to be like the "people of the God of Abraham" it must be due to their repentance and obedience.[31]

"To the choirmaster: with stringed instruments. A Psalm. A Song. May God be gracious to us and bless us and make his face to shine upon us, Selah.

That your way may be known on earth, **your saving power among all nations**.

Let the peoples praise you, O God; let all the peoples praise you!

Let the nations be glad and sing for joy, for you judge the peoples with equity and guide the nations upon earth. Selah.

Let the peoples praise you, O God; let all the peoples praise you!

The earth has yielded its increase; God, our God, shall bless us.

God shall bless us; let all the ends of the earth fear him!" (Ps 67:1-7, ESV)

> **"Kiss the son before he becomes angry, and you die where you stand. Indeed, his wrath can flare up quickly." (Ps 2:12, ISV)**

CONCLUDING REMARKS

The Bible is clear – the Biblical model for a relationship with God is consistent from Genesis to Revelation. Firstly, God defines the relationships. He calls people and nations, waking them to His ways and plan – an epiphany!

Any person or any nation must then submit to Him as Lord and Master, working cooperatively with Him to obey His laws and ways. As His chosen are today, they too will delight in developing Godly character. So it shall be during the Millennial reign of the Messiah:

"There is an eschatological, almost apocalyptic, dimension to the psalms anticipation of **a warfare of the faithful that will settle the conflict between the kingdoms of this world and the kingdom of God**. The expectation of a victory over nations and people that leaves kings and princes in chains as subdued captives is a vision that

---

[31] The *Cambridge Bible for Schools and Colleges* online: "The Massoretic text ot the next line must be rendered with R.V., 'To be *the people of the God of Abraham*': a bold phrase, reaching the very climax of Messianic hope, and hardly paralleled elsewhere. For though the nations are frequently spoken of as attaching themselves to Israel in the worship of Jehovah (Isa_2:2 ff; Isa_11:10; Isa_56:6 ff.; Isa_60:3 ff.; Zec_8:20 ff.; &c, &c), they are not called "the people of God." This title is reserved for Israel, and only in the N.T. are the promises made to Israel extended to the Gentiles (Rom_9:25). Yet see Isa_19:25, where Egypt receives the title 'my people.'"

transcends local conflicts and specific wars. Inspired by Psalms and prophecies of the coming kingdom, this psalmist has composed a hymn that calls the faithful to a praise and militancy that serves its coming ... Something wonderful and strange is afoot here, **the lowly becoming the warriors who fight for the kingdom and inherit the earth**" (James Mays, *Inspiration. A Bible Commentary for Teaching and Preaching. Psalms*, p. 448).

Figure 13 Christ will avenge Israel

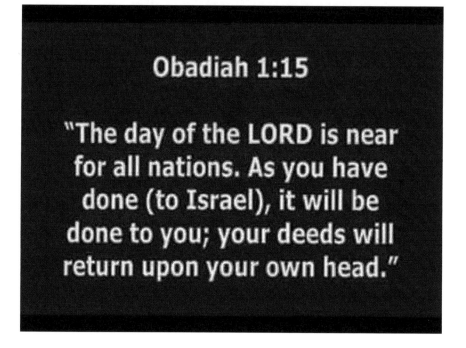

"Then I saw heaven opened, and behold, a white horse! The one sitting on it is called Faithful and True, and in righteousness he judges and makes war.

His eyes are like a flame of fire, and on his head are many diadems, and he has a name written that no one knows but himself.

He is clothed in a robe dipped in blood, and the name by which he is called is The Word of God.

And the armies of heaven, arrayed in fine linen, white and pure, were following him on white horses.

From his mouth comes a sharp sword with which to strike down the nations, and he will rule them with a rod of iron. He will tread the winepress of the fury of the wrath of God the Almighty.

On his robe and on his thigh he has a name written, King of kings and Lord of lords." (Rev 19:11-16, ESV. Cp Is 63:3-6)

Sometimes, end-time events appear blurred. However, when we assemble all the pertinent Scriptures and consider them, underpinned by the historical precedents associated with the First Exodus, the order emerges.

As He sets foot on the Mount of Olives, His reign commences. He then extends it gradually and methodically according to a plan, encompassing all the world.

He will rule from Mount Zion with love – but beware O nations! Step out of line and you will be dealt with.

"As the glory of the LORD entered the temple by the gate facing east,

the Spirit lifted me up and brought me into the inner court; and behold, the glory of the LORD filled the temple.

While the man was standing beside me, I heard one speaking to me out of the temple,

and he said to me, "Son of man, **this is the place of my throne and the place of the soles of my feet, where I will dwell in the midst of the people of Israel forever**. And the house of Israel shall no more defile my holy name, neither they, nor their kings, by their whoring and by the dead bodies of their kings at their high places. (Ezek 43:4-7, ESV)

"For the LORD has chosen Zion; he has desired it for his dwelling place:

"This is my resting place forever; here I will dwell, for I have desired it." (Ps 132:13-18, ESV)

A WAR EVEN AFTER THE MESSIAH'S RETURN!

VARIOUS INTERPRETATIONS

FOR MANY YEARS SOME TAUGHT that the armies of Ezekiel 38 and 39 come against the House of Israel some years following their regathering after the return of Christ. This was contrary to the teaching of most evangelists who proclaimed a different prophetic message.

For example this was covered early in the article "What's Prophesied about Russia," *Plain Truth*, Nov-Dec 1943:

"But this very fact – that this invasion will not come until *after* the Second Coming of Christ – will seem preposterous to many, at first thought.

That is because we have been accustomed to merely ASSUME things that are not true. We have blindly ASSUMED that when Christ comes, there will be no opposition. Every person and power on earth, we have thought, will simply submit meekly and instantly to Him and His power. But that is not true!

The very battle at Armageddon is a battle between the "BEAST" and Christ. The power who undoubtedly shall finally conquer and disperse Israel, *prior* to Christ's coming – the power who shall then enforce the "mark of the Beast" and martyr many saints (Mat. 24:9; Rev 6:11) – this last coming European revival of the Roman Empire by a federation of European nations, will fight Christ. The "Beast" and "False Prophet" who heads the organized religion Christ shall abolish, shall both CONTEST Christ's right to rule." (p. 7)

"… the Gentile nations who have schemed to conquer and rule the world – they shall not submit until forced to. The European Axis power shall be subdued and conquered at Armageddon. But Russia, and the populous Oriental nations who know not God or Christ, shall still have to be brought to submission!

… Notice, these heathen nations do not see and recognise the dread DIVINITY, the MIGHT, and POWER of the Eternal Christ, with supernatural power, even after He has returned. He has to TEACH them that He is the Eternal!" (p. 12)[32]

---

[32] This article was updated, re-titled and re-published over the years as "Why Russia will not attack America!" in the *Good News*, Jan 1952, pages 1-2, 13-15 and later as "Will Russia Attack America?" in later editions of the *Plain Truth*.

Although quoted in a previous chapter, it is worth repeating the following quote:

> "Gog and Magog refer to the tribes of the outer rim of civilization mentioned in Ezekiel 38 and 39. **There is no hint that all the earthly enemies of Christ are exterminated at His return; in fact, only the doom of the leaders is stated. Even under the universal reign of righteousness there could still be a smoldering discontent of evil which would burst into flame if opportunity were provided.** The integration of these factors indicates that the thousand years are an era in which the righteous dead will be resurrected; in which the former martyrs shall reign with Christ; in which the powers of evil shall be repressed and dormant; and during which the earth shall be governed by righteousness." ("The Importance and Exegesis of Revelation 20:1-8," Merrill Tenney, *Bibliotheca Sacra*, April 1954, pp. 144-45) [emphasis mine]

Later in other Church booklets such as *Russia and China in Prophecy* we read:

> "These ... Asian armies are also described in Ezekiel, chapters 38 and 39, where elements of those forces are prophesied to invade the Holy Land when all 12 tribes of Israel have returned ... These circumstances will be extant only after the coming of the Messiah, when surviving Eurasian forces will be supernaturally punished" (*Russia and China in Prophecy*, pp. 25, 31, 43).[33]

The Church of God, for example, taught that the book of Ezekiel followed a logical procession or "a time sequence flowing through the book" interspersed with inset chapters, somewhat like the book of Revelation. For instance:

- Chapter 33 – end-time warning
- Chapter 34 – scattering of Israel and the Church
- Chapter 35 – punishment upon Seir and Idumea
- Chapter 36 – return of Israel to the Holy Land
- Chapter 37 – Israel and Judah re-united and restored
- Chapters 38 and 39 – invasion by the forces of Gog and Magog
- Chapters 40-47 – Millennial Temple
- Chapter 48 – tribal land allocations

---

[33] Other sources: In *The Book of Revelation Unveiled at Last*, Herbert Armstrong wrote similarly:

"The second woe, with its symbols of horses and horsemen, is interpreted by Ezekiel 38:4, 15, and is also referred to as an event in the Day OF THE Eternal in Joel 2:4. This refers to a tremendous military power–also to the NORTH–due north! They come with an army of two hundred million! Think of it–an army of two hundred million!" (pp. 38-39).

The Church of God's *Systematic Theology Project* also made mention of these battles:

"Then begins the millennial rule of Christ and the saints over the earth. After some continuing confrontations and battles (described in Ezek. 38 and 39), God's Kingdom shall be set up over all peoples; and Jesus Christ shall teach them God's laws, the way of happiness and eventually of eternal salvation." (chapter on "Prophecy", p. 8 (or p. 108 of the entire document))

The sequence leads us to come to a logical conclusion, as we shall see. Below are some typical views of these chapters:

1. it occurs shortly after the return of Christ
2. it occurs prior to the Millennium, as they are the forces of the Beast
3. it occurs prior to the Millennium, as they are allies of the Beast
4. it occurs prior to the Millennium, as they are the former allies of Babylon and invade the Middle East after the fall out
5. it is entirely historical and will not occur again
6. it refers only to the events mentioned in Rev 20:7-9 after the Millennium
7. it is entirely symbolic of the forces of evil.

Given the above, the interpretation of these chapters may be confusing to some. So, let us turn to both commentaries and obviously, and most importantly, the Bible itself.

Personally, I was taught by various Protestant groups in my early youth - in sermons and books - that the chapters in Ezekiel 38 and 39 concerning the eastern and northern hordes occurred during the Great Tribulation, prior to the return of the Messiah. Some even equated these to the Beast.

Various prophecies about the blooming of the desert were interpreted as the Jewish improvement to the land of Israel; the return of the Jews; to the second exodus and fulfilment of Ezekiel 37; and the temple described in Ezekiel 40-48 as the pre-Tribulation temple.

It seemed to these teachers of prophecy that Ezekiel 38 and 39 referred to the invasion of the Holy Land by Russia and its allies prior to the return of Christ and they were to be equated with the King of the North. The Gomer mentioned in those chapters was interpreted as Germany and the young lions as Britain. The fall of the Berlin wall and the entry of eastern European states into the European Union has disproven this long held theory.[34]

Appendices at the end of this work provide additional information and pointers toward further

---

[34] Upon reading the old Church of God literature on the subject in 1973 and talking with their ministers I changed my understanding to see that the evangelical view was incorrect An old Church publication contained this information: **"Ezekiel 38 and 39 describe a war that will take place against Israel after they have been reestablished and will be living in peace and prosperity. Isaiah 30:20-21 shows how we will need to be constantly working with people who want to go their own way.**

All mankind will learn a new language (Zeph. 3:9). Have you ever tried to learn a foreign language? That will take much time and patience right there.

The waste cities will be rebuilt (Isa. 61:4), but they will be rebuilt properly. That means a lot of tearing down and cleaning up. We will solve massive problems of food and water supply, proper sanitary facilities — even providing vines and fig trees (Mic. 4:4)!

Problems? Certainly. But every Feast of Tabernacles will see more people coming to rejoice before the Lord. Every year greater numbers of people from every nation will venture to Jerusalem to learn the laws and ways of the God of Israel (Isa. 2:1-4, Mic. 4:1-5).

As the years pass there will be less sickness, fewer dying of famine, less rebellion, less suffering around the earth. It will take time, but at every Feast we will be able to look back at a year of tremendous progress and rejoice before the Lord in person." (Art Docken, "But What If 'Everything Goes Wrong'?" *Good News*, September 1982, pp. 8-9) [emphasis mine]

research and contemplation: One is a table **Comparing Ezekiel 38 and 39 with other Scriptures;** another **Ezekiel Chapters 38 and 39 with comments;** and **Ezekiel – Revelation Parallels** which shows there are some parallels in terms of structure between Ezekiel and Revelation. But that is to be expected when common language is used in the Scriptures for different event.

WHAT COMMENTARIES REVEAL

Commentaries, of course, have various views, such as those listed above. Evangelicals generally take a position that the prophecy refers to an attack upon the Jewish people prior to the return of Christ, during the Tribulation.

The more considered commentaries, more logical, scholarly and conservative in their outlook, take a position more-or-less similar to that of the Church of God. Here are quotes from some of them:

New Bible Commentary:

> "These two chapters are unique in OT prophecy in **that they describe an uprising of foreign powers against the people of God after the commencement of the Messianic kingdom**. The prophecy has already predicted the coming blessedness of Israel (33-37); he [Ezekiel] now portrays the nation as long settled in their land and transformed into a prosperous community (38:8, 11, 12, 14), a condition which, according to his earlier teaching, involves their prior repentance, regeneration and political revival (33-37).
>
> Whereas he had said that Israel's restoration would come 'soon' (36:8), he says that Gog will be mustered 'after many days … in the latter years' (38:8). The motive underlying the prophecy is the necessity of earlier prophecies concerning the destruction of hostile Gentile powers being fulfilled (38:17; 39:8) and for the nations of the world to learn the power, holiness and sole deity of Yahweh (see 39:7).
>
> The author of the book of Revelation has both used these chapters to vivify his description of Armageddon prior to the millennium (Rev. 19:17, 18), and adapted their essential idea so as to make it a final rebellion of the godless of humanity at the end of the millennium, before the new creation (20:7-9).
>
> In comparing the two writings it should be remembered that Ezekiel knew nothing of a new creation nor of a new Israel which was to inherit the kingdom; if John was to incorporate the prophecy he had of necessity to change its form. In conformity with his usage of OT prophecy generally, he has not hesitated to do so" (*New Bible Commentary*, "38:1-39:29 Prophecy against Gog", pp. 681-82) [emphasis mine].

J. Barton Payne in his famous *Encyclopedia of Biblical Prophecy* agrees with this position (p. 367). He also states that the Bible is 27% predictive, including typologies. But he does not include many of the types and 'hidden' prophetic messages. So, at least 33% of the Bible is prophecy. Payne lists Ezekiel as the most predictive book in the Bible with 821 verses devoted to the subject.

Halley's Bible Handbook:

"... A glance at the map makes it plain that he has in mind that part of the world known as Russia ... In these two chapters Ezekiel predicts Another Scythian invasion, on a far more stupendous scale, confederate with peoples from the East (38:5), into the Holy Land, against Restored Israel, "in the latter years" (38:8), **apparently during the Messianic Age**; and that with the help of God, they will be so overwhelmingly defeated that their weapons will supply fuel for 7 years (39:9), and it will take 7 months to bury their dead" (39:14).

"In the book of Revelation the same words, God and Magog, are used as representing all nations in Satan's final furious attack on the people of God (Revelation 20:7-10)" (pp. 333-34) [emphasis mine].

New Bible Dictionary:

"The linkage with peoples at the extremities of the then known world (Ezk, xxxviii. 5,6; cf Rev. xx.8) suggests that we are to regard them as eschatological figures rather than as a historically identifiable king, etc. This is the interpretation in Rev. xx. 8 and rabbinic literature.

Since we need not interpret Ezk. xxxviii, xxxix as earlier in time than Ezk. xl-xlviii, and rabbinic tradition places Gog after the days of the Messiah, we need see no contradiction between Ezekiel and Revelation, **provided we understand the millennium in the sense the Rabbis gave 'the days of the Messiah'**" (*New Bible Dictionary*, "Gog and Magog" pp. 480-81). [emphasis mine]

In principle, this *Dictionary* sees a rebellion against God sometime after the return of the Messiah if they interpret rabbinic literature correctly – it sees Ezekiel and Revelation as referring to the same event in that context.

The International Standard Bible Encyclopedia:

"Perhaps Ezekiel had in mind something of the eschatology of Zec. 14, in which the nations that represented "the ends of the earth" would rise against Jerusalem ... In Ezekiel **the invasion of Gog occurs during the messianic age, while in Revelation it occurs just at the close of the millennium**. In Ezekiel Gog and Magog are gathered by Yahweh for their destruction; in Revelation they are gathered by Satan. In both cases the number is vast, the destruction, by supernatural means, is complete and final" (Vol. 2, pp. 519-20) [emphasis mine].[35]

---

[35] Bullinger's *Companion Bible* states:

"... Israel will have then already been "gathered" ... It must therefore precede the Millennium; and on that account must be distinguished from Rev. 20:8, 10 ... after the "gathering" **but before the final "Restoration"**, and therefore before the Millennium" (pp. 1161, 1163). [emphasis mine]

Bullinger can see that it refers to a period after Israel returns from captivity, although prior to the Millennium.

One can, therefore, given the above commentaries and the sequence of events in Ezekiel, come to the following conclusion:

The invasion occurs some years after the return of Christ and the official commencement of the Millennium. This could be at least 3 ½ - 7 years after the return of Christ. In other words the invasion of these peoples occurs after the Great Tribulation and Day of the Lord, after the second Exodus and the gathering of Israel to the Holy Land - after a period of settlement and peace for Israel and probably other nations. Israel would have repented, had the Holy Spirit granted to her (Ezek 37:15-28) and have come into a Covenant relationship with God.

Finally, given that so much of Scripture is dual that these chapters, while referring to a time near the beginning of the Millennium, may also prefigure or type the Gog and Magog attack of Rev 20:7-9 which rises up in rebellion *after* the end of the Millennium.

However, Ezekiel 38 and 39 cannot be identical to that which arises after the end of the Millennium for the following reasons outlined in the table below:

Table 7 Comparison of Ezekiel 38 and 39 with Revelation 20:7-9

Comparison of Ezekiel 38 and 39 with Revelation 20:7-9	
Ezekiel 38 and 39:	**Revelation 20:7-9**:
As we have seen, according to the story flow of Ezekiel, chapters 38 and 39 occur near the beginning of the Millennium	Gog and Magog in Rev 20:7-9 occurs shortly after the end of the Millennium, which is explicitly stated
Based on their lusts, God (not Satan) will draw them into battle and defeat (Ezek 38:4; 39:2)	Satan deceives peoples after the Millennium (Rev 20:3)
According to 39:23-29, the captivity of Israel is still a recent event	The captivity of Israel occurred over 1,000 years earlier
Gog seems to be regarded as a ruler	Here Gog is a nation or symbolic of nations
Literal nations descended from Noah's sons including Meschech, Tubal etc, not only Gog and Magog	Apparently 'Gog and Magog' is symbolic of peoples[36] and rebels that may have been assigned to the former lands occupied by Gog and Magog and now attempt to wreak their revenge on God's people
Armies descend primarily from the north and south (Gog is of the land of Magog). NB Gog and Magog are seen supported by African armies; while the Beast is seen invading North Africa in Dan 11.	Armies are from all "four quarters" of the earth
These armies are defeated in the land of Israel and their weapons are burned for 7 years	They are burned up with fire from heaven immediately

---

[36] Unlike Ezekiel 38 and 39, Revelation 20:8-9 "… the chiastic parallel suggests that "Gog and Magog" should be seen as a metaphor and synonym of these kings and armies, rather than as specific nations." (Ed Christian, "A Chiasm of Seven Chiasms: The Structure of the Millennial Vision, Rev 19:1-21:8," *Andrews University Studies Seminary*, 1999, Vol. 37, No. 2, p. 220)

WHY WILL THE FORCES OF EZEKIEL 38 AND 39 INVADE THE HOLY LAND?

These armies must be the remnants of the forces of the Second Woe (Rev 9:13-21) which God would have used to conquer and punish the countries of Babylon and the Beast power. Perhaps after the first seven years or so of Israelites being settled back in the Holy Land, after Israel has swooped upon certain gentile peoples as we have read about previously, many of these peoples will rise up in rebellion, envying Israel, probably claiming discrimination and so on as justifying this invasion.

Just as God gives us enough time to repent or show our true colours; just as He allowed Lucifer plenty of time to foment rebellion; so He will allow these forces to develop. The picture we get is that these peoples are led by the forces that invaded and conquered the nations comprising the Beast power in Europe. As such, they no doubt comprise the remnants of the 200 million army pictured in Rev 9:16.

The bitterness and jealousy will well-up into a lust for war and conquest. They shall see the great blessings and wealth of Israel granted to them and want it for themselves (see Rev 18:11-13; Hag 2:7-9; Is 23:17-18; Ex 12:35-36; Jos 6:18-19).

"Wrath *is* cruel, and anger *is* overwhelming; but who *is* able to stand before envy?" (Prov 27:4, KJV)

Ezekiel reveals the following:

"So says the Lord Jehovah: And it shall be in that day that things shall come into your heart, and you shall devise an evil plan.

And you shall say, I will go up to the land of open spaces. I will go *to* those at ease [cp Lam 1:3], who dwell securely, all of them dwelling without walls, and there are no bars nor gates to them,

in order to take a spoil, and to steal a prize; to turn your hand on the inhabited waste places, and on the people gathered out of the nations, who have gotten cattle and goods, who dwell in the midst of the land." (Ezek 38:10-12, MKJV)

Notice: this rebellion is against the Israelites who have returned from captivity and who now have gathered much wealth. They are also dwelling in peace, which is hardly a description of the Holy Land or the world today.

And why does this war occur?

"And I will set My glory among the nations, and all the nations shall see My judgments which I have done, and My hand that I have laid on them.

So the house of Israel shall know that I *am* Jehovah their God from that day and forward. [there will be no more doubting Thomas's]

And the nations shall know that the house of Israel was exiled [i.e. prior to this **Gog and Magog invasion**] for their iniquity [therefore the nations must now also

not sin]. Because they sinned against Me, therefore I hid My face from them and gave them into the hand of their enemies. So they all fell by the sword." **[it follows on therefore that these gentile nations will now be called to repent and agree to God ruling over them through Israel]** (Ezek 39:21-23, MKJV)

One by one the nations will be conquered and brought into submission commencing with Israel during the Great Tribulation; followed by the coming Beast power and Babylon during the Day of The Lord; and then His government will extend to various Japhethite and Hamite nations.

The Messiah has returned and this is now His world and the last of the gentile nations must be brought into submission!

> "And it shall come to pass, *that* every one that is left of all the nations which came against Jerusalem shall even go up from year to year to worship the King, the LORD of hosts, and to keep the feast of tabernacles.
>
> And it shall be, *that* whoso will not come up of *all* the families of the earth unto Jerusalem to worship the King, the LORD of hosts, even upon them shall be no rain.
>
> And if the family of Egypt go not up, and come not, that *have* no *rain*; there shall be the plague, wherewith the LORD will smite the heathen that come not up to keep the feast of tabernacles.
>
> This shall be the punishment of Egypt, and the punishment of all nations that come not up to keep the feast of tabernacles." (Zech 14:16-19, KJV)

There may be parallel passages in Zechariah: Chapter 12 has a Trumpets theme and is read in synagogues on the Day of Trumpets; chapter 13 has an Atonement theme and read on the Day of Atonement; while chapter 14 is read during the Feast of Tabernacles.[37] It is also of interest to note that Ezek 38-39 is read in many synagogues during the Feast of Tabernacles, not prior to it.

In fact, according to Jewish understanding, Psalm 2 refers to Gog and Magog:

> "Why do the heathen rage, and the people imagine a vain thing?
>
> The kings of the earth set themselves, and the rulers take counsel together, against the LORD, and against his anointed, *saying*,
>
> Let us break their bands asunder, and cast away their cords from us.
>
> He that sitteth in the heavens shall laugh: the Lord shall have them in derision.
>
> Then shall he speak unto them in his wrath, and vex them in his sore displeasure.
>
> Yet have I set my king upon my holy hill of Zion.
>
> I will declare the decree: the LORD hath said unto me, Thou *art* my Son; this day have I begotten thee." (Ps 2:1-7, KJV)

---

[37] For instance: "According to the Prophet Zacharia, the nations who survive the final "War of Gog and Magog" will come to Jerusalem every year "to prostrate themselves to the King, Hashem...and to celebrate the Succot festival." (Zecharia 14:16)"

It seems that the above Psalm, like so many of them, is also a prophecy as we learned in the previous chapter. In fact, these appear to be nations that come against the Messiah after His return, not at His return. In the *Gemara* (the second part of the *Talmud*) we read:

> "… when the war of Gog and Magog will break out they will be asked, "Why have you come?" They will answer, "[To fight] against God and His anointed," as it says, "Why do nations assemble, and regimes talk in vain … to conspire against God and His anointed" (Psalms 2:1)."[38]

Similarly, each Sabbath, a selection of the *Prophets* is read in the synagogue services after the *Torah* lessons. This reading is known as the *Haftarah*. On the first day of the Feast of Tabernacles (Sukkot), Ezekiel 38 and 39 is read (first day of Tabernacles *Haftarah*).

It is interesting that this reading is on the **first** day – representing the first years of the Feast of Tabernacles. Not all is peaceful during the initial part of the Millennium.

The Jewish community considers the following issues during Tabernacles (Sukkot):

- The Kingdom of David as a type
- God's tests upon the nations during Sukkot
- Divine visitation
- The war with Gog and Magog (readings on First day of Sukkot)
- A special feast will be held for the righteous people of God – a special event during Tabernacles (perhaps typological of Matt 22:1-13 and Rev 19:9).

Jewish understanding for the timing of Ezekiel 38 and 39 parallels Christian interpretative diversity, ranging across several viewpoints:

- It refers to armies that attack the holy land prior to the Messiah; or
- Refers to a time shortly after the Messiah's arrival; or
- It is typological of evil doers in opposition to God.

In any event, it seems possible that Zechariah chapter 14:1-11 refers to the first few years of the Millennium and it specifically states that Jerusalem (symbolic of all Israel) will be safely inhabited (cp Ezek 38:11,14). Then we are told:

> "And this shall be the plague with which Jehovah will strike all the peoples who have fought against Jerusalem **[both before and after the return of Christ]**. Their flesh shall rot while they stand on their feet, and their eyes shall rot in their sockets. And their tongue shall rot in their mouth.

---

[38] According to the daily Jewish readings site, http://www.chabad.org/dailystudy/tehillim.asp?tDate=10/30/2006&Lang=, Psalms 46 and 47 refers to the period immediately after the Gog and Magog rebellion: "Following the battle of Gog and Magog (in the Messianic era), war will be no more. God will grant us salvation, and we will merit to go up to the Holy Temple for the festivals, Amen."

And it shall be in that day a great panic of Jehovah shall be among them And they shall each one lay hold of his neighbor, and his hand shall rise up against the hand of his neighbor.

And Judah also shall fight at Jerusalem; and the wealth of all the nations all around shall be gathered, gold, and silver, and clothing in great abundance. **[cp Eze 39:10]**

And so shall be the plague of the horse, the mule, the camel, and the ass, and of all the beasts which shall be in these tents, like this plague.

1And it shall be, everyone who is left of all the nations which came up against Jerusalem shall go up from year to year to worship the King, Jehovah of Hosts, and to keep the Feast of Tabernacles.

And it shall be, *that* whoso will not come up of *all* the families of the earth unto Jerusalem to worship the King, the LORD of hosts, even upon them shall be no rain.

And if the family of Egypt go not up, and come not, that *have* no *rain*; there shall be the plague, wherewith the LORD will smite the heathen that come not up to keep the feast of tabernacles. **[cp Is 19:4-5]**

This shall be the punishment of Egypt, and the punishment of all nations that come not up to keep the feast of tabernacles.

In that day shall there be upon the bells of the horses, HOLINESS UNTO THE LORD; and the pots in the LORD'S house shall be like the bowls before the altar.

Yea, every pot in Jerusalem and in Judah shall be holy to Jehovah of Hosts. And all those who sacrifice shall come and take of them, and boil in them. And in that day there shall no longer be a trader **[i.e. Canaanite – either spiritual or physical]** in the house of Jehovah of Hosts." (Zech 14:12-21, MKJV. Refer also to Ezekiel 38:21-23 for a parallel or similar event)

Zechariah 14 may also be paralleled with Isaiah 19. There is an issue with Egypt (or what is left of it): they must keep the Feast of Tabernacles (and the other laws of course), or bear the consequences. Starting with Israel, then the nations that formerly comprised Babylon, Assyria, Egypt etc, God commences a global theocracy nation-by-nation:

"The burden of Egypt. Behold, the LORD rideth upon a swift cloud, and shall come into Egypt: and the idols of Egypt shall be moved at his presence, and the heart of Egypt shall melt in the midst of it.

And I will set the Egyptians against the Egyptians: and they shall fight every one against his brother, and every one against his neighbour; city against city, *and* kingdom against kingdom.

And the spirit of Egypt shall fail in the midst thereof; and I will destroy the counsel thereof: and they shall seek to the idols, and to the charmers, and to them that have familiar spirits, and to the wizards." (Is 19:1-3, KJV)

The above indicates that this occurs after the return of the Messiah. Compare with Zech 14:13.

"And the Egyptians will I give over into the hand of a cruel lord; and a fierce king shall rule over them, saith the Lord, the LORD of hosts.

And the waters shall fail from the sea, and the river shall be wasted and dried up." (Is 19:4-5, KJV)

This may be cross-referenced to Zech 14:18. Isaiah continues:

"And they shall turn the rivers far away; *and* the brooks of defence shall be emptied and dried up: the reeds and flags shall wither.

The paper reeds by the brooks, by the mouth of the brooks, and every thing sown by the brooks, shall wither, be driven away, and be no *more*.

The fishers also shall mourn, and all they that cast angle into the brooks shall lament, and they that spread nets upon the waters shall languish.

Moreover they that work in fine flax, and they that weave networks, shall be confounded.

And they shall be broken in the purposes thereof, all that make sluices *and* ponds for fish." (Is 19:6-10, KJV)

Perhaps so perplexed at what is going on, they turn to evil guides for answers:

"Surely the princes of Zoan *are* fools, the counsel of the wise counsellors of Pharaoh is become brutish: how say ye unto Pharaoh, I *am* the son of the wise, the son of ancient kings?

Where *are* they? where *are* thy wise *men*? and let them tell thee now, and let them know what the LORD of hosts hath purposed upon Egypt.

The princes of Zoan are become fools, the princes of Noph are deceived; they have also seduced Egypt, *even they that are* the stay of the tribes thereof.

The LORD hath mingled a perverse spirit in the midst thereof: and they have caused Egypt to err in every work thereof, as a drunken *man* staggereth in his vomit.

Neither shall there be *any* work for Egypt, which the head or tail, branch or rush, may do.

In that day shall Egypt be like unto women: and it shall be afraid and fear because of the shaking of the hand of the LORD of hosts, which he shaketh over it." (Is 19:11-16, KJV)

Now Egypt learns to fear Judah which God uses to punish them:

"And the land of Judah shall be a terror unto Egypt, every one that maketh mention thereof shall be afraid in himself, because of the counsel of the LORD of hosts, which he hath determined against it." **[see Zech 14:14 where Judah are portrayed as fighters]** (Is 19:17, KJV)

Then we have Egypt's repentance:

"In that day shall five cities in the land of Egypt speak the language of Canaan, and swear to the LORD of hosts; one shall be called, The city of destruction.

In that day shall there be an altar to the LORD in the midst of the land of Egypt, and a pillar at the border thereof to the LORD.

And it shall be for a sign and for a witness unto the LORD of hosts in the land of Egypt: for they shall cry unto the LORD because of the oppressors, and he shall send them a saviour, and a great one, and he shall deliver them." (Is 19:18-20, KJV)

These oppressors are probably those referred to in verses 11-13.

> "And the LORD shall be known to Egypt, and the Egyptians shall know the LORD in that day, and shall do sacrifice and oblation; yea, they shall vow a vow unto the LORD, and perform *it*.
>
> And the LORD shall smite Egypt: he shall smite and heal *it*: and they shall return *even* to the LORD, and he shall be intreated of them, and shall heal them.
>
> In that day shall there be a highway out of Egypt to Assyria, and the Assyrian shall come into Egypt, and the Egyptian into Assyria, and the Egyptians shall serve with the Assyrians.
>
> In that day shall Israel be the third with Egypt and with Assyria, *even* a blessing in the midst of the land:
>
> Whom the LORD of hosts shall bless, saying, Blessed *be* Egypt my people, and Assyria the work of my hands, and Israel mine inheritance." (Is 19:21-25, KJV)

And so we have an alliance: Israel – the chief of all the nations; Egypt (Mizraim), probably chief of the Hamites and Assyria probably the chief of the Shemites. It seems that another will now join them – a nation descended from Japheth to become chief of the Japhethites under the overall leadership of Israel – this appears to be the world order that Christ will initiate. In other words the Messiah's dealing with the hordes of Ezekiel 38 and 39 follow next in the sequence of prophesied events. The chief of these nations may be Meschech (given the prominence it has compared to other Japhetic nations).

Gradually nation after nation will submit to God through Israel's conquests and leadership. Woe to them if they do not submit!

But only Egypt of the African nations is mentioned in Isaiah 19. While in Ezekiel 38 and 39 Egypt is not mentioned – this indicates that the prophecy in Isaiah 19 precedes that of Ezekiel where other African nations adjacent to Egypt are mentioned. Why? Because if Egypt was not repentant, it would have been part of these hordes along with their Hamitic brethren (Cush and Phut) – many of which dwell in adjacent lands.

TYPOLOGY CONTAINED WITHIN THE BOOK OF JOSHUA

Surprising as it may sound, further proof for the true timing of Ezekiel 38 and 39 is found in the book of Joshua.

This is how I figured it out as I have related to many for some years, so I might as well mention it here: I was reading old Church articles on Ezekiel around 1973 and trying to work out how these chapters could refer to a period some years after the Messiah's return to this earth rather than prior. After all I was influenced in my initial understanding of these chapters by evangelical authors. To me the clincher was two-fold:

1. the story flow of the book of Ezekiel;
2. the typology of Joshua as explained below.

The Exodus of Israel from Egypt, the crossing of the Red Sea, Wilderness wanderings, crossing of the Jordan and conquest of Canaan by Joshua are typological, as I am sure we have all heard. The typology follows two broad avenues:

1. spiritual Israelites undertake the same basic journey through life and are rescued from Satan. This is followed by baptism, life of trial, 'baptism' of the resurrection, entry into the spiritual Promised Land (Kingdom of God), finding rest for eternity;
2. physical Israelites in these last days will be rescued and set free from Babylon (and the Beast power) (Rev 18:4) as they were from ancient Egypt via the outpouring of plagues. Then they go through a wilderness wondering where they will be tried, cleansed and the Holy Spirit granted to the repentant. Following this they will enter the Promised Land of Israel led by Jesus Christ and His saints (Jesus is the Greek form of Joshua) and dwell there in peace (rest) protected by the Messiah; the land is conquered and the Temple and system of governance is re-established.

But what happens next? Here are the pertinent Scriptures that one can use to draw parallels between the first and second exoduses:

First of all, Israel passes through the Jordan and enters the Holy Land (compare Joshua 3-4) which typifies, in many ways (but not all) the Millennial age. Further enemies are encountered after the entry into the Holy Land (compare Joshua 5-6). Keil et al explains:

"… Jericho … the destruction of this town, the key to Canaan, was intended by God to become **a type** of the final destruction at the last day of the power of this world … [Christ] destroys one worldly power after another, and thus **maintains and extends His kingdom** upon the earth" (*Commentary of the Book of Joshua*, pp. 50-52) (emphasis mine).

Further hostile powers are encountered (compare Joshua 7–11). A northern alliance of enemies comes against Israel which Joshua destroys:

"And Jehovah troubled them before Israel, and killed them with a great slaughter at Gibeon, and chased them along the way that goes up to Beth-horon, and struck them to Azekah, and to Makkedah.

And it happened, as they fled from before Israel, and *were* in the descent of Bethhoron, Jehovah cast **down great stones from the heavens** on them to Azekah, and they died. The many who died from hailstones were more than the sons of Israel killed with the sword." **[compare this with Ezek 38:22]** (Jos 10:10, MKJV)

"And it happened when Jabin **[name means The Intelligent (one)]**, king of Hazor, had heard, he sent to Jobab king of Madon, and to the king of Shimron, and to the king of Achshaph, and to the kings on the north of the mountains, and on the plains south of Chinneroth, and in the valley, and in the borders of Dor on the west, *and to* the Canaanite on the east and on the west, and the Amorite, and the Hittite, and the Perizzite, and the Jebusite in the mountains, and to the Hivite under Hermon, in the land of Mizpeh.

And they went out, they and all their armies with them, many people, even as the sand on the seashore in multitude, with very many horses and chariots.

And when all these kings had met together, they came and pitched together at the waters of Merom, to fight against Israel." (Jos 11:1-5, MKJV)

"And these *are* the kings of the land, whom the sons of Israel struck and whose land they possessed on the other side Jordan toward **the rising of the sun**, from the river Arnon to mount Hermon, and all the plain on the east: **[cp with Judges 7:12]**

Sihon king of the Amorites, who lived in Heshbon *and* ruled from Aroer, which is on the bank of the river Arnon, and from the middle of the river, and from half Gilead, even to the river Jabbok, the border of the sons of Ammon; and from the plain to the sea of Chinneroth on the east, and to the sea of the plain, the Salt Sea on the east, the way to Beth-jeshimoth, and from the south, under The Slopes of Pisgah.

And they struck the coast of **Og king of Bashan, of the rest of the giants [great ones]**, who lived at Ashtaroth and at Edrei, and reigned in mount Hermon and in Salcah, and in all Bashan, to the border of the Geshurites and the Maachathites, and half Gilead, the border of Sihon king of Heshbon." (Joshua 12:1-5, MKJV)

Og is a related word to Gog. Ezekiel places him on an equal footing with Magog, yet he is not mentioned as being a descendant of Japheth in the Table of Nations nor anywhere else in Scripture. Little reference is made to this or similar names. However, in history there was a king Gyges of Lydia, called *Gugu* by the Assyrians (George Beasley-Murray, *New Bible Dictionary*, p. 480) who was ruler of a Cimmerian people (Donald Wiseman, *Peoples of Old Testament Times*, p. 165). Also, the Arabs referred to the 'Yajuj and Majuj' as living in Northeast Asia beyond the Tatars and Sclavonians.[39]

Amalek, the most infamous of the sons of Edom, also migrated into Turkestan naming a city *Amalek* after themselves according to Paul Herrmann's *Sieben vorbei und Acht Verweht* (p. 451). Amalek was borne from a union between Eliphaz and Timna, a Horite (Gen 36:12, 22). The Egyptians called the Amalekites *Amu*. In Turkestan the River Amu was probably named after them (the Oxus of the ancient Greeks); Amu is a Persian name. But that is not all. The Edomites inhabited Mount Seir region initially, as has already been mentioned. In Turkestan the Syr Dary river may be named after them as the meaning is "the river of Seir". There can be no doubt about it, a branch of the Amalekites dwell to this day in Central Asia, Turkestan and surrounding areas to be exact. Here then is the end-time Gog! We should expect a strong leader to emerge from this region in the future years and decades. Gog is not Russia and the Western peoples of the former Soviet Union as many speculate, but the peoples of central Asia, seeking independence from Russia and perhaps they may form their own federation in cooperation with Russia and China in due time?

The Assyrian texts refer to the King of Lydia (in western Turkey) as *Gugu* and there was also a mention of Gugians in the area of Mitanni. However, whether there is any connection to the Amalekites cannot be ascertained at this point in time although it could be pointed

---

[39] Gog may also be the Yao of ancient Chinese history.

out that the kings of Amalek were sometimes named Agag (Num 24:7; 1Sam 15:8). Josephus also sees Agag as a synonym for Amalek. We know from the Scriptures that one evil man Haman, tried to exterminate the Judahites in Persia. In the book of Esther, Haman was called an Agagite (3:1,10; 8:3,5; 9:24); Josephus, in fact explicitly calls Haman an Amalekite: "Now there was one Haman, the son of Amedatha, by birth an Amalekite, that used to go in to the king" (*Antiquities of the Jews*, Book 11, Section 209). All this positively indicates that many of the Edomites were migrating slowly toward Central Asia even at this time. The *International Standard Bible Encyclopedia* reveals that Haman's home was in an area adjacent to Media known as *Agazi* in the *Annals of Sargon* a name possibly associated with or derived from Agag or Gog.

Another son of Edom, Reuel, unlike his grandsons Amalek and Teman, is very difficult to trace specifically. As Reuel's mother was Bashemath, the Ishmaelitess, he may be among the Arabs, Ruwaleh specifically. Conversely, Jehush, Jaalam and Korah were borne by Aholibamah who was daughter of Anah and granddaughter of Zibeon, the Hivite, one of Esau's wives. They might well be among the Turkic tribes of Central Asia along with Amalek as a result. Korah may have given his name to the Karakum Desert, Karakul Lake, Karatau mountains, the Kirghiz and Khorasan in Turkestan. One division of the Kirghiz peoples is known as the Kara.

The name of Hivite could have lived on in the city of Khiva of Central Asia, which was the capital of the province of Khiva of the Turks.

The Edomites were also known as Idumaeans, probably due to some intermarriage between Edomites and Dumah, the descendant of Ishmael. In Turkey we find the areas of Duman, Duman Dagh mountain and Dumanli Dagh mountains. And in India there is the town of Dumagudiem and the Duma mountains possibly named after them.

Now that we have located where many of the descendants of Edom are today, let us find out what the name *Gog* means.

"Gog - it is a long o both in the Hebrew and in the Greek - is made from the old-world-root 'GG', which in the early languages implied something 'g-i-g-antic'. Russia has this long time been the colossus of the north'.

A potentate of bible history and prophecy was 'Agog'. That name, or rather, its title, comes from the same root. He was (in his own estimation), a, Aleph, + GG = No. 1 - GREAT! The Agagites, we are told in *Young's Analytical Concordance*, were an 'Amalekite tribe' and Agog, was 'a poetic name of Amalek, derived from a particular dynasty ...'.

Of course, it is always on the cards that some great military dictator [in Russian Central Asia] may arise - he would be the personal Gog". (Walter Milner, *The Russian Chapters of Ezekiel*, pp. 9-10).

It seems reasonable to assert that these northern armies are typified by Israel's experiences and confrontations in the Holy Land. They will invade after the commencement of the new age of Israel under Joshua (Jesus Christ).

3. After they are defeated, we are told:

    > "And Joshua took the whole land, according to all that Jehovah commanded Moses. And Joshua gave it for an inheritance to Israel according to their divisions by their tribes. And **the land rested from war**" [typological of the Messianic age after Gog & Magog are defeated – no more wars in or near the Holy Land until the end of the Millennium] (Jos 11:23, MKJV)

From the above brief summary of Joshua's typology, there can be no doubt that Ezekiel 38 and 39 are typed by foes primarily to the north of Israel a few years *after* Israel enters the Holy Land and has no pre- or post- Millennial application.

Evidently, these are people and nations that will yet be reached and converted at the outset of the Millennium. It makes clear sense that upon the Messiah's return, He will gather His people Israel which would have been scattered to the four corners and bring them to the Near East. Somewhere close to the Holy Land (probably Sinai), He will plead with them and purge out the rebels from among them.

Then He will lead the Priests, Levites, Judah and Israel into the Promised Land where a New Covenant will be forged. Followed by the training of Israel to become world servant leaders.

Treasures from all over the world will pour into the Holy Land swelling the wealth of Israel. Yet some nations not reached by God through Israel will rise up in jealous indignation. It will do them no good as Ezekiel 38 and 39 demonstrate. The 'rest will be history' as they say.

As with so much Scripture, these chapters of Ezekiel may be typological of later events found in Rev 20:

Table 8 Relevant chapter in Ezekiel and its Typology for the post-Millennial period

Relevant chapter in Ezekiel and its Typology for the post-Millennial period		
Joshua	**Ezekiel**	**Revelation**
Chs 3-4 -Crossing over the Jordan into the Holy Land	Ch 36-37 – Israel restored and relocated to the Holy Land (Second Exodus)	Ch 21:10-15 – First Resurrection
Chs 4-6, 11-12 – Seven Canaanite tribes defeated over seven years	Chs 38 and 39 – armies invade the Holy land after the Messiah returns and defeated	Ch 20:7-9 – post Millennial armies defeated
Ch 11- Land at peace	Ch 39:21-29 –peace reigns	Ch 21:10-15 – Second Resurrection -peace reigns & Third resurrection
Ch 18 - tabernacle relocated to Shiloh. David later plans to build a Temple in Jerusalem which was fulfilled by Solomon. Tribal allotments/inheritance (chs 18-19, 21). Seven years of settlement	Chs 40-48 – Millennial temple and tribal allotments/inheritance (ch 48)	Chs 21-22 – the New Jerusalem and inheritance of Israel (21:12)

Note: no typology is perfect or complete – they merely inform us of other or future events and demonstrate some similarities. By studying a given portion of Scripture as typology, we gain a greater insight into their counter-part prophecy.

Concerning chapter 37 of Ezekiel, evangelist Herbert Armstrong confirmed its duality:

> "In chapter 37, the first part pictures the "valley of dry bones." This represents (Verse 11), the whole House of Israel — including Judah. **It has a dual significance**. It pictures the re-birth and resurrection of Israel as a nation, from captivity, dispersion and slavery. It pictures, too, the literal bodily resurrection of the individual who has long since died, after which the knowledge of the Truth — spiritual knowledge — shall be revealed, and he shall be converted, and Gods Spirit shall enter within, and he shall be saved." (Herbert Armstrong, "Will Russia Attack America?" *Plain Truth*, July 1956, p. 6) [emphasis mine]

Many or most commentators would agree with this position. For example, John Taylor states under the sub-title "The spiritual re-birth of the nation (37:1-28)":

> "The bones represent the Israelites in exile. The have been there for ten years now, and what glimmerings of hope they had when first they arrived have now been altogether extinguished. Their hope was lost: as bones, they were very dry" (*Ezekiel. Tyndale Old Testament Commentaries*, p. 228)

Many other commentaries similarly explain that chapter. Hosea also uses resurrection as typological of a restoration of the nations in 6:2 and 13:14.

CONCLUDING REMARKS

Finally, an addition to this typology should be mentioned here: a Near Eastern king, Cushan-Rishathaim, was used by God to punish Israel (Judges 3).

> "The historical and textual evidence also suggests that the Indo-Aryan ethnic group that founded and ruled Mitanni called themselves originally by a name that sounded something like "Rish" or "Ras." This name is reflected in Judges 3:7-11 where Cushan is said to have been from an ethnic group called the "Rishathaim."" (Clyde Billington, "Othniel, Cushan-Rishathaim, and the Date of the Exodus," *Artifax*, Summer 2017, p. 19)

Figure 14 Gog and Magog, Royal Arcade, Melbourne

The Mitanni are descendants of Midian and prophetically, nothing much is said about Midian. Perhaps the peoples mentioned in the Book of Judges, where they are allies of the Amalekites (Gog), represent a foreshadowing of the future eastern hordes, as described in Judges 7:12. Through Habbakuk, God says that the Midianites (the Mitanni) will tremble at Him when He begins to intervene in world affairs (Habbakuk 3:7-8). They are also referred to in Jeremiah 25:25. Their kin, the Medes are prophesied to come against end-time Babylon in Jeremiah 51:28, undoubtedly as part of the prophesied eastern forces. The Medes descend from Medan and dwell alongside the Ukrainians (Madai) today.

Further information on these parallels is found in the appendix ***Ezekiel – Revelation Parallels***. Given all the evidence presented in this chapter, it is self-evident that the armies of Ezekiel 38 and 39 represent a threat to Israel ***after*** the return of the Messiah, and not beforehand.

CHIEF COMPONENTS OF THE MILLENNIUM

THE REIGN OF THE MESSIAH will usher in a new order of obedience to His Law and all people, upon repentance, will receive the holy spirit. As they grow in God's goodness, they develop the fruit of the spirit (Gal 5:16-26), develop the beautiful attitudes and blessings (of Matt 5-7) and learn to have outgoing concern for others. In addition, God bestows spiritual gifts upon His own, to be used for His glory and for the benefit of others (1 Cor 12:4-11). That is the way of GIVE versus the way of GET. The way of outgoing concern for others – in other words love!

This will be reflected in how God's way is 'rolled out' or enacted around the world.

This author thought it best to assemble a table that in effect summarises the way of life, system of government and various aspects or components of the Millennial reign. This, it is believed, is the most effective way for any Bible student to learn more about that period in an easy-to-follow format. I think you will find it unique and better than a very lengthy tome on the subject.[40]

Note that He, together with the saints, rule on earth (Rev 5:10. Cf IKings 8:27). This does not discount the possibility of Him appearing before God the Father in heaven as needed. But on the earth, as spirits, they dwell in the heavenlies – the spiritual sphere around the earth – the first heaven.

---

[40] Refer to the *Wonderful World Tomorrow* book by Herbert W Armstrong for further information .

Table 9 Analysing the Kingdom on Earth

Condition/System	Scriptures	Comments/References
Agricultural blessings	**Key Scripture:** "There shall be an handful of corn in the earth upon the top of the mountains; the fruit thereof shall shake like Lebanon: and *they* of the city shall flourish like grass of the earth. His name shall endure for ever: his name shall be continued as long as the sun: and *men* shall be blessed in him: all nations shall call him blessed. Blessed *be* the LORD God, the God of Israel, who only doeth wondrous things." (Ps 72:16-18, KJV) **Other Scriptures:** Ps. 67:6-7; Isa. 9:3; 35:1; 65:22; Ezek 34:27-29; Joel 2:24-26; 3:18; Amos 9:13-14	The land sabbath and other ecological laws will be restored
Animals and nature	**Key Scripture:** "The wolf also shall dwell with the lamb, and the leopard shall lie down with the kid; and the calf and the young lion and the fatling together; and a little child shall lead them. And the cow and the bear shall feed; their young ones shall lie down together: and the lion shall eat straw like the ox. And the sucking child shall play on the hole of the asp, and the weaned child shall put his hand on the cockatrice' den. They shall not hurt nor destroy in all my holy mountain: for the earth shall be full of the knowledge of the LORD, as the waters cover the sea." (Is 11:6-9, KJV) **Other Scriptures:** Is 30:23-24; 35:9; 65:25; Job 5:22; Ezek 34:25; Hos 2:18 (cp Prov 12:10; Lev 26:6)	For further information, refer to the chapter on *Animals in the World Tomorrow*

Condition/System	Scriptures	Comments/References
Capital of the world: Mt Zion in Jerusalem	**Key Scripture:** "And it shall come to pass in the last days, *that* the mountain of the LORD'S house shall be established in the top of the mountains, and shall be exalted above the hills; and all nations shall flow unto it. And many people shall go and say, Come ye, and let us go up to the mountain of the LORD, to the house of the God of Jacob; and he will teach us of his ways, and we will walk in his paths: for out of Zion shall go forth the law, and the word of the LORD from Jerusalem." (Is 2:2-3, KJV) **Other Scriptures:** Is 56:7; 62:1; 65:18-19; Jer 3:17-18; Ezek 20:40; 40:2; 48:15-19; Mic4:1-2; Zech 8:3; 14:4; Luke 21:24	
Cities rebuilt	**Key Scripture:** "And they shall build the old wastes, they shall raise up the former desolations, and they shall repair the waste cities, the desolations of many generations." (Is 61:4, KJV) **Other Scriptures:** Ps 69:35-36; Is 44:26, 28; 52:9; 54:3; 58:12 Ezek 36:10-11, 33-38; Amos 9:14	For further information, refer to the PPT presentation *Cities in the World Tomorrow*
Curses lifted	**Key Scripture:** "And to Adam he said, "Because you have listened to the voice of your wife and have eaten of the tree of which I commanded you, 'You shall not eat of it,' cursed is the ground because of you; in pain you shall eat of it all the days of your life; thorns and thistles it shall bring forth for you; and you shall eat the plants of the field. By the sweat of your face you shall eat bread, till you return to the ground, for out of it you were taken; for you are dust, and to dust you shall return."" (Gen 3:17-19), ESV[41] **Other Scriptures:** Is 11:6-9; 24:6; 65:23-25; Ezek 47:8-12; Zech 8:4; 14:8	No more plagues, fighting, lacking of basics, agricultural problems (e.g. fires, floods and droughts). Climate and weather will change for the better

---

[41] The curse here is different to that of Genesis 8:21 according to some commentaries. Genesis 8 is in reference to the Flood.

Condition/System	Scriptures	Comments/References
Environment like Eden and the deserts blooming	**Key Scripture:** "For the LORD shall comfort Zion: he will comfort all her waste places; and he will make her wilderness like Eden, and her desert like the garden of the LORD; joy and gladness shall be found therein, thanksgiving, and the voice of melody." (Is 51:3, KJV) **Other Scriptures:** Is 32:15; 35:1-2, 7-8; 41:19; 51:3; 55:12-13; 65:17, 25; Ezek 36:35-36; Acts 3:19-21	Refer to the *Wonderful World Tomorrow* book for further information
Evil conquered	**Key Scripture:** "The people that walked in darkness have seen a great light: they that dwell in the land of the shadow of death, upon them hath the light shined." (Is 9:2, KJV) **Other Scriptures:** Ps 45:3-6; 110:5-6; Is 9:3-5; 61:1 (cp Ps 147:3); Jer 50:17-19; Ezek 36:35; Dan 2:37-44; Zech 14:9	
Extent of the Kingdom	**Key Scripture:** "The LORD reigneth; let the earth rejoice; let the multitude of isles be glad *thereof*." (Ps 97:1, KJV) **Other Scriptures:** Ps 2:6-9; 72:8; 93:1-3; 97:1-12; Is 2:2; 9:6-7; 40:4-5; Dan 2:44; 4:34; 7:14, 27; Mic 4:1-2; Zech 9:10; Ps 72:8-11; Dan 7:13-14	
Gentiles: leaders and nations subject to the Messiah	**Key Scripture:** "Ask of me, and I shall give *thee* the heathen *for* thine inheritance, and the uttermost parts of the earth *for* thy possession. Thou shalt break them with a rod of iron; thou shalt dash them in pieces like a potter's vessel. Be wise now therefore, O ye kings: be instructed, ye judges of the earth. Serve the LORD with fear, and rejoice with trembling. Kiss the Son, lest he be angry, and ye perish *from* the way, when his wrath is kindled but a little. Blessed *are* all they that put their trust in him." (Ps 2:8-12, KJV) **Other Scriptures:** Ps 47:1-9; 67:1-7; Is 64:1-2; Zech 14:16-19; Hag 2:22; Rev 2:26-27	For further information, refer to the chapters *Status of the Nations in the World Tomorrow* and *Feast of the Nations* and *Invisible Rulers over the Nations* and the section *Why will the forces of Ezekiel 38 and 39 Invade the Holy Land?* See also West's comments in *The Thousand Years in both Testaments*, p. 7

Condition/System	Scriptures	Comments/References
Healing (physically and emotionally)	**Key Scripture:** "And the inhabitant shall not say, I am sick: the people that dwell therein *shall be* forgiven *their* iniquity." (Is 33:24, KJV) **Other Scriptures:** Is 29:17-19; 35:3-6; 61:1-2; Jer 31:8	Christ's healing miracles are a forerunner of the coming mass healings
Holy spirit poured out – holiness and righteousness extends across the world	**Key Scripture:** "And it shall come to pass afterward, *that* I will pour out my spirit upon all flesh; and your sons and your daughters shall prophesy, your old men shall dream dreams, your young men shall see visions: And also upon the servants and upon the handmaids in those days will I pour out my spirit." (Joel 2:28-29, KJV) **Other Scriptures:** Is 11:2-5; 32:15; 44:3; 59:21; Ezek 36:27; Ob 17	
Israel and Judah enter the Holy Land and reunite	**Key Scripture:** "Say unto them, Thus saith the Lord GOD; Behold, I will take the stick of Joseph, which *is* in the hand of Ephraim, and the tribes of Israel his fellows, and will put them with him, *even* with the stick of Judah, and make them one stick, and they shall be one in mine hand." (Ezek 37:19, KJV) **Other Scriptures:** Jer 31:1, 7-9; 50:4-5; Ezek 11:17; 34:12-13; 37:19-22. Other related Scriptures include: Lev 26: 42-46; Ps 14:7; 53:6; 68:6; 30:4; Jer 3:17-19; 12: 14-15; 16:15; 23:3-4, 7-8; 24:6-7; 30:3, 8-10; 33:6-9; 50:4-5, 19-20; Hos 1:11; 2:14; Mic 2:12; 5:4-7; Zech 8:7-8; 10:9-12; 12:10-14; Acts 15:16-17; Rom 11:26	For further information, refer to the chapter *Israel's Second Exodus* See also West's comments in *The Thousand Years in both Testaments*, p. 7

Condition/System	Scriptures	Comments/References

Israel: New Covenant entered into	**Key Scripture:**
	    "Not according to the covenant that I made with their fathers in the day *that* I took them by the hand to bring them out of the land of Egypt; which my covenant they brake, although I was an husband unto them, saith the LORD:
	    But this *shall be* the covenant that I will make with the house of Israel; After those days, saith the LORD, I will put my law in their inward parts, and write it in their hearts; and will be their God, and they shall be my people." (Jer 31:32-33, KJV)
	
	Other Scriptures:
	    Is 59:20-21; Heb 8:8; Ezek 16:59-60; 36:26-28; Hos 2:16-19
		Cf Dan 9:24-27 – Christ will complete His 3 ½ year ministry to Israel and enter into a New Covenant with them

Israel: global leadership and leading the gentile nations	**Key Scriptures:**
	    "So when they had come together, they asked him, "Lord, will you at this time restore the kingdom to Israel?"
	    He said to them, "It is not for you to know times or seasons that the Father has fixed by his own authority"" (Acts 1:6-7, ESV)
	    "Strangers shall stand and tend your flocks; foreigners shall be your plowmen and vinedressers; but you shall be called the priests of the LORD; they shall speak of you as the ministers of our God; you shall eat the wealth of the nations, and in their glory you shall boast.
	    Instead of your shame there shall be a double portion; instead of dishonor they shall rejoice in their lot; therefore in their land they shall possess a double portion; they shall have everlasting joy." (Is 61:5-7, ESV)
	
	Other Scriptures:
	    Deut 28:12-13; Is 14:1-2; 41:15; 55:4-5; 60:5-16; 19:17; 61:1-9; Ezek 25:13-17; Ob 1:17-21; Amos 9:11-12; Zeph 2:7-13; 8:23; Zech 9:11-14; 10:3-10; 12:7-8; 14:14; Luke 1:32-33
		For further information, refer to the chapter *Israel's Role after the Second Exodus*

Israel: Tribal Allocations	**Key Scriptures:**
	    "This is the land that you shall allot as an inheritance among the tribes of Israel, and these are their portions, declares the Lord GOD." (Ezek 48:29, ESV)
	
	Other Scriptures:
	    Jer 23:8; 31:10; Ezek 36:24; 48:1-35; Amos 9:14-15	

Condition/System	Scriptures	Comments/References
Judging of the Nations	**Key Scriptures:** "Before the Lord: for He cometh, for He cometh to judge the Earth: He shall judge the World with righteousness, and the people with His truth." (Ps 96:13, KJV) "But those mine enemies, which would not that I should reign over them, bring hither, and slay them before me." (Luke 19:12-14, 27, KJV) "Kiss the Son, lest he be angry, and ye perish from the way, when his wrath is kindled but a little. Blessed are all they that put their trust in him." (Ps 2:12, KJV) "And they shall go forth, and look upon the carcases of the men that have transgressed against me: for their worm shall not die, neither shall their fire be quenched; and they shall be an abhorring unto all flesh." (Is 66:24, KJV) **Other Scriptures:** Gen 49:1-2, 9-12; Ps 2:1-12; 21:7-13; 86:9; 110:1-7; 149:1-9; Is 2:12-22; 11:1-8; 30:33; 60:1-3; Hag 2:6-7; Ob 15-16; Zech 2:11-13	For further information, refer to the chapter *The Judging of the Nations* This fire will be burning throughout the Millennium (Rev 19:20; 20:10)
Judicial fairness, equity and justice	**Key Scripture:** "O let the nations be glad and sing for joy: for thou shalt judge the people righteously, and govern the nations upon earth. Selah." (Ps 67:4, KJV) **Other Scriptures:** Ps 72:2,12-13; Isa 9:7; 11:3-5; 32:1, 16; 42:3-4; Jer 23:5-6; 33:15-16	
Language	**Key Scripture:** "For then will I turn to the people a pure language, that they may all call upon the name of the LORD, to serve him with one consent." (Zeph 3:9, KJV) **Other Scriptures:** Is 19:18; Dan 7:14; Zech 8:23	It seems that there will be a single global language. But that the nations will possess their own national languages for language is a cultural transmitter and means of maintaining identity.
Length of the Messiah's reign	**Key Scripture:** "And cast him into the bottomless pit, and shut him up, and set a seal upon him, that he should deceive the nations no more, till the thousand years should be fulfilled: and after that he must be loosed a little season." (Rev 20:3, KJV) **Other Scriptures:** IISam 7:16; IIPet 3:8	

Condition/System	Scriptures	Comments/References
Melchizedek Priesthood	**Key Scriptures:** "For it is evident that our Lord was descended from Judah, and in connection with that tribe Moses said nothing about priests. This becomes even more evident when another priest arises in the likeness of Melchizedek, who has become a priest, not on the basis of a legal requirement concerning bodily descent, but by the power of an indestructible life. For it is witnessed of him, "You are a priest forever, after the order of Melchizedek." (Heb 7:14-17, ESV) **Other Scriptures:** Ps 110:1-7; Zech 6:12-13; Heb 6:20; ITim 2:5-6	Refer to *A Note on the Melchizedek Priesthood.* **What does this Priesthood do?:** 1. Sacrifice – Christ sacrificed Himself (Heb 8:3; 7:27; Rev 5:6, 12) 2. Sympathises with humans (Heb 4:15-16) 3. He makes intercession (Heb 7:25; Is 53:12) 4. He advocates (IJohn 2:12; Heb 4:16; 10:22) 5. We draw nigh to God through Him (Heb 7:25; John 14:6) **Credentials:** 1. Ascend to God (Heb 4:14; 6:20; Heb 1:3 13) 2. Divine (Heb 4:14; 1:14) 3. Was human (John 1:1, 14; Heb 2:9-10, 14-17; 4:15-16) 4. Learned obedience and perfection (Heb 5:7-9; 7:26) 5. Sacrifices (Heb 8:3; 7:27) 6. Possesses eternal life (Heb 7:25; 2:9) It follows that we, as embryonic priests in the Order of Melchizedek, likewise suffer in order to be able to be empathetic and fully understand the humans we will be representing. See Rev 1:5-6; 5:9-10. Notice the priestly garments of the saints: Rev 3:4, 18; 6:11; 7:9; 19:7

121

Condition/System	Scriptures	Comments/References
Messiah - return of Christ as global Messiah	**Key Scriptures:** Angels "said, "Men of Galilee, why do you stand looking into heaven? This Jesus, who was taken up from you into heaven, will come in the same way as you saw him go into heaven.""" (Acts 1:11, ESV) "Then I saw heaven opened, and behold, a white horse! The one sitting on it is called Faithful and True, and in righteousness he judges and makes war. His eyes are like a flame of fire, and on his head are many diadems, and he has a name written that no one knows but himself. He is clothed in a robe dipped in blood, and the name by which he is called is The Word of God. And the armies of heaven, arrayed in fine linen, white and pure, were following him on white horses. From his mouth comes a sharp sword with which to strike down the nations, and he will rule them with a rod of iron. He will tread the winepress of the fury of the wrath of God the Almighty. On his robe and on his thigh he has a name written, King of kings and Lord of lords." (Rev 19:11-16, ESV) **Other Scriptures:** Is 30:26-27; Rev 1:7-8	For further information, refer to the chapter *Kiss the son before he becomes angry, and you die where you stand: The Messiah and the Nations.*
Messiah ruling from David's throne	**Key Scripture:** "He shall be great, and shall be called the Son of the Highest: and the Lord God shall give unto him the throne of his father David: And he shall reign over the house of Jacob for ever; and of his kingdom there shall be no end." (Luke 1:32-33, KJV) **Other Scriptures:** Gen 49: 8-12; Is 2:3; Jer 33:14-17; Acts 1:6	For further information, refer to the chapter *Kiss the son before he becomes angry, and you die where you stand: The Messiah and the Nations.*

Condition/System	Scriptures	Comments/References

Peace - war no more	**Key Scripture:**
	    "And he shall judge among the nations, and shall rebuke many people: and they shall beat their swords into plowshares, and their spears into pruninghooks: nation shall not lift up sword against nation, neither shall they learn war any more." (Is 2:4, KJV)
	
	Other Scriptures:
	    Ps 72:3-7; Is 9:7; Ezek 37:26; Mic 4:3	

Peace unfurled across the world gradually	**Key Scripture:**
	    "Rejoice greatly, O daughter of Zion; shout, O daughter of Jerusalem: behold, thy King cometh unto thee: he *is* just, and having salvation; lowly, and riding upon an ass, and upon a colt the foal of an ass.
	    And I will cut off the chariot from Ephraim, and the horse from Jerusalem, and the battle bow shall be cut off: and he shall speak peace unto the heathen: and his dominion *shall be* from sea *even* to sea, and from the river *even* to the ends of the earth." (Zech 9:9-10, KJV)
	
	Other Scriptures:
	    Is 2:4; 32:17-18; 65:20-23; Jer 23:5-6; 33:15-16; Ezek 34:25-29; Mic 4:3-4	

Prosperity – the economic and financial system	**Key Scripture:**
	    "And it shall come to pass in that day, *that* the mountains shall drop down new wine, and the hills shall flow with milk, and all the rivers of Judah shall flow with waters, and a fountain shall come forth of the house of the LORD, and shall water the valley of Shittim." (Joel 3:18, KJV)
	
	Other Scriptures:
	    Ps 72:3; Is 4:2; Amos 9:13-15
		The financial system will be based on stability and slow, steady growth. Probably a gold standard with silver coinage. The years of release, Jubilee Years and ban on usury etc will be restored

Condition/System	Scriptures	Comments/References
Rulers: King David	**Key Scripture:** "And I will set up one shepherd over them, and he shall feed them, *even* my servant David; he shall feed them, and he shall be their shepherd. And I the LORD will be their God, and my servant David a prince among them; I the LORD have spoken *it*." (Ezek 34:23-24, KJV) **Other Scriptures:** Ps 89:20-28; Jer 23:5; 30:8-9; Ezek 34:11, 15, 23-24; Hos 3:5; Luke 1:32-33, 68-69; John 16: 11, 16, 27-29; IPet 5:4	NB: Some of these Scriptures may be referring indirectly to Christ as well given the dual nature of prophecy. Refer to the *Wonderful World Tomorrow* book for further information
Rulers: Twelve Apostles over Israel and saints over the world	**Key Scripture:** "Jesus said to them, "Truly, I say to you, in the new world, when the Son of Man will sit on his glorious throne, you who have followed me will also sit on twelve thrones, judging the twelve tribes of Israel." (Matt 19:28, ESV) **Other Scriptures:** Is 32:1; Dan 7:17-18, 7:21-22, 7:27; Mat 19:28; Luke 19:17-19; 22:30; Rev 2:26-27; 3:21; 5:10	
Temple Priesthood	**Key Scriptures:** "and the chamber that faces north is for the priests who have charge of the altar. These are the sons of Zadok, who alone among the sons of Levi may come near to the LORD to minister to him." (Ezek 40:46, ESV) "But the Levitical priests, the sons of Zadok, who kept the charge of my sanctuary when the people of Israel went astray from me, shall come near to me to minister to me. And they shall stand before me to offer me the fat and the blood, declares the Lord GOD." (Ezek 44:15, ESV) **Other Scriptures:** Is 66:21-24; Ezek 43:19; 48:11	"The prescribed worship services of Ezekiel's temple are also described for us in great detail by the prophet. The priests presiding over the temple services will be of the line of Zadok (44:15) who proved faithful after the failure of the Levitical priests in the line of Eli (1 Samuel 2:35, 1 Kings 2:26-27, 35). **The Millennial Temple will not have a separate High Priest. Instead the previously separate offices of King and Priest will be combined in the Messiah** as noted, (See Zechariah 6:9-15)" (Lambert Dolphin in *The Temple of Ezekiel*, p. 5).

Condition/System	Scriptures	Comments/References
Temple Restored	**Key Scripture:** "Then he brought me by way of the north gate to the front of the temple, and I looked, and behold, the glory of the LORD filled the temple of the LORD. And I fell on my face." (Ezek 44:4, ESV) **Other Scriptures:** Is 2:3; 33:15-22; 44:28; 66:21-24; Ezek 40-48; Zech 6:9-15. Other Scriptures on the glory of the Lord in the Temple are IIChron 7:1-3; Ezek 43:1-5	For further information refer to Leroy Neff's MA Thesis *God's Temple in Prophecy* available for free online at www.friendsofsabbath.org See also Randall Price, *The Program For The Last Days Temple.*
Temple Sacrifices	**Key Scripture:** "He will sit as a refiner and purifier of silver, and he will purify the sons of Levi and refine them like gold and silver, and they will bring offerings in righteousness to the LORD. Then the offering of Judah and Jerusalem will be pleasing to the LORD as in the days of old and as in former years." (Mal 3:3-4, ESV) **Other Scriptures:** Is 56:6-8; 66:19-21; Jer 3317-18; Ezekiel 20:40-41; Zech 14:19-21	An excellent book on the sacrificial system is *What about the Sacrifices?* by D. Thomas Lancaster.

From the above table the reader will have a thorough and more detailed understanding of the Millennium. Perhaps it will be a little different to what one anticipates.

CHAPTER EIGHT

THE ANIMALS IN THE WORLD TOMORROW

"But ask the beasts, and they will teach you; the birds of the heavens, and they will tell you; or the bushes of the earth, and they will teach you; and the fish of the sea will declare to you.

Who among all these does not know that the hand of the LORD has done this?

In his hand is the life of every living thing and the breath of all mankind." (Job 12:7-10, ESV)

INTRODUCTION

THE GARDEN OF EDEN, as graphically portrayed in Genesis, was a place which, by all reasonable deduction, was originally meant to eventually envelop the entire earth. The whole planet, it seems, was to become paradise – a garden of peace, of plenty, tender interaction between humans and animals, and sheer joy. But it was not to be.

Instead, under the influence of Satan man sinned and was driven from the garden. Animals became hostile to man and to each other. To this day male lions kill the cubs of rival male lions if they take over their pride. Lions hunt down and kill the cubs of other species and visa-versa. Infanticide is practiced by many species.

Many animals learnt to hunt, maim, kill and devour other species. Was this always meant to be the case? Or was the Garden of Eden a place without predatory animals? Speculation abounds regarding the origin of animals devouring each other. And the solution?

God will gradually change the nature and internal structure of these animals to dwell at peace with one another and with humans.

The Bible does not tell us exactly how some animals began to devour each other or how it will all end.

The very first chapter of Genesis suggests to some that both man and beast were totally vegetarians:

"And God blessed them, and God said unto them, Be fruitful, and multiply, and replenish the earth, and subdue it: and have dominion [does this include eating meat?] over the fish of the sea, and over the fowl of the air, and over every living thing that moveth upon the earth.

And God said, Behold! I have given you every herb seeding seed which *is* upon the face of all the earth, and every tree in which *is the* fruit of a tree seeding seed; to you it shall be for food. [does this preclude eating meat?]

And to every beast of the earth, and to every fowl of the heavens, and to every creeper on the earth which *has* in it a living soul every green plant *is* for food; and it was so." (Gen 1:28-30, KJV) [see also Job 38:39-41; 39:4, 8, 30; 40:15, 20; Ps 104:14; 145:15-16; 147:9]

Some commentaries and creation science organisations maintain that man did not even consume meat, milk products or eggs because fruit and vegetables may have been much more nourishing at that time than today. This is possible, but I fail to see the logic. Nor has any science substantiated this.

However, the very structure of human digestion and teeth suggests that we are meant to eat meat, as Christ Himself did.[42] And given that man was appointed dominion over all the creatures on the earth suggests that this may include eating those that God has sanctioned (Lev 11). There is not a word against the eating of meat and milk products anywhere in the scriptures.

Here is an example of the debate surrounding these verses:

> "The whole of the grasses and the green parts or leaves of the herbage are distributed among the inferior animals for food. Here, again, the common and prominent kind of sustenance only is specified. There are some animals that greedily devour the fruits of trees and the grain produced by the various herbs; and there are others that derive the most of their subsistence from preying on the smaller and weaker kinds of animals. Still, the main substance of the means of animal life, and the ultimate supply of the whole of it, are derived from the plant. Even this general statement is not to be received without exception, as there are certain lower descriptions of animals that derive sustenance even from the mineral world. But this brief narrative of things notes only the few palpable facts, leaving the details to the experience and judgment of the reader." (*Barnes Book Notes* on Genesis 1:30)

During the Millennium, according to Bible prophecy, animals will no longer hunt, kill or consume other animals.

---

[42] Refer to the article "Did Jesus Eat Meat?" *Got Questions*, 4 Jan 2022 www.gotquestions.org/did-Jesus-eat-meat.html

"Also the wolf shall dwell with the lamb, and the leopard shall lie down with the kid; and the calf and the cub lion and the fatling together; and a little child shall lead them.

And the cow and the bear shall feed; their young ones shall lie down together; and the lion shall eat straw like the ox.

And the suckling child shall play on the hole of the asp, and the weaned child shall put his hand on the adder's den.

They shall not hurt nor destroy in all My holy mountain; for the earth shall be full of the knowledge of Jehovah, as the waters cover the sea" (Is 11:6-9, MKJV) (compare Job 5:22-23; Is 35:1; Ezek 34:25; 44:31; Hos 2:18)

Here we are told that lions will eat straw, although that does not mean that is all they will eat, as straw certainly does not provide sufficient nutrients for cats and, particularly large, predatory cats. Rather, it seems that straw represents an increased vegetarian diet. Even in Ezekiel 39:4 the birds of prey and various animals eat dead human flesh.

But it is not only the Bible that shows that a golden age was once extant in the days of old.

Figure 15 Today animals devour one another – but not when the Messiah returns

A New Age for the Animals

Many early 'Christian' Fathers continued the belief of the original Apostles in the Millennium, such as Justin the Martyr (100-165AD):

> "But I and others, who are right-minded Christians on all points, are assured that there will be a resurrection of the dead, and **a thousand years** in Jerusalem, which will then be built, adorned, and enlarged, the prophets Ezekiel and Isaiah and others declare.
>
> For Isaiah spake thus concerning this space of a thousand years: 'For there shall be the new heaven and the new earth, and the former shall not be remembered, or come into their heart; but they shall find joy and gladness in it, which things I create' ... For as Adam was told that in the day he ate of the tree he would die, we know that he did not complete a thousand years. We have perceived, moreover, that the expression, 'The day of the Lord is as a thousand years,' is connected with this subject. And further, there was a certain man with us, whose name was John, one of the apostles of Christ, who prophesied, by a revelation that was made to him, that those who believed in our Christ would dwell a thousand years in Jerusalem; and that thereafter the general, and, in short, the eternal resurrection and judgment of all men would likewise take place." (*Dialogue*. Chapters 80-81)

Many Jews also believed in the concept. For instance Rabbi Ketina:

> "The world endures **six thousand years** and one thousand it shall be laid waste, whereof it is said 'The Lord alone shall be exalted in that day'. As out of seven years every seventh is a year of remission, that God alone may be exalted in that day."

Various religions and mythologies recall ancient events, although clouded by their beliefs. For example, Sumerian mythology contains a similar description to Isaiah, but of a past paradise, rather than a future one. At the mouth of the Euphrates, the pagan priests recalled a Golden Age of peace and plenty. They claimed that their predecessors dwelt in the paradise of Dilmun known as the *Pure Place*.

> "That place was pure, that place was clean. In Dilmun the raven utters no cry ... the lion mangled not. The wolf ravaged not the lambs".

Another Sumerian text noted:

> "There was no unrighteousness in the land, no crocodile seized, no snake bit in the time of the First Gods".

Figure 16 God's creatures living in harmony without fear of violence

Even the animals will enjoy a golden age:

> "And in that day will I make a covenant for them with the beasts of the field, and with the fowls of heaven, and *with* the creeping things of the ground: and I will break the bow and the sword and the battle out of the earth, and will make them to lie down safely." (Hos 2:18, KJV) [cp Job 5:23; Is 65:25; Ezek 34:25; Is 35:9; Lev 26:6]

There will be no more fear, tension or stress. All will enjoy harmony and a full, abundant life.

BIBLICAL EXAMPLES OF KINDNESS TOWARD ANIMALS

We must be kind and compassionate toward God's creatures which is what He expects and this will be implemented during His reign. The Scriptures inform us:

> "A righteous man has regard for the life of his beast, but the mercy of the wicked is cruel." (Proverbs 12:10, KJV)[43]

---

[43] After all, to dress and keep the earth (Gen 2:15) is not restricted to the vegetation but must include the animals.

Kindness is also demonstrated in Deut 11:13-15; Deut 22:4; 22:6-7; Job 24:7-8; 39:5-8. An example of this is found in Genesis and another from Matthew:

> "And he said, Let us take our journey, and let us go, and I will go before thee.
> And he said unto him, My lord knoweth that the children *are* tender, and the flocks and herds with young *are* with me: and if men should overdrive them one day, all the flock will die.
> Let my lord, I pray thee, pass over before his servant: and I will lead on softly, according as the cattle that goeth before me and the children be able to endure, until I come unto my lord unto Seir." (Gen 33:12-14, KJV)

> "He said to them, "Which one of you who has a sheep, if it falls into a pit on the Sabbath, will not take hold of it and lift it out?
> Of how much more value is a man than a sheep! So it is lawful to do good on the Sabbath."" (Matt 12:11-12, ESV)

God Himself has compassion on the animals! His creations were even to be rested on the Sabbath day (Ex 20:10; 23:12; Deut 5:13-14). While Deuteronomy 22:10 suggests that

> "pairing animals of different sizes and strengths would cause conflict and would place a strain on the weaker of them, or perhaps both." (Lewis Regenstein, *Replenish the Earth*, p. 21).

Notice also

> "Your righteousness is like the mountains of God; your judgments are like the great deep; man **and beast** you save, O LORD." (Ps 36:6, ESV. Cp Ps 145:9; Is 43:19-20)

> "Thus says the LORD: "Heaven is my throne, and the earth is my footstool; what is the house that you would build for me, and what is the place of my rest?
> All these things my hand has made, and so all these things came to be, declares the LORD. But this is the one to whom I will look: he who is humble and contrite in spirit and trembles at my word.
> **"He who slaughters an ox is like one who kills a man; he who sacrifices a lamb,** like one who breaks a dog's neck; he who presents a grain offering, **like one who offers pig's blood**; he who makes a memorial offering of frankincense, like one who blesses an idol. These have chosen their own ways, and their soul delights in their abominations;
> I also will choose harsh treatment for them and bring their fears upon them, because when I called, no one answered, when I spoke, they did not listen; but they did what was evil in my eyes and chose that in which I did not delight.""
> (Is 66:1-4, ESV)

Notice the kindness to animals demonstrated in Genesis:

"But God remembered Noah **and all the beasts** and all the livestock that were with him in the ark. And God made a wind blow over the earth, and the waters subsided." (Gen 8:1, ESV)

"And God said, "This is the sign of the covenant that I make between me and **you and every living creature that is with you**, for all future generations … God said to Noah, "This is the sign of the covenant that I have established between me **and all flesh that is on the earth**." (Gen 9:12, 17, ESV)

"When she had finished giving him a drink, she said, "I will draw water for your camels also, until they have finished drinking."

So she quickly emptied her jar into the trough and ran again to the well to draw water, and she drew for all his camels.

The man gazed at her in silence to learn whether the LORD had prospered his journey or not.

When the camels had finished drinking, the man took a gold ring weighing a half shekel, and two bracelets for her arms weighing ten gold shekels" (Gen 24:19-22, ESV. See also vv 31-33 where he looked after the animals before himself)

"Now the priest of Midian had seven daughters, and they came and drew water and filled the troughs to water their father's flock.

The shepherds came and drove them away, but Moses stood up and saved them, and watered their flock." (Ex 2:16-17, ESV)

"And should not I pity Nineveh, that great city, in which there are more than 120,000 persons who do not know their right hand from their left, and also much cattle?" (Jonah 4:11, ESV. Refer also to Num 22:28-35 – smiting of animals is not well regarded)

"save yourself like a gazelle from the hand of the hunter, like a bird from the hand of the fowler." (Prov 6:5, ESV)[44]

We can even learn lessons from wild creatures for instance in Jeremiah 8:7-8 (in this case admiring the way the flocks migrate from location to location) and Proverbs 6:6 (don't be lazy).

Isaiah 5:8 appears to warn governments and developers not to squeeze people into small spaces and of course, this also means that there is little room for animals or peaceful solitude. Notice that in Numbers 35:2-5 a "green belt" was required around the Levitical towns – this allows for animals to freely roam (cp Job 5:23; 30:29).

"Let everything that has breath praise the LORD! Praise the LORD!" (Ps 150:6, ESV)

---

[44] Human stewardship of nature is found in a number of Scriptures: Gen 1:26; Lev 25:23; Ps 8:6-8; Ps 24:1; 50:10-11.

CARNIVORES IN THE WORLD TOMORROW?

Certainly, at the end of the Day of the Lord, animals will be used as scavengers to eat the dead bodies (Rev 19:17-18), as well as a few years later (Ezekiel 39:17-20). This lends weight to the following discussion.

Let us return to Isaiah 11, where we are told that lions will eat straw and will dwell peacefully with other animals.

How can this be when lions' and other predators' physical build, teeth, internal organs and digestive systems are created for eating meat? If they suddenly changed to a vegetarian diet, they would conceivably wither away or become extremely slow and useless. Witness the giant Chinese Panda bear. Its digestive system and teeth demonstrate that it must have been an omnivore at some time, but somehow switched to a vegetarian diet. As such, they are now very slow and ponderous given that their diet does not contain the necessary proteins to provide adequate energy for such a large beast.

This suggests that meat will still be a necessity in their diet and by extended thinking, it is possible there will be carnivores and omnivores but no predators in the Millennium. What this means is that a carnivore can still be meat-eating without being a predatory hunter. Will they be fed meat by humans or will carnivores be miraculously changed to herbivore? Is it something they will learn gradually?

In a documentary on *"An animals world: Lions"* shown on Discovery Channel (Australia), January 2002, Sydney, Australia, the commentator lamented that too much emphasis was given to the predatory nature of lions. In fact, he said that a lion's food source can be up to 60% derived from scavenging dead animals rather than hunting. Other carnivores similarly scavenge, and this may be what they will do during the Millennium – eat dead meat to maintain a clean environment.

Figure 17 God's amazing animal creation

In Hosea 2:18 we find:

> "And I will make for them a covenant on that day with the beasts of the field, the birds of the heavens, and the creeping things of the ground. And I will abolish the bow, the sword, and war from the land, and I will make you lie down in safety." (ESV)

The means of hunting and hurting animals, causing stress, panic, mental torture and suffering will be abolished.

This fits in well with the well-known prophecy of Isaiah 11:6-8 which clearly shows that during the future utopia, animals will be at peace with one another and mankind, in turn, at peace with them. Compare this with Job 5:22-23.

However, some commentators try and explain the nature of animals in the Millennium in a typological fashion rather than as literal or dual. They view Isaiah 11:5-9 and Jeremiah 50:17 in this light:

> "The imagery changes again with verses 6-8, though verse 9 offers its explanation. Context suggests that the talk of harmony in the animal world is a metaphor for harmony in the human world. The strong and powerful live together with the weak and powerless because the latter can believe that the former are no longer seeking to devour them. The end to which verses 6-9 lead thus belongs to the same thought as verse 1-5 and fits with other themes from earlier chapters (e.g., 2:2-4).
>
> "Indeed, the book opened by using animals to stand for human beings (1:3) — also in connection with the question of knowledge, as here." (John Goldingay, *Isaiah. New International Bible Commentary*, p. 85. Hans Wilderberger sees it this way too in *Isaiah 1-12*, pp. 480-81).

A verse some turn to is Isaiah 65:25:

> "... it seems odd that this creature should also be present in the renewed Jerusalem. Perhaps the implication is that such life is no more designed to be challenge-free than life in Eden was." (John Goldingay, *Isaiah. New International Bible Commentary*, p. 369. Refer also to Jason A Staples, "'Rise, Kill, and Eat': Animals as Nations in Early Jewish Visionary Literature and Acts 10," *Journal for the Study of the New Testament*, Vol. 42, Issue 1, 26 June 2019, pp. 3-17)[45]

But one Bible student provides us with the correct understanding based on Biblical duality:

> "Indeed, Isaiah 11:6-9 explains **that the very nature and perhaps even physiology of many animals will be changed, thus requiring, it would seem, a restructuring of the global ecosystem. Isaiah repeats this amazing prophecy in Isaiah 65:25.**

---

[45] "Bruce writes, "The animals in the vision [Acts 10:9-28] are parabolic of human beings" (Ajith Fernando, *Acts. The NIV Application Commentary*, p. 321.

But, it should be noted, the animals here may well also be symbolic of the nations of the world, with their peacefully dwelling together representing an end of war between people. The lamb, kid, calf, fatling, ox and cow are often used in Scripture to symbolize the generally peace-loving Israelite peoples. The wolf (the wild dog-kind) may be a reference to the descendants of Esau or to certain other Arabs (the Edomite Herod was referred to as a fox by Christ in Luke 13:32). And the great cats (leopard and lion) and the bear are used in Daniel 7 to symbolize great gentile kingdoms. These parallels are perhaps most clearly seen in Jeremiah 5:6, where the lion, wolf and leopard are widely understood to represent Israel's enemies. In God's millennial reign the wild nature of the "beasts" among men will be changed, as was figuratively portrayed by Nebuchadnezzar when he (the Babylonian lion, compare Daniel 2 and 7) was made to eat grass with the oxen (Daniel 4:33)." (www.ucg.org/bible-study-tools/bible-commentary/bible-commentary-isaiah-11-12 *Beyond Today Bible Commentary. Isaiah*, by Tom Robinson, 24 March 2003) [emphasis mine]

"There can be no doubt that the prophet means here [Isaiah 11:8; 65:25 and see Acts 20:29] to describe the passions and evil propensities of people, which have a strong resemblance to the ferocity of the wolf, or the lion, and the deadly poison of the serpent, and to say that those passions would be subdued, and that peace and concord would prevail on the earth." (Albert Barnes' *Notes on the Bible* online)

Robinson is correct and is joined by others in this interpretation indicating duality in Scripture:

"... animals are common in apocalyptic visions, where they often symbolize various nations" (Craig Keener, *Acts: An Exegetical Commentary*, p. 1766)

This prophecy in its context and in relation to others is dual. It can refer to nations typed by animals of course. But that typology is based on actual, real animals. Christ is likened to a lion because it is regal, powerful, a leader and can devour its enemies. Satan is also likened to a lion because they can be predatory, violent and cruel.

But lions still exist and in real life exhibit those qualities.

Thus lions and other wild animals will still exist in the Millennium and the prophecies found in Isaiah demonstrate that these are also literal animals who have become tame. Some authors have little understanding of the Millennium, what it types, what the Garden of Eden was like and God's awesome capacity. He does not understand the restoration of all things.

In fact, most do not understand or believe in the Millennium and the groups, authors and commentaries that do expound this doctrine, represent a small minority.

CONCLUDING REMARKS

From the above I deduce the following:

- Today's predators (land, air, and water-based), which learnt to kill under the influence of Satan, will once again join the other scavengers to eat dead animals but with an increased vegetarian diet (of interest is that scientists are now saying that T-Rex was a scavenger and not a predator. They question whether T-Rex could even run at all to enable them to catch prey).
- There will be such a preponderance of wildlife, that there will be more dead animals to clean up than ever before. Carnivores and omnivores will be essential to maintain the ecological balance. No longer will they kill young animals, the sick and the aged.
- Hunting for pleasure by humans is contrary to God's nature, which rather is to help the young, sick and aged – whether they be animal or human. The spirit of competition, strife, killing, injuring and fear will no longer be extant when the Messiah returns to the earth.
- The prophecies seem to only refer to mammals and higher order animals. Whether it pertains to insects and many sea creatures, is something that would be interesting to discuss further, but insects have an important role in the ecological cycle, including eating other dead insects and animals. Isaiah's prophecy does not preclude foods other than straw being eaten by lions. It demonstrates and symbolises peace between animals and that none will be predators, however this does not negate them being scavenging carnivores.

As such, the earth shall be restored to its original beauty and peace shall reign:

> "Therefore repent and convert so that your sins may be blotted out, when the **times of refreshing [i.e. revival] shall come** from *the* presence of the Lord.
>
> And **He shall send Jesus Christ**, who before was proclaimed to you, whom Heaven truly needs to receive until the times of **restoration [i.e., reconstitution] of all things**, which God has spoken by *the* mouth of His holy prophets since the world began." (Acts 3:19-21, MKJV)

From time-to-time, we see cases of human service and love that must emulate what the world was supposed to be in the Garden of Eden. We even see this in the animal kingdom, where a dog goes around adopting other strays, including cats, or a cat adopts a bird, and so on.

About mid-2001, news emanating out of China was similarly fascinating. It detailed how a missing 2-year-old child was found in a bear's den. The bear had adopted the child and cared for it, even feeding it milk for some weeks! Not the slightest physical harm was detected on the child. Other similar stories of dolphins and dogs rescuing humans are wonderful testimonies to God's creation and foreshadow how humans will interact with animals in the Millennium.

Soon the world will be at peace, and no animal will devour another, but will live together with all other species in perfect harmony. The Garden of Eden will be restored and will extend its reach until the entire world – man and animal – which reflects the nature of God.

Figure 18 There will come a time when humans will play with wild animals

FURTHER READING

- Burke, J. (2016), "Does God Care for Oxen? Animal Welfare Ethics in the Bible," *Defence and Confirmation*, April, pp. 9-29.
- Grandin, T. & Johnson, C. (2009), *Animals Make Us Human. Creating the best life for Animals*. Houghton Mifflin Harcourt, New York, NY.
- Peters, G. N. H. (1884), *The Theocratic Kingdom of our Lord Jesus, the Christ, as Covenanted in the Old Testament and Revealed in the New, (Vol 1)*. Funk & Wagnalls, London & New York.
- Taylor, D. (1882), *Reign of Christ on Earth*. S. Bagster & Sons, London.
- Ward, H. D. (1841), *History and Doctrine of the Millennium. A discourse delivered in the conference on the Second Advent near*. Boston, MA.
- West, N. (1889), *The Thousand Years in Both Testaments*. Scripture Truth Book Company, Fincastle, VA.
- Whitcomb, J. C. (1994), "The Millennial Temple of Ezekiel 40-48," *The Diligent Workman Journal*, May, pp. 21-25.
- Wright, C. J. H. (2004), *Old Testament Ethics for the People of God*. Inter-Varsity, Leicester.

PART THREE

THE RELIGIOUS SYSTEM ESTABLISHED

THE RESTORATION OF GOD'S SYSTEM OF WORSHIP

Many have faithfully taught for decades[46] that the temple and its system of priests and sacrifices will be restored during the Millennial reign of the Messiah. There is nothing unique to this as many commentators and researchers have held to this view since the mid or early nineteenth century.

A casual reading of Ezekiel 40-48 must surely be taken literally because this particular temple detailed by Ezekiel is extremely difficult to apply mere symbolism to. Nor can it be the New Jerusalem despite some similarities (different epochs in prophetic fulfillment often have similarities. The 1,000-year reign, after all, is a firstfruit of the eternal Kingdom).

---

[46] Further information concerning this area of Biblical doctrine may be found in the following Church of God sources available here:

- http://bible.ucg.org/bible-reading-program/pdf/brp0402.pdf and read especially the final paragraph on p. 15 and also p. 16
- http://bible.ucg.org/bible-commentary/Ezekiel/Description-of-the-millennial-temple-complex/
- https://www.ucg.org/sermons/millennial-sacrifices-and-satans-fate
- https://www.ucg.org/sermons/sacrifices-in-the-millenium
- http://www.globalchurchofgod.co.uk/q-a-11376/

For instance the United Church of God's *Beyond Today* magazine published this in one of their articles:

"The final chapters of Ezekiel, starting in chapter 40, show that a rebuilt physical temple at Jerusalem will be functioning during the Millennium. Some dismiss this as mere spiritual symbolism, but the level of detailed description found in these chapters makes that idea untenable. The temple system always contained symbolic aspects, but it was nevertheless literal, as the new one will be.

The physical temple is regarded as the place of God's throne on earth—the mercy seat of the Ark of the Covenant between the cherubim modeled on God's throne in heaven. So Jerusalem will be the capital of the world: "At that time *Jerusalem shall be called The Throne of the Lord*, and all the nations shall be gathered to it, to the name of the Lord, to Jerusalem. No more shall they follow the dictates of their evil hearts" (Jeremiah 3:17, emphasis added throughout). From here Christ will rule: "For out of Zion shall go forth the law, and the word of the Lord from Jerusalem" (Isaiah 2:3)." ("Why Will Jesus Christ Return? (Part 2)," *Beyond Today*, Nov-Dec 2020, p. 25)

As one researcher put it:

> "... the NT texts on "temple" do not do away with the OT promises of a future temple as some sort of type to antitype." (Jason Beals, *National Restoration and the Divine Dwelling Place in Ezekiel 37:15-28*, p. 86).

Author George Beasley-Murray argued:

> "To tackle the vision verse by verse and try to take symbolically thirteen cubits, hooks a handbreadth long, the sixth part of an ephah, place names like Berothat and Hauran, is out of the question, to contradict all reason" ("Ezekiel," *The New Bible Commentary*, Donald Guthrie (ef, et al), 3rd ed, p. 663)

Because chapters 40-48 of Ezekiel are complicated, I shall endeavour to simplify this by using various resources. This will be undertaken for the following three aspects of these chapters, viz:

- The temple
- Sacrificial system
- Tribal land allotments

If we have a basic understanding of these areas, then these chapters are easy to understand rather than to be ignored or for one to struggle with. Many scholars are aware that the temple and sacrificial system will be restored during the Millennium, such as Ian Bacon in *The Plausibility of Animal Sacrifices in Ezekiel 40-48 Literally Operating in the Millennial Kingdom Under the New Covenant* noted

> "The apocalyptic nature of the passage reinforces the seriousness of God's punishment of the nation for their covenant disobedience, resulting in the disappearance of God's glory from the temple. Ezekiel 40-48 is a magnificent promise that the temple will be restored in the future. In contrast to those who claim that a dispensational hermeneutic misses the nuances of Ezekiel's symbolic language, it seems more likely that the symbolism demands a literal fulfillment based on the message of the rest of the book." (p. 16)

> "The animal sacrifices serve as means through which Israel may fulfill their mission in the Millennium." (p. 52)

IS THE TEMPLE OF EZEKIEL 40-48 MILLENNIAL OR PRE-MILLENNIAL?

This section explains why the temple of Ezekiel cannot be pre-Millennial or be the New Jerusalem (although it contains some typology for the New Jerusalem).

Ezekiel is a book in sequence with inset chapters, somewhat like the book of of Revelation, which leads the reader step-by-step from Israel's tribulation, restoration and ultimate glory with the establishment of the temple as the centre piece of the Messiah's global capital.

Below is a brief outline of the final chapters of Ezekiel to prove this point:

- Chapter 33 – end-time warning
- Chapter 34 – scattering of Israel and the Church
- Chapter 35 – punishment upon Seir and Idumea
- Chapter 36 – return of Israel to the Holy Land
- Chapter 37 – Israel and Judah re-united
- Chapters 38 and 39 – invasion by the forces of Meschech, Tubal, Magog etc
- Chapters 40-48 – Millennial Temple, Sacrifices and Tribal Land Allocations

An example of the typology of one event portraying or informing another is Isaiah 65:15-25 which is clearly Millennial. It probably includes the period after the Millennium but interestingly also parallels various statements at the end of the book of Revelation, which are post-Millennial and post-Great White Throne Judgement. The Scriptures below are compared with those of Revelation 21 and 22:

> "And ye shall leave your name for a curse unto my chosen: for the Lord GOD shall slay thee, and **call his servants by another name**:
> That he who blesseth himself in the earth shall bless himself in the God of truth; and he that sweareth in the earth shall swear by the God of truth; because **the former troubles are forgotten**, and because they are hid from mine eyes." (Is 65:15-16, KJV)

> "For, behold, **I create new heavens and a new earth: and the former shall not be remembered, nor come into mind.** " (Is 65:17, KJV. cp Rev 21:1, 4)

> "But be ye glad and rejoice for ever *in that* which I create: for, behold, I create Jerusalem a rejoicing, and her people a joy.
> And I will rejoice in Jerusalem, and joy in my people: and the **voice of weeping shall be no more heard in her,** nor the voice of crying." (Is 65:18-19, KJV. cp Rev 21:4)

> "There shall be no more thence an infant of days, nor an old man that hath not filled his days: for the child shall die an hundred years old; but the sinner *being* an hundred years old shall be accursed.
> And they shall build houses, and inhabit *them*; and they shall **plant vineyards, and eat the fruit** of them." (Is 65:20-21, KJV. cp Rev 22:2-3, 19)

> "They shall not build, and another inhabit; they shall not plant, and another eat: for as the days of a tree *are* the days of my people, and **mine elect** shall long enjoy the work of their hands." (Is 65:22, KJV. cp Rev 21:7; 22:14]

> "They shall not labour in vain, nor bring forth for trouble; for they *are* the seed of the blessed of the LORD, and their offspring with them.
> And it shall come to pass, that before they call, I will answer; and while they are yet speaking, I will hear." (Is 65:2-24, KJV. cp Is 11:6, 9)

Much of the above is similar to Revelation 21:1-7. Then it states:

> "**The wolf and the lamb shall feed together, and the lion shall eat straw like the bullock: and dust *shall be* the serpent's meat. They shall not hurt nor destroy in all my holy mountain, saith the LORD.**" (Is 65:25, KJV)

This verse parallels Millennial descriptions found in Isaiah 11:6-9 and Hosea 2:18. Another example is found in the following chapter where the Millennium is called a "new heavens and new earth":

> "And the Gentiles shall see thy righteousness, and all kings thy glory: and thou shalt be **called by a new name**, which the mouth of the LORD shall name …" (Is 62:, KJV 2. cp Rev 2:17; 3:12)

> "And I will also take of them for **priests *and* for Levites**, saith the LORD.
> For as **the new heavens and the new earth**, which I will make, shall remain before me, saith the LORD, so shall your seed and your name remain." (Is 66:21-22, KJV. cp Rev 21:1)

> "And it shall come to pass, *that* from one new moon to another, and from one sabbath to another, shall **all flesh come to worship before me**, saith the LORD.
> And they shall go forth, and **look upon the carcases of the men that have transgressed against me**: for their worm shall not die, neither shall their fire be quenched; and they shall be an abhorring unto all flesh." (Is 66:23-24, KJV. cp Rev 21:8; 22:11, 15)

This is clearly different to the new heavens and earth mentioned in Revelation 21:1 and IIPeter 3:10-11.

Similarity in language does not mean that these are the same events. When there is similarity in description, it is usually that one event portrays another or is a forerunner to the later event. The following quotes from scholars should be helpful in understanding these passages:

1. Note what Ralph Alexander states:

> "In the light of the whole Scripture, it appears that **the Millennium is like a "firstfruits" of the eternal state**. The Millennium will be like a preview of the eternal messianic kingdom that will be revealed fully in the eternal state. Therefore, because the two are alike in nature, they share distinct similarities. Yet because they are both different revealed time periods, they would likewise reflect some dissimilarities …" (*Ezekiel*, in *The Expositor's Bible Commentary*, Vol 6, p. 945). [emphasis mine]

2. Researcher Moore stated it this way:

> "**There are a number of statements by the sacred writers that are designed to apply to distinct facts**, successively occurring in history. If the words are limited to

anyone of these facts, they will seem exaggerated, for no one fact can exhaust their significance. They must be spread out over all the facts before their plenary meaning is reached.

There is nothing in this principle that is at variance with the ordinary laws of language. The same general use of phrases occurs repeatedly ... Every language contains these formulas, which refer not to anyone event, but a series of events, all embodying the same principle, or resulting from the same cause.

[Thus] ... the promise in regard to the "seed of the woman," (Gen. 3:15) refers to one event but runs along the whole stream of history, and includes every successive conquest of the religion of Christ ... [This] class of predictions ... is ... what the old theologians called the *novissima* ..." (*Haggai, Zechariah, Malachi*, pp. 396-99) [emphasis mine]

3. Willis Beecher, author:

"Thus, the "Day of Yahweh" is a generic or collective event which gathers together all the antecedent historical episodes of God's judgment and salvation along with the future grand finale and climactic event in the whole series. Every divine intervention into history before that final visitation in connection with the second advent of Christ constitutes only a preview, sample, downpayment or earnest on that climactic conclusion. **The prophet did not think of the day of the Lord as an event that would occur once for all, but one that could "be repeated as the circumstances called for it".**" (*The Prophets and the Promise*, p. 311) [emphasis mine]

4. One of my all-time favourite scholars, who has insights into various aspects of Scripture, Walter Kaiser:

"**That final time would be climactic and the sum of all the rest**. Though the events of their own times fitted the pattern of God's future judgment, that final day was nevertheless immeasurably larger and more permanent in its salvific and judgmental effects." (*Toward an Old Testament Theology*, p. 191). [emphasis mine]

He also demonstrates that the miracles of Acts chapter 2 are "samples" or "a preliminary fulfillment" or "mere harbingers" or "samples" portraying the coming outpouring of God's holy spirit upon the earth during the time of the Messiah (Walter Kaiser, *The Uses of the Old Testament in the New*, p. 99).[47]

Thus, given the above, there are obvious similarities in Ezekiel 40-48 and also Isaiah 65, to the New Jerusalem period. Also, the description of Old Testament events in Israel's destruction with events at the death and resurrection of Christ (i.e. Day of the Lord

---

[47] John Orr notes:

"An expression repeatedly used by Jesus in John (6:39f., 44, 54; 11:24; 12:48) for the day of resurrection and judgment (see "eschatology"). Cf. the usage in the OT of "latter days" (Isa. 2:2; Mic. 4:1) and in the NT (Acts 2:17; 2 Tim 3:1; 1 Pe 1:5; 2 Pet 3.3; 1 Jn 2:18; Jude 18) of "last days" and "last time" to denote the messianic age" ("Day, Last," *International Standard Bible Encyclopedia*, Vol. 1, p. 879).

typology etc) - similarities exist. Or the forces of Gog and Magog in Ezekiel 38 and 39 with Revelation 20.[48]

What we find is that the earlier event typifies a later event – a sort of prototype or "firstfruit" of it. Hence the similarity in language. Unfortunately, this sometimes 'trips up' people who get these various events mixed up because they don't understand the concept of typology and prophetic similarities where one event portrays or informs a later event.

Why the similarities? Because God works in patterns, styles and cycles where events rhyme. That is the way the Bible is inspired and written for our reading and spiritual education. It takes time and effort to understand.

SUPPLEMENTARY INFORMATION CONCERNING THE TEMPLE

Below is an outline of Ezekiel 40-48 which, I trust, assists the reader in understanding these amazingly detailed prophecies. Once one has a grasp of the big picture for that period, then one can drill deeper into these chapters and come to understand them.

On the surface they can be daunting, but this technique of grasping the overview and then analysing the details is very helpful.

Table 10 Outlining the Temple as described in Ezekiel

Chapter	Outline
40	The future is revealed to Ezekiel, and he is shown the outer courts, inner courts, gates, offerings.
41	The holy place (outer sanctuary), holy of holies (inner sanctuary), various aspects of the temple revealed.
42	Priests' chambers shown to Ezekiel and also the outer dimensions.
43	God's glory enters the temple! The altar of God is also shown.
44	The Prince and priests etc discussed as are various laws.
45	The holy area is divided and the temple, Jerusalem, lands etc. The offerings are described.
46	How the Lord is to be worshipped and approached!
47	The river of healing waters flowing from the temple to the Dead Sea.
48	How the holy land will be divided up among the tribes of Israel. There seems to be status or grading involved with the concubine tribes occupying the outer extremities of the allocation. The land divided among the Tribes of Israel. Also, the 12 gates of Jerusalem described.

Note that there will be some changes to the sacrificial system when one compares the

---

[48] There are also the fires of *gehenna* – the lake of fire at the beginning of the Millennium (Rev 19:20) which continues on to the end of it (IIPet 3:7; Rev 20:9-15) and possible recreation of the universe after it is uncreated by fire (IIPet 3:12).

sacrifices of Ezekiel with those of Leviticus and Numbers, including no need for a Levitical high priest:

> "The prescribed worship services of Ezekiel's temple are also described for us in great detail by the prophet. The priests presiding over the temple services will be of the line of Zadok (44:15) who proved faithful after the failure of the Levitical priests in the line of Eli (1 Samuel 2:35, 1 Kings 2:26-27, 35). **The Millennial Temple will not have a separate High Priest. Instead the previously separate offices of King and Priest will be combined in the Messiah** as noted, (See Zechariah 6:9-15)" (Lambert Dolphin, *The Temple of Ezekiel*, p. 5).

This indicates that Christ continues His Melchizedek priesthood into and through the Millennium.

> "And he [the Messiah] shall be a priest upon his throne - He shall, as the great high priest, offer the only available offering and atonement; and so **he shall be both king and priest, a royal king and a royal priest**; for even the priest is here stated to sit upon his throne." (Adam Clarkes *Commentary*)

In the Millennium there will be the

> "opening the door to the Melchizedekian High Priest of Ps 110:4 (cf. Ezek 21:26-27; Zech 6:13: "He will be a priest on His throne"), whose visible presence on earth during the coming Kingdom age will be the ultimate answer to this dilemma of the ages." (John Whitcomb, "Christ's Atonement and Animal Sacrifices in Israel," *Grace Theological Journal*, Vol. 6, No. 2, p 216)

Zadok (which means '*righteous*') indeed proved faithful to David and was a type of Christ in many ways. First of all, he was a direct descendant of Eleazor, son of Aaron from which the High Priests descended (IChron 27:17). It is Zadok who supported David during the time of Absalom's revolt (David's son) according to IISam 15:13-37. Later, when Adonijah set himself up as king, David had Zadok anoint Solomon (IKings 1:5, 32-40) and served as a temple priest under Solomon.

There are three priesthoods referred to in the Bible:

- Levitical – this is physical and will be restored upon His return
- Melchizedekian – Christ will be High Priest of this new order, with the saints occupying lower positions (IPet 2:5, 9; Rev 1:6; 5:10)
- False or pagan (including apostate Levites)

Of further interest is that not all the holy days are mentioned in Ezekiel – in fact 4 of the 7 are not mentioned. However, Ezekiel 46:11 indicates that all 7 will be observed.[49]

---

[49] Tova Ganzel comments: "Ezekiel never mentions these one-day festivals and certainly does not list any offerings related to them. It is possible that Ezekiel does not discuss these festivals because he is not making

Table 11 Comparing Holy Days of Leviticus 23 with those of Ezekiel 40-48

Holy Days of Leviticus 23	Holy Days of Ezekiel 40-48
Passover	Passover
Unleavened Bread	Unleavened Bread
Pentecost	Not listed
Trumpets	Not listed
Day of Atonement	Not listed
Tabernacles	Tabernacles
Last Great Day	Not listed

Let us now turn to the offerings. All the offerings which are mentioned in Ezekiel have differences to those in Leviticus and Numbers, this includes the number of sacrifices offered:

Table 12 Comparing the Sacrifices offered during the Feast of Ingathering with that of Unleavened Bread

Day	1	2	3	4	5	6	7
Ingathering (Num. 29:12-34)	13 bulls 2 rams 14 lambs 1 goat	12 bulls 2 rams 14 lambs 1 goat	11 bulls 2 rams 14 lambs 1 goat	10 bulls 2 rams 14 lambs 1 goat	9 bulls 2 rams 14 lambs 1 goat	8 bulls 2 rams 14 lambs 1 goat	7 bulls 2 rams 14 lambs 1 goat
Unleavened Bread (Num. 28:16-25)	2 bulls 1 ram 7 lambs 1 goat	2 bulls 1 ram 7 lambs 1 goat	2 bulls 1 ram 7 lambs 1 goat	2 bulls 1 ram 7 lambs 1 goat	2 bulls 1 ram 7 lambs 1 goat	2 bulls 1 ram 7 lambs 1 goat	2 bulls 1 ram 7 lambs 1 goat
Ingathering and Unleavened Bread (Ezek 45:21-25)	7 bulls 7 rams 1 goat	7 bulls 7 rams 1 goat	7 bulls 7 rams 1 goat	7 bulls 7 rams 1 goat	7 bulls 7 rams 1 goat	7 bulls 7 rams 1 goat	7 bulls 7 rams 1 goat

Key:

Bulls = by the princes
Rams = by the leaders/elders
Lambs = by the common folk
Goats = by the common folk

Concerning the difference between this and Solomon's temple, note the comments by Nathaniel West:

---

any changes to their rites. Alternatively, the omission may indicate that these festivals will not be observed in the future temple." (p. 3)

"**There is no Ark of the Covenant, no Pot of Manna, no Aaron's rod to bud, no Tables of the Law, no Cherubim, no Mercy-Seat, no Golden Candlestick, no Shew-bread, no Veil, no unapproachable Holy of Holies** where the High Priest alone might enter, nor is there any High-Priest to offer atonement to take away sin, or to make intercession for the people. None of this. The Levites have passed away as a sacred order. The priesthood is confined to the sons of Zadok, and only for a special purpose. **There is no evening sacrifice** [i.e., one per day]. The measures of the Altar of Burnt-Offerings differ from those of the Mosaic altar, and the offerings themselves are barely named. The preparation for the Singers is different from what it was. The social, moral and civil prescriptions enforced by Moses with such emphasis, are all wanting." (Nathaniel West, *The Thousand Years in Both Testaments*, p. 493) [emphasis mine. NB. Heb 10:20 – Christ's flesh is the veil] [emphasis mine]

God's law is perfect, but He can, and does make minor amendments to it as necessary and the above is one of them. In the Millennium His temple and sacrificial system are revived, but simplified.

CHAPTER TEN

WILL THE SACRIFICIAL SYSTEM BE RESTORED?

In Ezekiel 43:18-27 we find a description of the consecration of the new sanctuary prior to use (in similitude to Solomon's in IKings 8:62-66 and IIChronicles 7:4-10). In addition, there are offerings of the princes in chapter 45:10-17; and others on Unleavened Bread and Tabernacle (verses 18-25). There are even more announced for the Sabbath and new moon sacrifices as outlined in Ezekiel chapter 46.

SCRIPTURAL PROOF FOR SACRIFICIAL RESTORATION

A variety of Scriptures, in addition to Ezekiel 40-48, prove that there will be sacrifices during this period, even though some deny it. Refer to a Millennial prophecy in Isaiah 56:6-8:

> "And the foreigners who join themselves to the LORD, to minister to him, to love the name of the LORD, and to be his servants, everyone who keeps the Sabbath and does not profane it, and holds fast my covenant—
> these I will bring to my holy mountain, **and make them joyful in my house of prayer; their burnt offerings and their sacrifices** will be accepted on my altar; for my house shall be called a house of prayer for all peoples."
> The Lord GOD, who gathers the outcasts of Israel, declares, "I will gather yet others to him besides those already gathered." (ESV) [see also Is 44:28]

There are also a number of other supporting references in Isaiah:

> "and I will set a sign among them. And from them I will send survivors to the nations, to Tarshish, Pul, and Lud, who draw the bow, to Tubal and Javan, to the coastlands far away, that have not heard my fame or seen my glory. And they shall declare my glory among the nations.
> And they shall bring all your brothers from all the nations as an offering to the LORD, on horses and in chariots and in litters and on mules and on dromedaries, to

my holy mountain Jerusalem, says the LORD, just as the Israelites **bring their grain offering in a clean vessel to the house of the LORD**.

And some of them also I will take for priests and for Levites, says the LORD."(Is 66:19-21, ESV) [cp Zech 14:16]

Jeremiah likewise proves this case:

"In those days and at that time I will cause a righteous Branch to spring up for David, and he shall execute justice and righteousness in the land.

In those days Judah will be saved, and Jerusalem will dwell securely. And this is the name by which it will be called: 'The LORD is our righteousness.'

"For thus says the LORD: David shall never lack a man to sit on the throne of the house of Israel,

and the Levitical priests shall never lack a man in my **presence to offer burnt offerings, to burn grain offerings, and to make sacrifices forever**."

The word of the LORD came to Jeremiah:

"Thus says the LORD: If you can break my covenant with the day and my covenant with the night, so that day and night will not come at their appointed time,

then also my covenant with David my servant may be broken, so that he shall not have a son to reign on his throne, and my covenant with the Levitical priests my ministers.

As the host of heaven cannot be numbered and the sands of the sea cannot be measured, so I will multiply the offspring of David my servant, and the Levitical priests who minister to me." (Jer 33:15-22)

Ezekiel 20:40-41:

""For on my holy mountain, the mountain height of Israel, declares the Lord GOD, there all the house of Israel, all of them, shall serve me in the land. There I will accept them, and there I will require your contributions and the choicest of your gifts, **with all your sacred offerings**.

As a pleasing aroma I will accept you, when I bring you out from the peoples and gather you out of the countries where you have been scattered. And I will manifest my holiness among you in the sight of the nations." (ESV)

Zechariah 14:19-21:

"This shall be the punishment to Egypt and the punishment to all the nations that do not go up to keep the Feast of Booths.

And on that day there shall be inscribed on the bells of the horses, "Holy to the LORD." And the pots in the house of the LORD shall be as the bowls before the altar.

And every pot in Jerusalem and Judah shall be holy to the LORD of hosts, so **that all who sacrifice may come and take of them and boil the meat of the sacrifice in them**. And there shall no longer be a trader in the house of the LORD of hosts on that day." (ESV)

Malachi 3:3-4:

> "He will sit as a refiner and purifier of silver, and he will purify the sons of Levi and refine them like gold and silver, and they will bring offerings in righteousness to the LORD. **Then the offering of Judah and Jerusalem will be pleasing to the LORD as in the days of old and as in former years.**" (ESV)

Some churches and many conservative commentators have held to the view that the sacrificial system will be restored during the Millennial reign of the Messiah (presumably based on the above Scriptures).

For example:

> "Even though those who initially enter the Millennial kingdom are all regenerate (Jews- Ezekiel 20:33-38; Gentiles- Matthew 25:31-46), they are still mortal beings who intentionally or unintentionally can violate ceremonial standards." (Randall Price, *The Program for The Last Days Temple*, p. 554).

> "Ezekiel describes many aspects of Israel's future Temple as it will be when Christ is reigning on the earth. He vividly describes the Temple's physical dimensions, its ritualistic practices and rites, and its many functions in the ministry of the people in their worship of the Messiah in the millennial kingdom, which includes the reinstitution of animal sacrifices. In surmising Ezekiel's vision, Unger lists at least five distinct purposes for the future millennial Temple:
>
> (1) To demonstrate God's holiness.
> (2) To provide a dwelling place for God's glory (43:7).
> (3) To perpetuate the memorial of sacrifice.
> (4) To provide a center for the divine government (43:7).
> (5) To provide victory over the curse (47:1-12). [quoting from Merrill F. Unger, "The Temple Vision of Ezekiel," *Bibliotheca Sacra*, Vol. 106 (January 1949), pp. 57-64.]
>
> … Ezekiel's prophecy tells the reader that this will most certainly come to pass. **The burden of proof therefore falls on those who seek to refute what is clearly stated in the text.**

> … Sacrifices will be reinstated as memorial to Christ's finished work on the cross and it will be a symbolic act of ritualistic cleansing for those entering into close proximity to the Lord and His holiness at the Temple mount." (James Brooks, *The Millennial Sacrifice Controversy*, pp. 2-4). [emphasis mine][50]

---

[50] This topic was also mentioned from time-to-time in old Church of God sermons and in literature, eg:

"Notice it! The Levites shall never lack a man — "want a man" in the archaic wording of the King James Version — to present offerings continually. There will always be Levites available to do the job — or God's promise is not true. The Levites have been punished — there is now no temple or tabernacle whereupon to present their offerings, but they have never lacked a man who could perform the rituals whenever they might be required.

Note that Christ is the ultimate sacrifice and always will be for eternity: John 1:29; IICor 5:21; Heb 7:27-28; 10:1-6; Ps 40:6-8; 50:23; 51:16-10; 141:2. But physical sacrifices only provided forgiveness that is temporal and not eternal.

Despite the above Scriptures and more, some sources insist on taking a position opposite to clear Scriptural revelation:

> "The majority of dispensationalists have argued that the sacrifices are memorials to the sacrifice of Christ, with no atoning character. However, the idea that these are memorial sacrifices is no where apparent in Ezekiel, and it is specifically claimed by Ezekiel that these offerings will make atonement (45:15, 17, 20)" (Ian Duguid, *Ezekiel* in *The NIV Application Commentary*, p. 521).

> "In vv 15 and 17 the expiatory significance of the sacrifice is emphatically expressed … In 43:20 and 45:19f it can be seen that **the expiatory power is especially attributed to the blood**"" (Walther Zimmerli, *Ezekiel 2: A Commentary on the Book of the Prophet Ezekiel Chapters 25-48*, p. 479). [emphasis mine]

> "Though the priest could care for a dead family member, he would be defiled; and it would be necessary for him to be cleansed according to biblical guidelines (cf. Num 19:11-13) and wait seven days, the period for cleansing (v.26). When a priest returned to minister in the inner court after defilement and cleansing, it would be necessary for him to offer a sin offering as a purification offering for himself (v.27)" (Ralph Alexander, *Ezekiel. Everyman's Bible Commentary*, p. 978).

> "In Eze 44:25-27 there follow regulations concerning defilement from the dead, and its removal. Eze 44:25 is a simple repetition of Lev 21:1-3. But the instructions concerning the purification from defilement from the dead are sharpened, inasmuch as not only is the purification prescribed by the law (Num 19:1.), and which lasted seven days, required (this is meant by טהרתו), but a further period of seven days is appointed after these, at the expiration of which the presentation of a sin-offering is demanded before the service in the sanctuary can be resumed. By this demand for a heightened purification, the approach to a corpse permitted to the priests, which was prohibited to the high priest in the Mosaic law, even in the case of father and mother (Lev 21:11), is tolerably equalized." (Keil & Delitzsch, *Ezekiel. Bible Commentary on the Old Testament*, pp. 416-17).

In Ezekiel we find that after Christ's return the Levites will still be available to perform the physical duties of the priesthood as a reminder of Israel's failure as a nation to do God's will (Ezekiel 40.46; 43.19; and 44.9-21). **The very statutes which were perpetually, established upon the priesthood in Moses' day are still binding during the millennium upon the Levites (Eze 44.17-25)**. When God declares a statute everlasting, HE MEANS IT! Read these verses for yourself." (Herman Hoeh in "Are God's Festivals to be Observed Forever?" *The Good News*, March 1959, p. 6) [emphasis mine]

"And then, **beginning chapter 40, the remainder of the Book of Ezekiel reveals the ideal THEOCRACY — God's NEW ORDER of divine government upon earth** — the permanent forms and institutions which shall express the ideal relation between God and man!" (Herbert W Armstrong in "Will Russia Attack America?" *Plain Truth*, July 1956, p. 19) [emphasis mine]

Cleansing for expiation or atonement or making amends are not the same as complete forgiveness of sins - they are not the same thing. In any event, the sort of forgiveness that is complete and eternal, can only come through Christ's sacrifice.

OTHER INFORMATION BY RESEARCHERS

Researchers and commentators who have delved deeply into this complicated aspect of doctrine have come to a common-sense and inevitable conclusion. Some of these are quoted below:

Walter Kaiser:

"The blood by which the covenant was ratified and sealed was the basis for the union between Yahweh and the people" (*Exodus. The Expositor's Bible Commentary*, Vol 1, p. 449).[51]

Daniel Block:

"Third, the focus of the celebration [i.e. of Passover in Ezekiel] has changed. On the day of the Passover, the prince is to provide for himself and the people a bull for a purification offering (*hatta't*). This shift parallels the change in the nature of the sacrificial victims. Whereas the function of the original Passover was apotropaic, to ward off Yahweh's lethal actions, and subsequent celebrations provided annual reminders of the original event, in the Ezekielian ordinance the memorial purposes of the Passover are overshadowed by the purgative concern. **Thus, while the Passover, the most fundamental of all Israelite celebrations, is retained in Ezekiel's new religions order, its nature and significance has been changed** ...

"**Although Ezekiel retains the label of the ancient rite of Passover, his ordinance calls for a dramatic transformation of the festival.** Like the original Passover (Exod. 12-13), Ezekiel's celebration has inaugural significance. Through this celebration the nation of Israel becomes the people of God. **Whereas the function of the original Passover sacrifice was apotropaic (to ward off Yahweh), however, Ezekiel's is purgative.** Like the rest of this prophet's Torah, the cult of the new order is preoccupied with holiness: maintaining the sanctity of the temple (v.20) and of the worshippers (v.22). Before the rituals can be performed, viz., before the new spiritual relationship between Yahweh and his people can be celebrated, the defilement of the building and the people must be purged. Through the Passover celebration, the

---

[51] "... the blood not only became a bond of union between Jehovah and His people, but as the blood of the covenant, it became a vital power, holy and divine, uniting Israel and its God; the sprinkling of the blood with this blood was an actual renewal of life, a transposition of Israel into the kingdom of God, in which was filled with the powers of God's spirit of grace, and sanctified into a kingdom of priests, a holy nation of Jehovah (ch 19:6). And this covenant was made "upon all the words" which Jehovah had spoken, and the people promised to observe. Consequently it had for its foundation the divine law and right, as the rule of life for Israel" (Carl Keil, *Exodus. Bible Commentary on the Old Testament*, p. 424).

temple complex becomes sacred space and the Israelites become a holy people. In this newly constituted theocracy the role of the *nasi'* is pivotal. As the patron and guardian of the cult, he bears the responsibility for the sanctification of the temple and the nation..." (*The Book of Ezekiel Chapters 25–28* in *New International Commentary on the Old Testament*, pp. 664-66). [emphasis mine]

John Skinner:

"Nor should it be overlooked that Ezekiel's Torah omits all reference to the other great festival that figures in the Mosaic Torah, viz. that of Pentecost, or the Feast of Weeks, as well as to the Feast of Trumpets and the great Day of Atonement ... Why does Ezekiel require, in the cultus (which he sets up) so much less than Num 28:1-31 and Num 29:1-40? Where, in Ezekiel is the high priest, who for the priest code is the center of the theocracy? Where is the great Day of Atonement of Lev 16:1-34?" and so on. **The answer to these interrogations is that Ezekiel did not intend to republish the Mosaic Torah, but to modify it so as to meet the requirements of the new era, or (perhaps better) to express more adequately the new conceptions of religion and worship he had been commissioned to set before his fellow-exiles**; and that Ezekiel had a perfect right to deal in this way even with the Mosaic Torah, inasmuch as he distinctly claimed, in committing to writing the details of his temple- vision, to be acting under special Divine guidance (Eze 43:10, Eze 43:11; Eze 44:5).

"All true and lasting reformations are conservative at heart; their object never is to make a clean sweep of the past, but so to modify what is traditional as to adapt it to the needs of a new era ... Accordingly we find that the new theocracy is modelled from beginning to end after the pattern of the ancient institutions which had been destroyed by the Exile. If we ask, for example, what is the meaning of some detail of the Temple building, such as the cells surrounding the main sanctuary, the obvious and sufficient answer is that these things existed in Solomon's Temple, and there was no reason for altering them. On the other hand, **whenever we find the vision departing from what had been traditionally established, we may be sure that there is a reason for it, and in most cases we can see what that reason was** ..." (John Skinner, *The Book of Ezekiel*, pp. 387-88). [emphasis mine]

Iain M Duguid:

"In contrast to the Pentateuchal program, **Ezekiel's sacrifices appear to be more numerous and more focused on the concept of purification**. This is another way of conveying the same message as the temple building itself, which is larger and more restricted in access than the former temple. God is doing something greater than the former things, a greatness that shows itself in the dimensions of the holy space and the number of sacrifices. God is also doing something that will prevent any repetition of the contamination of the past that drove him from the land, through erecting high walls and buffer zones and inaugurating more rites of purgation." (*Ezekiel. The NIV Application Commentary*, pp. 523). [emphasis mine]

Bob Bolender:

> "It is the work of the Lord Jesus Christ to reveal God the Father (John 1:18; Colossians 1:15; Hebrews 1:3) and to bring people to the Father (John 14:6). Ultimately, the Lord's work will be to apply the teaching He received from the Father (John 5:20). The Son revealed the Father in His first-advent incarnation (John 1:18; 17:4). Accordingly, it makes sense to understand that the Son will reveal the Father with His work that follows His second advent. Simply stated, **the Lord Jesus Christ has been revealing the Father since creation. Why would He stop doing that in the Millennium?** ...
>
> "Whereas Old Testament animal sacrifices were shadow-Christology, millennial animal sacrifices will be shadow-Paterology." ("Memorials and Shadows. Animal Sacrifices of the Millennium," *Chafer Theological Journal*, April 2002, p. 40). [emphasis mine]

OVERVIEW

With the information provided above, it should be rather clear that Ezekiel was inspired to provide a detailed description of a yet future system that will be set up during the early years of the Millennium. The temple with its sacrificial system will be restored as well as the allotment of land to the tribes of Israel.

In addition, now armed with the basic outline and information about the temple, sacrifices and tribal allotments, it should be an easier for one to come to grips with and to comprehend these intriguing chapters.

These three areas of detail (temple, sacrifices and tribal allotment), once studied, understood and summarized, can be understood and thus help one to dig deeper into God's Word, uncovering many hidden treasures.

The Bible is a vast, detailed and sometimes difficult book to comprehend. But may we all at least try to understand all parts of it and come to be teachers of His Word, assisting one another in this life and in the next world, to a deeper appreciation of the Word.

FURTHER READING

- Alexander, R. H. (1976), "Ezekiel," *Everyman's Bible Commentary*, Vol. 6, p. 945, note on *Does Ezekiel 40-48 Relate to the Millennium or to the Eternal State?*
- Hullinger, J. M. (1995), "The Problem of Animal Sacrifices in Ezekiel 40-48," *Bibliotheca Sacra*, July-September, Vol. 152, pp. 279-89.
- Lancaster, D. T. (2011), *What about the Sacrifices?* First Fruits of Zion, Marshfield, MO.
- Whitcomb, J. C. (1985), "Christ's Atonement and Animal Sacrifices in Israel," *Grace Theological Journal*, Vol. 6, No. 2, pp. 201-217.
- Whitcomb, J. C. (1994), "The Millennial Temple of Ezekiel 40-48," *The Diligent Workman Journal*, May, pp. 21-25.

PART FOUR

THE NATIONS IN THE
WORLD TOMORROW

OUTLINE OF THIS SECTION

These chapters primarily explore the prophecies related to the peace and prosperity during the Messiah's reign, a theme often emphasised by preachers and writers. However, they tend not to delve into the numerous other prophecies. These overlooked prophecies detail the manner of the Messiah's governance and the specific actions the Messiah will undertake to establish and maintain His rule. These include, but are not limited to: punishments upon nations, the role of Israel, the length of time it will take for Him to conquer the entire world, the New Covenant with Israel, the Temple of Ezekiel and such like.

The oracles against the nations are virtually ignored or glanced over. While many or most of the oracles are historical, they foreshadow or type future end-time events including the Tribulation and Day of the Lord; others are clearly Millennial. As we read the prophecies it becomes clear that God wants to have a relationship with all the peoples and nations of mankind – but only after they are broken, repentant and turn to Him. They will need to repent, serve Him and live in peace with each other. Then, and only then, will the Millennial blessings be provided to the nations.

So much is overlooked about His method of rulership over the nations, including curses upon them for rebellion and punishments. The Millennium will not be a proverbial 'bed of roses' and it seems that world conquest will take some time. Gradually the nations will be brought to heel and national sins will decline over many decades as nations change their ways. After a few decades we will have relative peace as more and more nations surrender to the Messiah, put down their weapons and learn the way of outgoing love toward others.

For God is not only interested in personal relationships and repentance, but also national relationships and repentance. To achieve this, He may have to unleash fierce wrath:

> "I trampled down the peoples in my anger; I made them drunk in my wrath, and I poured out their lifeblood on the earth." (Is 63:6, ESV)

The gap in understanding of the Millennium, I hope, is filled to some degree by the following chapters. These are straight-forward Bible studies containing cross-references to other pertinent or parallel Scriptures, comments and references to assist the reader. They are not exhaustive studies or scholarly works as such. They are elementary and uncomplicated studies that are easy to follow and read.

The first in these series of chapters is titled *Feast of the Nations*, which delves into the role of Israel under Christ and the saints to lead and help educate the gentile nations – to assist in bringing them to national repentance. This is symbolised by the Feast of Ingathering referred to in Leviticus 23:33-44 (also known as the Feast of Tabernacles).

It concentrates on an issue which has been neglected or forgotten due to a number of reasons, not least political correctness.

The following chapter concerns the ***Judging of the Nations***. The purpose of this study is to seek clarity about Christ's management of the ingathering of the nations during His reign on earth.

Many or most Christians totally overlook the fact that God does not only work with individuals and families, but also with nations. In other words, He deals with societies or families that have expanded into nations as one block.

The interpretation of the word *judging* is determined by the context: it can be to sternly deal with; reign over with justice; settle disputes etc. There is so much written in the Bible about His judging of the nations that it behoves us to study this topic.

Status of the Nations represents the third and final chapter in this part and explores what each nations will be doing in the World Tomorrow. What will be their role? How will they relate to the House of Israel?

An elementary collation of the Millennial prophecies of the nations under the Messiah's reign will provide us with some information and insights into a topic seldom or never addressed.

In this short, straightforward study, all the various Scriptures concerning particular nations that are mentioned in Millennial prophecies are sought out and assembled under their names.

The nations mentioned in the Millennial prophecies are listed, and, where appropriate, they are cross-referenced or commented upon.

CHAPTER ELEVEN

FEAST OF THE NATIONS

INTRODUCTORY COMMENTS

It is evident from the Scriptures that the gentile peoples are not ignored or unwanted. God has a plan for them too, mentioned in Genesis 12:3:

> "Now the LORD said to Abram, "Go from your country and your kindred and your father's house to the land that I will show you.
>
> And I will make of you a great nation, and I will bless you and make your name great, so that you will be a blessing.
>
> I will bless those who bless you, and him who dishonors you I will curse, and **in you all the families of the earth shall be blessed**."" (Gen 12:1-3, ESV; cf Is 41:8-9; 51:2)

These families or nations that would be blessed are mentioned and listed just two chapters previous to this promise in Genesis 10 where 70 names are listed in that chapter representing the grandsons and great-grandsons etc of Noah. What this shows is that these different nations will still exist in a way that can be identified from their Genesis 10 origins, which continues into the Millennium. In the near future, amid the massive worldwide upheavals of the Great Tribulation and Day of the Lord, these various peoples will survive, even if only a small number, and be rescued from utter destruction:

> "For then there will be great tribulation, such as has not been from the beginning of the world until now, no, and never will be.
>
> And if those days had not been cut short, no human being would be saved. But for the sake of the elect those days will be cut short." (Matt 24:21-22, ESV)

So, God having developed all these different nations, wants to preserve them for His honour and glory – to demonstrate His creative capacity – and to express the different gifts and talents He has granted to all peoples.

Thus true nationalism/patriotism is of God – not extreme nationalism on the one hand nor globalisation on the other. It is God Who has developed or brought about the nations and as such He will ultimately see to it that their diverse characteristics continue.

Relying on the prophecies referred to in this chapter and the chapter on *Judging of the Nations*, I set out to prove that the Millennial rule of the Messiah will be a time that He tests and tries the various nations listed in Genesis 10. It is not just individuals' love and respect He is seeking, but that of all the nations. They will all have to repent and turn to Him with all their heart, sincerely and absolutely.

Although individuals, families, clans, tribes and sub-nations constitute nations, it is the collective nation that He is addressing and working with (in addition to individuals). In other words, all individuals have a national or collective (or 'corporate') responsibility for righteous acts. They must work together as a community or society, united in purpose: an order or system of rulers or Princes, country/nation, tribe, family, individual – it is clear from the Scriptures that God works with nations as a collective or community.

It is therefore rather obvious that God is not advocating "the triumph of the individual" or the "selfish gene theory" of the Left. His way is utterly different to man's and He has chosen to work through and with nations as well as families and individuals.

It is also evident that He is coming to judge the nations. Any negative attributes they have (e.g., warmongering, lying, stealing, under-handedness, jealousy, tearing down tall poppies etc) must be eschewed collectively; any good attributes must be maintained and enhanced. Everyone within a nation has a responsibility to work together with others toward that outcome. This process begins with the individual and progresses through families, clans, tribes, and sub-nations, until a collective national behavior and attitude of righteousness is expressed.

GENTILE NATIONS OFFERED SALVATION!

Many, or even most, people who have an understanding of God's overall plan that is outlined in the Biblical holy days are cognisant that the Feast of Tabernacles (also known as Sukkoth, Booths and Ingathering) portrays the future Millennial reign of the Messiah over the entire earth (a list of Scriptures on the Feast of Tabernacles may be found in the appendix *Feast of Tabernacles and Last Great Day*).

It is a festival that also commemorates the Sinai wanderings of Israel where God's presence was so real – His presence in the cloud by day and pillar of fire at night. Their clothes and shoes did not wear out and the Israelites dwelt in temporary abodes.

The Covenant was ratified, laws introduced and righteous judgment was enforced.

Bible students are aware that this particular Feast not only has historic reference, but it also embodies spiritual teaching concerning our temporal nature, Christ's central role in salvation, and various other typologies. None of these will be explored in much detail in this chapter due to its Millennial emphasis and because others have written on these vital aspects of this Feast.

The Feast of Tabernacles also portrays the future great 'harvest' of mankind – the bringing of all peoples under His reign and care. Israel is to be God's instrument in doing so.[52]

---

[52] "They [Israel] form the nucleus of the Kingdom of God on earth, into which all nations of the world are eventually absorbed … Deut. 32:8-9 indicates that God intended from the beginning of human history that

162

The nations are currently under the sway of Satan (Matt 4:8-9; IICor 4:4; Matt 13:5; Is 25:6-7) and as such they need to be brought under the helm of God through the Messiah, the saints and his instrument, Israel.[53]

This study emphasises the ingathering or harvest aspect of this feast. Some commentators and authors certainly understand this aspect of Christ's reign:

> "It is remarkable how many allusions to this feast occur in the writings of the prophets, as if its types were the goal of all their desire" (Alfred Edersheim, *The Temple: Its Ministry and Services*, p. 215, footnote 1).

> "In the great messianic future, many nations "will be joined with the LORD" (v.11) or "will join themselves to the Lord" (the Hebrew can be rendered either way). Such **an ingathering of the nations to the Lord** echoes the promise in the Abrahamic covenant: "All people on earth will be blessed through you" (Gen 12:3; cf. 18:18 and 22:18; see also Isa 2:2-4; 60:3; Zech 8:20-23). The result is that they too will become the people of God." (Kenneth Barker, *Zechariah. Expositor's Bible Commentary*, Vol. 7, p. 619) [emphasis mine][54]

> "Indirect messianic prophecy refers to passages that can be literally and fully realized only through the person and work of the Messiah - e.g., passages that speak of a personal coming of God to his people, as in v.10 and 9:9 (cf. Isa 40:9-11; Mal 3:1)...

various peoples should inhabit specific territories of the earth" (Rick Sherrod, *Review of United States and Britain in Prophecy. Part II*, pp. 45, 68). The conversion of the gentile nations during the 1,000 years of the Messiah's reign is nigh.

[53] "**The transformation of the initial state of the earth into complex human societies is not part of the fall, but rather the legitimate creational mandate of humanity**. Creation was never meant to be static, but was intended by God from the beginning to be developmental, moving toward a goal." (J. Richard Middleton, "A New Heaven and a New Earth: The case for a holistic reading of the Biblical Story of Redemption," *Journal for Christian Theological Research*, Vol. 11, 2006, p. 76)

"It is sometimes shocking for readers of the Bible to realize that the initial purpose and raison d'être of humanity is never explicitly portrayed in Scripture as the worship of God the distinctive way humans worship or render service to the Creator is by the development of culture through interaction with our earthly environment (in a manner that glorifies God)" (ibid, p. 81)

In a footnote he adds: ""Worship" in the narrow sense may be understood as part of human cultural activity. Second, we should not reduce human worship/service of God to verbal, emotionally charged expressions of praise (which is what we usually mean by the term). Note that Paul in Romans 12:1-2 borrows language of sacrifice and liturgy from Israel's cult in order to describe full-orbed bodily obedience (which, he says, is our true worship). This is the Bible's typical emphasis." (ibid) [emphasis mine]

[54] "God calls Abraham out from the now diversified human race (described as the nations or the families of the earth) to be a new agent or helper, precisely to impact the human race, the original agent. While God promises Abraham a large family—indeed a nation—with its own land, neither of these is the ultimate purpose for which Abraham has been called. In five texts in Genesis (starting with 12:1-3), **God tells Abraham, Isaac and Jacob that their purpose (including that of their descendants) is to mediate blessing to the human race—as if this new family will be God's priests in the world.**" In a footnote he adds "This is stated to Abraham in Genesis 12:1-3, 18:17-18, 22:17-18, to Isaac in Genesis 26:4-5, and to Jacob in Genesis 28:14." (ibid, p. 82) "... we find a re-articulation of the Abrahamic calling, applied to the entire nation in Exodus 19:3-6" (ibid, p. 83) [emphasis mine]

all passages that speak of a future rule of the Lord over Israel or to the earth, or that speak of a future rule of the Lord over Israel or over the whole earth, are ultimately messianic - indirectly or by extension - for to be fully and literally true, they require a future, literal messianic kingdom on the earth."

"The Messiah was the promised one who would embody in his own person the identity and mission of Israel, as their representative, King, leader and Savior. Through the Messiah as his anointed agent, YHWH, the God of Israel, would bring about all he intended for Israel. But what was that mission of Israel? Nothing less than to be "a light to the nations," the means of bringing redemptive blessings to the nations of the world, as originally promised in the title deeds of the covenant with Abraham. For the God of Israel is also the Creator God of all the world." (Barker, ibid, p. 619). [emphasis mine]

"Although the Messiah's mission is to establish his kingdom of "peace" (*salom*), he must first conquer all enemies and deliver his people. This he sets out to do (vv.11-16; cf. Ps 110). **Before he can reign in peace, he must fully deliver and restore Israel**. The passage is filled with battle terminology; prisoners (v.11), fortress (v.12), bow (v.13), arrow (v.14), trumpet (v.14), and slingstones (v.15). Here the Messiah is depicted as a conquering King (the divine Warrior motif)..."

"The basis for the hope is given in v.13, of which Laetsch (p.458) says, "in a bold metaphor the Lord compares Himself as a warrior using Judah as His bow, Ephraim His arrows... The point of this verse is that God's people will gain the victory over their enemies" (Barker, ibid, p. 666). [emphasis mine]

"In any treatment of this topic, we dare not treat the OT any differently than the NT treats it. NT writers took the OT seriously – and literally. So must we." (William Barrick, "The Kingdom of God in the Old Testament", *The Master's Seminary*, Fall 2012, p. 173)

"Our focus here is on *the physical aspects* of the messianic kingdom. **Covenantal promises clearly indicate that the future nation of Israel will inherit the land of Canaan again**." (Barrick, ibid, p. 185)

"Through the Messiah, therefore, the God of Israel would also bring about all he intended for the nations. **The eschatological redemption and restoration of Israel would issue in the ingathering of the nations**" (Christopher Wright, *The Mission of God*, p. 31). [emphasis mine]

"If revelation is to recommence in the millennial kingdom, converted Israel must head humanity. Jews and Gentiles stand on an equal footing, as both alike needing mercy; but as regards God's instrumentalities for establishing His kingdom on earth, Israel is His chosen people. The Israelite priest-kings on earth are what the transfigured priest-kings are in heaven... Earthly and heavenly glories shall be united in the twofold election. Elect Israel in the flesh shall stand at the head of the earthly; the elect spiritual church, the Bride, in the heavenly. These elections are not merely for the good of the elect, but for whom they minister. The heavenly Church is elected, not merely to salvation, but to rule in love, and minister blessings over the earth, as king-priests" (Andrew Fausset et al, "The Revelation of St. John the Divine," in *A Commentary, Critical and Explanatory, on the Old and New Testaments*, p. 722). [emphasis mine][55]

"Basically the promise consists of three elements: first, a "seed" or a line of heirs culminating in a chief *heir par excellence* which is promised to Eve, Abraham, Isaac, and Jacob (Gen 3:15; 12:3, 7 ; 13:14–16 ; 15:4, 5, 13, 18 ; 16:10; 17:2, 7, 9, 19 ; 21:12; 22:17 ; 26:24 ; 27:28, 29 ; 28:14); second, the land of Canaan which is given to the Patriarchs and their descendants forever as an *inheritance* (Gen 12:1, 7; 13:15, 17; 15:7, 18 ; 17:8; 24:7; 26:2, 3; 28:13; 49:8–12) and third, the climactic element: that the Patriarchs are the recipients of these basic three elements: (1) Abraham's seed through Isaac would by this *heritage* (Gen 12:3; 18:18; 22:18; 26:4; 28:14). This last item Paul clearly calls the "gospel" in Galatians 3:8.

There were additional items in Genesis which elaborated on these basic three elements: (1) Abraham's seed through Isaac would be countless as the stars and sand of the seashore, (2) they would be a great nation, (3) that kings would come from Abraham, Sarah, and Jacob, and (4) Abraham's name would be great.

God promises to be something and to do something for a select people so as to bring blessing to all mankind and creation.

The rest which God gives is at once historical (Canaan), soteriological (salvation), and eschatological (the kingdom and our reign with Christ). This is another beautiful illustration of the corporate solidarity of some of these themes in Scripture. Each step in the onward movement of such themes as the promise with its sub-themes such as the rest from God, the Messiah, and the Seed, points back to the beginning and to the ultimate goal intended by God. Each successive historical step harmoniously combines the beginning step in which the totality was programmatically announced with the end in which that totality shall be unfolded." (Walter Kaiser, "The Promise Theme and the Theology of Rest," *Bibliotheca Sacra*, Vol. 130-158, April 1973, p. 3) [emphasis mine]

It will take time to bring all the nations to heel. Recall that the House of Israel would have been severely dealt with in the Tribulation, liberated at the Second Exodus, and subsequently cleansed.

However, following that, the time will come for the nations to be brought into the fold, although this will take some time. As we have previously noted, one major rebellion during the

---

[55] "The elements of the covenant are threefold: making Abraham into a great nation, blessing Abraham personally, and blessing all nations in Abraham. The promises of the covenant are unconditional. The rest of the OT repeatedly refers back to God's oath to Abraham in the Torah. The NT does the same by pointing out that Jesus Christ, Abraham's seed, will make possible the final fulfillment of that covenant in the future." (Keith Essex, "The Abrahamic Covenant," *The Master's Seminary Journal*, Vol. 10, No. 2, 1999, p. 191)

early years of the Tribulation will be the famous battle outlined in Ezekiel 38 and 39 – these forces will probably be the recalcitrant remnants of the 200 million strong Eastern hordes referred to in Revelation 9:14-16 and 16:12.[56]

Keil and Delitzsch in their *Commentary on the Old Testament* state the following on Ezekiel 38:10-16:

> "Gog resolves to fall upon Israel, now living in peace and security, and dwelling in open unfortified places, and to rob and plunder it. ארץ, literally, land of plains, i.e., a land which has no fortified towns, but only places lying quite exposed (see the comm. on Zechariah 2:8); because its inhabitants are living in undisturbed peace and safe repose, and therefore dwell in places that have no walls with gates and bars (cf. Judges 18:7; Jeremiah 49:31). **This description of Israel's mode of life also points beyond the times succeeding the Babylonian captivity to the Messianic days,** when the Lord will have destroyed the horses and war-chariots and fortresses (Micah 5:9), and Jerusalem will be inhabited as an open country because of the multitude of the men and cattle, and the Lord will be a wall of fire round about her (Zechariah 2:8-9).

---

[56] The Church of God understands this. For instance, in the old booklet *Russia and China in Prophecy* we read:
"Notice, these nations [listed in Ezekiel 38 and 39] do not see and recognize the dread divinity, the might and power of the Eternal Christ, even after he has returned. He has to teach them that he is the Eternal!" (p. 25)

"These ... Asian armies are also described in Ezekiel, chapters 38 and 39, where elements of those forces are prophesied to invade the Holy Land when all 12 tribes of Israel have returned ... These circumstances will be extant only after the coming of the Messiah, when surviving Eurasian forces will be supernaturally punished" (p. 31).

"As we have seen, the coming Eurasian confederacy will devastate much of Western Europe. After Christ decimates the armies of all nations gathered at Armageddon, Gog will assemble a large army from among his surviving Eurasian forces ... The demise of Gog and his allies will furnish a powerful witness to the nations of the world." (p. 43)

In addition, there were *World Tomorrow* radio programs explaining this in the 1950s and early 1960s because the protestant evangelists of that time (and decades thereafter) promoted the idea that Communist Russia and China would invade America. Herbert Armstrong set them straight on this issue while also warning about Communist infiltration in the West. The *Good News* magazine contained an article that made reference to this as well:

"Ezekiel 38 and 39 describe a war that will take place against Israel after they have been reestablished and will be living in peace and prosperity. Isaiah 30:20-21 shows how we will need to be constantly working with people who want to go their own way ...

Problems? Certainly. But every Feast of Tabernacles will see more people coming to rejoice before the Lord. Every year greater numbers of people from every nation will venture to Jerusalem to learn the laws and ways of the God of Israel (Isa. 2:1-4, Mic. 4:1-5)." ("But what if 'everything goes wrong'?" *Good News*, Sept 1982, p. 9)

The *Systematic Theology Project* also made mention of these battles:
"Then begins the millennial rule of Christ and the saints over the earth. After some continuing confrontations and battles (described in Ezek. 38 and 39), God's Kingdom shall be set up over all peoples; and Jesus Christ shall teach them God's laws, the way of happiness and eventually of eternal salvation." (chapter on "Prophecy", p. 8 (or p. 108 of the entire document))

For *Ezekiel 38:12*, compare Isaiah 10:6. להשיב ידך is not dependent upon אעלה, like the preceding infinitives, but is subordinate to אמרת אעלה וגו: "thou sayest, I will go up ... to turn thy hand." השיב, to bring back, is to be explained from the fact that the heathen had already at an earlier period turned their hand against the towns of Israel, and plundered their possessions and goods. חרבות נושבות in this connection are desolate places which are inhabited again, and therefore have been rebuilt (cf. Ezekiel 12:20; Ezekiel 26:19). מקנה and קנין are synonyms; and מקנה does not mean flocks or herds, but gain, possession (cf. Genesis 36:6; Genesis 31:18; Genesis 34:23). One motive of Gog for making the attack was to be found in the possessions of Israel; a second is given in the words: who dwell upon the navel of the earth. This figurative expression is to be explained from Ezekiel 5:5: "Jerusalem in the midst of the nations." This navel is not a figure denoting the high land, but signifies the land situated in the middle of the earth, and therefore the land most glorious and most richly blessed; so that they who dwell there occupy the most exalted position among the nations. A covetous desire for the possessions of the people of God, and envy at his exalted position in the centre of the world, are therefore the motives by which Gog is impelled to enter upon his predatory expedition against the people living in the depth of peace." [emphasis mine]

JEWISH TRADITIONS AND EXPLANATIONS

To the Jews at the time of Christ, the Feast of Tabernacles was prophetic of the spiritual enlightenment that will be offered to the gentiles – with this task being granted to Israel on behalf of and guided by the Messiah and His representatives.

Pilgrims came from all over the region and in fact, some would take weeks to reach Jerusalem. Then they still had to prepare for the Feast by constructing a booth in which to dwell during this exciting and eventful period.

They dwelt in the booth for eight days which represented tabernacling with God Himself. Before you knew it there were thousands of booths all along the roofs, open areas and rooftops of Jerusalem.

Great celebrations took place at the Temple Mount and it is said that these spilled over into the Court of the Gentiles

Note what is expected for Feast of Tabernacle observation:

"On the fifteenth day of the seventh month, when you have gathered in the produce of the land, you shall celebrate the feast of the LORD seven days. On the first day shall be a solemn rest, and on the eighth day shall be a solemn rest.

And you shall take on the first day the fruit of splendid trees, branches of palm trees and boughs of leafy trees and willows of the brook, and you shall rejoice before the LORD your God seven days.

You shall celebrate it as a feast to the LORD for seven days in the year. It is a statute forever throughout your generations; you shall celebrate it in the seventh month.

You shall dwell in booths for seven days. All native Israelites shall dwell in booths, that your generations may know that I made the people of Israel dwell in booths when I brought them out of the land of Egypt: I am the LORD your God."

Thus Moses declared to the people of Israel the appointed feasts of the LORD." (Lev 23:39-44, ESV)

I would like to emphasise two aspects of these days, dwelling on verse 40:

1. It is the only festival where one is *required* to rejoice[57]
2. On the first day they had to take fruit from trees, branches of palms, boughs of leafy trees and willows.

As a backdrop, let us take a look at Jewish traditions which may sometimes prove helpful in studying and understanding certain aspects of holy day typologies:

"The Bible does not specify precisely which trees and fruits are to be taken.

"Jewish authorities have interpreted the 'fruit of goodly trees' to mean the etrog [i.e. large citrus fruit tree], and the 'branches of palms' to mean the lulav [i.e., date palms]. The 'boughs of thick trees' refers to the myrtle, and 'willows of the brook' are the familiar willow trees. These four species were to be held in the hand and blessed each day of the Sukkot holiday" (Alfred Kolotch, *The Jewish Book of Why*, p. 250).

In the book *Celebrate! The Complete Jewish Holidays Handbook*, we read:

"Khag HaAsif (Festival of Ingathering) was to take place once the produce of the vineyards and product of the threshing rooms was collected (Exo.23:14-17; 34:22). Beginning on the fifteenth of the seventh month, this Khag Adonai (Festival of God) would last seven days, the first a sacred occasion when no work was to be done. **The Israelites were to take the 'product of hadar trees, branches of palm trees, boughs of leafy trees, and willows of the brook' (later called the four species) and rejoice with them before God.**

"Then another dimension was added as a 'law for all time.' For the duration of the festival the Israelites were to live in booths (sukkot) 'so that future generations will know that I made the Israelite people live in sukkot when I brought them out of the land of Egypt, I the Lord your God' (Leviticus 23:39-43)" (p. 211). [emphasis mine]

"The specifics of the Jewish harvest festival were designed to protect the Israelites from the pagan influences they would encounter once they entered Canaan.[58] While

---

[57] For a good article on rejoicing during the Feast or Tabernacles, which is typological of what to expect during the Millennium, have a read of Clayton Steep, "Why should you rejoice at the Feast?" *Good News*, Sept 1982, pp. 7-10.
[58] The Canaanites may be regarded as the most degenerate of peoples in the Scriptures. Their carnality, lying, bullying, sublety, slander, forming gangs, cheating and such like are notorious. However, Paul Copan writing in *Is God a Moral Monster? Making Sense of the Old Testament God*, states: "Canaanite idolatry wasn't simply an abstract theology or personal interest carried out in the privacy of one's home. It was a worldview that profoundly influenced Canaanite society. Given this setting, it's no wonder God didn't want the Israelites to

heathens worshipped nature itself, the Jews were to worship the Creator and Renewer of nature. While the pagans celebrated with excess and debauchery, the Israelite pilgrims were to focus on the moral significance of the festivities.

"The purpose of rejoicing was not sensual abandon but to honor and thank God for His blessings, spread good fortune, and act with sensitivity" (p. 212). [emphasis mine and a lesson for us today][59]

An intriguing clue as to what all this means is found in Nehemiah:

"And they found it written in the Law that the LORD had commanded by Moses that the people of Israel should dwell in booths during the feast of the seventh month, and that they should proclaim it and publish it in all their towns and in Jerusalem, "Go out to the hills and bring branches of olive, wild olive, myrtle, palm, and other leafy trees to make booths, as it is written." (Neh 8:14-15, ESV)

An article at www.wildolive.co.uk/sukot.htm explains this:

"Literally translated it lists, "branches of *zayith* (wild olive), and branches of tree *shemen* (oil) (cultivated olive) and branches of *hadas* (Myrtle) and branches of *Tamarim* (palms) and branches of trees thickets.

It is interesting to see wild olive branches included in the Feast of Ingathering right back in the times of the prophets.

---

associate with the Canaanites and be led astray from obedience to the one true God. He wanted to have Israel morally and theologically separate from the peoples around them. In other words, the land of Canaan was no paradise before the Israelites got there. Israel had no inherent right to inhabit the land (as an undeserved gift from God), and neither did the Canaanites have a right to remain in it. In fact, both the Canaanites and the Israelites would experience (partial) removal from the land because of their wickedness." (p. 161)

"Though Esau didn't receive the inheritance rights, he was still reconciled to his trickster brother at story's end (Gen. 33:4). Esau succeeded while Cain failed. God shouldn't be blamed in either scenario. And when it comes to Israel and the nations, God's choosing Israel didn't exclude other nations from salvation (e.g., Rahab, Ruth, Nineveh in Jonah's day). Indeed, God's desire is to include all who will come to him. Even within Israel, God chose the tribe of Judah, through which the Davidic Messiah would come. Again, this was a means of bringing salvation to the Jews but also to the Gentiles. Just because God chose to work through Judah, who had a besmirched reputation (Gen. 37:23—27; 38), didn't mean that Joseph (a man of faith and integrity) couldn't experience salvation or receive God's blessing through trust and obedience. Besides this, consider how some persons are more intelligent, athletic, artistic, or pleasant looking than others. We don't have perfect equality here, except in the dignity and worth of each individual. Yes, those apparently less endowed can become resentful or jealous of those seemingly more endowed, or one can recognize the graces one has received and constructively deal with disappointments. In fact, some of the presumed assets of money, good looks, or intelligence can actually be spiritual hindrances and sources of pride and self-sufficiency." (pp. 200-01)

[59] Josephus adds to this historical knowledge:

"Upon the fifteenth day of the same month, when the season of the year is changing for winter, the law enjoins us to pitch tabernacles in every one of our houses, so that we preserve ourselves from the cold of that time of the year; as also that when we should arrive at our own country, and come to that city which we should have then for our metropolis, because of the temple therein to be built, and keep a festival of eight days, and offer burnt offerings, and sacrifice thank offerings, that **we should then carry in our hands a branch of myrtle, and willow, and a bough of the palm tree, with the addition of the pome citron**" (*Antiquities of the Jews*, bk.3, chap. 10, par. 4). [emphasis mine]

The Four Species

The Jews have a pictorial ritual using a citron (or Etrog) and branches from three trees, bound together, representing four sorts of people, all bound together in one (Jewish) nation under GOD'S care.

At various times during the celebrations, the four species (*Arba minim*) are waved in all six directions (North, South, East, West, up and down) to emphasise that God is everywhere. They are also carried in procession around the *bimah* in the synagogue. The processions, carrying the arba minim are called *Hoshannas* because a prayer including the refrain *Hosha na* is recited. *Hosha na* means "Save us". (Here we have the connection with palm branches and hosannas as *Yeshua* rode into Jerusalem)

The Nations

The bundle of the four species is waved to all four points of the compass, signifying that the ministry is to the whole world through God's chosen people of priests (Israel). Also, seventy bulls were sacrificed during *Sukkot*; seventy being the number of nations in the known world at that time. Thus *Sukkot* is a feast for the nations - not just Israel.

Tabernacles figures prominently in the last chapters of Zechariah. The prophet talks of the nations coming to attack Jerusalem and then, after God has defeated them, of the nations coming up to Jerusalem at Tabernacles. Clearly this talks of representatives of the nations (the armies first, and then the nations' chosen representatives)

Remember that Tabernacles is all about the culmination or completion of God's purposes, when Jerusalem is the metropolis of God's Kingdom on Earth - not just of Israel. Tabernacles is also about Ingathering. The *Talmud* and the *Mishna* single out Tabernacles as being prophetic of when, after Israel's national Day of Atonement, **the nation will be the channel of blessing for the world - spreading the knowledge of their Messiah over the whole earth.**" [emphasis mine]

Alfred Edersheim writing in *The Temple: Its Ministry and Services* throws additional light on this intriguing matter:

"As usual, we are met at the outset by a controversy between the Pharisees and the Sadducees. The law had it: 'Ye shall take you on the first day the fruit of goodly trees, branches of palm trees, and the boughs of thick trees, and willows of the brook,' which the Sadducees understood (as do the modern Karaite Jews) to refer to the materials whence the booths were to be constructed, while the Pharisees applied it to what the worshippers were to carry in their hands. The latter interpretation is, in all likelihood, the correct one; it seems borne out by the account of the festival at the time of Nehemiah, when the booths were constructed of branches of other trees than those mentioned in Leviticus 23; and it was universally adopted in practice at the time of Christ" (p. 273).

"The most joyous of all festive seasons in Israel was that of the 'Feast of Tabernacles.' It fell on a time of year when the hearts of the people would naturally be full of thanks- fulness, gladness, and expectancy. All the crops had been long stored; and now all fruits were also gathered, the vintage past, and the land only awaited the softening and refreshment of the 'latter rain,' to prepare it for a new crop ... If the beginning of the harvest had pointed back to the birth of Israel in their Exodus from Egypt, and forward to the true Passover-sacrifice in the future; if the corn harvest was connected to the giving of the law on Mount Sinai in the past, and the out-pouring of the Holy Spirit on the day of Pentecost; the harvest-thanksgiving of the Feast of Tabernacles reminded Israel, on the one hand, of their dwelling in booths in the wilderness, while, on the other hand, **it pointed to the final harvest when Israel's mission should be completed, and all nations gathered unto the Lord**" (pp. 268-269). [emphasis mine][60]

In the meantime, God's emphasis is on Israel (Matt 2:6; 10:23; 15:24; 19:28; Luke 2:32-34; 22:29-30; John 1:49; Acts 1:6; 15:16; 28:20; Rom 11:11-31). Paul, however, was sent to the gentiles (Acts 9:15; 22:21; Rom 15:15-18). Other Scriptures bear out that salvation was coming to the gentiles too (Matt 8:10; 15:21-28; 28:19; Mark 4:24-31; 8:27-30; Acts 10:28).[61]

During the Feast of Tabernacles 189 animals were sacrificed.

The figure of 189 animal sacrifices included 70 bullocks representing the 70 gentile nations (Noah's 3 sons, 16 grandsons and 51 other descendants). The offering of the bullocks represented the redemption of the nations and their being offered to God – to be accepted

---

[60] As Middleton wrote: "God sends his son, Jesus the Christ, as a helper or agent to restore Israel to their purpose and task. It is important to note that, in terms of the plot structure of the Bible, **Jesus did not come initially to save the world from sin, but to restore Israel—and this is confirmed by looking at the actual ministry and message of Jesus in the Gospels. Not only do we have Jesus' famous comments to a Canaanite woman about his mission to "the "lost sheep" of the house of Israel,"** (Matthew 15:21-28), but he also commissions the Twelve (symbolizing the core of a restored remnant) to aid him in this mission (Matthew 10:1-16). In this first commissioning of "apostles" (meaning "sent ones"), Jesus explicitly enjoins them not to go to the Gentiles or the Samaritans, but only to the towns of Israel.

"Plot Level 2: The Gentile Mission

Of course, by the end of Matthew, after the death and resurrection of Jesus, when a sufficiently large body of (Jewish) disciples have been gathered, the risen Jesus finally commissions **the apostles to take up the Abrahamic task, namely to go to the nations/Gentiles** with the message of the Gospel. The story of the Gentile mission then takes up much of the book of Acts and is the background to the Pauline and general epistles." (J. Richard Middleton, "A New Heaven and a New Earth: The case for a holistic reading of the Biblical Story of Redemption," *Journal for Christian Theological Research*, Vol. 11, 2006, p. 84)

"... (1 Peter 2:9) ... **This is a continuation of the Abrahamic calling. God's redeemed people are called to mediate blessing to the world** ...

The Gentile mission that was inaugurated with the call of Abraham/Israel is here portrayed as complete— the nations have received the blessing of salvation ... the redeemed human race will once again utilize their God-given power and agency to rule the earth as God intended." (ibid, p. 85) [emphasis mine]

[61] "... Thus in its reference to the harvest it is called 'the feast of ingathering' (Exo.23:16; 34:22); in that to the history of Israel in the past, 'the Feast of Tabernacles' (Lev. 23:34, and specifically verse 43; Deut.16:13, 16; 31:10; II Chron.8:13; Ezra 3:4); while its symbolic bearing on the future is brought out in its designation as emphatically 'the feast' (I Kings 8:2; II Chron.5:3; 7:8,9); and 'the Feast of Jehovah' (so literally in Lev.23:39). In this sense also Josephus, Philo, and the Rabbis (in many passages of the Mishnah) **single it out from all the other feasts**" (Alfred Edersheim, *The Temple: Its Ministry and Services,*pp. 269-70). [emphasis mine]

by Him. NB: 70 people from the household of Jacob journeyed as pilgrims to Egypt (Gen 46:27) – as if to portray that Israel was the first nation God dealt with and would eventually rule over the other nations.[62,63]

As pointed out above, there are a number of different categories of 182 sacrifices plus the meal offering that are divisible by 7, viz:

- 70 bulls = 7 x 10
- 14 rams = 7 x 2
- 98 lambs = 7 x 14
- In addition there are 7 purification offerings
- Plus meal offerings: 336 tenths of ephahs of flour = 7 x 48

We should also consider that this is the seventh holy day held in the seventh month.

> **"The sacrifices made throughout the week -- a total of seventy-- were understood to represent the seventy nations that then existed in the world**. Their well-being, like Israel's, depended on whether or not they would receive the rain needed for food supplies. Blessings like rain were understood as rewards for proper behavior (Deut. 11:13-15) (In his vision of messianic times, Zechariah presents lack of rain as punishment for the nations that fail to make pilgrimage to Jerusalem on Sukkot to worship God, which would show that they accept His sovereignty. This prophecy, and those of Isaiah and Micah calling on all nations to show their acceptance of God's sovereignty by going to His Temple -- combined with the connection between Sukkot and fulfillment, **the ultimate being messianic redemption -- encouraged many proselytes to join the pilgrims in Jerusalem**)" (*Celebrate! The Complete Jewish Holidays Handbook*, p. 214)

This will be the time when God calls all to salvation – a period of saving the world. It will be a time of true global evangelisation, when Israelite missions will be sent to nations in

---

[62] These 70 "descended from Noah's three sons, thereby indicating that the total population of the world came from Noah's seed" (Noga Ayali-Darshan, *Sukkot's Seventy Bulls*, p. 5). Note also her article "The Seventy Bulls Sacrificed at Sukkot (Num 29:12-34) in Light of a Ritual Text from Emar *(Emar 6, 373)*" demonstrates, to me, that the pagan nations round-about Israel, had religious system that may be termed a "counterfeit.""

[63] Another work to take note of is *The Fall Feasts of Israel*:

"The order of sacrifices on Sukkot is spelled out in minute detail in the book of Numbers. Never before had so many sacrifices been required of Israel on any one day. The vast number of sacrifices were commensurate with Israel's depth of thanksgiving for a bountiful harvest.

"A fascinating and mysterious pattern emerges from the seemingly endless list of sacrifices. **No matter how the offerings are grouped or counted, their number always remains divisible by the number seven.** During the week are offered 70 bullocks, 14 rams and 98 lambs -- altogether 182 sacrifices (26 x 7), to which must be added 336 (48 x 7) tenths of ephahs of flour for the meal offering …

"It was no coincidence that this seven-day holiday, which took place in the height of the seventh month, had the perfect number, seven, imprinted on its sacrifices. It was by divine design that the final holiday … bore on its sacrifices the seal of God's perfect approval" (Mitch & Zhava Glazer, *The Fall Feasts of Israel*, p. 163). [emphasis mine]

every corner of the world, reaching those who have 'not heard my fame or seen my glory' (Is 66:19, ESV). It will be a time when the nations will rejoice (Isaiah 12:4).

Of further interest is the Solomonic typology. Many scholars of Biblical typology are of the view that, amongst other things, the Solomonic era and Temple portrayed the Millennium in a number of ways.

For instance, the Temple was dedicated during this Feast, which pictures the Millennium. Notice:

> **"Likewise, when a foreigner, who is not of your people Israel, comes from a far country for your name's sake**
>
> **(for they shall hear of your great name and your mighty hand, and of your outstretched arm)**, when he comes and prays toward this house,
>
> hear in heaven your dwelling place and do according to all for which the foreigner calls to you, in order that all the peoples of the earth may know your name and fear you, as do your people Israel, and that they may know that this house that I have built is called by your name.
>
> "If your people go out to battle against their enemy, by whatever way you shall send them, and they pray to the LORD toward the city that you have chosen and the house that I have built for your name,
>
> then hear in heaven their prayer and their plea, and maintain their cause." (IKings 8:41-45, ESV)

This seems prophetic of the Millennium:

> "For I know their works and their thoughts, and **the time is coming to gather all nations and tongues. And they shall come and shall see my glory,**
>
> and I will set a sign among them. And from them I will send survivors to the nations, to Tarshish, Pul, and Lud, who draw the bow [Hebrew for *draw* is maw-shak' which may refer to the ancient Moschi or Meschech], to Tubal and Javan, to the coastlands far away, that have not heard my fame or seen my glory. And they shall declare my glory among the nations." (Is 66:18-19, ESV)

Other typologies include:

- His Temple was full of splendour, typing the Millennium (IKings 6:1-14. Cp Zech 6:12-13). It even contained 7 lamps on each of the 10 lampstands which equals to 70 (IKings 7:49; IIChron 4:7). Could this represent the spiritual light of God's Way offered to the gentiles?
- Solomon probably typed Christ as the Melchizedek Priest-King (Ps 110)
- Fair judgment and rulings were the order of the day (IKings 2:25-46. Cp Matt 25:31-32)
- Rule with great wisdom (IKings 3:5-13. Cp Is 11:1-5)
- A time of peace – as the Millennium will eventually be a time of peace (IChron 22:6-9; Cp Is 2:2-4; 9:6-8; 11:6-9)

- Glory of the Lord visible (IKings 8:6-11. Cp Is 24:23; 40:5; 60:1-3 Is 4:2-6; Ezek 43:1-5; Hag 2:3-9)
- Israel will reign supreme (IKings 10:23-27. Cp Mic 4:2; Zech 8:20-23).[64]

GATHERING IN OF THE NATIONS – THEIR TIME TO BE OFFERED SALVATION

As we can see, there was great rejoicing before the Lord and celebration during the Feast of Tabernacles because of the gathering in of all the nations – by offering them salvation. What a wonderful event to be happy about!

Starting in a small way, gentile peoples were being called during the time of the early Church and ever since:

> "Simeon has related how God first visited the Gentiles, to take from them a people for his name.
>
> And with this the words of the prophets agree, just as it is written,
>
> "After this I will return, and I will rebuild the tent of David that has fallen; I will rebuild its ruins, and I will restore it, that the remnant of mankind may seek the Lord, and all the Gentiles who are called by my name, says the Lord, who makes these things known from of old.'
>
> Therefore my judgment is that we should not trouble those of the Gentiles who turn to God" (Acts 15:14-19, ESV)

Over some period of time during the Messiah's reign, the nations will learn to repent gradually and sequentially. They will, at last, be considered to be like Israel, as a number of Scriptures demonstrate and which are presented below for your reading and study:

> "Blessed is the nation whose God is the Lᴏʀᴅ, the people whom he has chosen **as his heritage**!" (Ps 33:12, ESV. Cp Ps 47:7-9; Jer 18:6-10)

> **"All the ends of the earth shall remember and turn to the LORD, and all the families of the nations shall worship before you**.
>
> For kingship belongs to the LORD, and he rules over the nations." (Ps 22:27-28, ESV)

> **"For God is the King of all the earth**; sing praises with a psalm!
>
> **God reigns over the nations**; God sits on his holy throne.
>
> **The princes of the peoples gather as the people of the God of Abraham**. For the shields of the earth belong to God; he is highly exalted!" (Ps 47:7-9, ESV) [cp Ps 33:12; Ezek 25:14; Is 11:14; 19:24-25; Gen 27:29]

---

[64] Dr Rick Sherrod made reference to the Solomonic typologies in his article "Solomon's Splendor. A Type of God's Kingdom," *Good News*, September 1984, pp. 25-27.

"To the choirmaster: with stringed instruments. A Psalm. A Song. May God be gracious to us and bless us and make his face to shine upon us, Selah.

That your way may be known on earth, **your saving power among all nations**.

Let the peoples praise you, O God; let all the peoples praise you!

Let the nations be glad and sing for joy, for you judge the peoples with equity and guide the nations upon earth. Selah.

Let the peoples praise you, O God; let all the peoples praise you!

The earth has yielded its increase; God, our God, shall bless us.

God shall bless us; let all the ends of the earth fear him!" (Ps 67:1-7, ESV)

"On this mountain the LORD of hosts will make for all peoples a feast of rich food, a feast of well-aged wine, of rich food full of marrow, of aged wine well refined.

And he will swallow up on this mountain the covering that is cast over all peoples, the veil that is spread over all nations." (Is 25:6-7, ESV)

"Let not the foreigner who has joined himself to the LORD say, "The LORD will surely separate me from his people"; and let not the eunuch say, "Behold, I am a dry tree."

For thus says the LORD: "To the eunuchs who keep my Sabbaths, who choose the things that please me and hold fast my covenant,

I will give in my house and within my walls a monument and a name better than sons and daughters; I will give them an everlasting name that shall not be cut off.

"And the foreigners who join themselves to the LORD, to minister to him, to love the name of the LORD, and to be his servants, everyone who keeps the Sabbath and does not profane it, and holds fast my covenant—these I will bring to my holy mountain, and make them joyful in my house of prayer; their burnt offerings and their sacrifices will be accepted on my altar; for my house shall be called a house of prayer for all peoples."

The Lord GOD, who gathers the outcasts of Israel [Second Exodus], declares, **"I will gather yet others to him besides those already gathered**." (Is 56:3-8, ESV)

"For I know their works and their thoughts, and **the time is coming to gather all nations and tongues. And they shall come and shall see my glory**, and I will set a sign among them. And from them I will send survivors to the nations, to Tarshish, Pul, and Lud, who draw the bow, to Tubal and Javan, to the coastlands far away, that have not heard my fame or seen my glory. And they shall declare my glory among the nations.

And they shall bring all your brothers from all the nations as an offering to the LORD, on horses and in chariots and in litters and on mules and on dromedaries, to my holy mountain Jerusalem, says the LORD, just as the Israelites bring their grain offering in a clean vessel to the house of the LORD.

And some of them also I will take for priests and for Levites, says the LORD." (Is 66:18-21, ESV)

"At that time Jerusalem shall be called the throne of the LORD, and **all nations shall gather to it, to the presence of the LORD in Jerusalem**, and they shall no more stubbornly follow their own evil heart." (Jer 3:17, ESV)

"In that day I will raise up the booth of David that is fallen and repair its breaches, and raise up its ruins and rebuild it as in the days of old, that they may possess the remnant of Edom and **all the nations who are called by my name,**" declares the LORD who does this." (Amos 9:11-12, ESV)

"Sing and rejoice, O daughter of Zion, for behold, I come and I will dwell in your midst, declares the LORD.

And **many nations shall join themselves to the LORD in that day, and shall be my people.** And I will dwell in your midst, and you shall know that the LORD of hosts has sent me to you." (Zech. 2:10-11, ESV).

This great harvest of humans – the nations – to be converted, offered salvation and come under the control of the Messiah is one of the clear meanings of this holy day period!

How will it be executed? It will be accomplished through Israel as His instrument to rule and help convert the nations to Him. The nations conquered by Israel during the early part of the Messiah's reign will also be tried and tested to see where their hearts really are: with Him or with selfishness.

As explained in the chapter *Judging of the Nations*, this great harvest (and judgment) is God assessing the nations to see if they really do want to obey Him or not.

Metaphorically, a *harvest* is normally an allusion to some sort of judgment, assessment or punishment. He is God of harvests and Israel can be harvested (Hosea 6:11) and He can even take the harvest away (Hosea 2:9; Isaiah 18:4-6; Jeremiah 12:13).

His harvest can be severe such as that on sinful Babylon (Jeremiah 51:33). These sorts of harvests do not display the rejoicing that occurred during the Feast of Tabernacles – instead they portrayed severity of punishment. Christ uses similar language in Matthew 13:30, 38-39 and it is also used as a metaphor for judgment in Revelation 14:15.

But Israel must be punished and cleansed prior to them becoming upright and ready to execute the conquest and conversion of the nations. Their ultimate duty as a servant people to help uplift the nations will then be fulfilled.

"In that day the branch of the LORD shall be beautiful and glorious, and the fruit of the land shall be the pride and honor of the survivors of Israel.

And he who is left in Zion and remains in Jerusalem will be called holy, everyone who has been recorded for life in Jerusalem, when the Lord shall have washed away the filth of the daughters of Zion and cleansed the bloodstains of Jerusalem from its midst by a spirit of judgment and by a spirit of burning.

Then the LORD will create over the whole site of Mount Zion and over her assemblies a cloud by day, and smoke and the shining of a flaming fire by night; for over all the glory there will be a canopy.

There will be a booth for shade by day from the heat, and for a refuge and a shelter from the storm and rain." (Is 4:2-6, ESV)

Refer to the chapter *Israel's Role after the Second Exodus* for further information and detail. Now Israel will be prepared for anything. She will have faith in her Saviour and trust him after so many millennia. There will be an attempted invasion of gentile armies as we have seen, outlined in Ezekiel chapters 38 and 39, and Israel will be ready for this event when the Messiah uses this rebellion to bring to heel many nations (refer to the chapter *A War even after the Messiah's Return!*):

"I will cut off the chariot from Ephraim and the war horse from Jerusalem; and the battle bow shall be cut off, **and he shall speak peace to the nations; his rule shall be from sea to sea, and from the river to the ends of the earth.**

As for you also, because of the blood of my covenant with you, I will set your prisoners free from the waterless pit.

Return to your stronghold, O prisoners of hope; today I declare that I will restore to you double.

For I have bent Judah as my bow; I have made Ephraim its arrow. I will stir up your sons, O Zion, against your sons, O Greece, and wield you like a warrior's sword." (Zech 9:10-13, ESV)

Some conservative scholars explain this well:

"... the nations were portrayed in the Old Testament as witness of all that God was doing in, for or to Israel ... the expectation of Israel's faith and worship (if not always the outcome of their practice) was that the nations would come to benefit from that salvation and give thanks for it. **This meant that the nations would eventually acknowledge and worship Israel's God**, YHWH, with all the concomitant responsibilities and blessings of such worship"

"... **Israel definitely had a sense of mission**, not in the sense of *going* somewhere but of *being* something. They were to be the holy people of the living God YHWH. They were to know him for who he is, to preserve the true and exclusive worship [of] YHWH, and to live according to his ways and laws within loyal commitment to their covenantal relationship with him. In all these respects they would *be* a light and witness to the nations..." (Christopher Wright, *The Mission of God*, pp. 455, 504). [emphasis mine]

"For according to the prophet's meaning, to be ruled by the people of God is the true happiness of the nations, and to allow themselves to be so ruled is their true liberty" (Keil & Delitzsch, *Isaiah. Commentary on the Old Testament*, p. 199).

The expression "all peoples" [in Gen 12:3] did not mean that every person on earth would universally believe in the Messiah, but that every ethnic group would receive this blessing of God's grace and the joy of participating in worshiping and serving him. God would do this both by his own sovereignty (for he bound himself by a unilateral oath, as we shall see later) and through the instrumentality of those who had previously experienced the blessing of God." (Walter Kaiser, *Mission in the Old Testament. Israel as a Light to the Nations*, pp. 8-9. The entire book is worth a read)

"This election of the Jewish nation [i.e., Israel] was an absolute, unconditional (i.e. relating to the purpose of God) election so far as its national descent from Abraham is affected, i.e. **the kingdom is solely promised to the descendants of Abraham in** their national aspect (which is verified, as we shall see hereafter, by the covenants, confirmed by oath); and hence arises the necessity of Gentiles (as we shall show), who shall participate in this Kingdom, being grated in, becoming members of, the commonwealth of Israel." (George Peters, *The Theocratic Kingdom of our Lord Jesus, the Christ, as Covenanted in the Old Testament and Revealed in the New*, (Vol. 1), p. 209) [emphasis mine]

WHY REJOICING?

The Feast of Tabernacles is a time of special rejoicing by the Church of God groups, Messianics and Jews. Why is this the case?

Answer: they realize that God actually **commands** His people to rejoice during that Feast. It is a time to be happy, celebrate and demonstrate to Him your gratitude for all He has done for you, Israel and soon – all the nations of mankind.

Figure 19 Peace will eventually reign

Note the following Scriptures on rejoicing which are clearly Millennial prophecies. Read, study and rejoice in them:

"The wilderness and the solitary place shall be glad for them (Israel); and the desert shall blossom as the rose. It shall blossom abundantly, and **rejoice** even with joy and singing: the glory of Lebanon shall be given unto it, the excellency of Carmel and Sharon, they shall see the glory of the LORD, and the excellency of our God." (Is 35:1-2, KJV)

"Great is the LORD, and greatly to be praised, in the city of our God, His holy mountain. Beautiful in elevation, the joy of the whole earth, is Mount Zion in the far north, the city of the great King. God, in her palaces, has made Himself known as a stronghold … Let Mount Zion be glad, let the daughters of Judah **rejoice** because of Your judgments. Walk about Zion and go around her; count her towers; consider her ramparts; go through her palaces, that you may tell it to the next generation" (Ps 48:1-3, 11-13, ESV).

"Behold, this is our God, we have waited for Him and He will save us; this is the LORD; we have waited for Him, we will be glad and **rejoice** in His salvation" (Isa. 25: 9, KJV).

Let the heavens rejoice, let the earth be glad; Let the sea roar and the fulness thereof. Let the field be joyful, and all that is therein; Then shall all the trees of the wood **sing joyously** Before the Lord; for He is come. He is come to judge the earth. He judges the world in righteousness And the peoples in His faithfulness." (Ps 96:11-13, KJV)

"Jehovah reigneth, let the earth exult: Let the multitude of the isles **rejoice**. Cloud and darkness are round about Him, Righteousness and judgment are the foundations of His throne. A fire goeth before Him, And consumeth His adversaries all around. His lightnings flash over the world: The earth saw and trembled, The mountains melted like wax at the presence of Jehovah – At the presence of the Lord of the whole earth." (Ps 97:1-5, ASV)

"Let the sea roar and the fulness thereof; The world and its inhabitants. Let the rivers **clap their hands**, Let the hills together **sing for joy** Before Jehovah - For He came to judge the earth; He shall judge the world in righteousness. And the peoples with fairness." (Ps 97:7-9, ASV)

"… the mountains and the hill; shall break forth before you into **singing**, and all the trees of the field shall **clap their hands**" (Is 55: 12, ASV).

"**Sing and rejoice**, O daughter of Zion, for behold, I come and I will dwell in your midst, declares the LORD.

And **many nations shall join themselves to the LORD in that day, and shall be my people**. And I will dwell in your midst, and you shall know that the LORD of hosts has sent me to you." (Zech 2:10-11, ESV).

"For the LORD has ransomed Jacob and has redeemed him from hands too strong for him. [i.e., the Second Exodus]

They shall come and sing aloud on the height of Zion, and **they shall be radiant** over the goodness of the LORD, over the grain, the wine, and the oil, and over the young of the flock and the herd; their life shall be like a watered garden, and they shall languish no more.

Then shall the young women **rejoice in the dance**, and the young men and the old shall be merry. I will turn their mourning into joy; I will comfort them, and give them gladness for sorrow.

I will feast the soul of the priests with abundance, and my people shall be satisfied with my goodness, declares the LORD." (Jer 31:11-14, ESV)

Why rejoice so much? Because so many nations will be joined to the Lord during His reign. It will be a time of outgoing concern for others, prosperity and security for all. Happiness will be the order of the day.

> "To the choirmaster: with stringed instruments. A Psalm. A Song. May God be gracious to us and bless us and make his face to shine upon us, Selah.
>
> that your way may be known on earth, your saving power among all nations.
>
> **Let the peoples praise you, O God; let all the peoples praise you!**
>
> **Let the nations be glad and sing for joy**, for you judge the peoples with equity and guide the nations upon earth. Selah.
>
> **Let the peoples praise you, O God; let all the peoples praise you!**
>
> The earth has yielded its increase; God, our God, shall bless us.
>
> God shall bless us; let all the ends of the earth fear him!" (Ps 67:1-7, ESV) [65]

All of us should be so happy for what God will do among the nations. Rejoice in this future event!

CONCLUDING REMARKS

This study has highlighted a very important aspect of the Feast of Tabernacles: the ingathering or conversion of the gentile nations under guidance from Israel and the saints, during the Millennial reign of the Messiah.

Some have understood that God is not calling many people today to spiritual salvation whether they be Israelite or gentile. Here are extracts from the literature of that time:

> **"God's Spiritual Harvests**
>
> In the land settled by ancient Israel (later known as Palestine and now occupied by the modern state of Israel), there is a small spring grain harvest followed by a

---

[65] In another publication Kaiser is adamant that "**Israel was to be kings and priests to God on behalf of the nations; they were to be mediators of the gospel as missionaries to the world** ("in your seed shall all the nations of the earth be blessed," (Gen 12:3b) and they were to be partakers in the present aspects and coming reality of the "kingdom of God."" (*Exodus. Expositors Bible Commentary*, Vol. 2, p. 417) [emphasis mine]

Oswalt explains: "To whom are the promises given? Just to the people of Israel? Hardly. They are given to those of all flesh who worship him from month to month and Sabbath to Sabbath. This is the ultimate end [result] of Israel's religion, that everyone should have opportunity of joining Israel in worshiping the one God (cf. Zech. 14:16-21). Israel is not to be separate so that it can revel in its separateness, but so that its faith can survive to be declared" (John Oswalt, *The Book of Isaiah Chapters 40-66. The New International Commentary on the Old Testament*, p. 691).

much larger late summer and autumn harvest. These yearly agricultural harvests are symbolic of God's spiritual "harvests" of mankind!

Today, we can understand from the teachings of Christ and the apostles that God intends the spring festivals to illustrate that all those He has called to become His Spirit-begotten children before Christ's Second Coming are only the "firstfruits" harvest (Jas. 1:18)—only the relatively small beginning of His spiritual harvest of individuals into His divine Family.

The festivals of the much larger autumn harvest season picture God's calling of thousands of millions of humanity to salvation and Sonship in His glorious Family after Christ's return.

In Leviticus 23, we find a summary of these annual festivals. The first three, beginning with the Passover, are memorials of the first part of God's Master Plan. They picture the firstfruits of Christ's labors. The last four festivals look forward to the future and show how and when God will reap the great autumn harvest of people into His Family!" (*Ambassador College Bible Correspondence Course*, Lesson 23, "What is God's Purpose for Mankind?", pp. 4-5)

Herbert W Armstrong wrote the following in his famous booklet *Pagan Holidays – or God's Holy Days – Which?*

"Notice that the Festival of Tabernacles is to be held "at the year's end" (Ex. 34:22). In this verse the Festival of Tabernacles or Booths is specifically called the "feast of ingathering." The harvest year ended at the beginning of autumn. Just as Pentecost pictures the early harvest — this church age, so the Festival of Ingatherings or Tabernacles pictures the fall harvest — the great harvest of souls in the Millennium!" (p. 44)

The Jews, some scholars and many Messianics understand that to one degree or another. Yet many Churches have given very little attention to it. The Millennium, as we know, will be a time when Godly knowledge and practice will be spread by Israel across the entire world and engulf the gentiles:

"They shall not hurt or destroy in all my holy mountain; for the earth shall be full of the knowledge of the LORD as the waters cover the sea." (Is 11:9, ESV)

Yet the nations will be tested during this period, to see where their hearts are.

"As the Millennium, therefore, although a vast advance ... upon this present time, will not be a perfect state to the inhabitants of the earth because they will still be in the flesh; **it will be necessary ... that there should be ... a test of their obedience ... in the Millennium**." (Robert Brown, *Outlines of Prophetic Truth*)

This great 1,000-year period itself has a variety of purposes, including being a foretype of the eternal Kingdom itself as Professor James McGrath explains:

"... the **millennial period either foreshadows or symbolises this eternal ideal**" (James McGrath, *The Only True God: Early Christian Monotheism in its Jewish Context*, p. 74). [emphasis mine]

It will be a time of extraordinary splendour and happiness, though with some trials and tests. It will not be a 'bed of roses.' But it will be **the wonderful world tomorrow!**

"All the ends of the earth shall remember and turn to the LORD, and **all the families of the nations shall worship before you**.

For kingship belongs to the LORD, and **he rules over the nations**." (Ps 22:27-28, ESV)

"On this mountain the LORD of hosts will **make for all peoples** a feast of rich food, a feast of well-aged wine, of rich food full of marrow, of aged wine well refined. [foretyped by the Feast of Tabernacles]

And he will swallow up on this mountain the covering that is cast over all peoples, the veil that is spread over all nations." (Is 25:6-7, ESV)

In other words, there will be no more spiritual blindness. And as Joyce Baldwin claims

"**The one festival uniting all nations in worship is to be the feast of booths**... it was open to all, including 'the stranger'... The reference in Nehemiah shows that the festival was ... an occasion for hearing the law read. In God's kingdom, the gentiles would be brought within that covenant when they came to worship in the Temple *the King, the Lord of hosts*..." (*Haggai, Zechariah, Malachi: An Introduction and Commentary. Tyndale Old Testament Commentaries*, p. 206). [emphasis mine]

Then, and only then, will the nations be free of sin and come to salvation.

"Before the Lord: for He cometh, for **He cometh to judge the Earth**: He shall judge the World with righteousness, and the people with His truth." (Ps.96:13, KJV)

"But those mine enemies, which would not that I should reign over them, bring hither, and **slay them before me**." (Luke 19:12-14, 27, KJV)

Kiss the Son, lest he be angry, and **ye perish from the way, when his wrath is kindled but a little**. Blessed are all they that put their trust in him. (Ps 2:1-12, KJV)

And they shall go forth, and **look upon the carcases of the men that have transgressed against me**: for their worm shall not die, neither shall their fire be quenched; and they shall be an abhorring unto all flesh." (Is 66:24, KJV)

CHAPTER TWELVE

JUDGING OF THE NATIONS

INTRODUCTORY REMARKS

IN AUGUST 2018, SEVERAL YEARS after writing this chapter (it was initially a Bible Study), I noticed the following statement that dove-tailed perfectly with this study:

> "Matthew 25:31-34 ... Notice, all those called and saved *prior* to Christ's second appearing on earth had been SEPARATED from the unsaved before Christ stood upon earth – while still in the clouds of the air – *before* He sits upon the throne of His glory!
>
> The SEPARATION going on *after* He sits upon that throne ruling over THE NATIONS, therefore, is a different, and a succeeding separation!
>
> **Here are earth's nations – earth's mortals – *all* nations! And now begins a process of SEPARATION. It is according to the decisions they make, and the actions they take.** Those who turn to life of RIGHTEOUSNESS are set on the RIGHT hand. They are converted – given IMMORTALITY – because Christ says to them: *"Inherit* the Kingdom!"* – and mortal flesh and blood *cannot* inherit the Kingdom (ICor 15:50).
>
> Those who do evil then receive the full penalty of the law – DEATH! They are sentenced to depart into the lake of fire!
>
> Certainly this passage pictures nothing but a process of salvation going on, after Christ's return, DURING His millennial "Sabbath Day."
>
> That is the great "FALL Harvest of souls!"" ("Predestination ... Does the Bible Teach It?" *Plain Truth*, Nov-Dec 1943, pp. 10-11). [emphasis mine]

Another author explains

> "If, however, the passage [Matt 25:31-46] represents the rule of Christ during a period of time, in which **He deals with the nations as groups**, but judges the individuals in them by their conduct toward each other during the period in which He is personally present, the judgment on the basis of behavior becomes explicable. In the

light of His presence they cannot plead ignorance of His salvation or of His ethical standards, and **their misconduct is utterly without excuse**. As a description of Christ's administration during the millennium it would fit the existing requirements." (Merrill Tenney, "The Importance and Exegesis of Revelation 20:1-8," *Bibliotheca Sacra*, April 1954, pp. 146-47) [emphasis mine]

With that in mind, the reader should be aware that the purpose of this chapter is to attempt to find clarity about Christ dealing with the ingathering of the nations during His reign on earth.

As discussed earlier in this book, many or most Christians totally overlook the fact that God does not *only* work with individuals and families – but also with nations as a collective. In other words, He deals with societies or families that have grown big into nations – as one unit – which in turn means that they have collective responsibility. And collective blessings or suffering and punishment.

In fact, nations are even stereo-typed – just look at Habakkuk 1:5-6 and Titus 1:12-16 for two examples. Traits inherited from forefathers and from national experience imprint on the DNA and national memories and characteristics that carry on down through the centuries.

There is no evidence that the New Testament overturns this Biblical teaching; it continues the teachings of the patriarchs, Moses, King David and the prophets.

All nations have to come to realise that

"Righteousness exalts a nation, but sin is a reproach to any people." (Prov 14:34, ESV)

God Himself says that they are the "families of the earth" or "nations" for they are all unique and different. Some commentators remark accordingly:

"Since the rebellion of nations differ, the circumstance surrounding each situation is not the same, and God's purposes for each nation will vary. No one except a divinely inspired prophet can predict what God will do to other nations in the future." (Gary Smith, *Isaiah 1-39: An Exegetical and Theological Exposition of Holy Scripture*, p. 322)

"These prophecies about the punishment of various nations are actually oracles about God's sovereign power over all the nations of the earth." (p. 291)

One of the great sins was the attempt of nations to unite in Genesis 11:

"the rebellion against God's purpose is seen among the nations, not just among individuals. All nations are plotting to build a tower to reach heaven." (William Chalker, *Science and Faith*, p. 132)

It is self-evident from the Scriptures and the huge number of references to nations, that He has ultimate control and will both punish and bless as necessary.

This leads to many questions arising about this aspect of His Divine rule upon the earth, viz:

- What is meant by Christ ingathering and judging the nations?
- How does He gather?
- How does He separate them – judge them?
- Will this occur directly upon His return or gradually during the Millennium and even after it?
- How long will it take to do this?
- Will Israel be used to bring the nations to repentance?
- Which nations will be involved?
- Does the Old Testament provide clues to this event or series of events?

The Bible shows that over the centuries, He has brought judgment upon many nations. But this will climax during the Day of the Lord and on into the Millennium. It is ongoing, but the most awful and dreadful punishment is yet ahead.

In Matthew we read:

> "When the Son of man shall come in his glory, and all the holy angels with him, then shall he sit upon the throne of his glory:
> And before him shall be gathered all **nations**: and he shall separate them one from another, as a shepherd divideth *his* sheep from the goats:
> And he shall set the sheep on his right hand, but the goats on the left.
> Then shall the King say unto them on his right hand, Come, ye blessed of my Father, inherit the kingdom prepared for you from the foundation of the world" (Matt 25:31-34)

> "Behold my servant, whom I have chosen; my beloved, in whom my soul is well pleased: I will put my spirit upon him, and he shall shew judgment to the Gentiles." (Matt 12:18, KJV)

Nations here according to *Strong's Concordance*:

> "**1484 e;qnoj** ethnos {eth'-nos}
> **Meaning:** 1) a multitude (whether of men or of beasts) associated or living together 1a) a company, troop, swarm 2) a multitude of individuals of the same nature or genus 2a) the human race 3) a race, nation, people group 4) in the OT, foreign nations not worshipping the true God, pagans, Gentiles 5) Paul uses the term for Gentile Christians
> **Origin:** probably from 1486; TDNT - 2:364,201; n n
> **Usage:** AV - Gentiles 93, nation 64, heathen 5, people 2; 164."

Notice again what Christ says about the nations:

> "And seek not ye what ye shall eat, or what ye shall drink, neither be ye of doubtful mind.
> For all these things do the **nations** of the world seek after: and your Father knoweth that ye have need of these things.

But rather seek ye the kingdom of God; and all these things shall be added unto you." (Luke 12:29-31, KJV)

Finally, there will be a little repetition of matters discussed in previous chapters. But that is necessary.

ALL NATIONS TO BE SUBJECT TO CHRIST

The reign of Christ commences the 1,000 years or Millennium – it commences at Zion and quickly spreads into all of Jerusalem, the holy land and gradually radiates across the earth. Some commentators understand this and explain it well:

> "The feasts of Israel were given an eschatological meaning. The Feast of Tabernacles was not only an agricultural festival, a thanksgiving for the land and its harvest: it recalled the dwelling in tabernacles in the wilderness days, and God's provision for the people before they entered their land. The Fourth Gospel probably reflects the ceremonies that later Jewish practice added to the celebration of the feast, as well as the fulfilment of its meaning in Christ.
>
> But there is an eschatological hope connected with the Feast of Tabernacles even in Old Testament days. **In Zechariah xiv the thought of the Feast as the harvest is connected with the ingathering of the nations**. All the nations and families of the earth are summoned to go up to Jerusalem to keep it. Whether or not it can be said to be evident from this passage, it is clear that before the time of Christ, there was, connected with the Feast of Tabernacles, the hope of the future tabernacling of God in the midst of His people in a more glorious way than ever before. It has been sufficiently well established that the Jewish Lectionary antedates the Christian era, and in this Zechariah xiv and 1 Kings viii, Solomon's prayer at the dedication of the temple, were coupled as readings for the Feast of Tabernacles. There can be little doubt of the significance of this fact. The presence of the Lord with His people in the wilderness and in the temple was a picture, or a type, of that more glorious tabernacling in their midst in the day that was yet to be, **when the ingathering of the nations would be fulfilled**." (Francis Foulkes, *The Acts of God. A Study of the Basis of Typology in the Old Testament*, pp. 27-28)
>
> "In the great messianic future, many nations "will be joined with the LORD" (v.11) or "will join themselves to the Lord" (the Hebrew can be rendered either way). Such **an ingathering of the nations to the Lord** echoes the promise in the Abrahamic covenant: "All people on earth will be blessed through you" (Gen 12:3; cf. 18:18 and 22:18; see also Isa 2:2-4; 60:3; Zech 8:20-23). The result is that they too will become the people of God" (Kenneth Barker, *Zechariah, Expositor's Bible Commentary*, Vol. 7, p. 619). [emphasis mine]

It is only then that verse 9 of Isaiah 11 is fulfilled:

> "They shall not hurt nor destroy in all my holy mountain: for the earth shall be full of the knowledge of the LORD, as the waters cover the sea." (KJV)

Figure 20 The Messiah will take this planet forcibly

The context is clearly Millennial:

"And there shall come forth a rod out of the stem of Jesse, and a Branch shall grow out of his roots:

And the spirit of the LORD shall rest upon him, the spirit of wisdom and understanding, the spirit of counsel and might, the spirit of knowledge and of the fear of the LORD;

And shall make him of quick understanding in the fear of the LORD: and he shall not judge after the sight of his eyes, neither reprove after the hearing of his ears:

But with righteousness shall he judge the poor, and reprove with equity for the meek of the earth: **and he shall smite the earth with the rod of his mouth**, and with the breath of his lips shall he slay the wicked. [cp Rev 2:26-27; 19:15; Ob 20; Ezek 25:14; Jer 50:20-23]

And righteousness shall be the girdle of his loins, and faithfulness the girdle of his reins.

The wolf also shall dwell with the lamb, and the leopard shall lie down with the kid; and the calf and the young lion and the fatling together; and a little child shall lead them.

And the cow and the bear shall feed; their young ones shall lie down together: and the lion shall eat straw like the ox.

And the sucking child shall play on the hole of the asp, and the weaned child shall put his hand on the cockatrice' den." (Is 11:1-8, KJV)

Then, over time, all nations will learn His ways and have the knowledge they require for repentance, obedience, salvation and success. But will they all adopt His ways immediately? That is the question.

"**And many nations shall be joined to the LORD** in that day, and shall be my people: and I will dwell in the midst of thee, and thou shalt know that the LORD of hosts hath sent me unto thee.

And the LORD shall inherit Judah his portion in the holy land, and shall choose Jerusalem again.

Be silent, O all flesh, before the LORD: for he is raised up out of his holy habitation." (Zech 2:11-13, KJV)

"Arise, shine; for thy light is come, and the glory of the LORD is risen upon thee.

For, behold, the darkness shall cover the earth, and gross darkness the people: but the LORD shall arise upon thee, and his glory shall be seen upon thee.

And **the Gentiles shall come to thy light, and kings to the brightness of thy rising.**" (Is 60:1-3, KJV)

"**All nations whom thou hast made shall come and worship before thee**, O Lord; and shall glorify thy name." (Ps 86:9, KJV)

As we shall discover, whilst it is true that Christ and the saints will put down unruly and rebellious nations, they will likely also be tested to see if they are willing to observe His law and ways periodically during the Millennium, just as Christians are during their life. For this is how God works – he does not promise us a 'bed of roses' – but He does train and test us and this will not differ for the Messiah's reign.

Testing of the nations will reveal that a percentage of the nations and tribes of the world will harbour resentment toward God's government – they will possess a sort of obedience that is feigned and not genuine. They will have to be conquered and brought to full repentance. Zechariah 14:16-19 and Psalm 149:5-9 exemplify this.

For example:

"For thou, O God, hast proved [i.e. examined or tested] us: thou hast tried us, as silver is tried.

Thou broughtest us into the net; thou laidst affliction upon our loins." (Ps 66:10-11, KJV)[66]

He tests us to see if we really want to follow His way, to prove our faith. It is a very necessary and beneficial part of our walk – it helps us grow and strengthen spiritually. And this shows our true heart.

So it will be for the nations. He will be examining them to see if they really want to be His followers or continue in rebellion. Whether they be genuine or not. But He does not tempt us – i.e. lead us into sin. Satan and the demons do that – see James 1:2-3, 12-15. Rather, as we can see above, He does test us.

---

[66] Other pertinent verses include: Gen 22:1-2; Ex 15:25; 16:4; Deut 8:2-3, 16; 13:3; Jud 3:1, 4; IIChron 32:31; Job 23:10; Ps 26:2; 105:19; 114:4-5; Prov 17:3; Eccl 3:18; Is 48:10; Jer 9:7; 11:20; 12:13; 17:10; John 6:5-6; Rom 16:10; IICor 2:9; IThess 2:4.

This will not be a time of instant, complete peace – instead peace is installed gradually across the earth.

Notice Ps 110:

> "The LORD said unto my Lord, Sit thou at my right hand, until I make thine enemies thy footstool.
>
> The LORD shall send the rod of thy strength out of Zion: rule thou **in the midst of thine enemies**." (Ps110:1-2, KJV) [cp Rev 2:26-27; 19:15; Ob 20; Ezek 25:14; Jer 50:20-23][67]

The Messiah will triumph over His enemies who surround Him! He rules in their midst – this means that even during early period of the Millennium there will be enemy nations!

> "He said therefore, A certain nobleman went into a far country to receive for himself a kingdom, and to return.
>
> And he called his ten servants, and delivered them ten pounds, and said unto them, Occupy till I come.
>
> But his citizens hated him, and sent a message after him, saying, We will not have this *man* to reign over us …
>
> **But those mine enemies, which would not that I should reign over them, bring hither, and slay** *them* **before me.**" (Luke 19:12-14, 27, KJV)

> "For the king trusteth in the LORD, and through the mercy of the most High he shall not be moved.
>
> **Thine hand shall find out all thine enemies: thy right hand shall find out those that hate thee.**
>
> **Thou shalt make them as a fiery oven in the time of thine anger: the LORD shall swallow them up in his wrath, and the fire shall devour them.**
>
> Their fruit shalt thou destroy from the earth, and their seed from among the children of men.
>
> For they intended evil against thee: they imagined a mischievous device, *which* they are not able *to perform.*
>
> Therefore shalt thou make them turn their back, *when* thou shalt make ready *thine arrows* upon thy strings against the face of them.
>
> Be thou exalted, LORD, in thine own strength: *so* will we sing and praise thy power." (Ps 21:7-13, KJV)

Although there will be peace in Zion, Jerusalem, and the Holy Land, the nations outside of that area will not all be conquered at the outset of the Millennium. This global conquest and conversion to the ways of God is a gradual process.

How long it will take Christ, the saints and Israel to conquer the entire world is unknown, but possibly a few decades or even a century – who knows? But it will take time. So, when

---

[67] Further Scriptures to read which assists in understanding this concept of being *under His footstool* are: Ps 110:1; Dan 2:44; Matt 22:44; Mark 12:36; Luke 20:43; Acts 2:35; ICor 15:25; Heb 1:13; Rev 19:15.

does the Millennium officially commence? In attempt to answer this. The following questions are posed:

- When He sets foot upon the earth (Zech 14:4-9)?
- When Jerusalem and the land of Israel are conquered?
- Upon the completion and dedication of the new temple?
- When Israel and Judah are reunited and the New Covenant is made with them? or
- When the entire earth comes under the rule of Christ?

Whatever the case (and assuming the first point is the correct timing of the commencement), this means that the 1,000 years will not be a time of 1,000 years of peace over the entire world instantly, but 1,000 years of His presence upon the earth – because there will be battles to be won and nations to be conquered at His return. This does not take place in a single day or a single year. It takes time, but it is difficult for one to ascertain how long without some Biblical clues or guides. Perhaps 50 years (a Jubilee?)

Of course, there will be peace in territories close to His power base initially.

And Psalm 2:1-12 (KJV) tells us:

"Why do the heathen rage, and the people imagine a vain thing?

The kings of the earth set themselves, and the rulers take counsel together, against the LORD, and against his anointed, *saying,*

Let us break their bands asunder, and cast away their cords from us. He that sitteth in the heavens shall laugh: the Lord shall have them in derision.

Then shall he speak unto them in his wrath, and vex them in his sore displeasure.

Yet have I set my king upon my holy hill of Zion.

I will declare the decree: the LORD hath said unto me, Thou *art* my Son; this day have I begotten thee.

Ask of me, and I shall give *thee* the heathen *for* thine inheritance, and the uttermost parts of the earth *for* thy possession.

Thou shalt break them with a rod of iron; thou shalt dash them in pieces like a potter's vessel. [cp Rev 2:26-27; 19:15; Ob 20; Ezek 25:14; Jer 50:20-23]

Be wise now therefore, O ye kings: be instructed, ye judges of the earth.

Serve the LORD with fear, and rejoice with trembling.

Kiss the Son, lest he be angry, and ye perish *from* the way, when his wrath is kindled but a little. Blessed *are* all they that put their trust in him."

The above appears to relate to certain nations sometime during the Millennium who want to rebel against His Way - rather than referring to nations destroyed during the previous Day of the Lord. How can this be? Two probabilities come to mind:

1. God will test the nations throughout the Millennium, and some may choose to rebel – particularly early on during that period of His rule.
2. this may refer to the famous Gog and Magog invasion (Ezek 38 and 39).

As Israel and the resurrected saints gradually spread the Kingdom across the world, sometimes there will be resistance (and there will be sin) during the 1,000 years – those individuals and nations who rise up in rebellion will be put down and punished.

> **"They that dwell in the wilderness shall bow before him; and his enemies shall lick the dust.**
>
> **The kings of Tarshish and of the isles shall bring presents: the kings of Sheba and Seba shall offer gifts.**
>
> **Yea, all kings shall fall down before him: all nations shall serve him.**
>
> For he shall deliver the needy when he crieth; the poor also, and *him* that hath no helper.
>
> He shall spare the poor and needy, and shall save the souls of the needy." (Ps 72:9-13, KJV)

> **"For the day of the LORD of hosts *shall be* upon every *one that is* proud and lofty, and upon every *one that is* lifted up; and he shall be brought low:**
>
> And upon all the cedars of **Lebanon**, *that are* high and lifted up, and upon all the oaks of Bashan,
>
> And upon all the high mountains, and upon all the hills *that are* lifted up,
>
> And upon every high tower, and upon every fenced wall,
>
> And upon all the ships of **Tarshish**, and upon all pleasant pictures.
>
> And the loftiness of man shall be bowed down, and the haughtiness of men shall be made low: and the LORD alone shall be exalted in that day.
>
> And the idols he shall utterly abolish.
>
> And they shall go into the holes of the rocks, and into the caves of the earth, for fear of the LORD, and for the glory of his majesty, **when he ariseth to shake terribly the earth.**
>
> In that day a man shall cast his idols of silver, and his idols of gold, which they made *each one* for himself to worship, to the moles and to the bats;
>
> To go into the clefts of the rocks, and into the tops of the ragged rocks, for fear of the LORD, and for the glory of his majesty, **when he ariseth to shake terribly the earth**.
>
> Cease ye from man, whose breath *is* in his nostrils: for wherein is he to be accounted of?" (Is 2:12-22, KJV)

Following on from this, consider that researchers who have found a certain literary eschatological structure throughout the Old Testament know that Genesis 49 has primary end time application and only a proto-type application for the period Israel dwelt in the Holy Land. People who try and deride the Promises to Abraham/British-Israel doctrine claim that this prophecy does not really have end-time application.

However, an analysis of the literature structure of the books of the Pentateuch leads one to 'beg to differ.' There is much literature on the subject so this will not be delved into in this chapter.

Suffice to say that this structure demonstrates that the terms "in the end of days" and "in the last days" are truly applicable to the times at the Messiah's return.

"Because of the terminology he [Moses] uses (viz., 'the end of days'), we could call it an eschatological reading of his historical narratives. The narrative texts of past events are presented as pointers to future events. **Past events foreshadow the future**." (John Sailhamer, *The Pentateuch as Narrative*, p. 37) [emphasis mine]

Notice this prophecy of both Christ's first and second comings – His second coming will be fierce and destructive to start with:

"And Jacob called unto his sons, and said, Gather yourselves together, that I may tell you *that* which shall befall you in **the last days**.

Gather yourselves together, and hear, ye sons of Jacob; and hearken unto Israel your father.

…

Judah *is* a lion's whelp: from the prey, my son, thou art gone up: he stooped down, he couched as a lion, and as an old lion; who shall rouse him up?

The sceptre shall not depart from Judah, nor a lawgiver from between his feet, until Shiloh come; and unto him *shall* the gathering of the people *be*.

Binding his foal unto the vine, and his ass's colt unto the choice vine; **he washed his garments in wine, and his clothes in the blood of grapes**:

His eyes *shall be* red with wine, and his teeth white with milk." (Gen 49:1-2, 9-12, KJV)

Researcher Davidson believes that:

"This verse indicates a succession in the royal line of Judah that will not be interrupted till the appearance of Shiloh … **The picture of the Messiah is highlighted in the preceding verses (vv. 8-9), with the imagery of a warrior victorious over his enemies, and a lion resting after taking his prey**." (Richard Davidson "The Eschatological Literary Structure of the Old Testament," in *Creation, Life, and Hope: Essays in Honor of Jacques B. Doukhan*, pp. 353-54) [emphasis mine]

This awesome Messiah will rebuke many nations including Moabites, Amalakites and Kenites:

"He shall pour the water out of his buckets, and his seed *shall be* in many waters, and his king shall be higher than Agag, and his kingdom shall be exalted.

God brought him forth out of Egypt; he hath as it were the strength of an unicorn: he shall eat up the nations his enemies, and shall break their bones, and pierce *them* through with his arrows.

He couched, he lay down as a lion, and as a great lion: who shall stir him up? Blessed *is* he that blesseth thee, and cursed *is* he that curseth thee.

…

And now, behold, I go unto my people: come *therefore, and* I will advertise thee what this people shall do to thy people **in the latter days**.

…

"I shall see him, but not now: I shall behold him, but not nigh: there shall come a Star out of Jacob, **and a Sceptre shall rise out of Israel, and shall smite the corners of Moab, and destroy all the children of Sheth** [the meaning here may be the sons of tumult or Seth may represent all mankind].

And Edom shall be a possession, Seir also shall be a possession for his enemies; and Israel shall do valiantly.

Out of Jacob shall come he that shall have dominion, and shall destroy him that remaineth of the city.

And when he looked on Amalek, he took up his parable, and said, Amalek *was* the first of the nations; but his latter end *shall be* that he perish for ever.

And he looked on the Kenites, and took up his parable, and said, Strong is thy dwelling place, and thou puttest thy nest in a rock.

Nevertheless the Kenite shall be wasted, until Asshur shall carry thee away captive.

And he took up his parable, and said, Alas, who shall live when God doeth this!" (Num 24:7-9, 14, 17-23, KJV)

Davidson explains further:

"The identity of the "him" as conquering king is further clarified in vv. 8b-9 with the description of his conquering his enemies, the nations ("He shall consume the nations, his enemies") ... the messianic king is portrayed as experiencing a new eschatological Exodus, recapitulating in his life the events of historical Israel." (p. 357)

Israel itself will not escape the severity of His wrath either:

"For I know that after my death ye will utterly corrupt *yourselves*, and turn aside from the way which I have commanded you; and evil will befall you **in the latter days**; because ye will do evil in the sight of the LORD, to provoke him to anger through the work of your hands." (Deut 31:29, KJV)

They will be the first of all nations to "be cleaned up" and "put back on track" – you would have read more about this in the chapter *Israel's Second Exodus*. Notice:

"And he shall sit *as* a refiner and purifier of silver: and he shall purify the sons of Levi, and purge them as gold and silver, that they may offer unto the LORD an offering in righteousness.

Then shall the offering of Judah and Jerusalem be pleasant unto the LORD, as in the days of old, and as in former years.

And I will come near to you to judgment; and I will be a swift witness against the sorcerers, and against the adulterers, and against false swearers, and against those that oppress the hireling in *his* wages, the widow, and the fatherless, and that turn aside the stranger *from his right*, and fear not me, saith the LORD of hosts." (Mal 3:3-5, KJV)

Israel must also be dealt with commencing with the tribes of Levi and Judah – but before He deals with the non-Israelitish peoples.

RELEVANT SCRIPTURES

Christ is at the centre of Zion. In turn Zion is the centre of Jerusalem. Jerusalem the centre of Israel. The land of Israel is the centre of the earth politically and religiously (this restored Jerusalem is referred to in Isaiah 54[68]). Later, after the Millennium, the earth becomes the centre of the universe which is the New Heavens and New Earth.

This chapter now becomes more of a Bible study as many Scriptures are listed below to prove our point.

Upon His return, Christ smashes the nations:

These are the nations of the future German-led US of Europe and other Eastern forces in the Middle East, gathering around Armageddon.

> "These shall make war with the Lamb, and the Lamb shall overcome them: for he is Lord of lords, and King of kings: and they that are with him are called, and chosen, and faithful." (Rev 17:14, KJV)

> "And out of his mouth goeth a sharp sword, that with it **he should smite the nations**: and he shall rule them with a rod of iron: and he treadeth the winepress of the fierceness and wrath of Almighty God.
>
> And he hath on *his* vesture and on his thigh a name written, KING OF KINGS, AND LORD OF LORDS." (Rev 19:15-16, KJV) [cp Rev 2:26-27; 19:15; Ob 20; Ezek 25:14; Jer 50:20-23]

> "I saw in the night visions, and, behold, *one* like the Son of man came with the clouds of heaven, and came to the Ancient of days, and they brought him near before him.
>
> And there was given him dominion, and glory, and a kingdom, **that all people, nations, and languages, should serve him**: his dominion *is* an everlasting dominion, which shall not pass away, and his kingdom *that* which shall not be destroyed." (Dan 7:13-14, KJV)

> "For I *know* their works and their thoughts: it shall come, that **I will gather all nations and tongues**; and they shall come, and see my glory." (Is 66:18, KJV) [cf Zech 14:16-19]

> "Then shall **the LORD go forth, and fight against those nations**, as when he fought in the day of battle.
>
> And his feet shall stand in that day upon the mount of Olives, which *is* before Jerusalem on the east, and the mount of Olives shall cleave in the midst thereof toward the east and toward the west, *and there shall be* a very great valley; and half of the mountain shall remove toward the north, and half of it toward the south.
>
> And ye shall flee *to* the valley of the mountains; for the valley of the mountains shall reach unto Azal: yea, ye shall flee, like as ye fled from before the earthquake in the days of Uzziah king of Judah: and the LORD my God shall come, *and* all the saints with thee.

---

[68] Cp vv 11-12 with Rev 21:18-21.

And it shall come to pass in that day, *that* the light shall not be clear, *nor* dark:
But it shall be one day which shall be known to the LORD, not day, nor night:
but it shall come to pass, *that* at evening time it shall be light." [i.e. the Day of the Lord] (Zech 14:3-7, KJV)

Examples of judgments during the Tribulation and Day of the Lord include:

- Assyria –

  1. Isaiah 10:5-6 – God's instruments
  2. Isaiah 7:17-25 – land of Judah stripped
  3. Isaiah 8:1-10 – conquerors of Israel
  4. Isaiah 10:5-34 – judgment upon Assyria
  5. Isaiah 14:24-28 – Assyrians broken in the Holy Land
  6. Isaiah19:23-25 – the Assyrians will eventually learn the truth
  7. Isaiah 20:1-6 – conquest of Egypt
  8. Isaiah 30:27-33 – punishment at the hand of God
  9. Isaiah 31:8-9 – Divine intervention will bring Assyria to heel
  10. Isaiah 37:21-36 – Jerusalem and Assyria
  11. Jonah 3:1-4 – message to Nineveh via Jonah
  12. Nahum – prophesied destruction of Assyria and Nineveh
  13. Zephaniah 2:13-15 – the desolation of Assyria
  14. Zechariah 10:11 – the pride of Assyria laid low
  15. Hosea 8-9 – conquest of Israel by Assyria

- Ishmael: Jer 2:10; 3:2; 25:23-24; 49:28; Ezek 29:21; Is 42:11; 60:7.
- Cush: Ps 68:31; 72:10; 87:4; Is 11:11. See also Is 20:3-5; 43:3; 45:14; Ezek 29:10; 30:4-5, 9; 38:5; Jer 46:9; Dan 11:43; Amos 9:7; Hab 3:7; Nah 3:9; Zeph 2:12.

… and many others.

Author, Walter Kaiser, explains further about these judgments:

"Yahweh's purpose and plan embraced the whole earth with all its nations. Nations rose and fell in accordance with that plan (Isa 14:24-27). But when national pride became exalted and motivated by imperialistic aggression, these nations were reminded quickly that they could not continue on ruthlessly. Even when they were the God-ordained instruments of judgment aimed at Israel, they were not to burn, kill, and destroy at will whomever they wished; for in this case, Yahweh would again remind them that they were merely His axes. The axe must not pretend that it was equal to the one who chops with it any more than the saw was greater than the one who sawed with it (Isa 10:5). So Assyria would learn that she served at the pleasure of the living God and not her own" (*Towards an Old Testament Theology*, pp. 210-211).

Valley of Decision:

"For, behold, in those days, and in that time, when I shall bring again the captivity of Judah and Jerusalem, [the Great Tribulation]

I will also gather all nations, and will bring them down into the **valley of Jehoshaphat** [= Yhwh judges], and will plead with them there for my people and *for* my heritage Israel, whom they have scattered among the nations, and parted my land. [these are the nations of the German-led US of Europe that would have invaded the Israelitish nations]

...

Let the heathen be wakened, and come up to the valley of Jehoshaphat: for there will I sit to judge all the heathen round about [Matt 25:31-32].

Put ye in the sickle, for the harvest is ripe: come, get you down; for the press is full, the fats overflow; for their wickedness *is* great.

Multitudes, multitudes in the valley of decision: for the day of the LORD *is* near in the **valley of decision.**

The sun and the moon shall be darkened, and the stars shall withdraw their shining [Day of the Lord].

The LORD also shall roar out of Zion, and utter his voice from Jerusalem; and the heavens and the earth shall shake [earthquakes]: but the LORD *will be* the hope of his people, and the strength of the children of Israel." [Israel waking up to His intervention, rescue and the forthcoming 2nd Exodus] (Joel 3:1-2, 12-16, KJV)

This act of violence will also serve as a filter – removing those that would be deemed unworthy of entering the New World. Other nations will be filtered out later.

Figure 21 Valley of Jehoshaphat connects the Valley of Hinnom to the Kidron Valley

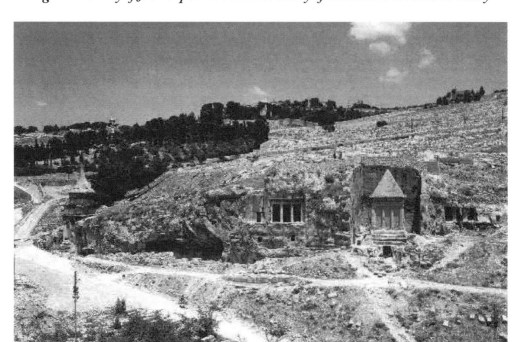

"And the fifth angel poured out his vial upon the seat of the beast; and his kingdom was full of darkness; and they gnawed their tongues for pain,

And blasphemed the God of heaven because of their pains and their sores, and repented not of their deeds.

And the sixth angel poured out his vial upon the great river Euphrates; and the water thereof was dried up, that the way of the **kings of the east** might be prepared.

And I saw three unclean spirits like frogs *come* out of the mouth of the dragon, and out of the mouth of the beast, and out of the mouth of the false prophet.

For they are the spirits of devils, working miracles, *which* go forth unto the kings of the earth and of the whole world, to gather them to the battle of that great day of God Almighty.

Behold, I come as a thief. Blessed *is* he that watcheth, and keepeth his garments, lest he walk naked, and they see his shame.

And he gathered them together into a place called in the Hebrew tongue Armageddon." (Rev 16:10-16, KJV)

Figure 22 Valley of Armageddon (Valley of Jezreel)

"And I saw an angel standing in the sun; and he cried with a loud voice, saying to all the fowls that fly in the midst of heaven, Come and gather yourselves together unto the supper of the great God;

That ye may eat the flesh of kings, and the flesh of captains, and the flesh of mighty men, and the flesh of horses, and of them that sit on them, and the flesh of all *men, both* free and bond, both small and great.

And I saw the beast, and the kings of the earth, and their armies, gathered together to make war against him that sat on the horse, and against his army.

And the beast was taken, and with him the false prophet that wrought miracles before him, with which he deceived them that had received the mark of the beast, and them that worshipped his image. These both were cast alive into a lake of fire burning with brimstone.

And the remnant were slain with the sword of him that sat upon the horse, which *sword* proceeded out of his mouth: and all the fowls were filled with their flesh." (Rev 19:17-21, KJV)

The nations of the German-led Europe and the Russian–led eastern forces will be in furious and desperate conflict with each other over world domination. Upon Christ's return they will turn and combine their military capabilities against him. This will be a futile attempt.

"For as the **lightning** cometh out of the east, and shineth even unto the west; so shall also the coming of the Son of man be.

For wheresoever the carcase is, there will the eagles be gathered together.

Immediately after the tribulation of those days shall the **sun be darkened, and the moon shall not give her light**, and the stars shall fall from heaven, and the powers of the heavens shall be shaken:

And then shall appear the sign of the Son of man in heaven: and **then shall all the tribes of the earth mourn**, and they shall see the Son of man coming in the **clouds** of heaven with power and great glory." (Matt 24:27-30, KJV)

During the subsequent Day of the Lord, giant earthquakes, volcanoes and tidal waves will sweep the globe, brilliantly reconstructing the earth's surface for a better world (i.e. for farming, natural beauty, navigation etc):

"Therefore will not we fear, **though the earth be removed,** and though the mountains be carried into the midst of the sea;

Though the waters thereof roar *and* be troubled, *though* **the mountains shake** with the swelling thereof. Selah." (Ps 46:2-3, KJV)

"The LORD reigneth; let the earth rejoice; let the multitude of isles be glad *thereof.*

Clouds and darkness *are* round about him: righteousness and judgment *are* the habitation of his throne. [cp Matt 24:30]

A fire goeth before him, **and burneth up his enemies round about**. [i.e. Day of the Lord volcanoes]

His **lightnings** enlightened the world: the earth saw, and trembled. [cp Matt 24:27; Rev 8:5; 16:18]

The hills melted like wax at the presence of the LORD, at the presence of the Lord of the whole earth.

The heavens declare his righteousness, and all the people see his glory." (Ps 97:1-6, KJV)

"In a little wrath I hid my face from thee for a moment; but with everlasting kindness will I have mercy on thee, saith the LORD thy Redeemer.

For this *is as* the waters of Noah unto me: for *as* I have sworn that the waters of Noah should no more go over the earth; so have I sworn that I would not be wroth with thee, nor rebuke thee.

For the mountains shall depart, and the hills be removed; but my kindness shall not depart from thee, neither shall the covenant of my peace be removed, saith the LORD that hath mercy on thee." (Isaiah 54:8-10, KJV)

"And the Lord GOD of hosts *is* **he that toucheth the land, and it shall melt [volcanic molten lava], and all that dwell therein shall mourn**: and it shall rise up wholly like a flood; and shall be drowned, as *by* the flood of Egypt.

It is he that buildeth his stories in the heaven, and hath founded his troop in the earth; he that calleth for the waters of the sea, and poureth them out upon the face of the earth [tidal waves – see Luke 21:25]: The LORD *is* his name." (Amos 9:5-6, KJV)

"For, behold, the LORD cometh forth out of his place, and will come down, and tread upon the high places of the earth.

And the mountains shall be molten under him, and the valleys shall be cleft, as wax before the fire [volcanoes], *and* as the waters *that are* poured down a steep place." (Micah 1:3-4, KJV)

"**The mountains quake at him, and the hills melt [volcanoes], and the earth is burned at his presence**, yea, the world, and all that dwell therein.

Who can stand before his indignation? and who can abide in the fierceness of his anger? his fury is poured out like fire, and the rocks are thrown down by him." (Nahum 1:5-6, KJV)

"And the LORD shall be king over all the earth: in that day shall there be one LORD, and his name one.

All the land shall be turned as a plain from Geba to Rimmon south of Jerusalem: and it shall be lifted up, and inhabited in her place, from Benjamin's gate unto the place of the first gate, unto the corner gate, and *from* the tower of Hananeel unto the king's winepresses." (Zech 14:9-10, KJV)

Israel will be rescued, cleansed, united, restored and granted world leadership:

"When they therefore were come together, they asked of him, saying, Lord, wilt thou at this time restore again the kingdom to Israel?

And he said unto them, It is not for you to know the times or the seasons, which the Father hath put in his own power." (Acts 1:6-7, KJV)

"Brethren, my heart's desire and prayer to God for Israel is, that they might be saved." (Rom 10:1, KJV)

"I say then, Hath God cast away his people? God forbid. For I also am an Israelite, of the seed of Abraham, *of* the tribe of Benjamin.

God hath not cast away his people which he foreknew." (Rom 11:1-2a, KJV)

The Second Exodus will then occur (refer to the chapter on this):

> "And the ransomed of the LORD shall return and come to Zion with singing; everlasting joy shall be upon their heads; they shall obtain gladness and joy, and sorrow and sighing shall flee away." (Is 35:10, KJV)

Previously we saw that after being rescued from the four corners of the earth, Israel is cleansed with the purging out of the rebels. As with Israel so with the gentiles. See Ezek 20:38, 42-44; Is 4:2-4; Is 35:10.

Israel then swoops upon ceertain nations to take them under their control: Is 14:1-2; 60:5-16; 19:17; 61:4-9; Ezek 25:13-17; Ob 1:17-21; Zech 9:11-14; 10:3-10; 12:7-8; 14:14; Amos 9:11-12; Zeph 2:7-13.

> "Praise ye the LORD: for *it is* good to sing praises unto our God; for *it is* pleasant; *and* praise is comely.
>
> The LORD doth build up Jerusalem: he gathereth together the outcasts of Israel. [the Second Exodus]
>
> He healeth the broken in heart, and bindeth up their wounds. [cp Is 61]
>
> …
>
> He sheweth his word unto Jacob, his statutes and his judgments unto Israel.
>
> He hath not dealt so with any nation: and *as for his* judgments, they have not known them. Praise ye the LORD." (Ps 147:1-3, 19-20, KJV)

> "For the day of the LORD *is* near upon all the heathen: as thou hast done, it shall be done unto thee: thy reward shall return upon thine own head.
>
> For as ye have drunk upon my holy mountain, *so* shall all the heathen drink continually, yea, they shall drink, and they shall swallow down, and they shall be as though they had not been.
>
> But upon mount Zion shall be deliverance, and there shall be holiness; and the house of Jacob shall possess their possessions.
>
> And the house of Jacob shall be a fire, and the house of Joseph a flame, and the house of Esau for stubble, and they shall kindle in them, and devour them; and there shall not be *any* remaining of the house of Esau; for the LORD hath spoken *it*.
>
> And *they of* the south shall possess the mount of Esau; and *they of* the plain the Philistines: and they shall possess the fields of Ephraim, and the fields of Samaria: and Benjamin *shall possess* Gilead.
>
> And the captivity of this host of the children of Israel *shall possess* that of the Canaanites, *even* unto Zarephath; and the captivity of Jerusalem, which *is* in Sepharad, shall possess the cities of the south.
>
> **And saviours shall come up on mount Zion to judge the mount of Esau; and the kingdom shall be the LORD'S."** (Ob 15-21, KJV)

Figure 23 Israelitish nations will be obliterated during the Tribulation

"Woe be unto the pastors that destroy and scatter the sheep of my pasture! saith the LORD. [political leaders responsible for Israel's destruction via globalisation and liberalism; also the ministers of the land. Spiritually, Church of God ministry have scattered the membership]

Therefore thus saith the LORD God of Israel against the pastors that feed my people; Ye have scattered my flock, and driven them away, and have not visited them: behold, I will visit upon you the evil of your doings, saith the LORD.

And I will gather the remnant of my flock out of all countries whither I have driven them, and will bring them again to their folds; and they shall be fruitful and increase.

And I will set up shepherds over them which shall feed them: and they shall fear no more, nor be dismayed, neither shall they be lacking, saith the LORD.

Behold, the days come, saith the LORD, that I will raise unto David a righteous Branch, and a King shall reign and prosper, and shall execute judgment and justice in the earth.

In his days Judah shall be saved, and Israel shall dwell safely: and this *is* his name whereby he shall be called, THE LORD OUR RIGHTEOUSNESS." (Jer 23:1-6, KJV)

"The Spirit of the Lord GOD *is* upon me; because the LORD hath anointed me to preach good tidings unto the meek; he hath sent me to bind up the brokenhearted, to proclaim liberty to the captives, and the opening of the prison to *them that are* bound; [i.e. Israel in captivity. Cp Ps 147]

To proclaim the acceptable year of the LORD, and the day of vengeance of our God; to comfort all that mourn;

To appoint unto them that mourn in Zion, to give unto them beauty for ashes, the oil of joy for mourning, the garment of praise for the spirit of heaviness; that they might be called trees of righteousness, the planting of the LORD, that he might be glorified.

And they shall build the old wastes, they shall raise up the former desolations, and they shall repair the waste cities, the desolations of many generations.

And strangers shall stand and feed your flocks, and the sons of the alien *shall be* your plowmen and your vinedressers.

But ye shall be named the Priests of the LORD: *men* shall call you the Ministers of our God: ye shall eat the riches of the Gentiles, and in their glory shall ye boast yourselves. [cp Is 66:21]

For your shame *ye shall have* double [birthright inheritances]; and *for* confusion they shall rejoice in their portion: therefore in their land they shall possess the double: everlasting joy shall be unto them." (Is 61:1-7, KJV)

"Behold, **a king shall reign in righteousness, and princes shall rule in judgment.**
And a man shall be as an hiding place from the wind, and a covert from the tempest; as rivers of water in a dry place, as the shadow of a great rock in a weary land." (Is 32:1-2, KJV)

"For thus saith the Lord GOD, the Holy One of Israel; In returning and rest shall ye be saved; in quietness and in confidence shall be your strength: and ye would not.

But ye said, No; for we will flee upon horses; therefore shall ye flee: and, We will ride upon the swift; therefore shall they that pursue you be swift.

One thousand *shall flee* at the rebuke of one; at the rebuke of five shall ye flee: till ye be left as a beacon upon the top of a mountain, and as an ensign on an hill.

And therefore will the LORD wait, that he may be gracious unto you, and therefore will he be exalted, that he may have mercy upon you: for the LORD *is* a God of judgment: blessed *are* all they that wait for him.

For the people shall dwell in Zion at Jerusalem: thou shalt weep no more: he will be very gracious unto thee at the voice of thy cry; when he shall hear it, he will answer thee.

And *though* the Lord give you the bread of adversity, and the water of affliction, yet shall not thy teachers be removed into a corner any more, but thine eyes shall see thy teachers:

And thine ears shall hear a word behind thee, saying, This *is* the way, walk ye in it, when ye turn to the right hand, and when ye turn to the left.

Ye shall defile also the covering of thy graven images of silver, and the ornament of thy molten images of gold: thou shalt cast them away as a menstruous cloth; thou shalt say unto it, Get thee hence.

Then shall he give the rain of thy seed, that thou shalt sow the ground withal; and bread of the increase of the earth, and it shall be fat and plenteous: in that day shall thy cattle feed in large pastures.

The oxen likewise and the young asses that ear the ground shall eat clean provender, which hath been winnowed with the shovel and with the fan.

And there shall be upon every high mountain, and upon every high hill, rivers *and* streams of waters in the day of the great slaughter, when the towers fall." (Is 30:15-25, KJV) [cp Jer 17:25-27; 32:3-5]

For additional reading on Israel's restoration and how she will rule the nations under Christ, refer to the chapter *Israel's Role after the Exodus.*

Figure 24 After the utter destruction of the House of Israel

Christ ruling Israel and the world:

Isaiah 59:18-20:

> "According to *their* deeds, accordingly he **will repay, fury to his adversaries,** recompence to his enemies; to the islands he will repay recompence.
>
> **So shall they fear the name of the LORD from the west, and his glory from the rising of the sun.** When the enemy shall come in like a flood, the Spirit of the LORD shall lift up a standard against him.
>
> And **the Redeemer shall come to Zion,** and unto them that turn from transgression in Jacob, saith the LORD." (KJV)

> "And it shall come to pass in the last days, *that* the mountain of the LORD'S house shall be established in the top of the mountains, and shall be exalted above the hills; and all nations shall flow unto it.
>
> And many people shall go and say, Come ye, and let us go up to the mountain of the LORD, to the house of the God of Jacob; and he will teach us of his ways, and

we will walk in his paths: for **out of Zion** shall go forth the law, and the word of the LORD from Jerusalem.

And **he shall judge among the nations, and shall rebuke many people** [this is during the Millennium]: and they shall beat their swords into plowshares, and their spears into pruninghooks: nation shall not lift up sword against nation, neither shall they learn war any more.

O house of Jacob, come ye, and let us walk in the light of the LORD [repentant Israel]." (Is 2:2-5, KJV)

Notice, He is judging the nations and rebuking them – then they learn the way of peace. Not all of this happens during the Day of the Lord or immediately upon His return. As we have seen, it all takes time – probably decades.

Similarly in Isaiah 60:1-22 (KJV):

"Arise, shine; for thy light is come, and the glory of the LORD is risen upon thee.

For, behold, the darkness shall cover the earth, and gross darkness the people: but the LORD shall arise upon thee, and his glory shall be seen upon thee.

And the Gentiles shall come to thy light, and kings to the brightness of thy rising.

Lift up thine eyes round about, and see: all they gather themselves together, they come to thee: thy sons shall come from far, and thy daughters shall be nursed at *thy* side.

Then thou shalt see, and flow together, and thine heart shall fear, and be enlarged; because the abundance of the sea shall be converted unto thee, the forces of the Gentiles shall come unto thee.

The multitude of camels shall cover thee, the dromedaries of Midian and Ephah; all they from Sheba shall come: they shall bring gold and incense; and they shall shew forth the praises of the LORD.

All the flocks of Kedar shall be gathered together unto thee, the rams of Nebaioth shall minister unto thee: they shall come up with acceptance on mine altar, and I will glorify the house of my glory.

Who *are* these *that* fly as a cloud, and as the doves to their windows?

Surely the isles shall wait for me, and the ships of Tarshish first, to bring thy sons from far, their silver and their gold with them, unto the name of the LORD thy God, and to the Holy One of Israel, because he hath glorified thee.

And the sons of strangers shall build up thy walls, and their kings shall minister unto thee: for in my wrath I smote thee [the Great Tribulation], **but in my favour have I had mercy on thee.** [restoration of Israel after the Exodus]

Therefore thy gates shall be open continually; they shall not be shut day nor night; that *men* may bring unto thee the forces of the Gentiles, and *that* their kings *may be* brought.

For the nation and kingdom that will not serve thee shall perish; yea, *those* **nations shall be utterly wasted.** [Israel will rule the world!]

The glory of Lebanon shall come unto thee, the fir tree, the pine tree, and the box together, to beautify the place of my sanctuary; and I will make the place of my feet glorious.

The sons also of them that afflicted thee shall come bending unto thee; and all they that despised thee shall bow themselves down at the soles of thy feet; and they shall call thee, **The city of the LORD, The Zion of the Holy One of Israel**.

Whereas thou hast been forsaken and hated, so that no man went through *thee*, I will make thee an eternal excellency, a joy of many generations.

Thou shalt also suck the milk of the Gentiles, and shalt suck the breast of kings: and thou shalt know that I the LORD *am* thy Saviour and thy Redeemer, the mighty One of Jacob.

For brass I will bring gold, and for iron I will bring silver, and for wood brass, and for stones iron: I will also make thy officers peace, and thine exactors righteousness.

Violence shall no more be heard in thy land, wasting nor destruction within thy borders; but thou shalt call thy walls Salvation, and thy gates Praise.

The sun shall be no more thy light by day; neither for brightness shall the moon give light unto thee: but the LORD shall be unto thee an everlasting light, and thy God thy glory. [typological of the Day of the Lord]

Thy sun shall no more go down; neither shall thy moon withdraw itself: for the LORD shall be thine everlasting light, and the days of thy mourning shall be ended. [symbolically speaking – and a type of the New Jerusalem]

Thy people also *shall be* all righteous: they shall inherit the land for ever, the branch of my planting, the work of my hands, that I may be glorified.

A little one shall become a thousand, and a small one a strong nation: I the LORD will hasten it in his time." [the might of Israel during the Millennium] [compare this chapter with Ps 60]

Christ rules out of Zion:

"The sun and the moon shall be darkened, and the stars shall withdraw their shining.

The LORD also shall roar out of Zion, and utter his voice from Jerusalem; and the heavens and the earth shall shake: but the LORD *will be* the hope of his people, and the strength of the children of Israel.

So shall ye know that I *am* **the LORD your God dwelling in Zion,** my holy mountain: then shall Jerusalem be holy, and there shall no strangers pass through her any more.

And it shall come to pass in that day *that* the mountains shall drop down new wine, and the hills shall flow with milk, and all the rivers of Judah shall flow with waters, and a fountain shall come forth of the house of the LORD, and shall water the valley of Shittim.

Egypt shall be a desolation, and Edom shall be a desolate wilderness, for the violence *against* the children of Judah, because they have shed innocent blood in their land.

But Judah shall dwell for ever, and Jerusalem from generation to generation.

For I will cleanse their blood *that* I have not cleansed: **for the LORD dwelleth in Zion**." (Joel 3:15-21, KJV)

"The mighty God, *even* the LORD, hath spoken, and called the earth from the rising of the sun unto the going down thereof.

Out of **Zion**, the perfection of beauty, God hath shined.

Our God shall come, and shall not keep silence: a fire shall devour before him, and it shall be very tempestuous round about him.

He shall call to the heavens from above, and to the earth, that he may judge his people.

Gather my saints together unto me; those that have made a covenant with me by sacrifice.

And the heavens shall declare his righteousness: for God *is* judge himself. Selah." (Ps 50:1-6, KJV)

See Ps 9:11; 50:1-4; 135:21, etc., for additional Scriptural proofs. Note: Jerusalem becomes the capital of the world, as seen in Zech 8:3, etc.

The nations are allocated their areas to flourish in, given that they are described as distinct peoples in prophecy. See Dan 7:13-14.

The Rebellion of Ezekiel 38 and 39:

For further details, read the chapter *A War even after the Messiah's Return!* that expands on this.

What are the origins and reasons for this invasion by these Eastern forces? Presumably these are the recalcitrant remnant of the 200 million horde as we have seen in chapter three.

After the establishment of Israel in the holy land, the remnants of the eastern forces attack the regathered Israel (Ezek 38 and 39):

> **"And I will set my glory among the heathen, and all the heathen shall see my judgment that I have executed, and my hand that I have laid upon them.**
>
> So the house of Israel shall know that I *am* the LORD their God from that day and forward.
>
> And the heathen shall know that the house of Israel went into captivity for their iniquity: because they trespassed against me, therefore hid I my face from them, and gave them into the hand of their enemies: so fell they all by the sword." (Ezek 39:21-23, KJV)

"God *is* our refuge and strength, a very present help in trouble.

Therefore will not we fear, though the earth be removed, and though the mountains be carried into the midst of the sea;

Though the waters thereof roar *and* be troubled, *though* the mountains shake with the swelling thereof. Selah.

There is a river, the streams whereof shall make glad the city of God, the holy *place* of the tabernacles of the most High.

God *is* in the midst of her; she shall not be moved: God shall help her, *and that* right early.

The heathen raged, the kingdoms were moved: he uttered his voice, the earth melted.

The LORD of hosts *is* with us; the God of Jacob *is* our refuge. Selah.

Come, behold the works of the LORD, what desolations he hath made in the earth.

He maketh wars to cease unto the end of the earth; he breaketh the bow, and cutteth the spear in sunder; he burneth the chariot in the fire.

Be still, and know that I *am* God: I will be exalted among the heathen, I will be exalted in the earth.

The LORD of hosts *is* with us; the God of Jacob *is* our refuge. Selah." (Ps 46:1-6, KJV)

Example of Egypt:

There are a number of prophecies dealing with Egypt (Mizraim): Isa 19:1-25; Jer 25:19; Hos 7:16; 9:6; 12:1; Joel 3:19; Amos 2:10; 3:1; Nah 3:9; Zech 10:11. Other scriptures dealing with the sons of Mizraim are: Ps 68:31; Jer 44:1; Ezek 29:14; Deut 2:43; Amos 9:7.

One that is rather intriguing is found in Zechariah 14:12-21. The preceding verses 1-11 seem to most likely refer to the first few years of the Millennium and it specifically states that Jerusalem (symbolic of all Israel) will be safely inhabited (cp Ezekiel 38:11,14). Then we are told that following this:

> "And this shall be the plague with which Jehovah will strike all the peoples who have fought against Jerusalem [both before and after the return of Christ]. Their flesh shall rot while they stand on their feet, and their eyes shall rot in their sockets. And their tongue shall rot in their mouth.
>
> And it shall be in that day a great panic of Jehovah shall be among them And they shall each one lay hold of his neighbor, and his hand shall rise up against the hand of his neighbor.
>
> And Judah also shall fight at Jerusalem; and the wealth of all the nations all around shall be gathered, gold, and silver, and clothing in great abundance. [cp Ezek 39:10]
>
> And so shall be the plague of the horse, the mule, the camel, and the ass, and of all the beasts which shall be in these tents, like this plague.
>
> And it shall be, everyone who is left of all the nations which came up against Jerusalem shall go up from year to year to worship the King, Jehovah of Hosts, and to keep the Feast of Tabernacles.
>
> And it shall be, *that* whoso will not come up of *all* the families of the earth unto Jerusalem to worship the King, the LORD of hosts, even upon them shall be no rain.
>
> And if the family of Egypt go not up, and come not, that *have* no *rain*; there shall be the plague, wherewith the LORD will smite the heathen that come not up to keep the feast of tabernacles. [cp Is 19:4-5]
>
> This shall be the punishment of Egypt, and the punishment of all nations that come not up to keep the feast of tabernacles.
>
> In that day shall there be upon the bells of the horses, HOLINESS UNTO THE LORD; and the pots in the LORD'S house shall be like the bowls before the altar.
>
> Yea, every pot in Jerusalem and in Judah shall be holy to Jehovah of Hosts. And all those who sacrifice shall come and take of them, and boil in them. And in that

day there shall no longer be a trader [i.e. Canaanite – either spiritual or physical] in the house of Jehovah of Hosts." (Zech 14:12-21, MKJV)

Compare the above with Ezekiel:

"And I will call for a sword against him on all My mountains, says the Lord Jehovah. *Each* man's sword shall be against his brother. [cp Hag 2:22]

And I will judge him with a plague and with blood. And I will rain on him, and on his bands, and on the many peoples with him, an overflowing shower, and great hailstones, fire and brimstone.

So I will magnify Myself and sanctify Myself. And I will be known in the eyes of many nations, and they shall know that I *am* Jehovah." [and they know God by loving Him and obeying Him e.g. by observing the Feast of Tabernacles] (Ezek 38:21-23, MKJV)

Zechariah 14 may also be paralleled to Isaiah 19. There is an issue with Egypt (or what is left of it): keep the Feast of Tabernacles (and the other laws of course) or bear the consequences. Starting with Israel, then Egypt, Assyria etc, God commences a global theocracy nation-by-nation. Of Egypt He warns:

"The burden of Egypt. Behold, the LORD rideth upon a swift cloud, and shall come into Egypt: and the idols of Egypt shall be moved at his presence, and the heart of Egypt shall melt in the midst of it.

And I will set the Egyptians against the Egyptians: and they shall fight every one against his brother, and every one against his neighbour; city against city, *and* kingdom against kingdom. [cp Zech 14:13]

And the spirit of Egypt shall fail in the midst thereof; and I will destroy the counsel thereof: and they shall seek to the idols, and to the charmers, and to them that have familiar spirits, and to the wizards." (Is 19:1-3, KJV)

The above indicates that this occurs after the return of the Messiah.

"And the Egyptians will I give over into the hand of a cruel lord; and a fierce king shall rule over them, saith the Lord, the LORD of hosts.

And the waters shall fail from the sea, and the river shall be wasted and dried up." (Is 19:4-5, KJV)

This may be cross-referenced to Zechariah 14:18. Isaiah continues:

"And they shall turn the rivers far away; *and* the brooks of defence shall be emptied and dried up: the reeds and flags shall wither.

The paper reeds by the brooks, by the mouth of the brooks, and every thing sown by the brooks, shall wither, be driven away, and be no *more*.

The fishers also shall mourn, and all they that cast angle into the brooks shall lament, and they that spread nets upon the waters shall languish.

Moreover they that work in fine flax, and they that weave networks, shall be confounded.

And they shall be broken in the purposes thereof, all that make sluices *and* ponds for fish." (Is 19: 6-10, KJV)

Perhaps so perplexed at what is going on, they turn to evil guides for answers:

"Surely the princes of Zoan *are* fools, the counsel of the wise counsellors of Pharaoh is become brutish: how say ye unto Pharaoh, I *am* the son of the wise, the son of ancient kings?

Where *are* they? where *are* thy wise *men*? and let them tell thee now, and let them know what the LORD of hosts hath purposed upon Egypt.

The princes of Zoan are become fools, the princes of Noph are deceived; they have also seduced Egypt, *even they that are* the stay of the tribes thereof.

The LORD hath mingled a perverse spirit in the midst thereof: and they have caused Egypt to err in every work thereof, as a drunken *man* staggereth in his vomit.

Neither shall there be *any* work for Egypt, which the head or tail, branch or rush, may do.

In that day shall Egypt be like unto women: and it shall be afraid and fear because of the shaking of the hand of the LORD of hosts, which he shaketh over it." (Is 19:11-16, KJV)

Now Egypt learns to fear Judah, which God uses to punish them:

"And the land of Judah shall be a terror unto Egypt, every one that maketh mention thereof shall be afraid in himself, because of the counsel of the LORD of hosts, which he hath determined against it." [see Zech 14:14 where Judah are portrayed as fighters] (Is 19:17, KJV)

Then we have Egypt's repentance:

"In that day shall five cities in the land of Egypt speak the language of Canaan, and swear to the LORD of hosts; one shall be called, The city of destruction.

In that day shall there be an altar to the LORD in the midst of the land of Egypt, and a pillar at the border thereof to the LORD.

And it shall be for a sign and for a witness unto the LORD of hosts in the land of Egypt: for they shall cry unto the LORD because of the oppressors, and he shall send them a saviour, and a great one, and he shall deliver them." (Is 19:18-20, KJV)

These oppressors are probably those referred to in verses 11-13.

"And the LORD shall be known to Egypt, and the Egyptians shall know the LORD in that day, and shall do sacrifice and oblation; yea, they shall vow a vow unto the LORD, and perform *it*.

And the LORD shall smite Egypt: he shall smite and heal *it*: and they shall return *even* to the LORD, and he shall be intreated of them, and shall heal them.

In that day shall there be a highway out of Egypt to Assyria, and the Assyrian shall come into Egypt, and the Egyptian into Assyria, and the Egyptians shall serve with the Assyrians.

In that day shall Israel be the third with Egypt and with Assyria, *even* a blessing in the midst of the land:

Whom the LORD of hosts shall bless, saying, Blessed *be* Egypt my people, and Assyria the work of my hands, and Israel mine inheritance." (Is 19:21-25, KJV)

Recall that we have an alliance: Israel, the chief of all the nations; Egypt, the chief of the Hamites; and Assyria, the chief of the Shemites. It seems that another will now join them – a nation descended from Japheth to become chief of the Japhethites under the overall leadership of Israel – this appears to be the world order that Christ will initiate. In other words, the Messiah's dealing with the populace of Ezekiel 38 and 39 follows next in the sequence of prophesied events of converting nations one-by-one. The chief of these nations may be Meschech (given the prominence it has compared to other Japhetic nations).

Gradually, nation after nation will submit to God through Israel's conquests and leadership. Woe to them if they do not submit!

Although only Egypt, among the African nations, is mentioned in Isaiah 19, it is not mentioned in Ezekiel 38 and 39. This indicates that the prophecy in Isaiah 19 precedes that of Ezekiel, where other African nations adjacent to Egypt are mentioned. Why? Because if Egypt was not repentant, it would have been part of these armies along with their Hamitic brethren (Cush and Phut) – many of which dwell in adjacent lands.

For more detailed information on the war expounded upon in Ezekiel 38 and 39 refer to the chapter ***A War even after the Messiah's Return!***

Rebellions continue through the Millennium, or at least the early portion:

How can this be?

Probably because human nature, still lingering from the pre-Millennial period, affects many nations that have not yet been reached to learn God's truths. Alternatively, they might be in the beginning phase of learning and initially resent Christ's Government, His saints, and Israel.

"And he that overcometh, and keepeth my works unto the end, **to him will I give power over the nations**:

And he shall rule them with a rod of iron; as the vessels of a potter shall they be broken to shivers: even as I received of my Father." (Rev 2:26-27, KJV)

"But in the last days it shall come to pass, *that* the mountain of the house of the LORD shall be established in the top of the mountains, and it shall be exalted above the hills; and people shall flow unto it.

And **many nations** shall come, and say, Come, and let us go up to the mountain of the LORD, and to the house of the God of Jacob; and he will teach us of his ways, and we will walk in his paths: for the law shall go forth of Zion, and the word of the LORD from Jerusalem.

And he shall judge among many people, and rebuke strong nations afar off; and they shall beat their swords into plowshares, and their spears into pruninghooks: nation shall not lift up a sword against nation, neither shall they learn war any more." (Mic 4:1-3, KJV)

Notice that certain nations are strong and they dwell in distant nations. Reaching them to bring them into submission may take a number of years.

The above appears to be after He establishes Himself in Jerusalem:

"For the LORD taketh pleasure in his people: he will beautify the meek with salvation. [Israel will be exalted, a type of Christians]

Let the saints be joyful in glory: let them sing aloud upon their beds.

Let the high *praises* of God *be* in their mouth, and a **twoedged sword** in their hand;

To execute vengeance upon the heathen, *and* punishments upon the people;

To bind their kings with chains, and their nobles with fetters of iron;

To execute upon them the judgment written: this honour have all his saints. Praise ye the LORD." (Ps 149:4-9, KJV)

All knees must bow toward the great King of the Earth – the Messiah. Bow, kneel, submit and serve – or face the terrible consequences.

Symbolically – and likely literally – rebellious national leaders will be dealt with during the Millennium. Uprisings against the King will not be tolerated.

"Mercy and truth preserve the king: and his throne is upholden by mercy." (Prov 20:28, KJV)

"A Psalm of David.> The LORD said unto my Lord, Sit thou at my right hand, until I make thine enemies thy footstool.

The LORD shall send the rod of thy strength **out of Zion: rule thou in the midst of thine enemies.**" [cp Rev 2:26-27; 19:15]

Thy people *shall be* willing in the day of thy power, in the beauties of holiness from the womb of the morning: thou hast the dew of thy youth.

The LORD hath sworn, and will not repent, Thou *art* a priest for ever after the order of Melchizedek.

The Lord at thy right hand shall strike through kings in the day of his wrath.

He shall judge among the heathen, he shall fill *the places* with the dead bodies; he shall wound the heads over many countries.

He shall drink of the brook in the way: therefore shall he lift up the head." (Ps 110:1-7, KJV)

"Therefore thy gates shall be open continually; they shall not be shut day nor night; that *men* may bring unto thee the forces of the Gentiles, and *that* their kings *may be* brought.

For the nation and kingdom that will not serve thee shall perish; yea, *those* nations shall be utterly wasted.

The glory of Lebanon shall come unto thee, the fir tree, the pine tree, and the box together, to beautify the place of my sanctuary; and I will make the place of my feet glorious.

The sons also of them that afflicted thee shall come bending unto thee; and all they that despised thee shall bow themselves down at the soles of thy feet; and they shall call thee, The city of the LORD, **The Zion** of the Holy One of Israel.

Whereas thou hast been forsaken and hated, so that no man went through *thee*, I will make thee an eternal excellency, a joy of many generations.

Thou shalt also suck the milk of the Gentiles, and shalt suck the breast of kings: and thou shalt know that I the LORD *am* thy Saviour and thy Redeemer, the mighty One of Jacob." (Is 60:11-16, KJV) [Israel will gather the 'nutrients' or blessings of other nations due to their servant leadership and assistance to these other peoples]

"**The LORD shall judge the people**: judge me, O LORD, according to my righteousness, and according to mine integrity that is in me." (Ps 7:8, KJV) [Christ will judge the nations - probably via His saints and Israel]

"Your hand will find all Your enemies; Your right hand will find those who hate You. You shall make them as a fiery oven in the time of Your anger; **The LORD shall swallow them up in His wrath**, And the fire shall devour them. Their offspring You shall destroy from the earth, And their descendants from among the sons of men." (Psalm 21:8-10, NKJV)

"The LORD has sworn And will not relent, "You are a priest forever According to the order of Melchizedek." The Lord is at Your right hand; **He shall execute kings in the day of His wrath**. He shall judge among the nations, He shall fill the places with dead bodies, He shall execute the heads of many countries." (Psalm 110:4-6, NKJV)

Christ is the Melchizedek Priest-King with the accompanying saints composing the Royal Priesthood (kings and priests) under Him (IPet 2:9; Rev 5:10):

"And they will be afraid. Pangs and sorrows will take hold of them; They will be in pain as a woman in childbirth; They will be amazed at one another; Their faces will be like flames. **Behold, the day of the LORD comes, Cruel, with both wrath and fierce anger, To lay the land desolate**; And He will destroy its sinners from it. For the stars of heaven and their constellations Will not give their light; The sun will be darkened in its going forth, And the moon will not cause its light to shine." (Isaiah 13:8-10, NKJV)

"Arise, O God, **judge the earth**: for thou shalt inherit all nations." (Ps 82:8, KJV)

"He shall subdue the people under us, and the nations under our feet! For God is the King of all the Earth: sing ye praises with understanding! God reigneth over the heathen: God sitteth upon the throne of His Holiness." (Ps.47:2,3,7,8, KJV)

"Yea, all kings shall fall down before Him: all nations shall serve Him. And blessed be His glorious Name for ever: and let the whole Earth be filled with His glory; Amen, and Amen!" (Ps.72:11,19, KJV)

"But the LORD shall endure for ever: he hath prepared his throne for judgment. And **he shall judge the world in righteousness, he shall minister judgment to the people in uprightness**." (Ps 9:7-8, KJV)

"Behold, the days come, saith the LORD, that I will raise unto David a righteous Branch, and a King shall reign and prosper, and **shall execute judgment and justice in the earth**." (Jer 23:5, KJV)

"But with righteousness shall he judge the poor, and reprove with equity for the meek of the earth: and he shall smite the earth with the rod of his mouth, and **with the breath of his lips shall he slay the wicked**." (Is 11:4, KJV) [he will judge individuals and nations with justice and fairness]

"Say among the heathen that the LORD reigneth: the world also shall be established that it shall not be moved: **he shall judge the people righteously**. Let the heavens rejoice, and let the earth be glad; let the sea roar, and the fulness thereof. Let the field be joyful, and all that is therein: then shall all the trees of the wood rejoice. Before the LORD: for he cometh, for he cometh to judge the earth: he shall judge the world with righteousness, and the people with his truth." (Ps 96:10-13, KJV)[69] [again, He will judge righteously and justly]

"That thy way may be known upon earth, thy saving health among all nations.
Let the people praise thee, O God; let all the people praise thee.
O let the nations be glad and sing for joy: **for thou shalt judge the people righteously**, and govern the nations upon earth. Selah.
Let the people praise thee, O God; **let all the people praise thee**.
Then shall the earth yield her increase; *and* God, *even* our own God, shall bless us.
God shall bless us; and all the ends of the earth shall fear him." (Ps 67:2-4, KJV)

"Before the LORD: for he cometh, **for he cometh to judge the earth: he shall judge the world with righteousness, and the people with his truth**." (Ps 96:13, KJV)

"Before the LORD; for **he cometh to judge the earth**: with righteousness shall he judge the world, and the people with equity." (Ps 98:9, KJV)

---

[69] "Psalm 96 is among a collection (Ps 93-100) known as the ""Apocalyptic Psalms" or "Theocratic Psalms" (Delitzsch), "Millennial Anthems" (Tholuck), "Songs of the Millennium" (Binnie), "Group of Millennial Psalms" (Herder), "Second Advent Psalms" (Rawlinson), "Enthronement Psalms" (Mowinckel) and "Royal Psalms" (Perowne). Whatever title is used, there can be no mistaking that the theme is eschatological and that it depicts a time when the Lord alone is King reigning over all peoples and lands (93:1; 96:10; 97:1; 99:1)." (Walter Kaiser, "The Promise Theme and the Theology of Rest," *Bibliotheca Sacra*, Vol. 130, April 1973, p. 6).

"Of the increase of his government and peace there shall be no end, upon the throne of David, and upon his kingdom, to order it, and **to establish it with judgment and with justice** from henceforth even for ever. The zeal of the LORD of hosts will perform this." (Is 9:7, KJV)

"And in mercy shall the throne be established: and he shall sit upon it in truth in the tabernacle of David, **judging, and seeking judgment, and hasting righteousness.**" (Is 16:5, KJV)

"And many people shall go and say, Come ye, and let us go up to the mountain of the LORD, to the house of the God of Jacob; and he will teach us of his ways, and we will walk in his paths: for out of Zion shall go forth the law, and the word of the LORD from Jerusalem. **And he shall judge among the nations, and shall rebuke many people**: and they shall beat their swords into plowshares, and their spears into pruninghooks: nation shall not lift up sword against nation, neither shall they learn war any more." (Is 2:3-4, KJV)

"And **he shall judge among many people, and rebuke strong nations afar off**; and they shall beat their swords into plowshares, and their spears into pruninghooks: nation shall not lift up a sword against nation, neither shall they learn war any more." (Mic 4:3, KJV)

"Until the Ancient of days came, **and judgment was given to the saints of the most High**; and the time came that the saints possessed the kingdom." (Dan 7:22, KJV)

The Judgment of the nations happens in conjunction with the 1000-year reign of Jesus Christ. This is not the Great White Throne Judgment, which happens after the Millennium. The *New King James Version Study Bible* note on Psalm 9:7 quoted above states:

"Judgment (also translated "justice") specifies what is right, not only as measured by a code of law, but also what makes for right relationships as well as harmony and peace. The OT prophets were champions of social justice. God's judgment is His just, fair and impartial treatment of all people. His actions and decisions are true and right … As Lord and Judge, God brings justice to nations (67:4)."

Repentant Nations side with the Messiah and offer Him gifts:
In many cultures, gifts to demonstrate friendship or submission are offered to leaders and kings. It is no different with the Messiah:

"**They that dwell in the wilderness shall bow before him; and his enemies shall lick the dust.**

The kings of Tarshish and of the isles shall bring presents: the kings of Sheba and Seba shall offer gifts.

Yea, all kings shall fall down before him: all nations shall serve him.

For he shall deliver the needy when he crieth; the poor also, and *him* that hath no helper.

He shall spare the poor and needy, and shall save the souls of the needy ..
His name shall endure for ever: his name shall be continued as long as the sun: and
men shall be blessed in him: all nations shall call him blessed." (Ps 72:9-13, 17, KJV)

"Surely the isles shall wait for me, and the ships of Tarshish first, to bring thy sons
from far, **their silver and their gold with them,** unto the name of the LORD thy
God, and to the Holy One of Israel, because he hath glorified thee." (Is 60:9, KJV)

We saw previously that the nations once part of the German-led United States of Europe,
warn Gog, Magog, Meschech and Tubal of their terrible fate if they attack God's people. A
fate of suffering at the hands of God which would be similar to their punishment some years
earlier. So, it seems that these former members of the US of Europe warn Gog and Magog
et al via emissaries not to do it but rather to learn from the lessons of history (Ezekiel 38:13).

Nations repentant – the saints rule:

There are three categories of saint in the Scriptures: Israel, the church and angels. In the
Old Testament Israel is called the saints as the Church is in the New Testament. As such,
the church is spiritual Israel – converted Israelites plus converted gentiles grafted into Israel,
spiritually speaking.

Below is a chart comparing the roles and duties of Israel with the Church:

Table 13 Comparing Israel and the Church

Israel – God's saints	Church (spiritual Israel) – God's saints
Tribulation	Tribulation and some in safety
Awaken	Resurrection
Rescued	Rescued at the resurrection
Cleansed	Cleansed finally at the resurrection
Restored	Inherit the Kingdom
Enter Holy Land	Enter Kingdom
Rewarded	Rewarded at the marriage supper
Rule the nations	Rule the world through Israel (as kings and priests under Christ the Priest-King (Melchizedek))
Attacked at the end of the Millennium	Attacked at the end of the Millennium

Unfortunately, replacement theology has infected Christianity. They see the Church
replacing Israel, rather than Christians being grafted into Israel spiritually and thus becoming
spiritual Israelites. Read the entirety of Romans 10 and especially 11 for the proof that the
Church and Israel become one – and therefore one bride of Christ.

Similarly, Christ will make the New Covenant with Israel.

It is this Bride of Christ – spiritual Israel together with physical Israel – that will rule the world in the Millennium under Christ, gradually enforcing God's will upon the world. It will take some time, but it will happen.

We may find this taught typologically by the bulls sacrificed during the Feast of Tabernacles (Numbers 29:12-38) - in reduced numbers each day, viz:

Day 1	**13**
Day 2	**12**
Day 3	**11**
Day 4	**10**
Day 5	**9**
Day 6	**8**
Day 7	**7**
Total	**70**

Another is counted for the Last Great Day, but of the 70 sacrificed during the Feast of Tabernacles, the Jewish *Talmud* asks: "To what do these seventy bullocks correspond? To the seventy nations" listed in the mysterious Table of Nations (Genesis 10).

A footnote reads: "Seventy is the traditional number of Gentile nations, and the seventy bullocks are offered to make atonement for them".

In Israel, the priests were the ruling class. In God's sacrificial system, bullocks were offered to make atonement for them (Leviticus 4:3) while Israel as a nation were also to sacrifice a bullock for national sins (Leviticus 4:13-14). In contrast a leader was to sacrifice a male goat (Leviticus 4:22-23) while the common people sacrificed a female kid or female lamb (Leviticus 4:27-28, 32). Therefore, the Jewish interpretation of the 70 bulls seems appropriate as they relate to rulers, leaders and nations. In Genesis 10 where we find the Table of Nations, we find, beside the name of Noah, 70 other names, representing the 70 nations.

Figure 25 Bulls – symbols of strength and power

Several other scriptures bear this out: in Ps 68:30 gentile kings are likened to bulls; as is the arrogance of Assyria (Isaiah 10:13); the rulers and leaders of Edom (Isaiah 34:7) and Babylon as well (Jeremiah 50:27). We know from the Scriptures that there is organisation in Satan's Kingdom (Ephesians 6:12; Colossians 1:16), which he uses to manipulate and control this world's nations. One such evil spiritual leader over a nation is described by Daniel as the 'prince of the kingdom of Persia,' a very powerful and senior demon who has been granted rulership over a nation or even an empire, as mentioned in Daniel 10:13, 20. Thus, the nations have demonic princes ruling over them.

These spirit rulers of nations may well be the bull demons of ancient mythology – very powerful gods in the religious belief systems of these civilisations. David himself may possibly have been surrounded and attacked by these vile bull forces – very senior prince demons that influence nations - when he cried out to God to deliver him from them (Psalm 22:12):

"Be not far from me; for trouble *is* near; for *there is* none to help.
Many bulls have compassed me: **strong *bulls*** of Bashan have beset me round.
They gaped upon me *with* their mouths, *as* a ravening and a roaring lion.
I am poured out like water, and all my bones are out of joint: my heart is like wax; it is melted in the midst of my bowels." (Ps 22:11-14, KJV).

If David was beset by immensely powerful bull demons (i.e., princely creatures near the top of Satan's brutal chain of command, influencing national leaders), then what about Christians? Due to his senior position as a national leader, it's possible that senior demons were unleashed upon him. Consequently, it follows that Christians might be assailed by lesser demons. Well, that's just a thought.

Continuing with the bull theme: All over the ancient Middle East we find reference to the bull which is used as a symbol of strength and fertility as well as to bull gods. El, the supreme deity and fertility god of the decadent Canaanite pantheon, was often called "the Bull El." Baal, the god of fertility, storms, rain and vegetation is also called the Bull. Also among the Hittites, Aramaeans and Babylonians, the bull gods were a dominant feature of their religions, not to mention the many bull and calf-cults linked closely to the Egyptian god Horus.

Cattle cults among the Cushitic peoples of Ethiopia and India may be found to this day! In Mithraism, bull worship was an important aspect of their beliefs.

In Babylonia, figures of bull gods guarded the entrance into temples, houses and gardens (in contrast, the lion of Judah was utilised extensively in the British Empire). During the Assyrian period, a human face was added. At Khorsabad, colossal human-headed winged bulls were found at the palace of Sargon II.

So, to come full circle, what do the 70 bulls represent in terms of the Millennium? It is this: there will be a continuous, ongoing repentance with a gradual reduction in sin and rebellion by the princes and leaders of the nations, and therefore also by the peoples they lead.

Eventually, the nations will worship the Lord and follow His ways:

"**Many nations shall come**, and say, Come, and let us go up to the mountain of the Lord, and to the house of the God of Jacob; and He will teach us of His ways, and we will walk in His paths: for the law shall go forth of Zion, and the Word of the Lord from Jerusalem." (Micah 4:2, KJV)

"And it shall come to pass, that **every one that is left of all the nations** which came against Jerusalem shall even go up from year to year to worship the King, the Lord of hosts, and to keep the feast of tabernacles." (Zech.14:16, KJV .)

"Until the Ancient of days came, **and judgment was given to the saints of the most High**; and the time came that the saints possessed the kingdom.
 And the kingdom and dominion, and the greatness of the kingdom under the whole heaven, shall be given to the people of the saints of the most High, whose kingdom *is* an everlasting kingdom, and all dominions shall serve and obey him. " (Dan 7:22, 27, KJV)

This demonstrates that nations that survived the Day of the Lord and Armageddon, now repentant, observe the Feast of Tabernacles – an overall indication of a deeper and broader repentance that will take time to extend over the entire earth.

Rebellion again at the end of the Millennium!

It is interesting to note that there are invading armies coming against the 'camp of the saints' and 'beloved city' (Revelation 20:9) holy land near the commencement and after the Millennium.

"And when the thousand years are expired, Satan shall be loosed out of his prison,
 And shall go out to deceive the nations which are in the four quarters of the earth, Gog and Magog, to gather them together to battle: the number of whom *is* as the sand of the sea.
 And they went up on the breadth of the earth, and compassed the camp of the saints about, and the beloved city: and fire came down from God out of heaven, and devoured them.
 And the devil that deceived them was cast into the lake of fire and brimstone, where the beast and the false prophet *are*, and shall be tormented day and night for ever and ever." (Rev 20:7-10, KJV)

It is clear that, in accordance with God's great love for all, He possesses a profound sense of justice and fairness. Therefore, it follows that the judgment to be meted out is, in reality, a sentencing. This is because they would have experienced the holy spirit and become acquainted with God's ways and laws.
 Having had the opportunity to fellowship with God, they now face sentencing. Notice

"For we must all appear before the judgment seat of Christ, that each one may receive the things done in the body, according to what he has done, whether good or bad." (IICor 5:10, KJV).

This is the final rebellion of the nations against God. His judgments at the Flood, Babel, ongoing over the millennia, Day of the Lord and during the Millennium come to finalisation after the Millennium.

God finally reigns as complete Sovereign and none can overthrow or withstand His power and glory forever and ever!

CONCLUDING REMARKS

From the above scriptures we can determine the following:

1. The Messiah – Christ – will make war with the nations during the Day of the Lord, in particular those that had attacked Israel and taken them into captivity.
2. Israel will be rescued in the Second Exodus and judged in the wilderness.
3. The other nations will be judged at the commencement of and during the Millennium.
4. Not all nations will be subject to His rule immediately upon the commencement of the 1,000 year period.
5. Peace will commence from Zion and gradually spread across the world which would, it seems, take a number of years or even decades to accomplish.
6. The nations of Ezekiel 38 and 39 will be conquered some years after His return.
7. other nations will be tested and given the opportunity to obey or rebel during the Millennium.
8. It would appear from the prophecies that various nations – or portions thereof – will choose to rebel even during the Millennial rule of the Messiah. They will be put down with force by the Divine King!
9. At the end of the Millennium the nations will be tested once more. This will be the final rebellion of the nations.

Since writing the original article that later formed this chapter, I came across an interesting article by Merrill Tenney which contains a number of essential points which I quote below:

> "There is no hint that all the earthly enemies of Christ are exterminated at His return; in fact, only the doom of the leaders is stated. **Even under the universal reign of righteousness there could still be a smoldering discontent of evil** which would burst into flame if opportunity were provided." ("The Importance and Exegesis of Revelation 20:1-8," *Bibliotheca Sacra*, April 1954, p. 144)

> ""For he must reign, till he hath put all enemies under his feet" (15:25). **This passage requires a period after Christ's return** during which He will reign until

He can complete the subjugation of evil and bring his enemies completely under his sovereignty. Such a period coincides quite exactly with the thousand years of Revelation." (p. 146)

"If, however, the passage represent the rule of Christ during a period of time, in which He deals with the nations as groups, but judges the individuals in them by their conduct toward each other during the period in which He is personally present, the judgment on the basis of behavior becomes explicable. In the light of His presence they cannot plead ignorance of His salvation or of His ethical standards, and their misconduct is utterly without excuse. As a description of Christ's administration during the millennium it would fit the existing requirements." (pp. 146-47)

"**The millennium, closely associated as it is with the return of Christ in judgment, is really the long Day of the Lord, or a period in which Christ and His servants will be occupied with judging evil**, in disentangling the complicated results of sin in human relationships, and in straightening out the moral affairs of humanity." (p. 147)

"The millennium, then, is not a useless excrescence on Scriptural Eschatology. It is a part of God's plan to vindicate His wisdom and to make redemption effective. It is intended to be a proving ground for the righteous administration **of the government of Christ, who will be purging the world of evil, and preparing it for the ultimate establishment of the city of God**." (p. 148) [emphasis mine]

These are excellent insights by Tenney and worthy of further exploration.

CHAPTER THIRTEEN

STATUS OF THE NATIONS

INTRODUCTORY COMMENTS

Following on from the book *In Search of … the Origin of Nations* which traces the nations of mankind after the great flood of Noah to their modern locations, it is important that we explore what these nations will be doing during the reign of the Messiah. The Scriptures do not reveal all that the nations will be doing, but they provide us enough information on the subject to be able to assemble an interesting picture of this 1,000 year period.

In this short chapter which is essentially a straightforward Bible study, all the various Scriptures concerning particular nations that are mentioned in Millennial prophecies are sought out and assembled by their names.

The nations as found in the Millennial prophecies are listed accordingly and where appropriate cross-referenced or commented upon.

> "Yea, all kings shall fall down before him: all nations shall serve him.
>
> For he shall deliver the needy when he crieth; the poor also, and *him* that hath no helper.
>
> He shall spare the poor and needy, and shall save the souls of the needy …
>
> His name shall endure for ever: his name shall be continued as long as the sun: and *men* shall be blessed in him: all nations shall call him blessed." (Ps 72:11-13, 17, KJV)

The rule of the Messiah commences when He first sets foot on the Mount of Olives, then slowly but methodically extends His reign. It begins with Jerusalem, spreads to Israel, the former Israelite colonies, and finally to the conquest of Gentile nations, one by one.

These nations will undergo trials and tests at various times during the Millennium. This process is to determine if they are truly converted and trust in His global leadership through Israel. For further biblical evidence, refer to the chapter 'Judging of the Nations'.

Overall, it will be a time of peace, harmony and prosperity. But God will not make anything too easy for anyone or any nation. He will test the heart of nations and individuals to see where they stand. Indeed, the nations will be tested to see if they are truly submissive to His rule through Israel and are building national character. All nations will have a part in God's great Plan. All nations will have a role in God's great Plan. This involves not becoming envious of Israel's blessings, rulership, and birthright inheritance. Similarly, it is important for Israel not to become haughty and arrogant.

This study will focus on specific Scriptures that relate to the nations mentioned explicitly in the prophecies.

During the Millennium, all the various races, peoples, and nations will maintain their distinct identities. The Bible does not express a 'one world' concept or the notion of 'humanity' et al. Instead, it speaks of 'all the nations' (Gen 22:18; 26:4; Zech 12:3) and 'all the families of the earth' (Gen 12:3; 28:14; Amos 3:2).[70] So it will be during the golden age of the Messiah!"

He sees commonalities, of course, but He also notices significant differences among the nations and peoples in terms of physiology, mentality, characteristics, and potential. We are not all the same; we are diverse. He, as Creator, wants diversity and it is up to us to both admire and protect it.

The process of separating out the nations to preserve their distinctiveness actually commences during the Day of the Lord, leading into the final intervention and world domination by the Messiah:

> "I will make a man more precious than fine gold; even a man than the golden wedge of Ophir.
>
> Therefore I will shake the heavens, and the earth shall remove out of her place, in the wrath of the LORD of hosts, and in the day of his fierce anger.
>
> And it shall be as the chased roe, and as a sheep that no man taketh up: **they shall every man turn to his own people, and flee every one into his own land**." (Is 13:12-14, KJV)

> "He made many to fall, yea, one fell upon another: and they said, Arise, **and let us go again to our own people, and to the land of our nativity**, from the oppressing sword." (Jer 46:16, KJV)

> "Cut off the sower from Babylon, and him that handleth the sickle in the time of harvest: for fear of the oppressing sword **they shall turn every one to his people, and they shall flee every one to his own land**." (Jer 50:16, KJV)

> "We would have healed Babylon, but she is not healed: forsake her, and **let us go every one into his own country**: for her judgment reacheth unto heaven, and is lifted up *even* to the skies." (Jer 51:9, KJV)

In this way all the nations will be preserved and be able to play their part in God's plan, according to the role He has assigned to each of them.

---

[70] The idea of a brotherhood of man et al are concepts from Communism and its twin, globalisation. The Bible, on the other hand, advocates nationhood with peoples of mankind cooperating while simultaneously maintaining their identities – God's true brotherhood of man.

This chapter reveals the Millennial roles of some of the nations referred to in the Bible. The appendix, *List of Tribulation and Day of the Lord Prophecies Concerning the Nations*, provides further Scriptures to study on the oracles against the nations. [71]

ASSYRIA

[NB: the Germans are the modern-day descendants of the Assyrians]

The Assyrians descend from Asshur, or Assur, second son of Shem (Genesis 10:22) and possibly the twin brother to Arphaxad. Traditionally, offspring are listed according to age: the firstborn is often listed first. In Genesis 10:22, we find listed five sons of Shem. Elam is clearly the firstborn. If Asshur was a twin brother of Elam, this would surely have been mentioned as with other twins in Scripture, but for some reason is not.

However, the historical antagonisms between Asshur and Israel (lineal descendants of Arphaxad) demonstrate that in all likelihood that they were twins with Asshur's birth possibly preceding Arphaxad's (compare with the example of Genesis 25:21-23). Arphaxad and Asshur were likely to have been twins for Scripture states that Arphaxad was begotten "two years after the Flood" (Genesis 11:10). In other words, Elam was begotten in the first year after the Flood and his two brothers begotten a year later. It is impossible for three separate births to have occurred within two years (24 months).

Not surprisingly, Asshur's name means 'strong' or 'powerful'. Or, as Josephus put it:

> "Ashur lived at the city Nineve; and named his subjects Assyrians, who became the most fortunate nation, beyond others." (Josephus *Antiquities*, I.vii.4)

This shows that they were a greatly blessed people, second only to the line of Arphaxad (and probably Aram it seems). God, by electing the line of Arphaxad to do His work and to lead the world, has led to Assur's jealousy of Arphaxad and an age-long antagonism which will culminate in a great show-down between their descendants in the years just ahead. Assur is likely just as capable as the descendants of Arphaxad in ruling and leading, with one exception: they are too warlike. As such, it is logical to conclude that God rejected Assur and chose the line of Arphaxad instead.

In the years ahead, Assyria together with their allies will attempt once and for all to subjugate the direct descendants of his twin brother Arphaxad (through Israel. i.e. the Anglo-Saxon-Kelts). But why? The age old resentment and envy that God had given the birthright blessing in place of Elam to Arphaxad, and not to himself (Assur) - that God chose that line, and not Assur's is still heaped up. Let there be no mistake: the modern descendants of Assur are an extremely gifted people who resemble the descendants of Arphaxad and Aram more so than any other nation. Their sense of order, discipline, ingenuity, cultural achievements and

---

[71] In addition - I have hand-written notes from the late 1970s on all the prophecies I could find on the end-time prophecies relating to all the non-Israelitish nations – that is during the Tribulation or the Messiah personally delivering excruciating punishment during the Day of the Lord. It is too easy to read over these parts of the Word of God without any reflection, thought or relating them to God's Plan.

cleanliness is superb and world-famous. But so is their warrior-image. From observation it seems probable that God chose Arphaxad because he had less of the military spirit and more leadership abilities.

But after WWIII, Assur will be one of the first to repent:

> "In that day there shall be a highway out of Egypt to **Assyria**, and **Assyria** shall come into Egypt, and Egypt into **Assyria**, and Egypt shall serve with **Assyria**.
>
> In that day Israel shall be the third with Egypt and with **Assyria**, a blessing in the midst of the land;
>
> whom Jehovah of Hosts shall bless, saying, Blessed *be* My people Egypt, and **Assyria** the work of My hands, and Israel My inheritance." (Is 19:23-25, MKJV)

So, the Germans will be granted their role in the World Tomorrow, like all other nations.

CUSH (ETHIOPIA)

[NB: the East Africans represent the western portion of the modern-day descendants of Cush. The southern Indians are the eastern portion of the Cushites]

> "Thus saith the LORD, The labour of Egypt, and merchandise of **Ethiopia** and of the Sabeans, men of stature, shall come over unto thee, and they shall be thine: they shall come after thee; in chains they shall come over, **and they shall fall down unto thee [Israel]**, they shall make supplication unto thee, saying, Surely God is in thee; and there is none else, there is no God.
>
> Verily thou art a God that hidest thyself, O God of Israel, the Saviour.
>
> They shall be ashamed, and also confounded, all of them: they shall go to confusion together that are makers of idols.
>
> But Israel shall be saved in the LORD with an everlasting salvation: ye shall not be ashamed nor confounded world without end." (Is 45:14-17, KJV)

> "Ah, land of whirring [Heb = "rustling"] wings that is **beyond the rivers of Cush**,
>
> which sends ambassadors by the sea, in vessels of papyrus on the waters! Go, you swift messengers, **to a nation tall and smooth [cp Is 45:14]**, to a people feared near and far, a nation mighty and conquering, whose land the rivers divide. [i.e. the sudd or swamps, hence the name Sudan, which probably means "black people of the swamps"]
>
> ...
>
> At that time tribute will be brought to the LORD of hosts from a people tall and smooth, from a people feared near and far, a nation mighty and conquering, whose land the rivers divide, to Mount Zion, the place of the name of the LORD of hosts." (Is 18:1-2, 7, KJV)

Notice, these are a tall, warrior people and the description seems to refer to the Nilotes. In fact, the Nilotes are considered to be among the tallest peoples in the world. Specifically, this prophecy is likely referring to the Dinka and Shilluk tribes who live on the floating cakes of Sudd. 'Beyond the rivers of Ethiopia' also refers to black peoples much further south, as those rivers were ultimately connected to the Zambezi at the time of the writing of that prophecy.

They dwell in eastern and northern Uganda, as well as southern Sudan. If the reader wishes to do some research himself, following is a list of the Nilote tribes to investigate: The Mittu, Abukaya, Luba (mixed with Lehabim?), Wira, Lendu, Mora, Shilluk, Anuok, Beir, Jur, Belanda, Acholi, Lango, Atura, Jaho, Dinka and the Nuer (a language of the Dinka is Ngok-**Sob**at which may relate to Sheba, son of Raamah, son of Cush).

CANAAN

[NB: the modern-day descendants of the Canaanites are scattered, though the core dwell along the Mediterranean rim]

> "And the captivity of this host of the children of Israel shall possess that of the **Canaanites**, even unto Zarephath; and the captivity of Jerusalem, which is in Sepharad, shall possess the cities of the south.
>
> And saviours shall come up on mount Zion to judge the mount of Esau; and the kingdom shall be the LORD'S." (Ob 20-21, KJV)

From this we can see that Israel will rule over them for at least an initial period of the Millennial reign of the Messiah.

> "Yea, and what have ye to do with me, **O Tyre, and Zidon**, and all the coasts of Palestine? will ye render me a recompence? and if ye recompense me, swiftly and speedily will I return your recompence upon your own head;
>
> Because ye have taken my silver and my gold, and have carried into your temples my goodly pleasant things:
>
> The children also of Judah and the children of Jerusalem have ye sold unto the Grecians, that ye might remove them far from their border.
>
> Behold, I will raise them out of the place whither ye have sold them, and will return your recompence upon your own head:
>
> And **I will sell your sons and your daughters into the hand of the children of Judah**, and they shall sell them to the Sabeans, to a people far off: for the LORD hath spoken it." (Joel 3:4-8, KJV)

This may seem rather odd, but a period of servitude must be necessary to break their rebellious will. They must learn to become subject to the Messiah!

> "Is it not yet a very little while, and **Lebanon** shall be turned into a fruitful field, and the fruitful field shall be esteemed as a forest?
>
> And in that day shall the deaf hear the words of the book, and the eyes of the blind shall see out of obscurity, and out of darkness.

> The meek also shall increase their joy in the LORD, and the poor among men shall rejoice in the Holy One of Israel." (Is 29:17-19, KJV)

> "The glory of **Lebanon** shall come unto thee, the fir tree, the pine tree, and the box together, to beautify the place of my sanctuary; and I will make the place of my feet glorious.
> The sons also of them that afflicted thee shall come bending unto thee; and all they that despised thee **shall bow themselves down at the soles of thy feet;** and they shall call thee, The city of the LORD, The Zion of the Holy One of Israel." (Is 60:13-14, KJV)

Both physically and spiritually, these people have afflicted the people of God – now judgment awaits them.

Edom (Esau)

[NB: various nations including most Turks and many Central Asians (mixed with Magog) are the modern-day descendants of the Edomites]

> "Therefore thus saith the Lord GOD; I will also stretch out mine hand upon **Edom**, and will cut off man and beast from it; and I will make it desolate from **Teman**; and they of Dedan shall fall by the sword.
> And **I will lay my vengeance upon Edom by the hand of my people Israel**: and they shall do in Edom according to mine anger and according to my fury; and they shall know my vengeance, saith the Lord GOD." (Ezek 25:13-14, KJV)

Israel will deal with this nation for the Messiah, Who will rule the entire world via His people (Revelation 2:26-27):

> "And thou shalt know that I am the LORD, and that I have heard all thy blasphemies which thou hast spoken against the mountains of Israel, saying, They are laid desolate, they are given us to consume.
> Thus with your mouth ye have boasted against me, and have multiplied your words against me: I have heard them.
> Thus saith the Lord GOD; When the whole earth rejoiceth, I will make thee desolate.
> As thou didst rejoice at the inheritance of the house of Israel, because it was desolate, so will I do unto thee: thou shalt be desolate, O mount **Seir**, and all **Idumea**, even all of it: and they shall know that I am the LORD." (Ezek 35:12-15, KJV)

Because they rejoice over the demise of God's people (Israel and the Church), their reckoning is approaching.

> "But upon mount Zion shall be deliverance, and there shall be holiness; and the house of Jacob shall possess their possessions.

And the house of Jacob shall be a fire, and the house of Joseph a flame, and the house of **Esau** for stubble, and they shall kindle in them, and devour them; and there shall not be any remaining of the house of **Esau**; for the LORD hath spoken it.

And they of the south shall possess the mount of **Esau**; and they of the plain the Philistines: and they shall possess the fields of Ephraim, and the fields of Samaria: and Benjamin shall possess Gilead.

And the captivity of this host of the children of Israel shall possess that of the Canaanites, even unto Zarephath; and the captivity of Jerusalem, which is in Sepharad, shall possess the cities of the south.

And saviours shall come up on mount Zion to judge the mount of **Esau**; and the kingdom shall be the LORD'S." (Ob 17-21, KJV)

GOG, MAGOG, MESCHECH, TUBAL ETC

[NB: these peoples generally inhabit the area of Russia today as well as Central Asia and China]

To understand Ezekiel 38:18-39:16, we need to note that they are read in many synagogues during the Feast of Tabernacles, providing the context for its fulfilment.

Also, these forces are likely the remnants of the Second Woe (Revelation 9:13-21), which God might have used to conquer and punish the nations under the Beast's power. Possibly, about seven years after the Israelites have resettled in the Holy Land, following Israel's actions towards certain Gentiles, many will likely rise in rebellion, probably citing discrimination and unfairness as reasons for this invasion.

Ezekiel reveals the following:

"And the word of the LORD came unto me, saying,

Son of man, set thy face against **Gog, the land of Magog**, the chief prince of **Meshech** and **Tubal**, and prophesy against him,

And say, Thus saith the Lord GOD; Behold, I *am* against thee, O Gog, the chief prince of Meshech and Tubal:

And I will turn thee back, and put hooks into thy jaws, and I will bring thee forth, and all thine army, horses and horsemen, all of them clothed with all sorts *of armour, even* a great company *with* bucklers and shields, all of them handling swords:

Persia, Ethiopia, and Libya with them; all of them with shield and helmet:

Gomer, and all his bands; the house of **Togarmah** of the north quarters, and all his bands: *and* many people with thee." (Ezek 38:1-6, KJV)

"So says the Lord Jehovah: And it shall be in that day that things shall come into your heart, and you shall devise an evil plan.

And you shall say, I will go up to the land of open spaces. I will go *to* **those at ease** [cp Lam 1:3], who **dwell securely**, all of them dwelling **without walls**, and there are no bars nor gates to them, in order to take a spoil, and to steal a prize; to turn your hand on the inhabited waste places, and **on the people gathered out of the nations, who have gotten cattle and goods**, who dwell in the midst of the land." (Ezek 38:10-12, MKJV)

Notice: as we have read previously, this rebellion is against the Israelites who have returned from captivity and who now have gathered much wealth as we have seen. They also are dwelling in peace.

And why does this war occur?:

> "And I will set My glory among the nations, and all the nations shall see My judgments which I have done, and My hand that I have laid on them.
>
> So the house of Israel shall know that I *am* Jehovah their God from that day and forward. [there will be no more doubting Thomas's]
>
> And the nations shall know that the house of Israel was exiled [i.e. prior to this Gog and Magog invasion] for their iniquity. Because they sinned against Me, therefore I hid My face from them and gave them into the hand of their enemies. So they all fell by the sword. [it follows on therefore that these gentile nations will now be called to repent and allow God to rule over them through Israel]" (Ezek 39:21-23, MKJV)

What of those nations that, prior to the liberation of Israel by Christ, would have enslaved Israel, but by now have repented and even assisted in the transporting of liberated Israelitish slaves to the Holy Land?:

> "**Sheba and Dedan**, and the merchants of **Tarshish**, with all their young lions [Assyria – Nah 2:11], shall say to you, Have you come to take a spoil? Have you gathered your company to steal a prize, to carry away silver and gold, to take away cattle and goods, to take a great spoil?" (Ezek 38:13, MKJV)

For more details, refer to the chapter *A War even after the Messiah's Return!*

ISHMAEL

[NB: the descendants of Ishmael dwell today in the Arabian peninsula as well as many millions scattered throughout North Africa and other countries such as Iran]

> "**They that dwell in the wilderness shall bow before him**; and his enemies shall lick the dust.
>
> The kings of Tarshish and of the isles shall bring presents: the kings of Sheba and Seba shall offer gifts." (Ps 72:9-10, KJV)

> "All the flocks of **Kedar** shall be gathered together unto thee, the rams of **Nebaioth** shall minister unto thee: they shall come up with acceptance on mine altar, and I will glorify the house of my glory." (Is 60:7, KJV)

As with all peoples, the rebellious will of the Arabs and related nations will be broken and they will then learn the true ways of God via the Messiah.

Mizraim (Egypt)

[NB: the Egyptians, in the main, are the modern-day descendants of the ancient Egyptians]

"And it shall come to pass, that every one that is left of all the nations which came against Jerusalem shall even go up from year to year to worship the King, the LORD of hosts, and to keep the feast of tabernacles.

And it shall be, that whoso will not come up of all the families of the earth unto Jerusalem to worship the King, the LORD of hosts, even upon them shall be no rain.

And if the **family of Egypt** go not up, and come not, that have no rain; there shall be the plague, wherewith the LORD will smite the heathen that come not up to keep the feast of tabernacles.

This shall be the punishment of **Egypt**, and the punishment of all nations that come not up to keep the feast of tabernacles." (Zech 14:16-19, KJV)

This shows that the observance of the Feast of Tabernacles will be obligatory upon all peoples and that the Law of God has not been done away.

"And **the land of Egypt** shall be desolate and waste; and they shall know that I am the LORD: because he hath said, The river is mine, and I have made it.

Behold, therefore I am against thee, and against thy rivers, and I will make the land of Egypt utterly waste and desolate, from the tower of Syene even unto the border of Ethiopia.

No foot of man shall pass through it, nor foot of beast shall pass through it, neither shall it be inhabited forty years.

And I will make the land of **Egypt** desolate in the midst of the countries that are desolate, and her cities among the cities that are laid waste shall be desolate forty years: and I will scatter the **Egyptians** among the nations, and will disperse them through the countries.

Yet thus saith the Lord GOD; At the end of forty years will I gather the Egyptians from the people whither they were scattered:

And I will bring again the captivity of **Egypt**, and will cause them to return into the land of Pathros, into the land of their habitation; and they shall be there a base kingdom.

It shall be the basest of the kingdoms; neither shall it exalt itself any more above the nations: for I will diminish them, that they shall no more rule over the nations.

And it shall be no more the confidence of the house of Israel, which bringeth their iniquity to remembrance, when they shall look after them: but they shall know that I am the Lord GOD." (Ezek 29:9-16, KJV)

Notice that even though they will be saved by God, yet they will be a base nation, overall.

"Thus saith the LORD, The labour of **Egypt**, and merchandise of Ethiopia and of the Sabeans, men of stature, shall come over unto thee [Israel], and they shall be thine: they shall come after thee; in chains they shall come over, and they shall fall down unto thee [Israel], they shall make supplication unto thee, saying, Surely God is in thee; and there is none else, there is no God.

Verily thou art a God that hidest thyself, O God of Israel, the Saviour.

They shall be ashamed, and also confounded, all of them: they shall go to confusion together that are makers of idols.

But Israel shall be saved in the LORD with an everlasting salvation: ye shall not be ashamed nor confounded world without end." (Is 45:14-17, KJV)

"**The burden of Egypt**. Behold, the LORD rideth upon a swift cloud, and shall come into Egypt: and the idols of Egypt shall be moved at his presence, and the heart of Egypt shall melt in the midst of it.

And I will set the Egyptians against the Egyptians: and they shall fight every one against his brother, and every one against his neighbour; city against city, *and* kingdom against kingdom.

And the spirit of Egypt shall fail in the midst thereof; and I will destroy the counsel thereof: and they shall seek to the idols, and to the charmers, and to them that have familiar spirits, and to the wizards." (Is 19:1-3, KJV)

The above indicates that this occurs after the return of the Messiah. Compare with Zechariah 14:13.

Now Egypt learns to fear Judah which God uses to punish them:

"And the land of Judah shall be a terror unto **Egypt**, every one that maketh mention thereof shall be afraid in himself, because of the counsel of the LORD of hosts, which he hath determined against it." [see Zech 14:14 where Judah are portrayed as fighters] (Is 19:17, KJV)

Then we have Egypt's repentance:

"In that day shall five cities in **the land of Egypt** speak the language of Canaan, and swear to the LORD of hosts; one shall be called, The city of destruction.

In that day shall there be an altar to the LORD in the midst of the land of **Egypt**, and a pillar at the border thereof to the LORD.

And it shall be for a sign and for a witness unto the LORD of hosts in the land of Egypt: for they shall cry unto the LORD because of the oppressors, and he shall send them a saviour, and a great one, and he shall deliver them." (Is 19:18-20, KJV)

These oppressors are likely those referred to in Is 19:11-13.

"And **the LORD shall be known to Egypt**, and the Egyptians shall know the LORD in that day, and shall do sacrifice and oblation; yea, they shall vow a vow unto the LORD, and perform *it*.

And the LORD shall smite Egypt: he shall smite and heal *it*: and they shall return *even* to the LORD, and he shall be intreated of them, and shall heal them.

In that day shall there be a highway out of Egypt to Assyria, and the Assyrian shall come into Egypt, and the Egyptian into Assyria, and the Egyptians shall serve with the Assyrians.

In that day shall Israel be the third with Egypt and with Assyria, *even* a blessing in the midst of the land:

Whom the LORD of hosts shall bless, saying, **Blessed *be* Egypt my people**, and Assyria the work of my hands, and Israel mine inheritance." (Is 19:21-25, KJV)

SHEBA, SEBA AND THE SABEANS

[NB: the descendants of Sheba are today dwelling in East Africa; Seba are the Dravidians (southern Indians) and Sabeans may be a collective name for Sheba, Seba etc]

"They that dwell in the wilderness shall bow before him; and his enemies shall lick the dust.

The kings of Tarshish and of the isles shall bring presents: the **kings of Sheba and Seba** shall offer gifts." (Ps 72:9-10, KJV)

"And the Gentiles shall come to thy light, and kings to the brightness of thy rising.

Lift up thine eyes round about, and see: all they gather themselves together, they come to thee: thy sons shall come from far, and thy daughters shall be nursed at *thy* side.

Then thou shalt see, and flow together, and thine heart shall fear, and be enlarged; because the abundance of the sea shall be converted unto thee, the forces of the Gentiles shall come unto thee.

The multitude of camels shall cover thee, the dromedaries of Midian and Ephah; **all they from Sheba shall come**: they shall bring gold and incense; and they shall shew forth the praises of the LORD." (Is 60:3-6, KJV)

"Behold, I will raise them out of the place whither ye have sold them, and will return your recompence upon your own head:

And I will sell your sons and your daughters into the hand of the children of Judah, and they shall sell them to **the Sabeans**, to a people far off: for the LORD hath spoken it." (Joel 3:7-8, KJV)

"Thus saith the LORD, The labour of Egypt, and merchandise of Ethiopia and **of the Sabeans**, men of stature, shall come over unto thee, and they shall be thine: they shall come after thee; in chains they shall come over, and they shall fall down unto thee, they shall make supplication unto thee, saying, Surely God is in thee; and there is none else, there is no God.

Verily thou art a God that hidest thyself, O God of Israel, the Saviour.

They shall be ashamed, and also confounded, all of them: they shall go to confusion together that are makers of idols.

But Israel shall be saved in the LORD with an everlasting salvation: ye shall not be ashamed nor confounded world without end." (Is 45:14-17, KJV)

TARSHISH, JAVAN, LUD

[NB: the Spanish are the western portion of the modern-day descendants of the descendants of Tarshish and the Japanese the eastern portion. Javan includes the core Greeks and southern Italians. Lud could also comprises some in south-east Europe]

"Surely the isles shall wait for me, and **the ships of Tarshish first, to bring thy sons from far**, their silver and their gold with them, unto the name of the LORD thy God, and to the Holy One of Israel, because he hath glorified thee." (Is 60:9, KJV)

"And I will set a sign among them, and I will send those that escape of them unto the nations, **to Tarshish, Pul, and Lud**, that draw the bow, to Tubal, and **Javan**, to the isles afar off, that have not heard my fame, neither have seen my glory; and they shall declare my glory among the Gentiles.

And they shall bring all your brethren for an offering unto the LORD out of all nations upon horses, and in chariots, and in litters, and upon mules, and upon swift beasts, to my holy mountain Jerusalem, saith the LORD, as the children of Israel bring an offering in a clean vessel into the house of the LORD.

And I will also take of them for priests and for Levites, saith the LORD." (Is 66:19-21, KJV)

"They that dwell in the wilderness shall bow before him; and his enemies shall lick the dust.

The kings of Tarshish and of the isles shall bring presents: the kings of Sheba and Seba shall offer gifts." (Ps 72:9-10, KJV)

Here we see that repentant Tarshish actually brings the remnants of Israel to the Holy Land as part of the Second Exodus. They even bring gifts to the Messiah demonstrating their obeisance and repentance.

OBSERVATIONS AND COMMENTS

The above represents most, if not all, of the Scriptures concerning specific nations that are named for the time of the Messiah as He rules supreme over the entire world.

They provide a mere glimpse of what will happen to particular nations after His arrival. It seems this occurs several years into the Millennium. These scriptures are a sample or representation of what the nations will be doing, including their roles and status.

It is important, though, to read the chapter *Israel's Role after the Second Exodus. Tomorrow?* to understand her role and place. Then match that with the roles of the non-Israelitish peoples which will help to more fully understand the prophecies listed or discussed within the pages of this book.

I hope this short chapter will expand one's thinking about the World Tomorrow and what will actually occur at that time. It demonstrates that God's Word has much more to say about this period than many would imagine, as it is all too easy to overlook the pertinent scriptures relating to these nations and their role during that period. What better way to complete this Bible study than by quoting a key scripture:

What better way to complete this Bible study than by quoting a key scripture:

"Arise, shine; for thy light is come, and the glory of the LORD is risen upon thee.

For, behold, the darkness shall cover the earth, and gross darkness the people: but the LORD shall arise upon thee, and his glory shall be seen upon thee.

And the Gentiles shall come to thy light, and kings to the brightness of thy rising.

Lift up thine eyes round about, and see: all they gather themselves together, they come to thee: thy sons shall come from far, and thy daughters shall be nursed at *thy* side.

Then thou shalt see, and flow together, and thine heart shall fear, and be enlarged; because the abundance of the sea shall be converted unto thee, the forces of the Gentiles shall come unto thee.

The multitude of camels shall cover thee, the dromedaries of Midian and Ephah; all they from Sheba shall come: they shall bring gold and incense; and they shall shew forth the praises of the LORD.

All the flocks of Kedar shall be gathered together unto thee, the rams of Nebaioth shall minister unto thee: they shall come up with acceptance on mine altar, and I will glorify the house of my glory.

Who *are* these *that* fly as a cloud, and as the doves to their windows?

Surely the isles shall wait for me, and the ships of Tarshish first, to bring thy sons from far, their silver and their gold with them, unto the name of the LORD thy God, and to the Holy One of Israel, because he hath glorified thee.

And the sons of strangers shall build up thy walls, and their kings shall minister unto thee: for in my wrath I smote thee [the Great Tribulation], **but in my favour have I had mercy on thee.** [restoration of Israel after the Exodus]

Therefore thy gates shall be open continually; they shall not be shut day nor night; that *men* may bring unto thee the forces of the Gentiles, and *that* their kings *may be* brought.

For the nation and kingdom that will not serve thee shall perish; yea, *those* nations shall be utterly wasted. [Israel will rule the world!]

The glory of Lebanon shall come unto thee, the fir tree, the pine tree, and the box together, to beautify the place of my sanctuary; and I will make the place of my feet glorious.

The sons also of them that afflicted thee shall come bending unto thee; and all they that despised thee shall bow themselves down at the soles of thy feet; and they shall call thee, **The city of the LORD, The Zion of the Holy One of Israel.**

Whereas thou hast been forsaken and hated, so that no man went through *thee*, I will make thee an eternal excellency, a joy of many generations.

Thou shalt also suck the milk of the Gentiles, and shalt suck the breast of kings: and thou shalt know that I the LORD *am* thy Saviour and thy Redeemer, the mighty One of Jacob.

For brass I will bring gold, and for iron I will bring silver, and for wood brass, and for stones iron: I will also make thy officers peace, and thine exactors righteousness. **Violence shall no more be heard in thy land, wasting nor destruction within thy borders; but thou shalt call thy walls Salvation, and thy gates Praise.**

The sun shall be no more thy light by day; neither for brightness shall the moon give light unto thee: but the LORD shall be unto thee an everlasting light, and thy God thy glory. [typological of the Day of the Lord]

Thy sun shall no more go down; neither shall thy moon withdraw itself: for the LORD shall be thine everlasting light, and the days of thy mourning shall be ended. [symbolically and also a type of the New Jerusalem]

Thy people also *shall be* all righteous: they shall inherit the land for ever, the branch of my planting, the work of my hands, that I may be glorified.

A little one shall become a thousand, and a small one a strong nation: I the LORD will hasten it in his time." [the might of Israel during the Millennium] (Is 60:1-22, KJV) [compare this chapter with Ps 60]

Prior to the Millennium, the world will experience the terrible Tribulation and Day of the Lord. Some prophecies that refer to specific nations are explained and listed in the appendix **List of Tribulation and Day of the Lord Prophecies concerning the Nations.**

But during the Millennium all nations will learn the hard way to serve and love the Son of God (Ps 2; 96; 97; 98; 99; 100; 150; Is 56:6-8).

FURTHER READING

- Kaiser, W. C. (1991), *Towards an Old Testament Theology*. Zondervan.
- Kaiser, W. C. (2000), *Mission in the Old Testament. Israel as a Light to the Nations*. Baker Books, Grand Rapids, MI.
- Kaiser, W. C. (1977), "The Davidic Promise and the Inclusion of the Gentiles (Amos 9:9-15 And Acts 15:13-18): A Test Passage for Theological Systems," *Journal of the Evangelical Theological Society*, Vol. 20, No. 2 (June), pp. 97-111.
- Mathewson, D. (2002), "The Destiny of the Nations in Revelation 21:1 – 22:5. A Reconsideration," *Tyndale Bulletin*, Vol. 53, No. 1, pp. 121-142.
- Tenney, M. (1954), "The Importance and Exegesis of Revelation 20:1-8," *Bibliotheca Sacra*, Vol. 111, pp. 137-148.
- White, C. M. (2021), *The Sanctity of Nationhood in the Bible* (Bible study), Sydney.
- White, C. M. (2015), *Days of the Lord* (Bible Study). Sydney.
- Worldwide Church of God. (1987), *Russia and China in Prophecy*. Worldwide Church of God, Pasadena, CA.

FINAL WORDS

We are now at the end of a book that the author hopes has been both enlightening and helpful in expanding the reader's understanding of the wonderful World Tomorrow.

The author particularly encourages readers to delve deeper into various aspects of the Millennium—to read the Scriptures contained herein, which pertain to the various facets of the Messiah's reign on Earth.

But what will occur after that 1,000 year period? Below I have assembled an outline in table form to make it easier to understand and follow:

Table 14 Sequence of Events After the Millennium

Order	Event	Supporting Scriptures
1.	Satan released	Rev 20:7
2.	Final Rebellion	Rev 20:8-9[72]
3.	Satan eliminated	Rev 20:10; Matt 25:41
4.	Demons judged	Jude 1:6; Matt 25:41; ICor 6:3 (see IPet 3:18-20); Is 24:21-23
5.	2nd resurrection	Rev 20:11-12; Matt 10:15; 11:21-24; 12:41-42; John 5:28-30; Acts 24:15; Dan 12:2
6.	3rd resurrection to Judgment	Rev 20:13-15; 21:7-8, 27; 22:14-15; Jude 1, 7-8, 14-16; Ps 11:5-6; 21:8-10; 68:3; 140:9-11; Prov 21:16; Dan 12:2; Mal 4:1-3; Matt 5:21-22; 7:18-23; 12:32; 13:39-42, 49-50; 18:8-10; Mark 3:28-30; 8:38; Acts 24:15; 2Thess 1:5-10; Heb 2:3; 6:4-8; 10:26-29; 12:28-29; IPet 4:17-19; IIPet 2:4-9, 20-21; 3:5-7
7.	Death abolished	Rev 20:14; ICor 15:25-26
8.	Earth cleansed by fire	IIPet 3:10-13; Matt 24:35[73]

---

[72] Refer to the chapter *A War after the Messiah's Return!* for proof that the army of Ezekiel 38 and 39 is a different army to that which invades after the Millennium, though seemingly typological of it.

[73] Similarly, Isaiah 51:6 states "Lift up your eyes to the heavens, and look upon the earth beneath: **for the heavens shall vanish away like smoke, and the earth shall wax old like a garment**, and they that dwell therein shall die in like manner: but my salvation shall be for ever, and my righteousness shall not be abolished" - clearly this refers to the Day of the Lord and not the universal event just prior to the New Heavens and New Earth referred to in IIPeter 3:10-13.

Order	Event	Supporting Scriptures
9.	Christ delivers up the Kingdom to the Father	ICor 15:24, 28; Eph 1:9-10; Heb 1:2
10.	New Heavens and New Earth	Rev 21:1-5; IIPet 3:13
11.	New Jerusalem established on the New Earth	Rev 21 and 22
12.	Christians inherit all things - the universe!	Rom 8:18-23; Rev 21:7

Concerning Revelation 21:1-5 and IIPeter 3:13 (in row 10 above), note the *New Living Translation* of Isaiah 65:20

> "No longer will babies die when only a few days old. No longer will adults die before they have lived a full life. No longer will people be considered old at one hundred! Only the cursed will die that young!"

This indicates that this Scripture may apply to both the Millennium and the Last Great Day. We also need to understand the difference between the *new heavens* mentioned in Isaiah 65:17 and 66:20 and that of the New Testament:

> "In the light of the whole Scripture, it appears that the Millennium is like a "firstfruits" of the eternal state. **The Millennium will be like a preview of the eternal messianic kingdom** that will be revealed fully in the eternal state. Therefore, because the two are alike in nature, they share distinct similarities. Yet because they are both different revealed time periods, they would likewise reflect some dissimilarities ..." (Ralph Alexander, *Ezekiel. Everyman's Bible Commentary*, Vol. 6, p. 945, note on *Does Ezekiel 40-48 Relate to the Millennium or to the Eternal State?)* [emphasis mine]

> "If apocalyptic represents a development, one would expect the earlier stage to fall by the wayside . . . **[Instead] the NT, while clearly availing itself of the expanded imagery and thought forms of apocalyptic, equally clearly retains a point of view fully consonant with OT prophecy** . . . [Thus] the [Biblical] apocalyptic view did not replace the prophetic one but rather existed beside it, enriching and expanding it, but never supplanting it" (John Oswalt, "Recent Studies in Old Testament Eschatology and Apocalyptic," *Journal of Evangelical Theological Society*, 1985, p. 301). [emphasis mine]

> "Various OT texts reveal conditions that are part of the millennial kingdom on earth but not part of the new heavens and new earth in the eternal state. Isaiah 65:17–25 and 66:22– 24 reveal **conditions that cannot be part of the eternal state. These descriptions require an intermediate kingdom prior to the eternal state.**
> Isaiah states that the child will die one hundred years old and the sinner being one hundred years old shall be accursed (Isa 65:20). The death of children at 100 years old shows the longevity of life in the millennial kingdom. This verse also shows

that King Jesus will judge those unbelieving children of the tribulation saints who physically survive the tribulation period and enter the kingdom in their physical bodies. Physical death will not happen in the new heavens and new earth. John wrote, "There will be no more death" (Rev 21:4)." (Gary Gromacki, "The fulfillment of the Abrahamic Covenant," *The Journal of Ministry and Theology*, Vol. 18, No. 2, 2006, pp. 100-01) [emphasis mine]

This will indeed be times of refreshing and restoration of God's Kingdom on earth (Acts 3:19-21).

From this, we can see that the refreshing and improvement of the earth, waters and its atmosphere is appropriately called new. It is indeed a renewing and the ultimate accomplishment of the Kingdom of God. It fulfills completely the testimony of the prophets that a future Messiah will come and rescue man from himself, sin, and all corruption.

Finally, a quote from George Ladd:

> "The physical world, with man, has fallen under the doom and decay of sin, and therefore in its present condition cannot be the scene of the perfected kingdom of God. A radical transformation is necessary, and the new transformed age of the kingdom will be so different from the present age as to constitute a new order of things ...
>
> **God has manifested his kingly power in the present for man's salvation, to bring to him in advance the blessings of the future kingdom** ... through the new people of God who experience the power of the kingdom ...
>
> men will enter the future kingdom because they have been confronted by the kingdom in the present and have embraced its reign in their lives." (George Ladd, "Why Not Prophetic-Apocalyptic?" *Journal of Biblical Literature*, Vol. 76, No. 3 (Sept 1957), pp. 192-200).[74] [emphasis mine]

This book is, in effect, a comprehensive Bible study and should be used for that purpose, as well as for further studies of the subject by the reader.

We have now completed a study on the Messiah's rule over the earth, and I hope and pray that the reader has learned more about this period, inspiring them to pray, "Thy Kingdom come!"

---

[74] Christopher Wright identifies four main categories that the prophets pronounce condemnation: idolatry; perversions; "that which was destructive of persons"; and the hardened approach toward the poor and needy (*Old Testament Ethics for the People of God*, p. 349).

PART FIVE

APPENDICES

THE RESURRECTIONS

At Christ's return, He will raise the saints to eternal life, but what actually occurs at that time? The table below outlines the steps to help us understand this stupendous event.

Table 15 Sequence of Events at the Resurrection

Order	Event	Supporting Scriptures
1.	A Christian falls asleep/dies	IISam 7:12; ICor 15:51
2.	Just prior to the resurrection they are given a new spiritual body (we will have glory beyond belief)	Ps 17:15; Is 26:19; 1Cor 15:51; Dan 12:1-3; Matt 13:41-43
3.	They then waken to eternal life to Christ's call and the trumpet	John 5:24-28; John 11:43; 1Th 4:16; 1Cor 15:40-55
4.	Graves will open and they will live again!	Job 14:10-15; Rom 8:20-29
5.	Angels appear at their graveside or place that they died	Matt 28:1-6; 13:26-27; 24:30-31
6.	Ascend into the clouds to be with Christ	Mark 14:61-62; IThess 4:16-18; Matt 24:30-31; Rev 1:7
7.	Singing with joy	Ps 30:3-6; 69:27-30; Is 38:18-19; 26:19-21; Rev 5:9; 15:3
8.	The Judgement or assessment of their lives	Rom 14:9-12; IICor 5:9-11; John 5:22-28; IPet 4:5; IJohn 2:28
9.	Rewarded and receive a new name	Ps 58:10-11; Is 62:10-12; Matt 6:17-18; ICor 3:14-15; Rev 22:12
10.	Marriage Feast	Rev 19:7-10; Matt 25:1-13; 26:29
11.	Descend to the earth to reign with Christ	Rev 15:3-8; 20:4; Dan 7:17-19, 27

The resurrections, as well as the rewards and punishments, appear to happen simultaneously in some scriptures. This is likely because Daniel 12:2, Acts 24:15, John 5:28-29, Matt 13:30-31, 39-43 and Mark 8:38 are examples of telescopic prophecies – a concept the Hebrew mind would understand and recognize as such. A telescopic prophecy makes future events appear as if they are occurring at the same time. For example, mountains in the distance may look close together, yet they can be 50 miles apart or more. Similarly, the prophetic event may seem to be a single occurrence but is actually composed of separate events.

If it were not for the book of Revelation, we would not have clarity of the sequence of end time events. It is chiefly because we have the book of Revelation that we know the sequence of events, more-or-less. I believe that it demonstrates that there are three resurrections representing three classes of people:

1. Resurrection to spirit life
2. Resurrection to physical life with an opportunity for salvation
3. Resurrection to condemnation and death.

That sequence makes sense to me. Belief in three (instead of two) resurrections is virtually unheard of in Christian theology. However, history records that some Sabbatarians believed in three resurrections in the 2nd century:

> "These Jewish Christian groups, referred to by Epiphanius (Williams, 1987) as Nazarenes or Elkasaites, professed the following beliefs: They proclaimed Jesus as prophet-Messiah; insisted upon the validity of the Torah & laws of ritual purity; **spoke of three resurrections;** professed a millennarian eschatology; looked forward to the restoration of the Temple; observed the feast of Sukkoth (Tabernacles), celebrated Easter at Passover, & observed the Sabbath; affirmed the primacy of James, brother of Jesus, over Peter in the leadership of the church; & preferred the designation "Nazarene" over "Christian." (Eric Meyers, "Early Judaism," *Biblical Archaeologist*, June 1988, pp. 69-79) [emphasis mine]

It would appear from the above quote that the Nazarenes believed in three resurrections.

It may be more than passing interest that there were three resurrections performed in the Old Testament (IKings 17:17-25; IIKings 4:32-37; 13:20-21); three by Christ (Luke 7:11-18; Mark 5:35; John 11); and three after Christ's death (Matt 27:51-53; Acts 9:36-42; 20:7-16). Bullinger in his superb *Number in Scripture* goes so far as to state that: "three is the number of resurrection" (p. 111) because Christ rose the 3rd day; he was perfected on the 3rd day, he was crucified at the 3rd hour; for three hours darkness shrouded the region at the time of His crucifixion; he raised three persons from the dead; and it was on the 3rd day that the earth was caused to rise up out of the waters in Genesis.

Daniel 12:2; Acts 24:15; Revelation 20:4-6, 12-15 have a consistent approach to resurrection.

> "Also Acts 24:15, where Paul speaks of the hope he shares with the Jewish people "that there will be a resurrection of both the righteous and the unrighteous," and Revelation 20:4-6 and 11-15, where the two resurrections are separated by a thousand years" (J. Ramsey Michaels, *The Gospel of John* in *The New International Commentary on the New Testament*, p. 322).

Now notice what some insightful commentators have to say about this in the context of John 4 and 5:

"Truly, truly, I say to you, **an hour is coming, and is now here**, when the dead will hear the voice of the Son of God, and those who hear will live ...

Do not marvel at this, for **an hour is coming** when all who are in the tombs will hear his voice and come out, those who have done good to the resurrection of life, and those who have done evil to the resurrection of judgment." (John 5:25, 28-29 ESV)

Compare with

"Jesus said to her, "Woman, believe me, **the hour is coming** when neither on this mountain nor in Jerusalem will you worship the Father.

But **the hour is coming, and is now here**, when the true worshipers will worship the Father in spirit and truth, for the Father is seeking such people to worship him." (John 4:21, 23 ESV)

"... "an hour is coming," echoing verse 25, except the transforming postscript, "and now is," is conspicuous by its absence... The same two expressions occurred in Jesus' dialogue with the Samaritan woman, but with a quite different rhetorical effect. There, Jesus first said, "an hour is coming" (4:21), and then used the longer expression, "an hour is coming and now is," to define what he meant (4:23). Here by contrast, the two expressions do not refer to the same "hour." The longer one comes first, announcing a future about to begin, or one that has begun for the readers (v.25). **The shorter expression, "an hour is coming" (v.28), points to a more remote future (equivalent to "the last day") and a literal, not just spiritual resurrection and judgment"** (Michaels, ibid p. 321). [emphasis mine]

The following chart, comparing John 5:24-25 with Revelation 20:4-6, is from William Hendriksen and sheds further light on the subject. This comparison is found in his work, *New Testament Commentary: Exposition of the Gospel According to John. Two Volumes Complete in One*, p. 200. Note: Hendriksen has aligned the words "and (he) does not come into condemnation..." from John 5 with Revelation 20:6 to demonstrate how these scriptures speak of the same event.

Table 16 Comparison of John and Revelation

Fourth Gospel (John)	Revelation
A. First Resurrection	A. First Resurrection
"I most solemnly assure you, he who hears my word and believes him who sent me has everlasting life ... has passed out of death unto life. I most solemnly assure you, the hour is coming – yea, has already arrived! – when the dead will hear his voice of the Son of God, and those who hear will live." "and (he) does not come into condemnation..."	"... and I saw the souls of them that had been beheaded ... and such as not as worshiped not the beast, neither his image, and received not the mark upon their forehead and upon their hand; and they lived and reigned with Christ a thousand years ... This is the first resurrection. "Blessed and holy is he who has part in the first resurrection: over these the second death has no power."

Fourth Gospel (John)	Revelation
B. Second Resurrection	**B. Second Resurrection**
(unto judgment)	(unto judgment)
"Stop being surprised about this, for the hour is coming when all who are in the tombs will hear his voice and will come out: those who have done good, for the resurrection of life, and those who have practised evil, for the resurrection of condemnation."	"And I saw a great white throne and him who sat upon it... Rev 20:12 And I saw the dead, the great and the small, standing before the throne; and books were opened: and another book was opened, which is the book of life: and the dead were judged out of the things which were written in the books, according to their works: And the sea gave up the dead that were in it; and death and Hades gave up the dead that were in them: and they were judged according to their works... And if any one was not found in the book of life, he cast into the lake of fire."

BIBLE STUDY. THE SECOND EXODUS AND THE LAST TRUMP

**The Last Trump may foretell the Second Exodus for the Houses of Israel and Judah.
An aspect of the Feast of Trumpets often overlooked**

1. VARIETY OF TRUMPET MEANINGS:

- Historical
- Warning of Doom/Invading Armies
- Day of the Lord
- Second Exodus
- Resurrection

2. STAGES IN THE SECOND EXODUS AND ISRAEL'S RESTORATION:

- **1. The house of Israel is scattered** in captivity in foreign lands – Assyria; Elam; Egypt, Pathros, Cush, Shinar, isles or coastlands of the sea and from the north country. (see Is 27:13; 10:20-22; 11:11-12; Jer 16:14-15; 23:3, 7-8; 31:8-9; 50:3-5)
- **2. Israel awakens to her destiny and repents.** The actual awakening to her identity and destiny may begin around the time of the Signs in the Heavens, which signals the soon-coming intervention of the Messiah to rescue Israel and to rain down plagues upon hostile gentile powers (Is 51:6; Luke 21:28; Lev 26:40-45; Hos 3:5; 6:1-3; Ps 121:1-8)
- **3. She is then rescued and rebels purged out** because Israel and Judah still need purging of rebels after the return of Christ (see Is 30:18; Jer 50:20; Ezek 20:35-38, 42-44). It seems that much of this may occur in a wilderness and in the Valley of Jezreel (Hos 1:4-11; 2:14; Is 40:2), also known as the plain of Megiddo.
- **4. A repentant Israel enters the Promised Land**

(a). Deut 4:26-29 (cp Is 55:1; Hos 6:1-3; Lam 3:23-24; Deut 30:1-5), 30-31; 30:4 (cp Matt 24:31); Is 10:20-22; Zeph 3:18-20; Is 35:1-10; 51:1-23.

(b). Is 1:11-16; 27:12-13 (it would appear that this will begin at the 7th Trump of Revelation). See also Zech 9:14-16; Is 10:20-22; 66:18-21; Jer 16:14-15; 23:3, 7-8; 31:8-9; 43:1-6; 50:3-5; Ezek 20:42-43.

(c). Is 42:1-6 (only then will Israel be in a position to become a light to the world)

- **5. Israel then swoops upon ceertain nations** either before or after entry into the Promised Land (Is 14:1-2; 41:15; 60:5-16; 19:17; 61:4-9; Ezek 25:13-17; Ob 1:17-21; Zech 9:11-14; 10:3-10; 12:7-8; 14:14; Amos 9:11-12; Zeph 2:7-13)
- **6. Millennial Temple established** and God's glory fills the Temple (see Ezek 40-48 (Ezek 43:5). Cp Acts 2:2; Is 44:28)
- **7. New Covenant made between Israel and her Messiah** after 3 ½ years of ministry. Christ completes His ministry of Dan 9:24-27 (Is 59:20-21; Jer 31:31-34; Heb 8:8; Ezek 16:59-60; 36:26-28; Hos 2:16-19)
- **8. Union of Israel and Judah** (see Jer 31:1, 7-9; 50:4-5; Ezek 11:17; 34:12-13; 37:19-22. Other related scriptures include: Jer 12: 14-15; 16:15; 23:3-4, 7-8; 24:6-7; 30:3, 8-10; 33:6-9; 50:4-5, 19-20; Ps 14:7; 53:6; 68:6; 30:4; Lev 26: 42-46); Jer 3:17-19; Zech 12:10-14; Rom 11:26; Acts 15:16-17; Hos 1:11; 2:14; Mic 2:12; 5:4-7; Zech 8:7-8; 10:9-12).

3. RELEVANT SCRIPTURES:

3.1 Captivity in Foreign Lands:

Jeremiah 16:13 Therefore will I cast you out of this land into a land that ye know not, *neither* ye nor your fathers; and there shall ye serve other gods day and night; where I will not shew you favour.

16:14 Therefore, behold, the days come, saith the LORD, that it shall no more be said, The LORD liveth, that brought up the children of Israel out of the land of Egypt;

16:15 But, The LORD liveth, that brought up the children of Israel from the land of the north, and from all the lands whither he had driven them: and I will bring them again into their land that I gave unto their fathers.

16 Behold, I will send for many fishers, saith the LORD, and they shall fish them; and after will I send for many hunters, and they shall hunt them from every mountain, and from every hill, and out of the holes of the rocks.

Leviticus 26:32 And I will bring the land into desolation: and your enemies which dwell therein shall be astonished at it.

26:33 And I will scatter you among the heathen, and will draw out a sword after you: and your land shall be desolate, and your cities waste.

26:38 And ye shall perish among the heathen, and the land of your enemies shall eat you up.

26:39 And they that are left of you shall pine away in their iniquity in your enemies' lands; and also in the iniquities of their fathers shall they pine away with them.

Deuteronomy 28:37 And thou shalt become an astonishment, a proverb, and a byword, among all nations whither the LORD shall lead thee.

28:41 Thou shalt beget sons and daughters, but thou shalt not enjoy them; for they shall go into captivity.

28:49 The LORD shall bring a nation against thee from far, from the end of the earth, *as swift* as the eagle flieth; a nation whose tongue thou shalt not understand;

28:50 A nation of fierce countenance, which shall not regard the person of the old, nor shew favour to the young:

28:64 And the LORD shall scatter thee among all people, from the one end of the earth even unto the other; and there thou shalt serve other gods, which neither thou nor thy fathers have known, *even* wood and stone.

28:65 And among these nations shalt thou find no ease, neither shall the sole of thy foot have rest: but the LORD shall give thee there a trembling heart, and failing of eyes, and sorrow of mind:

Hosea 5:8 Blow ye the cornet in Gibeah, [and] the trumpet in Ramah: cry aloud [at] Bethaven, after thee, O Benjamin.

5:9 Ephraim shall be desolate in the day of rebuke: among the tribes of Israel have I made known that which shall surely be.

3.2 Many Millions to be Delivered!:

Eze 34:11 For thus saith the Lord GOD; Behold, I, *even* I, will both search my sheep, and seek them out.

Eze 34:12 As a shepherd seeketh out his flock in the day that he is among his sheep *that are* scattered; so will I seek out my sheep, and will deliver them out of all places where they have been scattered **in the cloudy and dark day.**

Eze 34:13 And I will bring them out from the people, and gather them from the countries, and will bring them to their own land, and feed them upon the mountains of Israel by the rivers, and in all the inhabited places of the country.

Eze 34:14 I will feed them in a good pasture, and upon the high mountains of Israel shall their fold be: there shall they lie in a good fold, and *in* a fat pasture shall they feed upon the mountains of Israel.

Eze 34:15 I will feed my flock, and I will cause them to lie down, saith the Lord GOD.

Daniel 12:1 And at that time shall Michael stand up, the great prince which standeth for the children of thy people: and there shall be a time of trouble, such as never was since there was a nation *even* to that same time: **and at that time thy people shall be delivered**, every one that shall be found written in the book.

12:2 And many of them that sleep in the dust of the earth shall awake, some to everlasting life, and some to shame *and* everlasting contempt. [NB: the second exodus is a type of the first resurrection and these may both occur at the same time. Ezekiel 37 provides further information on the restoration of Israel as a type of the resurrection. This is when Israel and the Church are gathered at the same time: Matt 24:31; Mark 13:27]

Zechariah 9:13 When I have bent Judah for me, filled the bow with Ephraim, and raised up thy sons, O Zion, against thy sons, O Greece, and made thee as the sword of a mighty man.

9:14 And the LORD shall be seen over them, and his arrow shall go forth as the lightning: and the Lord GOD shall **blow the trumpet**, and shall go with whirlwinds of the south.

9:15 The LORD of hosts shall defend them; and they shall devour, and subdue with sling stones; and they shall drink, *and* make a noise as through wine; and they shall be filled like bowls, *and* as the corners of the altar.

9:16 And the LORD their God shall save them in that day as the flock of his people: for they *shall be as* the stones of a crown, lifted up as an ensign upon his land.

9:17 For how great *is* his goodness, and how great *is* his beauty! corn shall make the young men cheerful, and new wine the maids.

Isaiah 11:11 And it shall come to pass in that day, [that] the Lord shall set his hand **again the second time** to recover the remnant of his people, which shall be left, from Assyria, and from Egypt, and from Pathros, and from Cush, and from Elam, and from Shinar, and from Hamath, and from the islands of the sea.

11:12 And he shall set up an ensign for the nations, and shall assemble the outcasts of Israel, and gather together the dispersed of Judah from the four corners of the earth.

11:16 And there shall be an highway for the remnant of his people, which shall be left, from Assyria; like as it was to Israel in the day that he came up out of the land of Egypt.

Isaiah 27:13 And it shall come to pass in that day, [that] **the great trumpet shall be blown**, and they shall come which were ready to perish in the land of Assyria, and the outcasts in the land of Egypt, and shall worship the LORD in the holy mount at Jerusalem.

Isaiah 10:20 And it shall come to pass in that day, [that] the remnant of Israel, and such as are escaped of the house of Jacob, shall no more again stay upon him that smote them; but shall stay upon the LORD, the Holy One of Israel, in truth.

10:21 The remnant shall return, [even] the remnant of Jacob, unto the mighty God.

10:22 For though thy people Israel be as the sand of the sea, [yet] a remnant of them shall return: the consumption decreed shall overflow with righteousness.

Isaiah 48:20 Go ye forth of Babylon, flee ye from the Chaldeans, with a voice of singing declare ye, tell this, utter it *even* to the end of the earth; say ye, The LORD hath redeemed his servant Jacob. [cp Rev 18:4]

Jeremiah 23:3 And I will gather the remnant of my flock out of all countries whither I have driven them, and will bring them again to their folds; and they shall be fruitful and increase.

23:4 And I will set up shepherds over them which shall feed them: and they shall fear no more, nor be dismayed, neither shall they be lacking, saith the LORD.

23:5 Behold, the days come, saith the LORD, that I will raise unto David a righteous Branch, and a King shall reign and prosper, and shall execute judgment and justice in the earth.

23:6 In his days Judah shall be saved, and Israel shall dwell safely: and this [is] his name whereby he shall be called, THE LORD OUR RIGHTEOUSNESS.

23:7 Therefore, behold, the days come, saith the LORD, that they shall no more say, The LORD liveth, which brought up the children of Israel out of the land of Egypt;

23:8 But, The LORD liveth, which brought up and which led the seed of the house of Israel out of the north country, and from all countries whither I had driven them; and they shall dwell in their own land.

23:9 They shall come with weeping, and with supplications will I lead them: I will cause them to walk by the rivers of waters in a straight way, wherein they shall not stumble: for I am a father to Israel, and Ephraim *is* my firstborn.

23:10 Hear the word of the LORD, O ye nations, and declare *it* in the isles afar off, and say, He that scattered Israel will gather him, and keep him, as a shepherd *doth* his flock.

23:11 For the LORD hath redeemed Jacob, and ransomed him from the hand of *him that was* stronger than he.

23:12 Therefore they shall come and sing in the height of Zion, and shall flow together to the goodness of the LORD, for wheat, and for wine, and for oil, and for the young of the flock and of the herd: and their soul shall be as a watered garden; and they shall not sorrow any more at all.

23:13 Then shall the virgin rejoice in the dance, both young men and old together: for I will turn their mourning into joy, and will comfort them, and make them rejoice from their sorrow.

23:14 And I will satiate the soul of the priests with fatness, and my people shall be satisfied with my goodness, saith the LORD.

Jeremiah 50:3 For out of the north there cometh up a nation against her, which shall make her land desolate, and none shall dwell therein: they shall remove, they shall depart, both man and beast.

4 In those days, and in that time, saith the LORD, the children of Israel shall come, they and the children of Judah together, going and weeping: they shall go, and seek the LORD their God.

5 They shall ask the way to Zion with their faces thitherward, *saying*, Come, and let us join ourselves to the LORD in a perpetual covenant *that* shall not be forgotten.

6 My people hath been lost sheep: their shepherds have caused them to go astray, they have turned them away *on* the mountains: they have gone from mountain to hill, they have forgotten their restingplace.

7 All that found them have devoured them: and their adversaries said, We offend not, because they have sinned against the LORD, the habitation of justice, even the LORD, the hope of their fathers.

8 Remove out of the midst of Babylon, and go forth out of the land of the Chaldeans, and be as the he goats before the flocks.

9 For, lo, I will raise and cause to come up against Babylon an assembly of great nations from the north country: and they shall set themselves in array against her; from thence she shall be taken: their arrows *shall be* as of a mighty expert man; none shall return in vain.

10 And Chaldea shall be a spoil: all that spoil her shall be satisfied, saith the LORD.

Leviticus 26:40 If they shall confess their iniquity, and the iniquity of their fathers, with their trespass which they trespassed against me, and that also they have walked contrary unto me;

26:41 And *that* I also have walked contrary unto them, and have brought them into the land of their enemies; if then their uncircumcised hearts be humbled, and they then accept of the punishment of their iniquity:

Lev 26:42 Then will I remember my covenant with Jacob, and also my covenant with Isaac, and also my covenant with Abraham will I remember; and I will remember the land.

26:43 The land also shall be left of them, and shall enjoy her sabbaths, while she lieth desolate without them: and they shall accept of the punishment of their iniquity: because, even because they despised my judgments, and because their soul abhorred my statutes.

26:44 And yet for all that, when they be in the land of their enemies, I will not cast them away, neither will I abhor them, to destroy them utterly, and to break my covenant with them: for I *am* the LORD their God.

26:45 But I will for their sakes remember the covenant of their ancestors, whom I brought forth out of the land of Egypt in the sight of the heathen, that I might be their God: I *am* the LORD.

Zep 3:5 The just LORD *is* in the midst thereof; he will not do iniquity: every morning doth he bring his judgment to light, he faileth not; but the unjust knoweth no shame.

Zep 3:6 I have cut off the nations: their towers are desolate; I made their streets waste, that none passeth by: their cities are destroyed, so that there is no man, that there is none inhabitant.

Zep 3:7 I said, Surely thou wilt fear me, thou wilt receive instruction; so their dwelling should not be cut off, howsoever I punished them: but they rose early, *and* corrupted all their doings.

Zep 3:8 Therefore wait ye upon me, saith the LORD, until the day that I rise up to the prey: for my determination *is* to gather the nations, that I may assemble the kingdoms, to pour upon them mine indignation, *even* all my fierce anger: for all the earth shall be devoured with the fire of my jealousy.

Zep 3:9 For then will I turn to the people a pure language, that they may all call upon the name of the LORD, to serve him with one consent.

Zep 3:10 From beyond the rivers of Ethiopia my suppliants, *even* the daughter of my dispersed, shall bring mine offering.

Zep 3:11 In that day shalt thou not be ashamed for all thy doings, wherein thou hast transgressed against me: for then I will take away out of the midst of thee them that rejoice in thy pride, and thou shalt no more be haughty because of my holy mountain.

Zep 3:12 I will also leave in the midst of thee an afflicted and poor people, and they shall trust in the name of the LORD.

Zep 3:13 The remnant of Israel shall not do iniquity, nor speak lies; neither shall a deceitful tongue be found in their mouth: for they shall feed and lie down, and none shall make *them* afraid.

Zep 3:14 Sing, O daughter of Zion; shout, O Israel; be glad and rejoice with all the heart, O daughter of Jerusalem.

Zep 3:15 The LORD hath taken away thy judgments, he hath cast out thine enemy: the king of Israel, *even* the LORD, *is* in the midst of thee: thou shalt not see evil any more.

Zep 3:16 In that day it shall be said to Jerusalem, Fear thou not: *and to* Zion, Let not thine hands be slack.

Zep 3:17 The LORD thy God in the midst of thee *is* mighty; he will save, he will rejoice over thee with joy; he will rest in his love, he will joy over thee with singing.

Zep 3:18 I will gather *them that are* sorrowful for the solemn assembly, *who* are of thee, *to whom* the reproach of it *was* a burden.

Zep 3:19 Behold, at that time I will undo all that afflict thee: and I will save her that halteth, and gather her that was driven out; and I will get them praise and fame in every land where they have been put to shame.

Zep 3:20 At that time will I bring you *again,* even in the time that I gather you: for I will make you a name and a praise among all people of the earth, when I turn back your captivity before your eyes, saith the LORD.

3.3 Repentance and the New Covenant:

Zech 13:9 9 And I will bring the third part through the fire, and will refine them as silver is refined, and will try them as gold is tried: they shall call on my name, and I will hear them: I will say, It *is* my people: and they shall say, The LORD *is* my God." [cp Amos 5:3; Zech 12]

Ezek 20:34 And I will bring you out from the people, and will gather you out of the countries wherein ye are scattered, with a mighty hand, and with a stretched out arm, and with fury poured out.

20:35 And I will bring you into the wilderness of the people, and there will I plead with you face to face.

20:36 Like as I pleaded with your fathers in the wilderness of the land of Egypt, so will I plead with you, saith the Lord GOD.

20:37 And I will cause you to pass under the rod, and I will bring you into the bond of the covenant: [cp Lev. 27:32]

20:38 And I will purge out from among you the rebels, and them that transgress against me: I will bring them forth out of the country where they sojourn, and they shall not enter into the land of Israel: and ye shall know that I *am* the LORD.

20:42 And ye shall know that I [am] the LORD, when I shall bring you into the land of Israel, into the country [for] the which I lifted up mine hand to give it to your fathers.

20:43 And there shall ye remember your ways, and all your doings, wherein ye have been defiled; and ye shall lothe yourselves in your own sight for all your evils that ye have committed.

20:44 And ye shall know that I *am* the LORD, when I have wrought with you for my name's sake, not according to your wicked ways, nor according to your corrupt doings, O ye house of Israel, saith the Lord GOD.

4. ISAIAH 40 – A PROPHECY ABOUT THE 2ND EXODUS:

"Comfort, comfort my people, says your God.

Speak tenderly to Jerusalem, and cry to her that her **warfare is ended**, that her iniquity is pardoned, that she has received from the LORD's hand double for all her sins.

A voice cries: "In the wilderness **prepare the way of the LORD**, make straight in the desert a highway for our God. [return of Christ]

Every valley shall be lifted up, and every mountain and hill be made low; the uneven ground shall become level, and the rough places a plain. [symbolic and literal]

And **the glory of the LORD shall be revealed**, and all flesh shall see it together, for the mouth of the LORD has spoken."

A voice says, "Cry!" And I said, "What shall I cry?" All flesh is grass, and all its beauty is like the flower of the field.

The grass withers, the flower fades, when the breath of the LORD blows upon it; surely the people is grass.

The grass withers, the flower fades; but the word of our God will stand for ever.

Get you up to a high mountain, O Zion, herald of good tidings [i.e. Good News]; lift up your voice with strength, O Jerusalem, herald of good tidings, lift it up, **fear not**; say to the cities of Judah, "Behold your God!" [Christ setting up His Government on the earth]

Behold, the Lord GOD comes with might, and his arm rules for him; behold, **his reward is with him**, and his recompense before him. [return of Christ]

He will feed his flock like a shepherd, he will gather the lambs in his arms, he will carry them in his bosom, and gently lead those that are with young. [the Second Exodus]

Who has measured the waters in the hollow of his hand and marked off the heavens with a span, enclosed the dust of the earth in a measure and weighed the mountains in scales and the hills in a balance?

Who has directed the Spirit of the LORD, or as his counselor has instructed him?

Whom did he consult for his enlightenment, and who taught him the path of justice, and taught him knowledge, and showed him the way of understanding?

Behold, the nations are like a drop from a bucket, and are accounted as the dust on

the scales; behold, he takes up the isles like fine dust." (Is 40:1-15) [destruction of rebellious nations]

"Lebanon would not suffice for fuel, nor are its beasts enough for a burnt offering.

All the nations are as nothing before him, they are accounted by him as less than nothing and emptiness. [destruction of rebellious nations again]

To whom then will you liken God, or what likeness compare with him?

The idol! a workman casts it, and a goldsmith overlays it with gold, and casts for it silver chains.

He who is impoverished chooses for an offering wood that will not rot; he seeks out a skilful craftsman to set up an image that will not move.

Have you not known? Have you not heard? Has it not been told you from the beginning? Have you not understood from the foundations of the earth?

It is he who sits above the circle of the earth, and its inhabitants are like grasshoppers; who stretches out the heavens like a curtain, and spreads them like a tent to dwell in; **who brings princes to nought, and makes the rulers of the earth as nothing**. [the overthrow of this world's leaders and governments. It does not refer to Israel which is in captivity]

Scarcely are they planted, scarcely sown, scarcely has their stem taken root in the earth, when he blows upon them, and they wither, and the tempest carries them off like stubble.

To whom then will you compare me, that I should be like him? says the Holy One.

Lift up your eyes on high and see: who created these? He who brings out their host by number, calling them all by name; by the greatness of his might, and because he is strong in power not one is missing.

Why do you say, O Jacob, and speak, O Israel, "My way is hid from the LORD, and my right is disregarded by my God"?

Have you not known? Have you not heard? The LORD is the everlasting God, the Creator of the ends of the earth. He does not faint or grow weary, his understanding is unsearchable.

He gives power to the faint, and to him who has no might he increases strength.

Even youths shall faint and be weary, and young men shall fall exhausted;

but they who wait for the LORD shall renew their strength, they **shall mount up with wings like eagles, they shall run and not be weary, they shall walk and not faint**." (Is 40:16-31) [cp Rev 3:8. Refers to both the refreshing of God's people and the resurrection]

Israel restored, will rule the world under the Messiah, helping to bring the nations under His rule (Acts 1:6-7; Matt 19:28).

Addendum

An article worth reading is "Exodus Typology in Second Isaiah" by Bernard W Anderson (Chapter XII of B. Anderson & W. Harrelson, eds., *Israel's Prophetic Heritage: Essays in Honor of James Muilenburg*. Harper & Brothers, 1962, pp. 177-195)

"While there are numerous linguistic echoes of the Exodus tradition throughout the poems of Second Isaiah, the theme of the new exodus is the specific subject in several passages.

1. 40.3-5 The highway in the wilderness.
2. 41.17-20 The transformation of the wilderness.
3. 42.14-16 Yhwh leads his people in a way they know not.
4. 43.1-3 Passing through the waters and the fire.
5. 43.14-21 A way in the wilderness.
6. 48.20-21 The exodus from Babylon.
7. 49.8-12 The new entry into the Promised Land.
8. 51.9-10 The new victory at the sea.
9. 52.11-12 The new exodus.
10. 55.12-13 Israel shall go out in joy and peace. The historical setting of Second Isaiah's prophecy is the Babylonian Exile— Israel's captivity, which the prophet likens to the oppression in Egypt." (p. 3)

God the Father

Jesus Christ

Abraham

Jacob

Isaac

Noah

Job

Zerrubabel

Joseph

Amos

Moses

Joshua

David

Peter, James, John

Apostles

12 Tribes of Israel

Elijah

John the Baptist

Daniel

Shadrach, Meschach, Abed-nego

Paul

Thyatira Church

GOD'S GOVERNMENTAL STRUCTURE IN THE WORLD TOMORROW (SPECULATIVE)

Explanation of the above chart: the old Church of God thought that the following might be part of God's governmental structure during the Millennium.

Table 17 God's Governmental System

Function	Personage	Others
Supreme Universal Leader	God the Father	
Messiah and Supreme King over Israel	Jesus Christ	Assisted the saints (Old Testament and New Testament (i.e. the 7 churches))
Chairman	Abraham	Should Shem be included in this list, above Abraham?
Assistant to Abraham	Isaac	
Assistant to Abraham	Jacob	
World Economy	Joseph	Amos (assistant to Joseph – especially in Agricultural Affairs)
Urban Renewal	Job	Zerubbabel (assistant to Job)
Relations between Nations	Noah	
Religious System (Church educational arm)	Elijah	John the Baptist and HQ Church (Philadelphia Era) under Elijah
State Affairs	Moses	Joshua (assistant to Moses)
King of Israel	David	Under Moses
Rulers over chief tribes of Israel	Peter, James, John	Under David. Peter over Ephraim and Manasseh, the leading tribes
Rulers over the tribes of Israel	Apostles	Israel. Judah the administrative princes and leaders; Levi the priestly class; Ephraim and Manasseh the leading tribes. Israel in turn heading up 12 groups of gentile nations divided into the 3 races
Rulers over the gentile nations	Daniel	Under Moses. Shadrach, Meshach, Abed-nego (assistants to Daniel). Paul and Thyatira Church ruling the gentile nations under Daniel

You can find these details in the following: *The Wonderful World Tomorrow* by Herbert W Armstrong, the *Ambassador College Bible Correspondence Course* and some sermons.

1. Sermons

Too many to list, but you can find them online, free to download.

2. The *Ambassador College Bible Correspondence Course* (lesson 51):

"What reward will Jesus Christ give to all who overcame and "held fast" in the Thyatira Era? Rev 2:26-27.

COMMENT: The authority of Jesus Christ Himself — the very "power over the nations" which JEZEBEL sought by harlotry — will be given to God's Church — the Thyatira Era — who learned by repentance and long-suffering (PATIENCE does not adequately convey the meaning — verse 19) to show love and mercy."

3. In *The Wonderful World Tomorrow* (chapter 4) we find the following (upon which the above chart is based) information (extracts):

"The Pattern of Government Organization

God has not told us, in so many words, precisely how His coming world super government will be organized. Yet He has given us the general pattern. He has told us specifically where 14 high executives (including Christ) will fit in. And from them we may deduce a great deal of the remaining governmental structure. Much of the coming structure of government is at least strongly indicated by what is plainly revealed. We know it will be the Government of God. God Almighty — the Father of Jesus Christ — is Supreme Lawgiver, and Head over Christ, and over all that is.

We know that Christ is to be King of kings, and Lord of lords — over both state and church, united through Him. We know that King David of ancient Israel (details later) will be king over the twelve great nations composed of literal descendants of the twelve tribes of Israel. We know the twelve apostles will each be a king, sitting on a throne, over one of those great nations descended from the tribes of Israel.

We know it will be government from the top down. There is to be a definite chain of authority. No one will be elected by the people. Mortal humans have proved they do not know how to judge qualifications, and do not know the inner minds, hearts, intents, and abilities, of men. All will be divinely appointed from above. All, in positions of governmental authority, will be resurrected immortals, born of God — no longer flesh-and-blood humans.

With this in mind — with the knowledge that Abraham is (humanly) the father of all who are Christ's and heirs of salvation — it becomes plain that Abraham will be given a greater position of authority in God's Kingdom than David — and that he will be over both Israelites and Gentiles. He is "father" of Gentile converts as well as Israelites.

Then again, repeatedly the Bible uses the phrase, "Abraham, Isaac and Jacob," grouping them together as a team, and calling them, together, "The Fathers." For the promises were repromised, also, to Isaac and Jacob, whose name was changed to Israel.

What is plainly revealed indicates, then, that **Abraham, Isaac and Jacob, will function as a topflight team**, with Abraham as chairman of the team, next under Christ in the coming world Government of God. Jesus Himself said, definitely, that Abraham, Isaac and Jacob shall be in that glorious and glorified Kingdom (Luke 13:28).

Joseph qualified in a very special way, but we shall come back to him a little later.

Both Church and State

Another principle is made clear in God's Word: Church and State will be united under Christ. There will be one government, over all nations. There will be one Church — one God — one religion — one educational system — one social order. And, as in God's original pattern in ancient Israel, they will be united.

Three men — **Peter, James and John**, among the original twelve disciples — were privileged to see the Kingdom of God in a vision. In this vision, Jesus, who was actually with them in person, became transfigured — appearing as the glorified Christ. His face became bright, shining as the sun, His clothing white as light. Two others appeared with Him in this vision (Matt 17:9) — this glimpse into the coming Kingdom — and they were Moses and Elijah. These two, in the vision, represented the offices of Church and State, with and under Christ, as they will be in God's Kingdom. Both **Moses and Elijah** qualified in their human lifetime for very high positions in the Kingdom of God. Moses was the one through whom Christ (yes, He was the God of the Old Testament, as many, many Scriptures prove) gave the laws and the statutes of government for the nation Israel. Moses was trained as a son of a pharaoh (king of Egypt). His training and experience was among Gentiles, as well as the children of Israel.

Elijah, above all others, is represented in Scripture as the prophet who restored the worship of the true God — and obedience to His Commandments. When Elijah ordered King Ahab to gather on Mount Carmel "all Israel" (IKings 18:19-21) and the prophets of Baal and of Asherah (Easter), he said: "How long halt ye between two opinions? if the [Eternal] be God, follow him: but if Baal, then follow him ...." (verse 21). And when, at Elijah's 18-second prayer (verses 36-37), the fire fell miraculously from heaven consuming Elijah's sacrifice, the people fell on their faces, and said, "The [Eternal], he is the God; the [Eternal], he is the God" (verse 39).

The vision of the Transfiguration (Matt 16:27 through 17:9), gave the Apostles Peter, James, and John a preview of Christ coming in His Kingdom — as He shall come. The indication is thus given that Moses and Elijah represented the heads, under Christ, of state or national world government (under Moses), and church or religious activity (under Elijah).

These two men, like the "fathers," Abraham, Isaac and Israel, will then be resurrected immortal, in power and glory. Certainly the indication is given us that, under Christ as King of kings, and under Christ's top team — the "fathers" — will be Moses over all organized national and international government; and Elijah, over all organized church, religious and educational activity.

Actually, the Gospel and religious development is merely spiritual education. And it is significant that Elijah had organized and headed three schools or colleges (IIKings 2:3, 5; 4:38 — at Bethel, Jericho, and Gilgal) teaching God's Truth in a world corrupted by false pagan education.

On the National Level

Now we gain further insight into God's coming world government organization.

On the purely national level, the nations descended from **the two tribes of Ephraim and Manasseh (descended from Joseph), will become the two leading nations of the world** (Jeremiah 30:16-18; 32:4-11, 18-20; Isaiah 14:1-2; Deuteronomy 28:13).

But, next to them will be the nations descended from the other tribes of Israel. And, after them, but still prosperous and full of abundant blessings, the Gentile nations.

King David, resurrected, immortal, in power and glory, will be king, under Moses, over all twelve nations of Israel (Jeremiah 30:9; Ezekiel 34:23-24; 37: 24-25). **Each of the original twelve apostles will be king, under David, over one of these then super-prosperous nations** (Matt 19:28).

Under the apostles, each now king over a great nation, will be the rulers over districts, states, shires, counties or provinces, and over cities…

But what of all the Gentile nations? Who will be given top positions of rule over them?

There is strong indication — not a definite, specific statement — but indication, according to principles and specific assignments that are revealed, that the **Prophet Daniel** will be made king over them all, directly under Moses. What prophet — what man of God — did God send to be trained at top-level government authority, in the world's very first world empire? And what man refused to follow pagan ways and customs, even while serving next in authority to the king himself? What man proved loyal to God, and the worship of God, and obedient to the laws of God — even while serving at the top in the first world empire?

Why, of course it was the Prophet Daniel.

At first thought, one might suppose Christ will put the Apostle Paul at the head — under Moses and under Christ — of all Gentile nations. And indeed Paul qualified for high position over Gentiles.

But Daniel was thrown into almost daily contact with the king in the world's first world government. And though that was human government, Daniel proved completely loyal and obedient to God and God's rule. He was used, to reveal to King Nebuchadnezzar, and immediate successors, that it is God who rules over all kingdoms. Daniel refused the king's rich food and delicacies — including what was unclean according to God's health laws. He prayed three times a day to God, even though it meant being thrown into the den of lions. He trusted God to protect and deliver him from the lions. He gained knowledge and wisdom in the affairs and administration of government over nations.

When God, through the Prophet Ezekiel, named three of the most righteous men who ever lived, He named Daniel as one of them. The other two were Noah and Job (Ezekiel 14:14, 20). And it is evident that God will assign Noah and Job to offices of very great magnitude. More of that, later.

God in His Word gave Daniel the assurance that he shall be in the Kingdom of God, at the time of resurrection (Dan 12:13).

It is an interesting possibility, in passing, to consider that Daniel's three colleagues in this Chaldean Empire service — Shadrach, Meshach, and Abednego — might serve as a team directly with and under Daniel, even as the three "fathers" very possibly may serve as a team directly with and under Christ Himself. In fact there are a number of such teams which appear to be possibilities.

But what about Paul? As the twelve original apostles were sent to the "lost" House of Israel, **Paul was the apostle to the Gentiles.** That is the key. Christ Himself said specifically that each of the twelve shall be a king over one of the nations of Israel. It is inconceivable that Paul would be over no more than one Gentile nation. It might even be inferred that Paul rated a little higher in ability and accomplishment than any one of the Twelve Apostles. And, again, no Gentile nation will be as great as one of the Israelite nations.

The indication, then, seems to be that Paul will be given position over all Gentile nations, but under Daniel.

Of course there will be kings appointed by Christ over every Gentile nation. And district rulers under them, and rulers over cities. There is no indication as to the identity of any of these, except that those apostles and evangelists who worked with and directly under Paul — Barnabas, Silas, Timothy, Titus, Luke, Mark, Philemon, etc. undoubtedly will be given offices of importance. And what of other saints of that same time, in the first flush years of the Church, when its membership at first multiplied in number of converts? And what of many converted since, and down to our present day?

We can mention, here, only what seems to be rather clearly indicated from what God has already revealed.

The International Level

Beside these revealed and indicated assignments of government over nations and groups of nations on the national level, there will be positions of great magnitude on the international level in the areas of scientific and social functions. And there are a few indications of what some of those operations will be, and the possible — if not probable — personnel.

Since Noah lived first, we now take a look at Noah... God had set the boundary lines for the nations and the races at the beginning (Deut 32:8-9; Acts 17:26). But men had refused to remain in the lands to which God had assigned them. That was the cause of the corruption and violence that ended that world. For 120 years Noah had preached God's ways to the people — but they didn't heed.

At that time, even as today, that world faced a population explosion. It was when men began to multiply on the face of the earth" (Gen 6:1). Jesus said, of our time, right now, "But as the days of Noe [Noah] were, so shall the coming of the Son of man be" (Matt 24:37) — or, as in Luke 17:26, "And as it was in the days of Noe, so shall it be also in the days of the Son of man." That is, the days just before Christ returns. Today race wars, race hatreds, race riots, and race problems are among the world's greatest social troubles.

Noah merely preached to people in his human lifetime. But Noah, in the resurrection, immortal, in power and glory, will be given the power to enforce God's ways in regard to race.

It seems evident that the resurrected Noah will head a vast project of the relocation of the races and nations, within the boundaries God has set, for their own best good, happiness, and richest blessings. This will be a tremendous operation. It will require great and vast organization, reinforced with power to move whole nations and races. This time, peoples and nations will move where God has planned for them, and no defiance will be tolerated…

Joseph became food administrator of the greatest nation on earth of that time — Egypt. Joseph was synonymous with "prosperity." "And the [Eternal] was with Joseph, and he was a prosperous man; and … the [Eternal] made all that he did to prosper in his hand" (Gen 39:2-2-3). He was made actual ruler for the pharaoh of the world's greatest nation. But his specialty was dealing with the economy — with prosperity. And what he did, he did God's way.

It seems evident, therefore, that **Joseph will be made director of the world's economy — its agriculture, its industry, its technology, and its commerce — as well as its money and monetary system.** These systems will be on the international level, the same in every nation.

Undoubtedly Joseph will develop a large and perfectly efficient organization of immortals made perfect, with and under him in this vast administration. This will be an administration that will eliminate famine, starvation, poverty. There will be no poverty-stricken slums. There will be universal prosperity!

Another tremendous project on the worldwide international level will be that of rebuilding the waste places, and the construction of whatever really great and large buildings or structures Christ will require for the world He will create. "And they shall build the old wastes, they shall raise up the former desolations, and they shall repair the waste cities, the desolations of many generations" (Is 61:4).

Job was the wealthiest and greatest man of the east (Job 1:3) and a noted builder. He was so upright and perfect, God even dared Satan to find a flaw in his character. Actually, there was a terrible sin in his life — self-righteousness. But God brought him to repentance. (See Job chapters 38-42.) Once this man, of such strength of self- mastery that he could be so righteous in his own strength, was humbled, brought to reliance on God, filled with God's Spirit — well, surely no man who ever lived could equal him as an engineer over vast stupendous world projects.

Indication is strong, therefore, **that Job will be director of worldwide urban renewal, rebuilding the waste places and the destroyed cities,** not as they are now, but according to God's pattern; vast engineering projects, such as dams and power plants — or whatever the ruling Christ shall decree.

At least one other man seems indicated as a top assistant in this vast administration. That is Zerubbabel (Haggai, and Zechariah 4)." [emphasis mine]

EXTRACTS FROM COMMENTARIES AND ARTICLES

Renald E. Showers, *Maranatha, Our Lord Come*.

"In Matthew 19:28 Jesus declared that 'the regeneration' would take place 'when the Son of man shall sit on the throne of his glory.' His terminology is significant. It indicates that when Christ, as the Son of man (as a human, a kinsman of mankind) rules the earth, there will be a return to the original state that existed when the earth was born, which is recorded in Genesis and involved mankind's tenant possession or administration of the earth as God's representative. Christ taught that He will begin to exercise that rule when He returns in glory with His holy angels (Mtt. 25:31) ... Peter declared that 'the times of refreshing' and 'the times of the restitution of all things' will come when God sends Christ back to be personally present on the earth ... F. F. Bruce wrote that 'the restitution' to which Peter referred in Acts 3:21 'appears to be identical with' 'the regeneration' to which Jesus referred in Mat. 19:28, and that the restoration involved will include 'a renovation of all nature.'" (Renald E. Showers in *Maranatha, Our Lord Come*, pp. 86-87)

Alva J. McClain, *The Greatness Of The Kingdom*.

"In Holy Scripture there are two Jerusalems: the one is on earth in the land of Palestine; the other is 'above' in heaven (Gal. 4:25-26; Heb. 12:22). Now the Old Testament prophets speak of a city which, in the coming Kingdom, shall be reclaimed from Gentile power, rebuilt, restored to the historic nation of Israel, and made the religious center of the world. This Jerusalem cannot be the 'heavenly Jerusalem,' for that city is impeccably holy, the eternal dwelling of the true God, and has never been defiled or marred by human sin and rebellion. Any such notion is to the highest degree impossible and absurd. All predictions of a restored and rebuilt Jerusalem must therefore refer to the historical city of David on earth." (Alva J. McClain in *The Greatness Of The Kingdom*, p. 244)

LaHaye in "A Literal Millennium as Taught in Scripture, Part 4".

"This passage in Isaiah either describes the regeneration of the heavens and earth (cf. Mtt. Mat. 19:28) since it precedes the description of the millennium which follows, or Isaiah saw the final heavens and earth and the millennium (Rev. Rev. 21:1+), but the order of their presentation in this passage is reversed. Some believe that only unbelievers will die during the Millennial

Kingdom: Rev. 20:4-6+)."—LaHaye in "A Literal Millennium as Taught in Scripture, Part 4," in Thomas Ice (ed), *Pre-Trib Perspectives*, Vol. 8, No. 10, Pre-Trib Research Center, February, p. 2.)

Charles C. Ryrie, *Basic Theology*.

"Some allege that the Millennial Kingdom cannot be a spiritual one if it is earthly. But 'earthly' and 'spiritual' are not necessarily mutually exclusive. If the two concepts were incompatible, Christians today could not be expected to live spiritual lives in earthly bodies. During the millennium, God will join the spiritual and the earthly in a full display of His glory on this earth. The earthly kingdom will manifest the highest standards of spirituality." (Charles C. Ryrie, *Basic Theology*, p. 510)

A. R. Fausset, "The Revelation of St. John the Divine," *A Commentary, Critical and Explanatory, on the Old and New Testaments.*

"If revelation is to recommence in the millennial kingdom, **converted Israel must stand at the head of humanity**. In a religious point of view, Jews and Gentiles stand on an equal footing as both alike needing mercy; but as regards God's instrumentalities for bringing about His kingdom on earth, Israel is His chosen people for executing His plans." (A. R. Fausset, "The Revelation of St. John the Divine," in *A Commentary, Critical and Explanatory, on the Old and New Testaments* (note on Rev. 20:6)) [emphasis mine]

Merrill F. Unger, *Unger's Commentary on the Old Testament* **(note on Zeph 3:9).**

"Here not only giving the millennial nations 'cleansed' or 'purified' lips, as regenerated peoples, but apparently also in the sense that 'lip' signifies 'language' (Gen. 11:1, Gen. 11:6-7, Gen. 11:9) ... That would be not all that surprising, since **Israel will be the chief nation in that economy (Deu. 28:13) and Jerusalem in that day will be the religious and governmental capital of the millennial earth** (Isa. 2:2-3; Zec. 8:20-23). Moreover, it is all the more probable since the judgment of the nations at the second advent will eventuate in the destruction of the satanic world system ... That system had its beginning in ancient Babylon with its pride, idolatry, and rebellion (Gen. 10:8-10; Gen. 11:1-6). The gift of a pure speech will remove the curse of Babel, and it will anticipate the great millennial outpouring of the Spirit (Joel 2:28-32), of which Pentecost (Acts 2:1-11) was an illustration." (Merrill F. Unger, *Unger's Commentary on the Old Testament* (note on Zeph 3:9) [emphasis mine]

***The Acts of God. A Study of the Basis of Typology in the Old Testament* by Francis Foulkes, Tutor of Immanuel College, Ibadan, Nigeria The Tyndale House Old Testament Lecture for 1955 The lecture was delivered in Cambridge on 1st July 1955 at a meeting convened by the Tyndale Fellowship for Biblical Research).**

"In a different way we find in Ezekiel xl - xlviii the vision of a new and finer temple than that which had been destroyed. The temple of the prophet's vision was to be greater in dimensions and grander in structure than the old. But the one fact of transcendent importance was that to this house the glory of the Lord's presence would return and consequently the city would be called 'The Lord is there'. In various parts of the Old Testament, however, we find the expression of the hope that, since the Lord's presence cannot be thought of as limited in any way to the temple, His tabernacling presence would in future be known in a more glorious way than could be realized in the temple. God's dwelling is apart from men, and 'heaven' is the place of His temple; and no earthly shrine can adequately express or manifest the presence of God. In 1 Kings viii. 27, in the prayer of dedication of the temple, we have these words, 'But will God in very deed dwell on the earth? behold, heaven and the heaven of heavens cannot contain thee; how much less this house that I have builded.' The prophet Isaiah clearly felt this as, in his vision, he saw that just the 'skirts' or the 'train' of the Lord filled the temple, and as he heard the seraphs cry, 'The fulness of the whole earth is His glory.' Yet perhaps the greatest expression of this in the Old Testament is in the words of Isaiah lxvi. 1, 'The heaven is my throne, and the earth is my footstool; what manner of house will ye build unto me? and what place shall be my rest?' As the sense of God's transcendence grew, so developed the awareness that the tabernacling of the holy and omnipotent God among men was yet to be more wonderful than the temple could express." (Francis Foulkes, *The Acts of God. A Study of the Basis of Typology in the Old Testament*, The Tyndale House Old Testament Lecture for 1955, p. 29).

Ed Hindson & David Hocking, "Premillennialism," *The Popular Encyclopedia of Bible Prophecy.*

"The throne of David will be set up in Jerusalem with Jesus Christ, the messiah of Israel, the Son of David, literally ruling upon it in His millennial kingdom (2 Sam 7:12-16; Luke 1:32-33)" (Ed Hindson & David Hocking, "Premillennialism," *The Popular Encyclopedia of Bible Prophecy*, p. 280).

Walter C Kaiser, *Micah – Malachi. The Preacher's Commentary.*

"The second wonderful word of hope and comfort for God's people is *"My house shall be built in [Jerusalem]"* (Zec 1:16). The project of rebuilding the so-called "second temple" in the days of Haggai and Zechariah was only a partial fulfillment of the command to build a temple when our Lord returns to rule and reign in the Millennium. God's glorious promise of a temple - the details and dimensions of which had never before been seen (Ezek. 40-48) - was to be realized far in the future ...

"The third comforting word promises that Jerusalem's boundaries would expand (Zec 1:16). This city, ravaged as it was by the Babylonians in 587 B.C., the Romans in A.D. 70, and many other conflicts since - and still ravaged in our present day - would experience unusual urban renewal and expansion. The surveyor's line would *"be stretched out"* to measure an enlarged Jerusalem" (Walter C Kaiser, *Micah - Malachi, The Preacher's Commentary*, p. 480).

Sigmund Mowinckel, *He that Cometh.*

The entire book is worth reading in this context.

O. R. L. Crozier, "The Sanctuary. Part One of Four. The Law of Moses."

Crozier wrote about the Millennium as a time of restitution – a period of gradual transition of the world prior to the New Heavens and New Earth. It will be "an age of repairs, in which immortal saints will engage." He also understood is as the time when "the captives of Zion" – literal Israel - will return to the land of Israel to "possess their 'own land,' and the wastes shall be builded." After that time Satan will stir up forces against the Lord and be crushed. ("Rothschild and the City of Jerusalem," *Advent Harbinger*, Vol. 4, No. 6, 24 July 1852, p. 45).

David Guzik *Commentary on the Bible* (2014).

"c. **Till the thousand years were finished**: This thousand-year period is often known as the *Millennium*. Through church history, there has been many different ways of understanding the Millennium.

i. The Bible speaks powerfully to other aspects of the millennial earth. Tragically, the Church through history has often ignored or denied the promise of the millennial reign of Jesus Christ. The early church until Augustine almost universally believed in an earthly, historical reign of Jesus, initiated by His return. Tyconius (in the late 300's) was the first to influentially champion a spiritualized interpretation, saying that this Millennium is *now* (*amillennialism*) and must be understood as a *spiritual* reign of Jesus, not a literal reign. His view was adopted by Augustine, the Roman Catholic Church and most Reformation theologians.

ii. Growing out of *amillennialism* is the doctrine of *postmillennialsim* is an outgrowth of amillennialism, saying the millennium will happen in *this* age, before Jesus' return - but that the church will bring it to pass. But the clear teaching of the Bible isn't *amillennialism* or *postmillennialism*, but what is called *premillennialism* - the teaching that Jesus Christ will return to this earth *before* the millennial earth, and *He* is establish and govern it directly.

iii. But there is no need to say that Satan is only bound in a spiritual sense, and Jesus only rules in a spiritual sense. When we consider the rest of the Scriptures, the earthly reign of Christ and His people on this earth is plainly taught in the Old and New Testaments. In the Old Testament, we see it Psalms 72:1-20, Isaiah 2:2-4, Isaiah 11:4-9, Jeremiah 23:5-6, and many, many more passages. In the New Testament we see it in Luke 1:32-33, Matthew 5:18, Luke 19:12-27, among other passages. All in all, there are more than 400 verses in more than 20 different passages in the Old Testament which deal with this time when Jesus Christ rules and reigns personally over planet earth.

iv. Who will be on the earth in the Millennium? Even after the rapture and the vast judgments of the Great Tribulation, there will be many people left on earth. After Jesus returns in glory, He will judge those who survive the Great Tribulation in the judgment of the nations (Matthew 25:31-46). This is not a judgment unto salvation, but a judgment of moral worthiness, and entrance into the Millennial Kingdom of Jesus. The unworthy will be sent into eternal damnation, and the worthy will be allowed in Jesus' Millennial Kingdom.

d. **Some of what we know of the Millennium from other passages of Scripture.**

i. During the Millennium, Israel will be the "superpower" of the world. It will be the leading nation in all the earth, and the center of Israel will be *the mountain of the LORD's house* - the temple mount, which will be the "capital" of the government of the Messiah. *All nations shall flow* to the "capital" of the government of Jesus. (Isaiah 2:1-3, Ezekiel 17:22-24)

ii. During the Millennium, the citizens of earth will acknowledge and submit to the

Lordship of Jesus. It will be a time of perfectly administrated enforced righteousness on this earth. (Isaiah 2:1-5)

iii. During the Millennium, there will be no more war. There will still be conflicts between nations and individuals, but they will be justly and decisively resolved by the Messiah and those who reign with Him. (Isaiah 2:1-5) It isn't the reign of the Messiah itself that will change the heart of man. Citizens of earth will still need to trust in Jesus and His work on their behalf for their personal salvation during the millennium. But war and armed conflict will not be tolerated.

iv. During the Millennium, the way animals relate to each other and to humans will be transformed. A little child will be safe and able to lead a wolf or a leopard or a young lion or a bear. Even the danger of predators like cobras and vipers will be gone. In Genesis 9:2-3, the LORD gave Noah, and all mankind after him, the permission to eat meat. At the same time, the LORD put the *dread* of man in animals, so they would not be effortless prey for humans. Now, in the reign of the Messiah, that is reversed. For this reason, many think that in the reign of the Messiah, the Millennium, humans will return to being vegetarians, as it seems they were before Genesis 9:2-3. (Isaiah 11:6-9)

v. During the Millennium, King David will have a prominent place in the millennial earth, ruling over Israel (Isaiah 55:3-5, Jeremiah 30:4-11, Ezekiel 34:23-31, Ezekiel 37:21-28, Hosea 3:5).

vi. During the Millennium, there will be blessing and security for national Israel in the millennial earth (Amos 9:11-15).

vii. The Millennium a time of purity and devotion to God (Zechariah 13:1-9).

viii. During the Millennium, there will be a rebuilt temple and restored temple service on the millennial earth as a memorial of God's work in the past. (Ezekiel 40:1-49; Ezekiel 41:1-26; Ezekiel 42:1-20; Ezekiel 43:1-27; Ezekiel 44:1-31; Ezekiel 45:1-25; Ezekiel 46:1-24; Ezekiel 47:1-23; Ezekiel 48:1-35, Ezekiel 37:26-28, Amos 9:11, Ezekiel 20:39-44).

ix. During the Millennium, saints in their resurrected state will be given responsibility in the Millennial Earth according to their faithful service (Luke 19:11-27, Revelation 20:4-6, Revelation 2:26-28; Revelation 3:12; Revelation 3:22, 1 Corinthians 6:2-3).

e. **Thousand years**: Is it a literal 1,000 years? We should take a number literally *unless* there is clear reason or evidence to do otherwise. We should take this **thousand years** literally, because God has an important work to accomplish during the Millennium.

i. The Millennium is important because it will demonstrate Jesus' victory and worthiness to rule the nations.

ii. The Millennium is important because it will reveal the depths of man's rebellious nature in a perfect environment. Some people seem to believe that man is basically good, and deep down he really *wants* God's righteous rule. Many believe that man is really innocent, and corrupted only by a bad environment. The Millennium will answer these questions *before* the great judgment (Revelation 20:11-15).

iii. The Millennium is important because it will display the eternal depravity of Satan, who continues his evil as soon as he is released from his incarceration.

iv. The Millennium is important because it will show the invulnerability of the city of God and God's new order.

v. "Let us rejoice that Scripture is so clear and so explicit upon this great doctrine of the future triumph of Christ over the whole world . . . We believe that the Jews will be converted, and that they will be restored to their own land. We believe that Jerusalem will be the central metropolis of Christ's kingdom; we also believe that all the nations shall walk in the light of the glorious city which shall be built at Jerusalem. We expect that the glory which shall have its center there, shall spread over the whole world, covering it as with a sea of holiness, happiness, and delight. For this we look with joyful expectation." (Spurgeon)"

Merrill C. Tenney, *The Importance and Exegesis of Revelation 20:1-8.*

"The premillenarian position has also been criticized adversely because the current concept of the millennium was devoid of purpose. If the saints of God are to reign ultimately in the eternal heavenly city of spiritual light, if the devil and his hosts are to be remanded to the lake of fire, and if there is a general resurrection and judgment at the end of the age, why bother with a reign of a thousand years on earth? If the millennium is simply a protracted spiritual vacation for the saints, does it serve any useful end?

One or two suggestions are proffered here for further consideration by Bible students. They are not to be regarded as dogmatic pronouncements, but rather as exploratory ventures of thought.

The millennium, closely associated as it is with the return of Christ in judgment, is really the long Day of the Lord, or a period in which Christ and His servants will be occupied with judging evil, in disentangling the complicated results of sin in human relationships, and in straightening out the moral affairs of humanity. If men since the fall have spent several millennia in involving themselves in a hopeless snarl of social, economic, and moral evils it will take at least one millennium to right the wrongs, to judge the causes, and to put a redeemed humanity to work in a cleansed world. Such is the implied meaning of the phrase "till he hath put all enemies under His feet" (1 Cor. 15:25).

The millennium will fulfill the divine promise of Israel contained in Zechariah 14 and in Isaiah 11. In the former passage the personal coming of Jehovah is predicted: "His feet shall stand in that day upon the Mount of Olives, which is before Jerusalem on the east . . . and the Lord my God shall come, and all the saints with thee . . . and the Lord shall be king over all the) earth : in that day shall there be one Lord, and his name one" (Zech. 14:4, 5, 9).The reign of Jehovah shall be personal and visible. Israel shall possess its land as a sanctuary to which the nations shall come up in pilgrimage to worship.

Isaiah 11 predicts the renewal of the Davidic kingdom by the "branch" or shoot out of the stump of Jesse's house. In that kingdom peace and righteousness shall prevail, equity shall be administered to all, and wickedness shall not be tolerated. The promise was given by Isaiah to Israel; but the entire earth shall benefit by the reign, for the passage says that "the earth shall be full of the knowledge of the Lord as the waters cover the sea" (Isa. 11:9).

The millennium, then, is not a useless excrescence on Scriptural Eschatology. It is a part of God's plan to vindicate His wisdom and to make redemption effective. It is intended to be a proving ground for the righteous administration of the government of Christ, who will be purging the world of evil, and preparing it for the ultimate establishment of the city of God. It is the last stage of human history prior to the completion of the divine purpose and the manifestation of eternal life in its personal and social fulness. Perhaps no more is known about it now than was known about this age prior to the first coming of Christ. Perhaps the prophecies concerning it are scanty and are ignorantly interpreted. Its place in the purpose of God is assured, however, and with that reign in mind we all can unite in the prayer, "Thy kingdom come!"" ("The Importance and Exegesis of Revelation 20:1-8," *Bibliotheca Sacra*, April 1954, pp. 147-48)

Daniel Taylor, *The Reign of Christ on Earth (1882).*
The book entails a detailed look at the various millennial views over the centuries including Waldensians, Paulicians, Protestants, Catholics as well as various well-known men such as Luther, Tyndale, Foxe, Wesley etc. The book is 647 pages packed with information worth delving into.

"The Kingdom of God in the Old Testament", by William D. Barrick, *The Master's Seminary*, Fall 2012, pp. 173-92.
"In any treatment of this topic, we dare no treat the OT any differently than the NT treats it. NT writers took the OT seriously – and literally. So must we." (p. 173)

"Our focus here is on *the physical aspects* of the messianic kingdom. Covenantal promises clearly indicate that the future nation of Israel will inherit the land of Canaan again." (p. 185) He also points out that there will still be sinful people during the Millennium (p. 188)

On page 184 he provides a succinct outline of the future Kingdom of God on earth (which he terms "The Messianic Kingdom"):

"The Messianic Kingdom's Physical Blessings Before describing the physical aspects of the Messianic kingdom, we must not neglect its other characteristics:

- The messianic kingdom is primarily soteriological (Isa 52:7–10). It is a kingdom of grace, of unmerited divine favor (Zech 12:10). In addition, God establishes the messianic kingdom in holiness and His holiness pervades the kingdom (Ezek 28:25; Zech 14:20). He initiates the kingdom by pouring out His Holy Spirit upon all flesh (Joel 2:28–29).
- Due to the spiritual nature of the messianic kingdom, sinful and immoral values give way to readjusted moral values in accord with divine perfection (Isa 51:4–5). Yahweh's own objective standard will measure all ethical thought and behavior (Isa 2:3; 30:20–21), so that Messiah will judge on the basis of an accurate appraisal (Isa 32:5; Mal 3:18). Personal responsibility will dominate interpersonal relationships (Jer 31:29–30) and truth will characterize all matters (Ps 89:14; Zech 8:3).
- In the realm of society, Messiah will abolish warfare and establish peace (Isa 9:7; Mic 4:3–4). Social justice will prevail in every class and race of mankind (Isa 65:21–22;

Ps 72:4) and God will reclaim social wastes (Ps 72:16; Isa 61:4). Messiah will teach mankind to emphasize worthwhile relationships (Isa 42:3; Mal 4:6).

- In the political venue, the Messiah will establish Himself as the international authority (Isa 2:2–4; Ps 2:8–10) and will establish a world capital at Jerusalem (Jer 3:17). In His kingdom, the Messiah will put an end to the perennial "Jewish problem" (Zech 8:13, 23).32 As a reversal of the curse at Babel, language will cease to be a barrier to all human interaction and relationships (Isa 19:18; Zeph 3:9).
- Ecclesiastically, Messiah will rule as priest-king over Israel and the world community (Zech 6:12–13; Ps 110:4). In the messianic kingdom, Israel will become the religious leader of the world (Exod 19:6; Isa 61:6, 9) and the world's religious capital will be Jerusalem (Zech 14:16–17). As a result, the Temple in Israel will be the focal point of worship (Hag 2:6–9; Ezek 40–48)."

George Peters, *The Theocratic Kingdom of our Lord Jesus, the Christ, as Covenanted in the Old Testament and Revealed in the New* (1884).

This election of the Jewish nation was an absolute, unconditional (i.e. relating to the purpose of God) election so far as its national descent from Abraham is affected, i.e. the kingdom is solely promised to the descendants of Abraham in their national aspect (which is verified, as we shall see hereafter, by the covenants, confirmed by oath); and hence arises the necessity of Gentiles (as we shall show), who shall participate in this Kingdom, being grated in, becoming members of, the commonwealth of Israel." (p. 109).

Other Sources

A number of other sources could be cited on the historical development of the understanding of the Millennium. Three which stand out are:

- *History and Doctrine of the Millennium* by Henry Dana Ward
- *A historical review of early non-Sabbatarian Adventists' dispute over Israel in prophecy (1844-1850)* by Julia Neuffer, available at https://adventistbiblicalresearch.org/materials/adventist-heritage/gathering-israel-historical-study-early-writings-pp.-74-76
- *Doctrinal Development of Millennium in Adventism Between 1831-1850* a paper written by Miguel Patiño, AIIAS/Universidad de Montemorelos, 6 January 2014

OLD CHURCH ARTICLES ON THE MILLENNIUM

In addition to booklets, sermons and broadcasts on the subject, the Church of God published a number of articles in *Plain Truth* and *Good News* magazines.

These articles covered various aspects of the Millennium including outlines on the structure of the Kingdom, agriculture, the economy and cities.

General articles about the Kingdom and the Millennium:

- "After The Millennium - New Heavens and a New Earth," *Good News*, January 1981.
- "The Millenium...Fact Or Fiction?" *Plain Truth*, February 1956.
- "The Neglected Utopia," *Plain Truth*, February 1973.
- "The Teenager's Tomorrow-What It Will Be Like?" *Tomorrow's World*, September 1970.
- "The World Tomorrow-What Will It Be Like?" *Plain Truth*, October 1959.
- "Tips: Relax-Or Suffer Heart Disease," *Plain Truth*, March 1972.
- "Tomorrow's World-A Global Garden of Eden," *Good News*, July 1975.
- "Universal Prosperity In 15 Years," *Plain Truth*, July 1964.
- "Urban Ills Can Be Cured-Here's How," *Plain Truth*, June 1973.
- "What Is The Millenium?" *Good News*, May 1952.
- "What Will You Be Doing In The Next Life?" *Tomorrow's World*, September 1969.
- "What Will Your Job Be In The Kingdom?" *Good News*, February 1958.
- "Where Are We Headed?" *Plain Truth*, January 1947.
- "Where Will The Millenium Be Spent?" *Good News*, September 1981.

Cities and the World Tomorrow:

- "Can Our Cities Be Saved?" *Plain Truth*, December 1970.
- "Cities Waiting To Die," *Plain Truth*, April 1980.
- "Cities: Can We Save Them From Financial Disaster?" *Plain Truth*, December 1971.
- "How One Modern City Skirted The Ragged Edge Of Energy Disaster," *Plain Truth*, April 1974.
- "Newark: A Dying American City," *Plain Truth*, December 1971.

- "Public Housing Projects-Why Some Become High Rise Slums," *Plain Truth*, January 1972.
- "Sneak Preview: The Cities of Tomorrow," *Plain Truth*, April 1981.
- "Supercities: Growing Pains of The Population Crisis," *Plain Truth*, January 1991.
- "The Rural Exodus," *Plain Truth*, December 1972.
- "Tomorrow's Cities - What Will They Be Like?" *Good News*, Oct-Nov 1986.
- "Urban Ills Can Be Cured-Here's How," *Plain Truth*, June 1973.
- "What Cities Do To Us And What We Do To Cities," *Plain Truth*, July 1971.
- "Why City Problems?" *Tomorrow's World*, November 1970.
- "Why The Crisis In The Cities Threatens Rural Areas," *Plain Truth*, October 1968.

The Millennium

From the Living Church of God website:

Question:

"Where do you get the idea that mankind has been appointed 6,000 years of self-rule to be followed by a 1,000-year reign of Christ?"

Answer:

As Genesis shows, God reformed the earth and created the progenitors of all present life upon it in a six-day period, then rested on the seventh-day Sabbath. This began a weekly cycle in which man is to work for six days and rest every Sabbath (Ex. 20:9–11). In Hebrews 4:5–11, the Apostle Paul explained how the seventh-day Sabbath pictures the wonderful era of peace and rest that will follow the current age of man's activity. In the book of Revelation, John was inspired to write that this coming era, beginning with Christ's return to set up His Kingdom, will last 1,000 years (20:1–4)—often referred to as simply the "Millennium."

As the seventh day of the week, then, represents a thousand-year period in God's plan it follows that the previous six days of the week represent thousand-year periods as well. In explaining what some would perceive as a delay in Christ's return, Peter brought up this principle as something the Church should not be ignorant of: "But, beloved, be not ignorant of this one thing, that one day is with the Lord as a thousand years, and a thousand years as one day" (2 Peter 3:8 KJV).

The idea of each day of the week representing a thousand years of God's plan was well-known to the Jews of Peter's day. About 200 years before Christ, Rabbi Elias wrote, "The world endures six thousand years: two thousand before the law, two thousand under the law, and two thousand under Messiah." The famed historian, Edward Gibbon, wrote that "the tradition was attributed to the prophet Elijah" (Decline and Fall of the Roman Empire, p. 403). The Encyclopedia of the Jewish Religion (art. "Millennium," Adama Books, 1986, p.263) reports that the tannaim—rabbis of Christ's day—based such an interpretation on

Psalm 90, written by Moses: "For a thousand years in Your sight are like yesterday when it is past, and like a watch in the night" (v. 4). The tannaim said that, as there were six days of creation, the world would last for 6,000 years. The seventh "world day" would be 1,000 years of the Messiah (Sanhedrin 97a; Avodah Zarah 5a)...

As a final scriptural point, God told Adam that in the "day" he ate of the forbidden fruit, he would die (Genesis 2:17). Yet Adam lived to be 930 years old (Genesis 5:5)! How is that possible? One way is just as Methodius and other early church commentators explained: since a day with God was a thousand years, Adam had to die before the first 1,000-year day was completed—and he did.

[Comment by this author: it may be that the 6,000 years commences after the expulsion of Adam and Eve from the Garden of Eden rather than from when they were created. This could have been any number of years after their creation making it impossible for any human to know when that 6,000 year period was to expire].

COMPARING EZEKIEL 38 AND 39
WITH OTHER SCRIPTURES

There are various prophecies (not all about the same event) which use either similar wording or are parallel events. I list them below to illustrate that the Bible uses similar terminology for different events:

Table 18 Parallel or Similar Scriptures

Ezekiel 38 & 39	Other Scriptures	Comment
38:4	Zech 14:12-21; Hag 2:22	The parallel scripture in Zech represents a time after Christ's return
38:6	Jer 50:41-42; 51:27-28; Dan 11:44; Rev 16:12	From this, we see that these hordes are the remnants of the 200 million strong armies
38:11	Ezek 36:35-36; Zech 2:4-5; 14:11	The land is at rest (cp Lam 1:3), which is not the case in the end times
38:13	Is 60:3-14	These appear to be the repented nations who formerly composed the Beast Power or who were part
38:20	Rev 16:18, 20	The earthquake in Rev is against Babylon. The one in Ezek is against the northern armies
38:21	Zech 14:12-15	Parallel events seem to be described here
38:22	Rev 16:8, 21; Ps 140:10-11; Jos 10:11	Similar type of plagues poured upon Babylon and the Beast power, will be poured later upon these armies
39:16-21	Is 18:6	Similar wording and concepts in Is do not necessarily refer to the same event, but could do
39:17	Rev 19:17-21	The 'feast' for the animals referred to in Rev is for the Beast armies, but a similar fate awaits the northern armies which are not part of Babylon

EZEKIEL CHAPTERS 38 AND 39 WITH COMMENTS

Note the parts highlighted, showing that its application refers to a period after the return of Christ.

Eze 38:1 And the Word of Jehovah came to me, saying,

2 Son of man, set your face against Gog **[Central Asia]**, the land of Magog **[China]**, the chief ruler of Rosh **[Byelorussians]**, Meshech **[Great Russians around Moscow]**, and Tubal **[Great Russians around Tobolosk]**, and prophesy against him.

3 And say, So says the Lord Jehovah: Behold, I *am* against you, O Gog, the chief ruler of Rosh, Meshech and Tubal.

4 And I will turn you back **[this indicates that the remnants of the 200 million horde of Rev 9:16 return to the holy land for battle – this time God Himself will bring them back, not Satan, to humble them and force repentance]**, and put hooks into your jaws, and I will bring you out, and all your army, horses and horsemen, all of them clothed most perfectly, a great assembly *with* buckler and shield, all of them swordsmen;

5 Persia **[modern Persia or peoples near Byelorussia]**, Ethiopia **[Cush in East African and India]**, and Libya **[Phut – the Africans and northern Indians]** with them, all of them *with* shield and helmet; **[no mention of Egypt here as it would have previously repented and come under the authority of the Messiah]**

6 Gomer **[Southeast Asia]** and all his bands; the house of Togarmah **[Caucasus and also in Siberia]** *from* the recesses of the north, and all his bands; *and* many peoples with you.

7 Be prepared; yea, prepare for yourself, you and all your assembly that are assembled to you, and be a guard to them.

8 After many days you will be visited. In the latter years **you shall come into the land turned back from the sword**, gathered out of many peoples, on the mountains of Israel, **which have always been waste**. (But he has been brought out of the peoples, and they shall dwell securely, all of them.)

9 And you shall go up, coming like a storm. You shall be like a cloud to cover the land, you and all your bands, and many peoples with you.

10 So says the Lord Jehovah: And it shall be in that day that things shall come into your heart, and you shall devise an evil plan.

11 And you shall say, I will go up to the land of open spaces. **I will go *to* those at ease, who dwell securely, all of them dwelling without walls, and there are no bars nor gates to them, [this must be a time after the Second Exodus]**

12 in order to take a spoil, and to steal a prize; **to turn your hand on the inhabited waste places, and on the people gathered out of the nations, who have gotten cattle and goods, who dwell in the midst of the land.**

13 Sheba **[Schwabian Germans]** and Dedan **[Prussians]**, and the merchants of Tarshish **[Japanese and/or Spanish]**, with all their young lions **[Assyrians (Nah 2:8-12; Is. 5:29; Hos 5:13-14; Jer 2:14-15, 18; 4:7; 50:17; Zech 11:3; Joel 1:6) and perhaps other former nations and allies of the US of Europe]**, shall say to you, Have you come to take a spoil? Have you gathered your company to steal a prize, to carry away silver and gold, to take away cattle and goods, to take a great spoil? **[i.e. "don't you know what happened to us when we attacked Israel in the Tribulation?"]**

14 So, son of man, prophesy and say to Gog, So says the Lord Jehovah: In that day when My people of Israel dwells securely, shall you not know *it*?

15 And you shall come from your place out of the recesses of the north, you and many peoples with you, all of them riding on horses, a great company and a mighty army.

16 And you shall come up on My people Israel like a cloud, to cover the land. It shall be in the last days, and I will bring you against **My land [Holy Land, not North America and Britain]**, so that the nations may know Me when I shall be sanctified in you, O Gog, before their eyes.

17 So says the Lord Jehovah: *Are* you he of whom I have spoken in former days, by the hand of My servants the prophets of Israel, who prophesied in those days *and* years that I would bring you against them? **[these prophecies appear to be lost]**

18 And it shall be on that day, when Gog comes against the land of Israel, says the Lord Jehovah, My fury shall come up in My face.

19 For in My jealousy *and* in the fire of My wrath I have spoken, Surely in that day there shall be a great quaking in the land of Israel,

20 so that the fish of the sea, and the birds of the heavens, and the beasts of the field, and all creeping things that creep on the earth, and all the men on the face of the earth, shall quake at My presence. And the mountains shall be thrown down, and the steep places shall fall, and every wall shall fall to the ground. **[a giant earthquake]**

21 And I will call for a sword against him on all My mountains, says the Lord Jehovah. *Each* man's sword shall be against his brother.

22 And I will judge him with a plague and with blood. And I will rain on him, and on his bands, and on the many peoples with him, an overflowing shower, and great hailstones, fire and brimstone. **[cp Jos 10:11]**

23 So I will magnify Myself and sanctify Myself. And I will be known in the eyes of many nations, and they shall know that I *am* Jehovah.

Eze 39:1 Therefore, son of man, prophesy against Gog and say, So says the Lord Jehovah: Behold, I *am* against you, O Gog, the chief ruler of Rosh, Meshech and Tubal.

2 And I will turn you back, and lead you on. And I will bring you up from the recesses of the north, and I will bring you on the mountains of Israel.

3 And I will strike your bow out of your left hand, and will cause your arrows to fall out of your right hand.

4 You shall fall on the mountains of Israel, you and all your bands, and the people with you. I will give you for food to the birds of prey of every kind, and *to* the beasts of the field.

5 You shall fall on the face of the field, for I have spoken, says the Lord Jehovah.

6 And I will send a fire on Magog, and on the secure inhabitants of the coasts. And they shall know that I *am* Jehovah. **[volcanoes or meteorites?]**

7 And I will make My holy name known in the midst of My people Israel. And I will not *let them* profane My holy name any more. And the nations shall know that I *am* Jehovah, the Holy One in Israel.

8 Behold, it is coming, and it will be done, says the Lord Jehovah. This *is* the day of which I have spoken.

9 And the inhabitants of the cities of Israel shall go out and shall set on fire and burn the weapons, both the shields and the bucklers, the bows and the arrows, and the javelins, and the spears. And they shall burn them with fire **seven years [the Biblical number of completeness]**,

10 so that they shall take no wood out of the field, nor cut down *any* out of the forests for they shall burn the weapons for fire **[these weapons will provide fuel]**. And they shall plunder those who plundered them, and rob those who robbed them, says the Lord Jehovah.

11 And it will be in that day I will give to Gog a place there, a grave in Israel, the valley of those who pass by, east of the sea. And it shall stop the *noses* of those who pass by. And there they shall bury Gog and all his multitude. And *they* shall call *it*, The Valley of the Multitude of Gog.

12 And the house of Israel shall bury them, to cleanse the land, seven months.

13 And all the people of the land shall bury. And it shall be a name to them, the day when I am glorified, says the Lord Jehovah.

14 And men shall separate those who continually pass through the land, burying those who passed through, who remain on the face of the earth, to cleanse it. At the end of seven months they shall search.

15 And *as* they pass, those who pass through the land, and *any* man sees a bone, then he shall build a post beside it, until the buriers have buried it in The Valley of the Multitude of Gog.

16 And also the name of the city *is* The Multitude. And they shall cleanse the land.

17 And you, son of man, So says the Lord Jehovah. Speak to the bird of every wing, and to every beast of the field: Gather yourselves and come; gather yourselves from all around to My sacrifice that I sacrifice for you, a great sacrifice on the mountains of Israel, so that you may eat flesh and drink blood.

18 You shall eat the flesh of the mighty and drink the blood of the rulers of the earth, of rams, lambs, goats, *and* bulls, all of them fatlings of Bashan.

19 And you shall eat fat until you are full, and drink blood until you are drunk, of My sacrifice which I have sacrificed for you.

20 And you shall be filled at My table with horses and chariots, with mighty men, all the men of war, says the Lord Jehovah.

21 And I will set My glory among the nations, and all the nations shall see My judgments which I have done, and My hand that I have laid on them.

22 So the house of Israel shall know that I *am* Jehovah their God from that day and forward.

23 And the nations shall know that the house of Israel was exiled for their iniquity. Because they sinned against Me, therefore I hid My face from them and gave them into the hand of their enemies. So they all fell by the sword.

24 According to their uncleanness and according to their sins I have done to them, and have hidden My face from them.

[possibly from about here onward, we have an insert section in Ezekiel]

25 Therefore so says the Lord Jehovah: And I will return the captivity of Jacob, and will have mercy on the whole house of Israel, and will be jealous for My holy name;

26 *after* they have borne their shame and all their sins by which they have sinned against Me, when they dwell securely in their land and no one terrifies;

27 when I have brought them again from the peoples, and gathered them out of their enemies' lands, and am sanctified in them in the sight of many nations;

28 then they shall know that I *am* Jehovah their God **who exiled them among the nations**. But I have gathered them to their own land, and have not left any of them there.

29 Nor will I hide My face from them any more, for I have poured out My Spirit on the house of Israel, says the Lord Jehovah.

EZEKIEL – REVELATION PARALLELS

The book of Revelation has some parallels with Ezekiel – not because the two books concern the exact same events – but because there are similarities in events that occur that have similar consequences, parallels and as forerunners or types. Ian Boxall brings this out:

"The influence of the Book of Ezekiel on the last book of the Christian Bible is indisputable. It can be detected most obviously in the many allusions to and echoes of the Old Testament writing, permeating virtually every chapter of Revelation. Isolating these allusions with precision is not always straightforward, given John's stubborn refusal to actually quote Old Testament texts, and his tendency to evoke a range of texts from across the prophetic corpus in the same passage. Nevertheless, few would deny Ezekiel's role as at least one dominant source for the seer of Patmos. The 4th edition of the UBS Greek New Testament, for example, lists no less than 84 allusions and verbal parallels to Ezekiel in the Apocalypse, spread across every chapter except 12-13. More recent scholarship, however, has not been content with exploring verbal connections between the two works. A number of scholars, notably Albert Vanhoye [1962], Jeffrey Marshall Vogelgesang [1981], Michael Goulder [1981], and Jean-Pierre Ruiz [1989], have argued that this influence even extends to the structural level, and (though disagreeing to the extent of this phenomena) that Revelation follows Ezekiel's order." ("Exile, Prophet, Visionary: Ezekiel's Influence on the Book of Revelation" in *The Book of Ezekiel and its Influence*, p. 147)

Here is Boxall's chart ("The Revelation of Saint John," *Black's New Testament Commentaries*, p. 255):

Revelation 1	Ezekiel 1
Revelation 4	Ezekiel 1
Revelation 5	Ezekiel 2
Revelation 6	Ezekiel 5-7
Revelation 7:1-2	Ezekiel 7:2-3
Revelation 7-8	Ezekiel 9-10
Revelation 10	Ezekiel 2-3
Revelation 10-13	Ezekiel 11-14 (echoes)

Revelation 11:1-2	Ezekiel 40
Revelation 13:11-18	Ezekiel 14
Revelation 17	Ezekiel 16, 23
Revelation 18	Ezekiel 26-28
Revelation 19:11-21	Ezekiel 29, 32 (39)
Revelation 20:1-3	Ezekiel 29, 32
Revelation 20:4-6	Ezekiel 37
Revelation 20:7-10	Ezekiel 38:1-39:20
Revelation 20:11-15	Ezekiel 39:21-29
Revelation 21-22	Ezekiel 40-48

KEIL & DELITZSCH COMMENTARY ON THE OLD TESTAMENT – PSALM 2

Psalm 2

Introduction

The Kingdom of God and of His Christ,
to Which Everything Must Bow

The didactic Psalm 1:1-6 which began with אַשְׁרֵי, is now followed by a prophetic Psalm, which closes with אַשְׁרֵי. It coincides also in other respects with Psalm 1:1-6, but still more with Psalms of the earlier time of the kings (Psalm 59:9; Psalm 83:3-9) and with Isaiah's prophetic style. The rising of the confederate nations and their rulers against Jahve and His Anointed will be dashed to pieces against the imperturbable all-conquering power of dominion, which Jahve has entrusted to His King set upon Zion, His Son. This is the fundamental thought, which is worked out with the vivid directness of dramatic representation. The words of the singer and seer begin and end the Psalm. The rebels, Jahve, and His Anointed come forward, and speak for themselves; but the framework is formed by the composer's discourse, which, like the chorus of the Greek drama, expresses the reflexions and feelings which are produced on the spectators and hearers. The poem before us is not purely lyric. The personality of the poet is kept in the background. The Lord's Anointed who speaks in the middle of the Psalm is not the anonymous poet himself. It may, however, be a king of the time, who is here regarded in the light of the Messianic promise, or that King of the future, in whom at a future period the mission of the Davidic kingship in the world shall be fulfilled: at all events this Lord's Anointed comes forward with the divine power and glory, with which the Messiah appears in the prophets.

The Psalm is anonymous. For this very reason we may not assign it to David (Hofm.) nor to Solomon (Ew.); for nothing is to be inferred from Acts 4:25, since in the New Testament "hymn of David" and "psalm" are co-ordinate ideas, and it is always far more hazardous to ascribe an anonymous Psalm to David or Solomon, than to deny to one inscribed לדוד or לשלמה direct authorship from David or Solomon. But the subject of the Psalm is neither David (Kurtz) nor Solomon (Bleek). It might be David, for in his reign there is at least one coalition of the peoples like that from which our Psalm takes its rise, vid., 2 Samuel 10:6: on the contrary it cannot be Solomon, because in his reign, though troubled towards its close (1 Kings 11:14.), no such event occurs, but would then have to be inferred to have happened from this Psalm. We might rather guess at Uzziah (Meier) or Hezekiah (Maurer), both of whom inherited the kingdom in a weakened condition and found the neighbouring peoples alienated from the house of David. The situation might correspond to these times, for the rebellious peoples, which are brought before us, have been hitherto subject to Jahve and His Anointed. But all historical indications which might support the one supposition or the other are wanting. If the God-anointed one, who speaks in Psalm 2:7, were the psalmist himself, we should at least know the Psalm was composed by a king filled with a lofty Messianic consciousness. But the dramatic movement of the Psalm up to the ועתה (Psalm 2:10) which follows, is opposed to such an identification of the God-anointed one with the poet. But that Alexander Jannaeus (Hitz.), that blood-thirsty ruler, so justly hated by his people, who inaugurated his reign by fratricide, may be both at the same time, is a supposition which turns the moral and covenant character of the Psalm into detestable falsehood. The Old Testament knows no kingship to which is promised the dominion of the world and to which sonship is ascribed (2 Samuel 7:14; Psalm 89:28), but the Davidic. The events of his own time, which influenced the mind of the poet, are no longer clear to us. But from these he is carried away into those tumults of the peoples which shall end in all kingdoms becoming the kingdom of God and of His Christ (Revelation 11:15; Revelation 12:10).

In the New Testament this Psalm is cited more frequently than any other. According to Acts 4:25-28, Acts 4:1 and Acts 4:2 have been fulfilled in the confederate hostility of Israel and the Gentiles against Jesus the holy servant of God and against His confessors. In the Epistle to the Hebrews, Psalm 110:1-7 and Psalm 2:1-12 stand side by side, the former as a witness of the eternal priesthood of Jesus after the order of Melchisedek, the latter as a witness of His sonship, which is superior to that of the angels. Paul teaches us in Acts 13:33, comp. Romans 1:4, how the "to-day" is to be understood. The "to-day" according to its proper fulfilment, is the day of Jesus' resurrection. Born from the dead to the life at the right hand of God, He entered on this day, which the church therefore calls *dies regalis*, upon His eternal kingship.

The New Testament echo of this Psalm however goes still deeper and further. The two names of the future One in use in the time of Jesus, ὁ Χριστὸς and ὁ υἱὸς τοῦ θεοῦ, John 1:50; Matthew 26:63 (in the mouth of Nathanael and of the High Priest) refer back to this Ps. and Daniel 9:25, just as ὁ υἱὸς τοῦ ἀνθρώπου incontrovertibly refers to Psalm 8:5 and Daniel 7:13. The view maintained by De Wette and Hupfeld, that the Psalm is not applicable to the Christian conceptions of the Messiah, seems almost as though these were to be gauged according to the authoritative utterances of the professorial chair and not according to the language of the Apostles. Even in the Apocalypse, Ps 19:15; Psalm 12:5, Jesus appears exactly as this Psalm represents Him, as ποιμαίνων τὰ ἔθνη ἐν ῥάβδῳ σιδηρᾷ. The office of the Messiah is not only that of Saviour but also of Judge. Redemption is the beginning and the judgment the end of His work. It is to this end that the Psalm refers. The Lord himself frequently refers in the Gospels to the fact of His bearing side by side with the sceptre of peace and the shepherd's staff, the sceptre of iron also, Matthew 24:50., Matthew 21:44, Luke 19:27. The day of His coming is indeed a day of judgment-the great day of the ὀργὴ τοῦ ἀγνίου, Revelation 6:17, before which the ultra-spiritual Messianic creations of enlightened exegetes will melt away, just as the carnal Messianic hopes of the Jews did before His first coming.

Verses 1-3

The Psalm begins with a seven line strophe, ruled by an interrogative Wherefore. The mischievous undertaking condemns itself, It is groundless and fruitless. This certainty is expressed, with a tinge of involuntary astonishment, in the question. למה followed by *a praet.* enquires the ground of such lawlessness: wherefore have the peoples banded together so tumultuously (Aquila: å)? And followed by *a fut.*, the aim of this ineffectual action: wherefore do they imagine emptiness? ריק might be adverbial and equivalent to לריק, but it is here, as in Psalm 4:3, a governed accusative; for הגה which signifies in itself only quiet inward musing and yearning, expressing itself by a dull muttering (here: something deceitful, as in Psalm 38:13), requires an object. By this ריק the involuntary astonishment of the question justifies itself: to what purpose is this empty affair, i.e., devoid of reason and continuance? For the psalmist, himself a subject and member of the divine kingdom, is too well acquainted with Jahve and His Anointed not to recognise beforehand the unwarrantableness and impotency of such rebellion. That these two things are kept in view, is implied by Psalm 2:2, which further depicts the position of affairs without being subordinated to the למה. The *fut.* describes what is going on at the present time: they set themselves in position, they take up a defiant position (התיצב as in 1 Samuel 17:16), after which we again (comp. the reverse order in Psalm 83:6) have a transition to the *perf.* which is the more uncoloured expression of the actual: נוסד (with יחד as the exponent of reciprocity) prop. to press close and firm upon one another, then (like Arab. *(sâwada), which, according to the correct observation of the Turkish Kamus, in its signification clam cum aliquo locutus est, starts from the very same primary meaning of pressing close to any object): to deliberate confidentially together (as Psalm 31:14 and נועץ; Psalm 71:10). The subjects* מלכי־ארץ *and* רוזנים *(according to the Arabic (razuna), to be weighty: the grave, dignitaries, σεμνοί, augusti) are only in accordance with the poetic style without the article. It is a general rising of the people of the earth against Jahve and His* משיח, Χριστὸς, *the king anointed by Him by means of the holy oil and most intimately allied to Him. The psalmist hears (Psalm 2:3) the decision of the deliberating princes. The pathetic suff. (êmō) instead of (êhém) refers back to Jahve and His Anointed. The cohortatives express the mutual kindling of feeling; the sound and rhythm of the exclamation correspond to the dull murmur of hatred and threatening defiance: the rhythm is iambic, and then anapaestic. First they determine to break asunder the fetters (מוסרות = מאסרות) to which the* את, *which is significant in the poetical style, points, then to cast away the cords from them (ממנו a nobis, this is the Palestinian mode of writing, whereas the Babylonians said and wrote mimeenuw a nobis in distinction from* ממנו *ab eo, B. Sota 35a) partly with the vexation of captives, partly* with the triumph of freedmen. They are, therefore, at present subjects of Jahve and His Anointed, and not merely because the whole world is Jahve's, but because He has helped His

283

Anointed to obtain dominion over them. It is a battle for freedom, upon which they are entering, but a freedom that is opposed to God.

Verses 4-6

Above the scene of this wild tumult of battle and imperious arrogance the psalmist in this six line strophe beholds Jahve, and in spirit hears His voice of thunder against the rebels. In contrast to earthly rulers and events Jahve is called יושב בשמים: He is enthroned above them in unapproachable majesty and ever-abiding glory; He is called אדני as He who controls whatever takes place below with absolute power according to the plan His wisdom has devised, which brooks no hindrance in execution. The *futt.* describe not what He will do, but what He does continually (cf. Isaiah 18:4.). למו also belongs, according to Psalm 59:9; Psalm 37:13, to ישחק (שׂחק) which is more usual in the post-pentateuchal language = צחק). He laughs at the defiant ones, for between them and Him there is an infinite distance; He derides them by allowing the boundless stupidity of the infinitely little one to come to a climax and then He thrusts him down to the earth undeceived. This climax, the extreme limit of the divine forbearance, is determined by the אז, as in Deuteronomy 29:19, cf. שׁם; Psalm 14:5; 36:13, which isa "then" referring to the future and pointing towards the crisis which then supervenes. Then He begins at once to utter the actual language of His wrath to his foes and confounds them in the heat of His anger, disconcerts them utterly, both outwardly and in spirit. בהל, Arab. *(bhl), cogn.* בלה, *means originally to let loose, let go, then in Hebrew sometimes, externally, to overthrow, sometimes, of the mind, to confound and disconcert.*

Psalm 2:5-6

Psalm 2:5 is like a peal of thunder (cf. Isaiah 10:33); בחרונו, *Psalm 2:5,* like the lightning's destructive flash. And as the first strophe closed with the words of the rebels, so this second closes with Jahve's own words. With ואני begins an adverbial clause like Genesis 15:2; Genesis 18:13; Psalm 50:17. The suppressed principal clause (cf. Isaiah 3:14; Ew. §341, *c*) is easily supplied: ye are revolting, whilst notwithstanding I ... . With ואני He opposes His irresistible will to their vain undertaking. It has been shown by Böttcher, that we must not translate "I have anointed" (Targ., Symm.). נסך, Arab. *(nsk), certainly means to pour out, but not to pour upon, and the meaning of pouring wide and firm (of casting metal, libation, anointing) then, as in* הציג ה*, ציק, goes over into the meaning of setting firmly in any place (fundereintofundare, constituere, as lxx, Syr., Jer., and Luther translate), so that consequently* נסיך *the word for prince cannot be compared with* משׁיח, *but with* נציב.

(Note: Even the Jalkut on the Psalms, §620, wavers in the explanation of נסכתי between אמשחתיה I have anointed him, (after Daniel 10:3), אתיכתיה (I have cast him (after Exodus 32:4 and freq.), and גדלתיו I have made him great (after Micah 5:4). Aquila, by rendering it καὶ ἐδιασάμην (from διάζεσθαι= ὑφαίνειν), adds a fourth possible rendering. A fifth is נסך to purify, consecrate (Hitz.), which does not exist, for the Arabic *nasaka* obtains this meaning from the primary signification of cleansing by flooding with water (e.g., washing away the briny elements of a field). Also in Proverbs 8:23 נסכתי means I am cast = placed.)

The Targum rightly inserts ומניתיה (*et praefeci eum*) after רביתי (unxi), for the place of the anointing is not על־ציון. History makes no mention of a king of Israel being anointed on Zion. Zion is mentioned as the royal seat of the Anointed One; there he is installed, that He may reign there, and rule from thence, Psalm 110:2. It is the hill of the city of David (2 Samuel 5:7, 2 Samuel 5:9; 1 Kings 8:1) including Moriah, that is intended. That hill of holiness, i.e., holy hill, which is the resting-place of the divine presence and therefore excels all the heights of the earth, is assigned to Him as the seat of His throne.

Verses 7-9

The Anointed One himself now speaks and expresses what he is, and is able to do, by virtue of the divine decree. No transitional word or formula of introduction denotes this sudden transition from the speech of Jahve to that of His Christ. The psalmist is the seer: his Psalm is the mirrored picture of what he saw and the echo of what he heard. As Jahve in opposition to the rebels acknowledges the king upon Zion, so the king on Zion appeals to Him in opposition to the rebels. The name of God, יהוה, has *(Rebia) (magnum) and, on account of the compass of the full intonation of this accent, a (Gaja) by the Shebâ (comp.* אלהי *Psalm 25:2,* אלהים*; Psalm 68:8,* אדני *Psalm 90:1).*

(Note: *We may observe here, in general, that this Gaja (Metheg) which draws the Shebâ into the intonation is placed even beside words with the lesser distinctives (Zinnor) and (Rebia) (parvum) only by the Masorete Ben-Naphtali, not by Ben-Asher (both about 950 a.d.). This is a point which has not been observed throughout even in Baer's edition of the Psalter so that consequently e.g., in Psalm 5:11 it is to be written* אלהים*; in Psalm 6:2 on the other hand (with Dechî)* יהוה*, not* יהוה*.)*

The construction of ספר with אל (as Psalm 69:27, comp. אמר; Genesis 20:2; Jeremiah 27:19, 2 ;דבר Chronicles 32:19, הודיע Isaiah 38:19): to narrate or make an announcement with respect to ... is minute, and therefore solemn. Self-confident and fearless, he can and will oppose to those, who now renounce their allegiance to him, a חק, i.e., an authentic, inviolable appointment, which can neither be changed nor shaken. All the ancient versions, with the exception of the Syriac, read חק־יהוה together. The line of the strophe becomes thereby more symmetrical, but the expression loses in force. אל־חק rightly has *Olewejored*. It is the amplificative use of the noun when it is not more precisely determined, known in Arabic grammar: such a decree! majestic as to its author and its matter. Jahve has declared to Him: בניאתה,

(Note: Even in pause here אתה remains without a lengthened *(ā) (Psalter* ii. 468), but the word is become *Milel*, while out of pause, according to Ben-Asher, it is *Milra*; but even out of pause (as in Psalm 89:10, Psalm 89:12; Psalm 90:2) it is accented on the *penult.* by Ben-Naphtali. The *Athnach* of the books תאם(Ps., Job, Prov.), corresponding to the *Zakeph* of the 21 other books, has only a half pausal power, and as a rule none at all where it follows *Olewejored*, cf. Psalm 9:7; Psalm 14:4; Psalm 25:7; Psalm 27:4; Psalm 31:14; Psalm 35:15, etc. (Baer, *Thorath Emeth p.* 37).)

and that on the definite day on which He has begotten or born him into this relationship of son. The verb ילד (with the changeable vowel *i*)

(Note: The changeable *i* goes back either to a primary form שָׁאַל, יְרַשׁ, יְלַד, or it originates directly from *Pathach*; forms like יְרֻשָּׁה and שְׁאֵלָךְ favour the former, (ē) in a closed syllable generally going over into Segol favours the latter.))

unites in itself, like γεννᾶν, the ideas of begetting and bearing (lxx γεγέννηκα, Aq. ἔτεκον); what is intended is an operation of divine power exalted above both, and indeed, since it refers to a setting up (נסך) in the kingship, the begetting into a royal existence, which takes place in and by the act of anointing (משׁח). Whether it be David, or a son of David, or the other David, that is intended, in any case 2 Sam 7 is to be accounted as the first and oldest proclamation of this decree; for there David, with reference to his own anointing, and at the same time with the promise of everlasting dominion, receives the witness of the eternal sonship to which Jahve has appointed the seed of David in relation to Himself as Father, so that David and his seed can say to Jahve: אבי אתה, Thou art my Father, Psalm 89:27, as Jahve can to him: בני אתה, Thou art My son. From this sonship of the Anointed one to Jahve, the Creator and Possessor of the world, flows His claim to and expectation of the dominion of the world. The cohortative, natural after challenges, follows upon שׁאל, Ges. §128, 1. Jahve has appointed the dominion of the world to His Son: on His part therefore it needs only the desire for it, to appropriate to Himself that which is allotted to Him. He needs only to be willing, and that He is willing is shown by His appealing to the authority delegated to Him by Jahve against the rebels. This authority has a supplement in Psalm 2:9, which is most terrible for the rebellious ones. The suff. refer to the גוים, the ἔθνη, sunk in heathenism. For these his sceptre of dominion (Psalm 90:2) becomes a rod of iron, which will shatter them into a thousand pieces like a brittle image of clay (Jeremiah 19:11). With נפץ alternates רעע (= רעע frangere), fut. תרע; whereas the lxx (Syr., Jer.), which renders ποιμανεῖς αὐτοὺς ἐν ῥάβδῳ (as 1 Corinthians 4:21) σιδηρᾷ, points it תרעם from רעה. The staff of iron, according to the Hebrew text the instrument of punitive power, becomes thus with reference to שׁבט as the shepherd's staff Psalm 23:4; Micah 7:14, an instrument of despotism.

Verses 10-12

The poet closes with a practical application to the great of the earth of that which he has seen and heard. With ועתה, êaéiō(1 John 2:28), *itaque* appropriate conclusions are drawn from some general moral matter of face (e.g., Proverbs 5:7) or some fact connected with the history of redemption (e.g., Isaiah 28:22). The exhortation is not addressed to those whom he has seen in a state of rebellion, but to kings in general with reference to what he has prophetically seen and heard. שׁפטי ארץ are not those who judge the earth, but the judges, i.e., rulers (Amos 2:3, cf. 1:8), belonging to the earth, throughout its length or breadth. The *Hiph.*השׂכיל signifies to show intelligence or discernment; the *Niph.* נוסר as a so-called *Niph. tolerativum*, to let one's self be chastened or instructed, like נועץ; Proverbs 13:10, to allow one's self to be advised, נדרשׁEzekiel 14:3, to allow one's self to be sought, נמצא to allow one's self to be found, 1 Chronicles 28:9,and frequently. This general call to reflection is followed, in 1 Chronicles 28:11, by a special exhortation in reference to Jahve, and in Psalm 2:12, in reference to the Son. עבדו and גילו answer to each other: the latter is not according to Hosea 10:5 in the sense of חילו; Psalm 96:9, but, - since "to shake with trembling" (Hitz.) is a tautology, and as an imperative גִּילוּ everywhere else signifies: rejoice, - according to Psalm 100:2, in the sense of rapturous manifestation of joy at the happiness and honour of being permitted to be servants of such a God. The lxx correctly renders it: ááõâôñï Their rejoicing, in order that it may not run to the excess of security and haughtiness, is to be blended with trembling (בּ as Zephaniah 3:17), viz., with the trembling of reverence and self-control, for God is a consuming fire, Hebrews 12:28.

The second exhortation, which now follows, having reference to their relationship to the Anointed One, has been missed by all the ancient versions except the Syriac, as though its clearness had blinded the translators, since they render בַר, either בֹּר purity, chastity, discipline (lxx, Targ., Ital., Vulg.), or בַּר pure, unmixed (Aq., Symm., Jer.: *adorate pure*). Thus also Hupfeld renders it "yield sincerely," whereas it is rendered by Ewald "receive wholesome warning," and by Hitzig "submit to duty" (בַר like the Arabic *birr* =בִּר); Olshausen even thinks, there may be some mistake in בַר, and Diestel decides for בוֹ instead of בַר. But the context and the usage of the language require *osculamini filium*. The *Piel* נָשַׁק means to kiss, and never anything else; and while בֹּר in Hebrew means purity and nothing more, and בַּר as an adverb, *pure*, cannot be supported, nothing is more natural here, after Jahve has acknowledged His Anointed One as His Son, than that בַר (Proverbs 31:2, even בְּרִי = בְּנִי) - which has nothing strange about it when found in solemn discourse, and here helps one over the dissonance of פ בֶּן וּ - should, in a like absolute manner to חֹק, denote the unique son, and in fact the Son of God.

(Note: Apart from the fact of בַר not having the article, its indefiniteness comes under the point of view of that which, because it combines with it the idea of the majestic, great, and terrible, is called by the Arabian grammarians Arab. *('l) -(tnkîr) (lt'dîm) or (ltktîr) or (lthwîl); by the boundlessness which lies in it it challenges the imagination to magnify the notion which it thus expresses. An Arabic expositor would here (as in Psalm 2:7 above) render it "Kiss a son and such a son!" (vid., (Ibn) (Hishâm) in De Sacy's Anthol.Grammat. p. 85, where it is to be translated hic est vir, qualis vir!). Examples which support this doctrine are בְּיַר; Isaiah 28:2 by a hand, viz., God's almighty hand which is the hand of hands, and Isaiah 31:8* מִפְּנֵי־חֶרֶב before a sword, viz., the divine sword which brooks no opposing weapon.)*

The exhortation to submit to Jahve is followed, as Aben-Ezra has observed, by the exhortation to do homage to Jahve's Son. To kiss is equivalent to to do homage. Samuel kisses Saul (1 Samuel 10:1), saying that thereby he does homage to him.

(Note: On this vid., Scacchi *Myrothecium*, to. iii. (1637) c. 35.)

The subject to what follows is now, however, not the Son, but Jahve. It is certainly at least quite as natural to the New Testament consciousness to refer "lest He be angry" to the Son (vid., Revelation 6:16.), and since the warning against putting trust (חֲסוֹת) in princes, Psalm 118:9; Psalm 146:3, cannot be applied to the Christ of God, the reference of בוֹ to Him (Hengst.) cannot be regarded as impossible. But since חָסָה is the usual word for taking confiding refuge in Jahve, and the future day of wrath is always referred to in the Old Testament (e.g., Psalm 110:5) as the day of the wrath of God, we refer the *ne irascatur* to Him whose son the Anointed One is; therefore it is to be rendered: lest Jahve be angry and ye perish דֶּרֶךְ. This דֶּרֶךְ is the *accus.* of more exact definition. If the way of any one perish. Psalm 1:6, he himself is lost with regard to the way, since this leads him into the abyss. It is questionable whether כִּמְעַט means "for a little" in the sense of *brevi* or *facile*. The *usus loquendi* and position of the words favour the latter (Hupf.). Everywhere else כִּמְעַט means by itself (without such additions as in Ezra 9:8; Isaiah 26:20; Ezekiel 16:47) "for a little, nearly, easily." At least this meaning is secured to it when it occurs after hypothetical antecedent clauses as in Psalm 81:15; 2 Samuel 19:37; Job 32:22. Therefore it is to be rendered: for His wrath might kindle easily, or might kindle suddenly. The poet warns the rulers in their own highest interest not to challenge the wrathful zeal of Jahve for His Christ, which according to Psalm 2:5 is inevitable. Well is it with all those who have nothing to fear from this outburst of wrath, because they hide themselves in Jahve as their refuge. The construct state חוֹסֵי connects בּוֹ, without a genitive relation, with itself as forming together one notion, Ges. §116, 1. חסה the usual word for fleeing confidingly to Jahve, means according to its radical notion not so much *refugere, confugere, as se abdere, condere*, and is therefore never combined with אֶל, but always with בְּ.

(Note: On old names of towns, which show this ancient חסה. Wetzstein's remark on Job 24:8 [Comm. on Job, en loc.]. The Arabic still has hsy in the reference of the primary meaning to water which, sucked in and hidden, flows under the sand and only comes to sight on digging. The rocky bottom on which it collects beneath the surface of the sand and by which it is prevented from oozing away or drying up is called Arab. (ḥasâ) or (ḥisâ) a hiding-place or place of protection, and a fountain dug there is called Arab. (ʿyn) (ʾl) -(ḥy).)

E.W. BULLINGER'S *COMPANION BIBLE* NOTES – PSALM 2

Psalm 2

Verse 1

The second Psalm of each book has to do with the enemy. See App-10.

Why. ? Figure of speech *Erotesis*. App-6. Repeat at beginning of Psalms 2:2. Compare Acts 4:25, Acts 4:26.

heathen = nations. Note the quadruple *Anabasis* (App-6): nations, peoples, kings, rulers. Compare Psalms 1:1.

rage = tumultuously assemble.

people = peoples.

imagine. Same as meditate in Psalms 1:2.

Verse 2

set themselves = take their stand.

take counsel together = have gathered by appointment. So the Septuagint and Aramaean. Compare Psalms 48:4.

the LORD. Hebrew. *Jehovah.* App-4.

Anointed = Messiah. So Psalms 18:50; Psalms 20:6; Psalms 28:8; Psalms 84:9; Psalms 89:38, Psalms 89:51; Psalms 132:10, Psalms 132:17. In Daniel 9:25, Daniel 9:26, rendered Messiah.

saying. The Figure of speech *Ellipsis* (App-6) correctly supplied.

Verse 3

their: i.e. Jehovah"s, and Messiah"s.

Verse 4

laugh. Figure of speech *Anthropopatheia*. App-6.

The LORD*. Primitive text was Jehovah. Altered by the *Sopherim* to Adonai. See App-32.

Verse 6

set = founded. Not the same word as Psalms 2:2.

My holy hill. Figure of speech *Antimeria* (App-6). Hebrew = "mount of my Sanctuary".

holy. See note on Exodus 3:5.

Zion. The mount immediately south of Moriah. See note on 2 Samuel 5:7. Occurs thirty-eight times in Psalms. "Jerusalem" occurs seventeen times.

Verse 7

the = for a.

Thou art my Son. Quoted in Acts 13:33. Hebrews 1:5; Hebrews 5:5. This is the Divine formula for anointing. Compare Matthew 3:17, for Prophet; Matthew 17:5, for Priest; and Hebrews 1:5, Hebrews 1:6, for King.

begotten Thee. Figure of speech *Anthropopatheia* (App-6). It refers to resurrection (Acts 13:33. Romans 1:3, Romans 1:4. Colossians 1:18. Revelation 1:5).

Verse 8

Ask of me. Referring not to this present dispensation of grace, but to coming dispensation of judgment.

I shall give, &c. Quoted in Revelation 2:27; Revelation 12:5; Revelation 19:15.

Verse 9

break them = rule, or govern them. So Septuagint, Syriac, and Vulgate.

rod = sceptre.

iron. Put by Figure of speech *Metonymy* (of Adjunct), for unbending authority.

Verse 10

Be wise. Figure of speech *Apostrophe*. App-6.

Verse 11

the LORD. Hebrew. *"eth* Jehovah. App-4. (objective).

Verse 12

Kiss = submit to, or be ruled by. Hebrew. *nashak*. Occurs thirty-two times (first in Genesis 27:26, Genesis 27:27). Always so rendered except 1 Chronicles 12:2. 2 Chronicles 17:17. 2 Chronicles 78:9 (where it is Poel Part.) "armed"; Ezekiel 3:13 "touched" (margin "kissed"); and Genesis 41:40, "be ruled" (margin "be armed", or "kiss").

Son. Aramaean. *bar*, a *Homonym* with two meanings: (1) *s*on (Daniel 3:25. Ezra 5:1, Ezra 5:2, Ezra 5:2;Ezra 6:14. Daniel 3:25; Daniel 5:22; Daniel 7:13, and Proverbs 31:2, Proverbs 31:2, Proverbs 31:2 (king Lemuel); (2) *ground*, Daniel 2:38; Daniel 2:4, Daniel 2:12, Daniel 2:15, Daniel 2:21, Daniel 2:23, Daniel 2:23, Daniel 2:25, Daniel 2:32. See note on Job 39:4. So here in Psalms 2:12 = kiss the ground, Figure of speech *Metonymy* (of Adjunct), App-6, for prostrate yourselves in submission. The usual Hebrew for "son"is *ben*, and is translated "son" or "sons" 2,890 times, and "child" or "children" (where it ought always to be "son" or "sons"), 1,549 times: making 4,439 in all. The Aramaean *ben* is also used for "son".

He: i.e. Jehovah, Psalms 2:11.

from the way. No Figure of speech *Ellipsis* (App-6) here, "from" not needed = "perish, way [and all]". Ending like Psalms 1:6. Compare Psalms 146:9. So 2 Kings 3:4 = wool [and all].

When His wrath is kindled: or, His wrath will soon be kindled (Revised Version)

a little = quickly. See note on "almost", Proverbs 5:14.

Blessed = How happy. Figure of speech *Beatitude*. See note on Psalms 1:1.

put their trust = flee for refuge to. Hebrew. *hasah*. See App-69.

TREASURY OF SCRIPTURE KNOWLEDGE – PSALM 2

Psalm 2

Introduction
1   The kingdom of Christ.
10   Kings are exhorted to accept it.

Verse 1

Why do the heathen *rage*, and the *people imagine* a vain thing?
    A. M. 2963. B.C. 1042. Why
    18:42; 46:6; 83:4-8; Isaiah 8:9; Luke 18:32; Acts 4:25
    rage
    or, tumultuously assemble.
    Luke 22:1,2,5,22,23; Acts 16:22; 17:5,6; 19:28-32
    people
    Matthew 21:38; John 11:49,50; Acts 5:33; Revelation 17:14
    imagine
    Heb. meditate.

Verse 2

The *kings* of the earth set themselves, and the *rulers* take counsel together, against the LORD, and against his *anointed*, saying,
    kings
    10; 48:4; 110:5; Matthew 2:16; Luke 13:31; 23:11,12; Acts 12:1-6; Revelation 17:12-14
    rulers
    Matthew 26:3,59; 27:1; Acts 4:5-8
    Lord
    Exodus 16:7; Proverbs 21:30; John 15:23; Acts 9:4
    anointed
    45:7; 89:20; Isaiah 61:1; John 1:41; 3:34; Acts 10:38; Hebrews 1:9

Verse 3

Let us break their bands asunder, and cast away their cords from us.

Jeremiah 5:5; Luke 19:14,27; 1 Peter 2:7,8

Verse 4

He that sitteth in the heavens *shall laugh*: the Lord shall have them in derision.

He that

11:4; 68:33; 115:3; Isaiah 40:22; 57:15; 66:1

shall laugh

37:13; 53:5; 59:8; 2 Kings 19:21; Proverbs 1:26

Verse 5

Then shall he speak unto them in his wrath, and *vex* them in his sore displeasure.

Then

50:16-22; Isaiah 11:4; 66:6; Matthew 22:7; 23:33-36; Luke 19:27,43,44; Revelation 1:16;19:15

vex

or, trouble. sore.

110:5,6; Zechariah 1:15

Verse 6

Yet have I *set* my king upon my holy hill of Zion.

Yet

45:6; 89:27,36,37; 110:1,2; Isaiah 9:6,7; Daniel 7:13,14; Matthew 28:18; Acts 2:34-36;5:30,31; Ephesians 1:22; Philippians 2:9-11

set

Heb. anointed. my, etc. Heb. Zion, the hill of my holiness.

48:1,2; 50:2; 78:68; 132:13,14; Hebrews 12:22; Revelation 14:1

Verse 7

I will declare *the decree*: the LORD hath said unto me, *Thou* art my Son; *this* day have I begotten thee.

the decree

or, for a decree.

148:6; Job 23:13; Isaiah 46:10

Thou

Matthew 3:17; 8:29; 16:16; 17:5; Acts 8:37; 13:33; Romans 1:4; Hebrews 1:5; 3:6; Hebrews 5:5,8

this

89:27; John 1:14,18; 3:16; Hebrews 1:6

Verse 8

Ask of me, *and I* shall give thee the heathen for thine inheritance, and the uttermost parts of the earth for thy possession.

    Ask

    John 17:4,5

    and I

    22:27; 72:8; Daniel 7:13

Verse 9

Thou shalt break them with a rod of iron; thou shalt dash them in pieces like a potter's vessel.

    21:8,9; 89:23; 110:5,6; Isaiah 30:14; 60:12; Jeremiah 19:11; Daniel 2:44; Matthew 21:44;Revelation 2:26,27; 12:5

Verse 10

Be wise now therefore, *O* ye kings: *be instructed*, ye judges of the earth.

    Be wise

    Jeremiah 6:8; Hosea 14:9

    O

    45:12; 72:10,11; Isaiah 49:23; 52:15; 60:3,10,11

    be instructed

    82:1-8

Verse 11

Serve the LORD with fear, and *rejoice* with trembling.

    Serve

    89:7; Hebrews 12:28,29

    rejoice

    95:1-8; 97:1; 99:1; 119:120; Philippians 2:12; Hebrews 4:1,2; 12:25

Verse 12

Kiss the *Son*, lest he be angry, and *ye perish* from the way, *when* his wrath is kindled but a little. *Blessed*are all they that put their trust in him.

    Kiss

    Genesis 41:40,43,44; 1 Samuel 10:1; 1 Kings 19:18; Hosea 13:2; John 5:23

    Son

    and, etc

    Or, "and ye lose the way," or, "and ye perish in the way." The LXX., and Vulgate have, "and ye perish from the righteous way:" and the Syriac, "and ye perish from his way."

    ye perish

1:6; John 14:6

when

5; 2 Thessalonians 1:8,9; Revelation 6:16,17; 14:9-11

Blessed

40:4; 84:12; 146:3-5; Proverbs 16:20; Isaiah 26:3,4; 30:18; Jeremiah 17:7; Romans 9:33;Romans 10:11; Ephesians 1:12; 1 Peter 1:21; 2:6.

ZION IN PROPHECY AND TYPOLOGY

"This is the word that the LORD has spoken against him: 'She has despised you and mocked you, The virgin daughter of **Zion**; She has shaken her head behind you, The daughter of Jerusalem! 'Whom have you reproached and blasphemed? And against whom have you raised your voice, And haughtily lifted up your eyes? Against the Holy One of Israel!' (2 Kings 19:21-22)

"That I may tell of all Your praises, That in the gates of the daughter of **Zion** I may rejoice in Your salvation." (Psalm 9:14)

"There is a river whose streams make glad the city of God, The holy dwelling places of the Most High. God is in the midst of her, she will not be moved; God will help her when morning dawns. The nations made an uproar, the kingdoms tottered; He raised His voice, the earth melted." (Psalm 46:4-7)

"Great is the LORD, and greatly to be praised, In the city of our God, His holy mountain. Beautiful in elevation, the joy of the whole earth, Is Mount **Zion** in the far north, The city of the great King. God, in her palaces, Has made Himself known as a stronghold." (Psalm 48:1-14)

"His tabernacle is in Salem; His dwelling place also is in **Zion**." (Psalm 76:2)

"But chose the tribe of Judah, Mount **Zion** which He loved." (Psalm 78:68)

"The LORD loves the gates of **Zion** More than all the other dwelling places of Jacob. Glorious things are said of you, city of God: I shall mention Rahab and Babylon among those who know Me; Behold, Philistia and Tyre with Ethiopia: 'This one was born there.'" But of **Zion** it shall be said, "This one and that one were born in her"; And the Most High Himself will establish her. The LORD will count when He registers the peoples, "This one was born there." Selah." (Psalm 87:2-6)

"You will arise and have compassion on **Zion**; For it is time to be gracious to her, For the appointed time has come. Surely Your servants find pleasure in her stones And feel pity for her dust. So the nations will fear the name of the LORD And all the kings of the earth Your glory." (Psalm 102:13-16)

"That men may tell of the name of the LORD in **Zion** And His praise in Jerusalem, When the peoples are gathered together, And the kingdoms, to serve the LORD." (Psalm 102:21-22)

"Those who trust in the LORD Are as Mount **Zion**, which cannot be moved but abides forever. As the mountains surround Jerusalem, So the LORD surrounds His people From this time forth and forever." (Psalm 125:1-2)

"When the LORD brought back the captive ones of **Zion**, We were like those who dream. Then our mouth was filled with laughter And our tongue with joyful shouting; Then they said among the nations, "The LORD has done great things for them." The LORD has done great things for us; We are glad." (Psalm 126:1-3)

"For the LORD has chosen **Zion**; He has desired it for His habitation. "This is My resting place forever; Here I will dwell, for I have desired it. "I will abundantly bless her provision; I will satisfy her needy with bread." (Psalm 132:13-16)

"It is like the dew of Hermon Coming down upon the mountains of **Zion**; For there the LORD commanded the blessing--life forever." (Psalm 133:3)

"Blessed be the LORD from **Zion**, Who dwells in Jerusalem. Praise the LORD!" (Psalm 135:21)

"Praise the LORD, O Jerusalem! Praise your God, O **Zion**! For He has strengthened the bars of your gates; He has blessed your sons within you. He makes peace in your borders; He satisfies you with the finest of the wheat." (Psalm 147:12-14)

"The daughter of **Zion** is left like a shelter in a vineyard, Like a watchman's hut in a cucumber field, like a besieged city. Unless the LORD of hosts Had left us a few survivors, We would be like Sodom, We would be like Gomorrah." (Isaiah 1:8-9)

"Now it will come about that In the last days The mountain of the house of the LORD Will be established as the chief of the mountains, And will be raised above the hills; And all the nations will stream to it. And many peoples will come and say, "Come, let us go up to the mountain of the LORD, To the house of the God of Jacob; That He may teach us concerning His ways And that we may walk in His paths." For the law will go forth from **Zion** And the word of the LORD from Jerusalem. And He will judge between the nations, And will render decisions for many peoples; And they will hammer their swords into plowshares and their spears into pruning hooks Nation will not lift up sword against nation, And never again will they learn war." (Isaiah 2:2-4)

"Then He shall become a sanctuary; But to both the houses of Israel, a stone to strike and a rock to stumble over, And a snare and a trap for the inhabitants of Jerusalem." (Is 8:14)

"Therefore thus says the Lord GOD, "Behold, I am laying in **Zion** a stone, a tested stone, A costly cornerstone for the foundation, firmly placed. He who believes in it will not be disturbed." (Is 28:16)

"this is the word that the LORD has spoken against him: "She has despised you and mocked you, The virgin daughter of **Zion**; She has shaken her head behind you, The daughter of Jerusalem! "Whom have you reproached and blasphemed? And against whom have you raised your voice And haughtily lifted up your eyes? Against the Holy One of Israel!" (Isaiah 37:22-23)

"I bring near My righteousness, it is not far off; And My salvation will not delay And I will grant salvation in **Zion**, And My glory for Israel." (Isaiah 46:13)

"Awake, awake, Clothe yourself in your strength, O **Zion**; Clothe yourself in your beautiful garments, O Jerusalem, the holy city; For the uncircumcised and the unclean Will no longer come into you. Shake yourself from the dust, rise up, O captive Jerusalem; Loose yourself from the chains around your neck, O captive daughter of **Zion**." (Isaiah 52:1-2)

"Let not the foreigner who has joined himself to the LORD say, "The LORD will surely separate me from His people " Nor let the eunuch say, "Behold, I am a dry tree." For thus says the LORD, "To the eunuchs who keep My sabbaths, And choose what pleases Me, And hold fast My covenant, To them I will give in My house and within My walls a memorial, And a name better than that of sons and daughters; I will give them an everlasting name which will not be cut off." (Isaiah 56:3-7)

"Behold, the LORD has proclaimed to the end of the earth, Say to the daughter of **Zion**, "Lo, your salvation comes; Behold His reward is with Him, and His recompense before Him." And they will call them, "The holy people, The redeemed of the LORD"; And you will be called, "Sought out, a city not forsaken."" (Isaiah 62:11-12)

"How the Lord has covered the daughter of **Zion** With a cloud in His anger! He has cast from heaven to earth The glory of Israel, And has not remembered His footstool In the day of His anger." (Lamentations 2:1)

"The LORD determined to destroy The wall of the daughter of **Zion**. He has stretched out a line, He has not restrained His hand from destroying, And He has caused rampart and wall to lament; They have languished together. Her gates have sunk into the ground, He has destroyed and broken her bars Her king and her princes are among the nations; The law is no more Also, her prophets find No vision from the LORD. The elders of the daughter of **Zion** Sit on the ground, they are silent They have thrown dust on their heads; They have girded themselves with sackcloth The virgins of Jerusalem Have bowed their heads to the ground." (Lamentations 2:8-10)

"The comely and dainty one, the daughter of **Zion**, I will cut off. "Shepherds and their flocks will come to her, They will pitch their tents around her, They will pasture each in his place. "Prepare war against her; Arise, and let us attack at noon. Woe to us, for the day declines, For the shadows of the evening lengthen!" (Jeremiah 6:2-5)

"Have You completely rejected Judah? Or have You loathed **Zion**? Why have You stricken us so that we are beyond healing? We waited for peace, but nothing good came; And for a time of healing, but behold, terror! (Jeremiah 14:19)

"Micah of Moresheth prophesied in the days of Hezekiah king of Judah; and he spoke to all the people of Judah, saying, 'Thus the LORD of hosts has said, "**Zion** will be plowed as a field, And Jerusalem will become ruins, And the mountain of the house as the high places of a forest."' (Jeremiah 26:18)

"For thus says the LORD, 'When seventy years have been completed for Babylon, I will visit you and fulfill My good word to you, to bring you back to this place. 'For I know the plans that I have for you,' declares the LORD, 'plans for welfare and not for calamity to give you a future and a hope. 'Then you will call upon Me and come and pray to Me, and I will listen to you. (Jeremiah 29:10-14)

"'For I will restore you to health And I will heal you of your wounds,' declares the LORD, 'Because they have called you an outcast, saying: "It is **Zion**; no one cares for her."' "Thus says the LORD, 'Behold, I will restore the fortunes of the tents of Jacob And have compassion on his dwelling places; And the city will be rebuilt on its ruin, And the palace will stand on its rightful place. 'From them will proceed thanksgiving And the voice of those who celebrate; And I will multiply them and they will not be diminished; I will also honor them and they will not be insignificant." (Jeremiah 30:17-22)

"Behold, days are coming," declares the LORD, "when the city will be rebuilt for the LORD from the Tower of Hananel to the Corner Gate. "The measuring line will go out farther straight ahead to the hill Gareb; then it will turn to Goah. "And the whole valley of the dead bodies and of the ashes, and all the fields as far as the brook Kidron, to the corner of the Horse Gate toward the east, shall be holy to the LORD; it will not be plucked up or overthrown anymore forever." (Jeremiah 31:38-40)

"Blow a trumpet in **Zion**, And sound an alarm on My holy mountain! Let all the inhabitants of the land tremble, For the day of the LORD is coming; Surely it is near, A day of darkness and gloom, A day of clouds and thick darkness As the dawn is spread over the mountains, So there is a great and mighty people; There has never been anything like it, Nor will there be again after it To the years of many generations." (Joel 2:1-2)

"The LORD roars from **Zion** And utters His voice from Jerusalem, And the heavens and the earth tremble But the LORD is a refuge for His people And a stronghold to the sons of Israel." (Joel 3:16)

"Therefore, on account of you **Zion** will be plowed as a field, Jerusalem will become a heap of ruins, And the mountain of the temple will become high places of a forest." (Micah 3:12)

"And it will come about in the last days That the mountain of the house of the LORD Will be established as the chief of the mountains It will be raised above the hills, And the peoples will stream to it. Many nations will come and say, "Come and let us go up to the mountain of the LORD And to the house of the God of Jacob, That He may teach us about His ways And that we may walk in His paths " For from **Zion** will go forth the law, Even the word of the LORD from Jerusalem. And He will judge between many peoples And render decisions for mighty, distant nations Then they will hammer their swords into plowshares And their spears into pruning hooks; Nation will not lift up sword against nation, And never again will they train for war." (Micah 4:1-3)

""In that day," declares the LORD, "I will assemble the lame And gather the outcasts, Even those whom I have afflicted. "I will make the lame a remnant And the outcasts a strong nation, And the LORD will reign over them in Mount **Zion** From now on and forever. "As for you, tower of the flock, Hill of the daughter of **Zion**, To you it will come-- Even the former dominion will come, The kingdom of the daughter of Jerusalem." (Micah 4:6-8)

"Rejoice greatly, O daughter of **Zion**! Shout in triumph, O daughter of Jerusalem! Behold, your king is coming to you; He is just and endowed with salvation, Humble, and mounted on a donkey, Even on a colt, the foal of a donkey. I will cut off the chariot from Ephraim And the horse from Jerusalem; And the bow of war will be cut off And He will speak peace to the nations; And His dominion will be from sea to sea, And from the River to the ends of the earth." (Zechariah 9:9-10)

"Then it will come about that any who are left of all the nations that went against Jerusalem will go up from year to year to worship the King, the LORD of hosts, and to celebrate the Feast of Booths." (Zechariah 14:16)

"Say to the daughter of **Zion**, 'Behold your king is coming to you gentle, and mounted on a donkey, even a colt, the foal of a beast of burden.'" (Matthew 21:5)

"Fear not, daughter of **Zion**; Behold, your king is coming, seated on a donkey's colt." (John 12:15) "just as it is written, "Behold, I lay in **Zion** a stone of stumbling and a rock of offense, and he who believes in him will not be disappointed." (Romans 9:33)

"But as it is, they desire a better country, that is, a heavenly one Therefore God is not ashamed to be called their God; for He has prepared a city for them." (Hebrews 11:16)

"But you have come to Mount **Zion** and to the city of the living God, the heavenly Jerusalem, and to myriads of angels, to the general assembly and church of the firstborn who are enrolled in heaven, and to God, the Judge of all, and to the spirits of the righteous made perfect." (Hebrews 12:22-23)

"For this is contained in Scripture: "Behold, I will lay in **Zion** a choice stone, a precious corner stone, And he who believes in Him will not be disappointed."" (1 Peter 2:6)

"Then I looked, and behold, the Lamb was standing on Mount **Zion**, and with Him one hundred and forty-four thousand, having His name and the name of His Father written on their foreheads." (Revelation 14:1)

SCRIPTURES ON THE FEAST OF TABERNACLES

Exodus 23:14

"Three times a year you shall celebrate a feast to Me."

Exodus 23:16

"Also you shall observe the Feast of the Harvest of the first fruits of your labors from what you sow in the field; also the Feast of the Ingathering at the end of the year when you gather in the fruit of your labors from the field."

Exodus 34:22-23

"You shall celebrate the Feast of Weeks, that is, the first fruits of the wheat harvest, and the Feast of Ingathering at the turn of the year. "Three times a year all your males are to appear before the Lord GOD, the God of Israel."

Leviticus 23:33-34

"Again the LORD spoke to Moses, saying, "Speak to the sons of Israel, saying, 'On the fifteenth of this seventh month is the Feast of Booths for seven days to the LORD."

Leviticus 23:40

"Now on the first day you shall take for yourselves the foliage of beautiful trees, palm branches and boughs of leafy trees and willows of the brook, and you shall rejoice before the LORD your God for seven days."

Leviticus 23:37

"These are the appointed times of the LORD which you shall proclaim as holy convocations, to present offerings by fire to the LORD--burnt offerings and grain offerings, sacrifices and drink offerings, each day's matter on its own day"

Numbers 29:12-15

"Then on the fifteenth day of the seventh month you shall have a holy convocation; you shall do no laborious work, and you shall observe a feast to the LORD for seven days."

You shall present a burnt offering, an offering by fire as a soothing aroma to the LORD:

thirteen bulls, two rams, fourteen male lambs one year old, which are without defect; and their grain offering, fine flour mixed with oil: three-tenths of an ephah for each of the thirteen bulls, two-tenths for each of the two rams, and a tenth for each of the fourteen lambs"

Deuteronomy 16:13

"You shall celebrate the Feast of Booths seven days after you have gathered in from your threshing floor and your wine vat"

2 Chronicles 8:12-13

"Then Solomon offered burnt offerings to the LORD on the altar of the LORD which he had built before the porch; and did so according to the daily rule, offering them up according to the commandment of Moses, for the sabbaths, the new moons and the three annual feasts--the Feast of Unleavened Bread, the Feast of Weeks and the Feast of Booths."

Ezra 3:4

"They celebrated the Feast of Booths, as it is written, and offered the fixed number of burnt offerings daily, according to the ordinance, as each day required"

Nehemiah 8:17-18

"The entire assembly of those who had returned from the captivity made booths and lived in them. The sons of Israel had indeed not done so from the days of Joshua the son of Nun to that day And there was great rejoicing. He read from the book of the law of God daily, from the first day to the last day And they celebrated the feast seven days, and on the eighth day there was a solemn assembly according to the ordinance."

John 7:2-3

"Now the feast of the Jews, the Feast of Booths, was near. Therefore His brothers said to Him, "Leave here and go into Judea, so that Your disciples also may see Your works which You are doing."

FEAST OF TABERNACLES
AND LAST GREAT DAY

Extract from *Pagan Holidays - or God's Holy Days? - Which* by Herbert W Armstrong (pp. 43-47)

NOW WE come to the festival of Tabernacles — or Feast of Booths — the sixth festival. Let us notice the instruction concerning this occasion:

"Thou shalt observe the feast of tabernacles seven days, after that thou hast gathered in thy corn and thy wine. And thou shalt rejoice in thy feast, thou, and thy son, and thy daughter .... Seven days shalt thou keep a solemn feast unto the Lord thy God in the place which the Lord shall choose: because the Lord thy God shall bless thee in all thine increase, and in all the works of thine hands, therefore thou shalt surely rejoice ... and they shall not appear before the Lord empty: every man shall give as he is able, according to the blessing of the Lord thy God which he hath given thee" (Deut. 16:13-17).

Here is the Festival of Tabernacles, to be kept for seven days, beginning the 15th day of the seventh month of God's sacred calendar. Notice Leviticus 23:33-35: "And the Lord spake unto Moses, saying, Speak unto the children of Israel, saying, The fifteenth day of this seventh month shall be the feast of tabernacles for seven days unto the Lord. On the first day shall be an holy convocation; ye shall do no servile work therein."

On the first of these days is a holy convocation — a commanded assembly. No work is to be done. "... And ye shall rejoice before the Lord your God seven days .... It shall be a statute for ever in your generations: ye shall celebrate it in the seventh month" (Lev. 23:40-41).

Notice that it is commanded forever.

Here are pictured those final culminating events in God's great plan: after Christ has died for our sins to redeem mankind — after He has sent us the Holy Spirit and picked out a people for His Name to become kings and priests through the thousand years — after His glorious Second Coming — after He has finally restored the redeemed by placing all the sins upon the head of Satan, their real author, and separating both him and the sins from the presence of God and His people, thus finally perfecting the at-one-ment, making us finally joined in one — then we are ready for that final series of events, the commencement of the "Marriage of the Lamb," the actual making of the New Covenant, the establishment of the Kingdom of God on earth and the reaping of the great harvest of souls for a thousand years.

This festival is the picture of the Millennium!

Pictures the Millennium

To portray His plan, God took the yearly material harvest seasons in ancient Israel as the picture of the spiritual harvest of souls. In the Holy Land there are two annual harvests. The first is the spring grain harvest. Second comes the main harvest.

Notice that the Festival of Tabernacles is to be held "at the year's end" (Ex. 34:22). In this verse the Festival of Tabernacles or Booths is specifically called the "feast of ingathering." The harvest year ended at the beginning of autumn. **Just as Pentecost pictures the early harvest — this church age, so the Festival of Ingatherings or Tabernacles pictures the fall harvest — the great harvest of souls in the Millennium!**

Today is not the only day of salvation. Today is a day of salvation. Isaiah said so: chapter 49, verse 8. In fact, the original Greek words of Paul in II Corinthians 6:2 should be translated "a day of salvation," not "the day of salvation."

Turn to the book of Zechariah to understand this more thoroughly. In the 12th and 13th chapters we have a picture of Christ returning and the reconciliation of the world commencing. Here the meaning of the Festivals of Trumpets and Atonement is made plain.

Next, notice the 14th chapter. The time is the Millennium. "And the Lord shall be king over all the earth: in that day shall there be one Lord, and his name one ... there shall be no more utter destruction; but Jerusalem shall be safely inhabited" (verses 9, 11). It is the time when "living waters" — salvation, the Holy Spirit — "shall go out from Jerusalem" (verse 8). The "waters" are literal as well as figurative. God often pictures His spiritual plan by material events.

In that day, when the earth is safely inhabited, when the Holy Spirit is granted to all mortal flesh, what happens? "And it shall come to pass, that every one that is left of all the nations which came against Jerusalem shall even go up from year to year to worship the King, the Lord of hosts, and to keep the feast of tabernacles" (verse 16).

Gentiles Forced to Keep the Feast of Tabernacles

Notice this 16th verse of Zechariah 14. After Christ returns, the nations — mortal Gentiles who have not yet received salvation — will come to Jerusalem to keep the Feast of Tabernacles! How could they keep a festival that was abolished at the cross? They could keep it only if it were commanded forever.

And what will happen if they refuse to obey God? "And it shall be, that whoso will not come up of all the families of the earth unto Jerusalem to worship the King, the Lord of hosts, even upon them shall be no rain" (verse 17). Strong words these!

The nations will be forced to keep the Feast of Tabernacles, from year to year, when Christ is ruling with a rod of iron!

And if the nations still won't obey? "... there shall be the plague, wherewith the Lord will smite the heathen" — there are still heathen nations just beginning to learn the way of salvation — "that come not up to keep the feast of tabernacles. This shall be the punishment ... of all nations that come not up to keep the feast of tabernacles" (verses 18-19).

To receive salvation even the Gentiles will have to keep this festival. Of course, it is commanded forever!

Now we customarily quote Isaiah 66:23, showing that the Sabbath will be kept in the Millennium, as proof we must keep it now. Will we, then, when we read Zechariah 14:16, showing that the Feast of Tabernacles will be kept in the Millennium, be consistent by keeping it today?

Can we qualify as a son of God — a king and priest — ruling with Christ on His throne, assisting Christ at that time, if we now refuse to keep these festivals? Notice that Christ kept the Feast of Tabernacles. The Apostle John devoted an entire chapter of his gospel — the seventh chapter — to describe what Jesus said and did during the Feast of Tabernacles in the last year of His ministry.

Why Called the Feast of Tabernacles

During the Millennium, the Kingdom of God into which we may be born will rule the nations which are composed of mortal men begotten by the Spirit of God. The billions of mortal men alive during the Millennium will still be heirs to the Kingdom of God. They will not yet have inherited it as long as they remain mortal flesh, for "flesh and blood cannot inherit the kingdom of God" (I Cor. 15:50). "Ye must be born again" — "of the Spirit" — to inherit the Kingdom, said Jesus.

Remember that Abraham, Isaac and Jacob were merely heirs when they dwelled on earth (Heb. 11:9). While heirs they dwelled in tabernacles or booths, sojourning in the land of promise. Booths or temporary dwellings pictured that they were not yet inheritors. Thus we read of the Feast of Tabernacles that "ye shall dwell in booths seven days ... that your generations may know that I made the children of Israel to dwell in booths, when I brought them out of the land of Egypt" (Lev. 23:42-43). Israel dwelled in booths in the wilderness before they entered the promised land. Those booths pictured that they were only heirs. Even during the Millennium, when the Kingdom of God is ruling over mortal nations, the people will be only heirs to the Kingdom. They must overcome and grow in knowledge and wisdom to inherit the promises.

What a marvelous picture. God says of Ephraim (a type of all Israel) that they will "dwell in tabernacles, as in the days of the solemn feast" (Hosea 12:9). Israel, in the wilderness, was a type of all people who must go through trials and tribulations to inherit the promises. They were wanderers, waiting to inherit the promises of salvation.

The contention, held by some sects, that mortal human beings in the Millennium will remain flesh and blood forever is plainly denied by the Feast of Tabernacles, for the festival itself points toward an eternal inheritance.

Besides, after Jesus gathers the Church to Himself, and after He is seated on His throne where we will be ruling with Him, He will gather the nations before Him and say: "Inherit the Kingdom" (Matt. 25:34). [emphasis mine]

THE TEMPLE OF EDEN

By Tony Reinke
12 October 2009

In his book *The Temple and the Church's Mission* (IVP/Apollos, 2004), G. K. Beale argues that the Garden of Eden was the "first archetypal temple." He provides 14 conceptual and linguistic parallels between Eden and future tabernacle/temple structures. My brief summary:

1. **The Garden as the unique place of God's presence**. Eden was the place where God walked back and forth with man, paralleled this with later references to the Tabernacle (Gen. 3:8 with Lev. 26:12, Deut. 23:14; 2 Sam. 7:6–7**)**.

2. **The Garden as the place of the first priest**. Adam was placed in the garden to "cultivate and keep it" (Gen. 2:15). Taken alone, "cultivation" has obvious agricultural meaning. But this pair of terms ("cultivate/keep" also translated "serve/guard") is used elsewhere in the OT to describe the work of the priest (Num. 3:7–8; 8:25–26; 18:5–6; 1 Chr. 23:32; Ezek. 44:14). Thus "the task of Adam in Genesis 2:15 included more than mere spadework in the dirt of a garden. It is apparently that priestly obligations in Israel's later temple included the duty of 'guarding' unclean things from entering (cf. Num. 3:6–7, 32, 38; 18:1–7), and this appears to be relevant for Adam, especially in view of the unclean creature lurking on the perimeter of the Garden and who then enters" (p. 69).

3. **The Garden as the place of the first guarding cherubim**. After sin was introduced into the garden, Adam and Eve are barred from the tree of life by cherubim. This reveals that Adam's work included more than gardening—he was to protect the garden from evil and uncleanness. (Gen. 3:24 with Ex. 25:18–22; 1 Kgs. 6:29-35, 8:6–7; Ezek. 28:14–16, 41:18).

4. **The Garden as the place of the first arboreal lampstand**. Likely, the Tree of Life provides the model for the lampstand placed directly outside the holy of holies (Ex. 25:31–36).

5. **The Garden as formative for garden imagery in Israel's temple**. Temple references in the OT possess botanical, garden-like features (1 Kgs. 6:18, 29, 32; 7:20–26, 42, 47; Zech. 1:8–11; Ps. 74:3–7; 52:8; 92:13–15; Lam. 2:6; Isa. 60:13, 21).

6. **Eden as the first source of water**. Like Eden, the eschatological temples feature a source of water (Gen. 2:10 with Ezek. 47:1–12; Rev. 21:1–2).

7. **The Garden as the place of precious stones**. Note the correlation between precious stones in Eden and the building materials of the later tabernacle and temple (Gen. 2:12 with 1 Kgs. 6:20–22, Ex. 25:7, 11–39; 28:6–27; 1 Chr. 29:2).

8. **The Garden as the place of the first mountain**. Eden was situated upon a mountain (Ezek. 28:14, 16) just like Mount Zion (Ex. 15:17) and the eschatological temple (Ezek. 40:2; 43:12; Rev. 21:10).

9. **The Garden as the first place of wisdom**. "The ark in the holy of holies, which contained the Law (that led to wisdom) echoes the tree of the knowledge of good and evil (that also led to wisdom). Both the touching of the ark and the partaking of the tree's fruit resulted in death" (pp. 73–74).

10. **The Garden as the first place with an eastern facing entrance**. Like the future tabernacle and temples, Eden was entered from the east (Gen. 3:24 with Ezek. 40:6).

11. **The Garden as part of a tripartite sacred structure**. Genesis 2:10 reveals that "a river flowed out of Eden to water the garden." This reference formally distinguishes Eden from the garden. From this Beale builds the case that Eden and its adjoining garden "formed two distinct regions" (p. 74). He sees here tripartite degrees of holiness, similar to the temple complex, comprised of (a) the region outside the garden (the outer court); (b) the garden representing a sacred place (the holy place); and (c) Eden, where God dwells (the holy of holies).

12. **Ezekiel's view of the Garden of Eden as the first sanctuary**. In Ezekiel 28:13–18, the prophet draws a number of parallels between Eden and Israel's tabernacle/temple. Specifically, the prophet references Eden as a sanctuary and pictures Adam dressed as a priest (v. 13). And "Ezekiel 28:18 is probably, therefore, the most explicit place anywhere in canonical literature where the Garden of Eden is called a temple" (pp. 75-76).

13. **The Ancient Near Eastern concept of temples in association with garden-like features**. "Gardens not untypically were part of temple complexes in the Ancient Near East" (p. 76).

14. **Early Judaism's view of the garden as the first sanctuary**. Beale provides evidence from the non-canonical Jewish literature to further prove that "Judaism in various ways also understood the Garden to be the first sanctuary in line with the above Old Testament evidence" (p. 27).

Conclusion: "The cumulative effect of the preceding parallels between the Garden of Genesis 2 and Israel's tabernacle and temple indicates that Eden was the first archetypal temple, upon which all of Israel's temples were based" (pp. 79-80).

Read more on these conceptual and linguistic parallels on pages 66–80 of Beale's *The Temple and the Church's Mission: A Biblical Theology of the Dwelling Place of God* (IVP/Apollos, 2004).

====================================

Following is a pertinent extract from Beale's book:

"If Ezekiel and Revelation are developments of the first garden-temple ... then Eden, the area where the source of water is located, may be comparable to the inner sanctuary of Israel's later temple and the adjoining garden to the holy place...

"I would add to this that the land and seas to be subdued by Adam outside the Garden were roughly equivalent to the outer court of Israel's subsequent temple, which would lend further confirmation to the above identification of Israel's temple courtyard being symbolic of the land and seas throughout the earth. Thus, one may be able to perceive an increasing gradation in holiness from outside the garden proceeding inward:... the garden itself is a sacred space separated from the outside world (= the holy place), where God's priestly servants worships God by obeying him, by cultivating and guarding; Eden is where God dwells (= the holy of holies) as the source of both physical and spiritual life (symbolized by the waters)" (pp. 74-75).

LIST OF TRIBULATION AND DAY OF THE LORD PROPHECIES CONCERNING THE NATIONS

Ammon and Moab (sons of Lot):

Ammon: Jer 49:1-6; Ezek 25:1-7 Dan 11:41; Amos 1:13-15; Zeph 2:8-11
Moab: Isaiah 15, 16; Jer 48:1-47; Ezek 25:8-11; Dan 11:41; Amos 2:1-3; Zeph 2:8-11
Prophecies on Jordan: Is 11:14; 16:1-5, 13-14; Jer 9:26; 12:5; 25:21; 27:3; 48:9-11; 49:1-3, 6-9; 50:44; Ezek 25:1-10; 21:30; Zeph 2:8-11; Zech 11:3; Amos 2:1-3

Aram:

Isaiah 17:1-14; Jer 49:23-27; Amos 1:3-5

Assyria:

Isaiah 10:5-16; 10:24-34; 14:24-27; 19:23-25; 31:7-9; Micah 5:1-6; Nahum 1:1-3:19; Zeph 2:13-15; Zech 10:6-11

Babylonians (a combination of several nations and tribes):

Isaiah 13:1-14:11; 14:16-23; 21:1-10; 47:1-15; 48:20-21; Jer 50:1-46; 51:1-64; Ezek 12:10-16; Dan 2:31-38; 5:24-31; 7:1-4; Hab 1:1-11; Rev 17:1-18; 18:1-24
Rome: Dan 2:31-45; 7:1-7; 7:17-27; 8:22-25; 11:36-45; Rev 9:1-12; 13:1-18; 17:1-18:24

Canaan:

Lebanon: Isaiah 29:17-19; 60:13-14; Is 10:34; 14:18; 33:9; 37:24; 40:16; Ezek 26:5; Jer 47:4; Hab 2:17; Zech 11
Tyre & Sidon: Isaiah 23:1-18; Ezek 26:1-21; 27:1-36 ; 28:1-10; 28:20-26; Joel 3:4-8; Amos 1:9-10; Zech 9:3-4

Cush (Ethiopia):

Isaiah 18:1-7; Dan 11:41-43; Zeph 2:11-12;

Edom (Esau):

Isaiah Is 11:14; 34:5-8; 63:1, 6; Jer 9:26; 25:21; 49:7-24; Lam 4:21-22; Ezek 25:12-14; 35:1-15; 36:5; Dan 11:41; Amos 1:6-12; Ob 1:1-21; Joel 3:19; Amos 2:1; 9:12; Mic 1:12; Mal 1:2-4.

Elam:

Jer 49:34-39

Gog and Magog, etc:

Ezek 38:1-39:29; Dan 11:44-45; Rev 9:13-21; 16:12

Ishmael (Arabs):

Isaiah 21:13-17; Jer 2:10; 3:2; 25:23-24; 49:28; Ezek 29:21; Is 42:11; 60:7
Kedar: Jer 49:28-33

Javan (Greece):

Dan 2:31-39; 7:1-6; 8:1-14; 8:20-25; 11:1-35; Zech 9:13

Medes:

Is 13:17; Jere 51:11, 28

Mizraim (Egypt):

Isaiah 19; 20; Isaiah 45:14-17; Jer 46:1-28; Ezek 29:1-21; 30:1-26; 31:1-18; 32:1-32; Dan 11:41-43; Zech 10:6-11; 14:16-19
Philistia: Isaiah 14:29-32; Jer 47:1-7; Ezek 25:15-17; Amos 1:6-8; Zeph 2:4-7; Zech 9:5-8

Persia (descendants of Abraham through Keturah):

Dan 2:31-39; 5:24-31; 7:1-5; 11:1-4

Tarshish:

Isaiah 60:9; 66:19-21

REFERENCES

Alexander, J. A. (1864).   *The Psalms Translated and Explained.* Andrew Elliot and James Thin, Edinburgh.

Alexander, R. H. (1976).   *Ezekiel, Everyman's Bible Commentary*, Vol. 6 (p. 945, note on *Does Ezekiel 40-48 Relate to the Millennium or to the Eternal State?).* Moody Press, Chicago, IL.

Alexander, T. D. (2017).   *Exodus. Apollos Old Testament Commentary.* IVP Academic, London.

Anderson, B. W. (1962).   "Exodus Typology in Second Isaiah," Chapter XII of B. Anderson & W. Harrelson, eds., *Israel's Prophetic Heritage: Essays in Honor of James Muilenburg.* Harper & Brothers, New York, NY. pp. 177-195.

Armstrong, H. W. (1943).   "What's Prophesied about Russia," *Plain Truth*, Nov-Dec, pp. 5-7, 12.

Armstrong, H. W. (1952).   "Why Russia will not attack America!" *Good News*, Jan, pp. 1-2, 13-15.

Armstrong, H. W. (1956).   "Will Russia Attack America?" *Plain Truth,* July, pp. 3-6, 18-19.

Armstrong, H. W. (1971).   *Will Russia Attack America?* Ambassador College, Pasadena, CA (article reprint).

Armstrong, H. W. (1972).   *The Book of Revelation Unveiled at Last!* Ambassador College, Pasadena, CA.

Armstrong, H. W. (1976).   *Pagan Holidays - or God's Holy Days - Which?* Worldwide Church of God, Pasadena, CA.

Armstrong, H. W. (1979).   *The Wonderful World Tomorrow.* Worldwide Church of God, Pasadena, CA.

Aune, D. E. (1998).   *Revelation 17-22. World Bible Commentary.* Thomas Nelson, Nashville, TN.

Ayali-Darshan, N. (2015).   "The Seventy Bulls Sacrificed at Sukkot (Num 29:12-34) in Light of a Ritual Text from Emar *(Emar 6, 373),*" *Vetus Testamentum*, Vol. 65, No. 1, pp. 9-19.

Ayali-Darshan, N. (2016).   *Sukkot's Seventy Bulls.* TheTorah.com

Babcock, B. C. (2017).   "Who is "My Lord" in Psalm 110?" *Crucible*, Nov, pp. 1-23.

Bacon, I. (2018).   *The Plausibility of Animal Sacrifices in Ezekiel 40-48 Literally Operating in the Millennial Kingdom Under the New Covenant.* MA thesis. Rawlings School of Divinity, Lynchburg, VA.

Baldwin, J. G. (1972).   *Haggai, Zechariah, Malachi: An Introduction and Commentary. Tyndale Old Testament Commentaries.* InterVarsity Press, Downers Grove, IL.

Barker, K. L. (1985).   *Zechariah. Expositor's Bible Commentary. Vol 7: Daniel and the Minor Prophets.* Zondervan, Grand Rapids, MI.

Barnes, A. (c1850).   *Albert Barnes' Notes on the Whole Bible.* www.studylight.org/commentaries/bnb.html

Barratt, C. K. (1978).   *The Gospel According to St. John: An Introduction with Commentary and Notes on the Greek Text.* Westminster John Knox Press, Louisville, KY.

Barrick, W. D. (2012).   "The Kingdom of God in the Old Testament," *The Master's Seminary*, Fall, pp. 173-92.

Barton-Payne, J. (1973). *Encyclopedia of Biblical Prophecy*. Hodder and Stoughton, London.

Beale, G. K. (2004). *The Temple and the Church's Mission: A Biblical Theology of the Dwelling Place for God*, (*New Studies in Biblical Theology* series). IVP Academic, London.

Beals, J. E. (2013). *National Restoration and the Divine Dwelling Place in Ezekiel 37:15-28*. A thesis submitted to the Faculty in Partial Fulfillment for the Degree of Master of Theology, The Master's Seminary, Sun Valley, CA.

Beasley-Murray, G. R. (1970). "Ezekiel," *The New Bible Commentary* (Guthrie, G & Motyer, JA (eds)), W.B. Eerdmans Publishing, Grand Rapids, MI.

Beecher, W. J. (1905). *The Prophets and the Promise*. Thomas Y Crowell & Co, New York, NY.

Billington, C. (2017). "Othniel, Cushan-Rishathaim, and the Date of the Exodus," *Artifax*, Summer, pp. 14-20.

Blenkinsopp, J. (1990). *Ezekiel*. Westminster John Knox Press, Louisville, KY.

Block, D. I. (1998). *The Book of Ezekiel Chapters 25-28, New International Commentary on the Old Testament*. Eerdmans Publishing Co, Grand Rapids, MI.

Bolender, B. (2002). "Memorials and Shadows Animal Sacrifices of the Millennium," *Chafer Theological Journal*, April, pp. 26-41.

Boxall, I. (2006). "The Revelation of Saint John," *Black's New Testament Commentaries* General Editor: M D. Hooker. Hendrickson Publishers, Peabody, MA.

Boxall, I. (2007). "Exile, Prophet, Visionary: Ezekiel's Influence on the Book of Revelation" in *The Book of Ezekiel and its Influence*, eds: H. J. de Jonge, J Tromp. Ashgate Publishing Ltd, Farnham, UK.

Bright, J. (1951). "Faith and Destiny. The meaning of history in Deutero-Isaiah," *Interpretation. A Journal of Bible and Theology*, Vol. 5, Issue 1 (Jan), pp. 3-26.

Brodsky, H. (2006). "The Utopian Map in Ezekiel (48:1-35)," *Jewish Bible Quarterly*, Vol. 34, No. 1, pp. 20-26.

Bromiley, G. W. (1982). *The International Standard Bible Encyclopedia*. Vol. 2. William B Eerdmans, Grand Rapids, MI.

Brooks, J. (c2000). *The Millennial Sacrifice Controversy*. USA.

Brown, R. (1883). *Outlines of Prophetic Truth: Viewed Practically and Experimentally in the Light of the Divine Word: From Creation to Redemption* (Vols 1 & 2). S. W. Partridge & Co, London. (original 1770)

Broyles, C. C. (1999). *Psalms, New International Biblical Commentary*. Hendrickson Publishers, Peabody, MA.

Bullinger, E. W. (c1920). *The Companion Bible*. Samuel, Bagster and Sons Ltd, London.

Burgos, M. (2021). "An Exposition of the Second Psalm," *Academia Letters*, Oct, pp. 1-7.

Burke, J. (2016). "Does God Care for Oxen? Animal Welfare Ethics in the Bible," *Defence and Confirmation*, April, pp. 9-29.

Cambridge University. (1877). *Cambridge Bible for Schools and Colleges*. Cambridge University Press.

Chalker, W. H. (2006). *Science and Faith*. Westminster John Knox Books, Louisville, KY.

Christian, E. (1999). "A Chiasm of Seven Chiasms: The Structure of the Millennial Vision, Rev 19:1-21:8," *Andrews University Studies Seminary*, Vol. 37, No. 2, pp. 209-225.

Clarke, A. (1810-1826). *Commentary on the Bible* www.preteristarchive.com/Books/1810_clarke_commentary.html

Copan, P. (2011). *Is God a Moral Monster? Making Sense of the Old Testament God.* Baker Books, Grand Rapids, MI.

CR Moss, C. R. (2012). Baden, J. S. "1 Thessalonians 4.13-18 in Rabbinic Perspective," *New Testament Studies*, Vol. 58, Issue 2, April, pp. 199-212.

Crozier, O. R. L. (1852). "Rothschild and the City of Jerusalem," *Advent Harbinger*, Vol. 4, No. 6, 24 July, p. 45.

Davidson, R. M. (2000). "The Eschatological Literary Structure of the Old Testament," in *Creation, Life, and Hope: Essays in Honor of Jacques B. Doukhan*, pp. 349-366. Old Testament Department, Seventh-day Adventist Theological Seminary, Andrews University, Berrien Springs, MI.

Docken, A. (1982). *"But what if 'everything goes wrong'?" Good News*, Sept, Vol. 29, No. 8, pp. 8-9.

Dolphin, L. (2004). *The Temple of Ezekiel.* http://www.templemount.org/ezektmp.html

Douglas, J. D. (1972). *The New Bible Dictionary.* Inter-Varsity Press, England.

Duguid, I. M. (1999). *Ezekiel, The NIV Application Commentary.* Zondervan Publishing House, Grand Rapids, MI.

Dunn, H. (1868). *The Kingdom of God.* Simpkin, Marshall & Co, London.

Edersheim, A. (1879). *The Temple: Its Ministry and Services.* Hodder & Stoughton, New York, NY.

Essex, K. H. (1999). "The Abrahamic Covenant," *The Master's Seminary Journal*, Vol. 10, No. 2 (Fall), pp. 191-212.

Fausset, A. R. (et al) (1997). "The Revelation of St. John the Divine," in *A Commentary, Critical and Explanatory, on the Old and New Testaments* (note on Rev. 20:6), by R Jamieson, AR Fausset and D Brown, Logos Research Systems, Oak Harbour, WA (original 1877).

Fernando, A. (1998). *Acts. The NIV Application Commentary.* Zondervan Academic, Grand Rapids, MI.

Foulkes, F. (1955). *The Acts of God. A Study of the Basis of Typology in the Old Testament.* Tyndale House Old Testament Lecture for 1955 (1 July), Tyndale Fellowship for Biblical Research.

Gaebelein, F. E. (1991). *The Expositor's Bible Commentary* (Vol. 5). Zondervan Publishing House, Grand Rapids, MI.

Ganzel, T. (ND). *The Discrepancies between the Sacrifices in Ezekiel and the Torah.* https://thetorah.com/the-discrepancies-between-the-sacrifices-in-ezekiel-and-the-torah/

Glaser, M. (1987). Glaser, Z. *The Fall Feasts of Israel.* Moody Press, Chicago, IL.

Goldingay, J. (2002). *Isaiah. New International Bible Commentary.* Hendrickson Publishers, Carol Stream, IL.

Grandin, T. (2009). Johnson, C. *Animals Make Us Human. Creating the best life for Animals.* Houghton Mifflin Harcourt, New York, NY.

Gromacki, G. (2014). "The Fulfillment of the Abrahamic Promise," *The Journal of Ministry and Theology*, Vol. 18, No. 2, (Fall), pp. 77-119.

Guthrie, D. (et al) (1972). *The New Bible Commentary Revised.* Inter-Varsity Press, London.

Guzik, D. (2014). *Commentary on the Bible.* USA.

Halley, H. H. (1965). *Halley's Bible Handbook.* Zondervan, Michigan.

Hendriksen, W. (2002). *New Testament Commentary Exposition of the Gospel According to John: Two Volumes Complete in One.* Baker Publishing Group, Grand Rapids, MI.

Herrmann, P. (1952).   *Sieben vorbei und Acht Verweht.* Hoffmann & Campe.

Hilliker, J. (2009).   *A Visit to Millennial Headquarters!* (Sept). Philadelphia Church of God, Edmond, OK.
www.pcog.org/articles/308/a-visit-to-millennial-headquarters

Hindson, E. (2004).   "Premillennialism," *The Popular Encyclopedia of Bible Prophecy.* Tim LaHaye & Edward E. Hindson (eds). Harvest House Publishers, Eugene, OR.
Hocking, D.

Hoeh, H. L. (1959).   "Are God's Festivals to be Observed Forever?" *The Good News*, March, pp. 1-2, 5-6.

Hullinger, J. M. (1995).   "The Problem of Animal Sacrifices in Ezekiel 40-48," *Bibliotheca Sacra*, July-September, Vol. 152, pp. 279-89.

Kaiser, W. C. (1972).   "The Old Promise and the New Covenant: Jeremiah 31:31-34," *Journal of the Evangelical Theological Society*, Vol. 15, No. 1, pp. 11-23.

Kaiser, W. C. (1973).   "The Promise Theme and the Theology of Rest," *Bibliotheca Sacra*, Vol. 130, Dallas Theological Seminary, April, pp. 135-150.

Kaiser, W. C. (1977).   "The Davidic Promise and the Inclusion of the Gentiles (Amos 9:9-15 And Acts 15:13-18): A Test Passage For Theological Systems," *Journal of the Evangelical Theological Society*, Vol. 20, No. 2 (June), pp. 97-111.

Kaiser, W. C. (1978).   *Toward an Old Testament Theology.* Zondervan, Grand Rapids, MI.

Kaiser, W. C. (1985).   *The Uses of the Old Testament in the New.* Moody, Chicago, IL.

Kaiser, W. C. (1990).   *Exodus* in *Genesis, Exodus, Leviticus, Numbers. Expositors Bible Commentary.* Vol. 2. Zondervan, Grand Rapids, MI.

Kaiser, W. C. (1996).   "The Great Commission in the Old Testament," *International Journal of Frontier Missions*, Vol. 13, Jan-Mar, pp. 3-7.

Kaiser, W. C. (2000).   *Mission in the Old Testament. Israel as a Light to the Nations.* Baker Books, Grand Rapids, MI.

Kaiser, W. C. (2002).   *Micah – Malachi. The Preacher's Commentary.* Thomas Nelson, Nashville, TN,

Kaiser, W. C. (2008).   *Exodus in The Expositor's Bible Commentary.* Vol 1. Zondervan, Grand Rapids, MI.

Keener, C. S. (2019).   *Acts: An Exegetical Commentary.* Baker Academic, Ada, MI.

Keil, C. F.   *Ezekiel. Zechariah, Commentary on the Old Testament.* T & T Clark, Edinburgh.
& Delitzsch, F. (1866).

Keil, C. F.   *Isaiah. Commentary on the Old Testament.* T & T Clark, Edinburgh.
& Delitzsch, F. (1884).

Keil, C. F. (1857).   *A Commentary on the Book of Joshua.* T&T Clark, Edinburgh. Reprinted 1996 by Henderickson Publishers, Peabody, MA.

Keil, C. F. (1864).   *Exodus. Bible Commentary on the Old Testament.* Eerdmans, Grand Rapids, MI.
Delitzsch, F.

Keil, C. F. (1866-91).   *Biblical Commentary on the Old Testament.* T & T Clark, Edinburgh.
Delitzsch, F.

Kolatch, A. J. (2000).   *The Jewish Book of Why.* Penguin Group, New York, NY.

Ladd, G. E. (1957).   "Why Not Prophetic Apocalyptic?" *Journal of Biblical Literature*, Vol. 76, No. 3 (Sept), pp. 192-200.

LaHaye, T. (2004).   "A Literal Millennium as Taught in Scripture, Part 4," in Thomas Ice (ed), *Pre-Trib Perspectives.* Vol. 8, No. 10, Pre-Trib Research Center, February, p. 2.

LaHaye, T. M. (2006). Hindson, E. (eds). *Exploring Bible Prophecy from Genesis to Revelation.* Harvest House Publishers, Eugene, OR.

Lancaster, D. T. (2011). *What about the Sacrifices?* First Fruits of Zion, Marshfield, MO.

Martin, E. (1965). "The Sacrificial System in Israel," *Good News*, Sept, pp. 15-18, 24.

Martin, W. (1977). *The Temple Symbolism in Genesis.* Edited and expanded by David Sielaff, March 2004. Internet article. Portland, OR.

Mays, J. L. C. (2011). *Inspiration. A Bible Commentary for Teaching and Preaching. Psalms.* John Knox Press, Louisville, KY.

Mc Clain, A. J. (1959). *The Greatness of the Kingdom.* BMH Books, Winona Lake, IN.

McGrath, J. (2009). *The Only True God: Early Christian Monotheism in its Jewish Context*, University of Illinois Press, Champaign, Ill.

McNeile, A. H. (2010). *The Problem of the Future Life.* Kessinger Publishing, Whitefish, MT.

Meyers, E. (1988). "Early Judaism," *Biblical Archaeologist*, June, pp. 69-79.

Michaels, J. R. (2010). *The Gospel of* John in *The New International Commentary on the New Testament.* Wm B Eerdmans Publishing Co, Grand Rapids, MI.

Middleton, J. R. (2006). "A New Heaven and a New Earth: The case for a holistic reading of the Biblical Story of Redemption," *Journal for Christian Theological Research*, Vol. 11, pp. 73-97.

Milner, W. (1941). *The Russian Chapters of Ezekiel.* Destiny Publishers, Merrimac, MA. (First Published 1923)

Mittwede, S. K. (2014). "Will you rage with the Nations, or Will you kiss the Son?" *Old Roads*, May, pp. 12-15.

Moore, T. V. (1994). *Haggai, Zechariah, Malachi (Geneva Series of Commentaries).* Reprinted by The Banner of Truth Trust. (Original published in the 1800s)

Mowinckel, S. (1956). *He that Cometh.* Abingdon Press, New York, NY.

Neff, L. (1961). *God's Temple in Prophecy.* MA Thesis, Ambassador College, Pasadena, CA. (Revised 1986, 2005) Available online at www.friendsofsabbath.org/

Neuffer, J. (ND). *A historical review of early non-Sabbatarian Adventists' dispute over Israel in prophecy (1844-1850).* Biblical Research Institute General Conference of Seventh-day Adventists, available at https://adventistbiblicalresearch. org/materials/adventist-heritage/gathering-israel-historical-study-early-writings-pp. 74-76

Nielsen, S. (2014). *The Redistribution of the Land of Israel in the Millennial Kingdom* (17 Aug). https://studyingbibleprophecy.wordpress.com/2014/08/17/ the-redistribution-of-the-land-of-israel-in-the-millennial-kingdom/

NN. (2011). "The Feast of Tabernacles. Sukkot," www.wildolive.co.uk/sukot.htm

NN. (2022). "Did Jesus Eat Meat?" *Got Questions*, 4 Jan www.gotquestions.org/did-Jesus-eat-meat.html

NN. (ND). "Hysteron Proteron," *Wikipedia.*

North, C. R. (1946). *The Old Testament Interpretation of History.* The Epworth Press, London.

Orr, J. (1994). "Day, Last," *International Standard Bible Encyclopedia, Vol. 1.* Hendrickson Publishers, Peabody, MA. (reprint)

Oswalt, J. N. (1985). "Recent Studies in Old Testament Eschatology and Apocalyptic," *Journal of Evangelical Theological Society*, pp. 289-301.

Oswalt, J. N. (1998).   *The Book of Isaiah Chapters 40-66. The New International Commentary on the Old Testament.* Eerdmans, Grand Rapids, MI.

Patiño, M. (2014).   *Doctrinal Development of Millennium in Adventism Between 1831-1850.* AIIAS/ Universidad de Montemorelos, 6 Jan.

Peters, G. N. H. (1884).   *The Theocratic Kingdom of our Lord Jesus, the Christ, as Covenanted in the Old Testament and Revealed in the New.* (Vol. 1). Funk & Wagnalls, London & New York, NY.

Price, R. (1999).   *The Program for the Last Days Temple.* Harvest House, Eugene, OR.
Wlvoord, J.

Regenstein, L. G. (1991).   *Replenish the Earth.* SCM Press, London.

Reinke, T. (2009).   *The Temple of Eden.* Minneapolis, MI.

Robinson, T. (2003).   www.ucg.org/bible-study-tools/bible-commentary/bible-commentary-isaiah-11-12 *Beyond Today Bible Commentary. Isaiah,* 24 March.

Robinson, T. (2020).   "Why Will Jesus Christ Return? (Part 2)," *Beyond Today,* Nov-Dec, p. 25.

Ross, L. K. (1994).   *Celebrate! The Complete Jewish Holidays Handbook.* Jason Aronson Inc, New York, NY.

Ryrie, C. C. (1986).   *Basic Theology.* SP Publications, Wheaton, IL.

Sailhamer, J. H. (1995).   *The Pentateuch as Narrative. A Biblical-Theological Commentary.* Zondervan Academic, Grand Rapids, MI.

Sayce, A. H. (1928).   *Races of The Old Testament.* Lutterworth Press, Surrey, UK.

Sherrod, R. (1984).   "Solomon's Splendor. A Type of God's Kingdom," *Good News,* Sept, pp. 25-27.

Sherrod, R. (1996).   *Review of United States and Britain in Prophecy. Part II.* United Church of God. USA.

Showers, R. E. (1995).   *Maranatha, Our Lord Come.* Bellmawr, The Friends of Israel Gospel Ministry, NJ.

Smith, G. V. (2007).   *Isaiah 1-39: An Exegetical and Theological Exposition of Holy Scripture.* B & H Publishing Group, Nashville, TN.

Staples, J. A. (2019).   "Rise, Kill, and Eat': Animals as Nations in Early Jewish Visionary Literature and Acts 10," *Journal for the Study of the New Testament,* Vol. 42, Issue 1, 26 June, pp. 3-17.

Steep, C. D. (1982).   "Why should you rejoice at the Feast?" *Good News,* Sept, pp. 7-10.

Stevenson, K. R. (1996).   *Vision of Transformation. The Territorial Rhetoric of Ezekiel 40-48.* Scholar's Press.

Swanson, D. (1996).   "The Millennial Position of Spurgeon," *The Master's Seminary.* Vol. 7, No. 2, pp. 183-212.

Taylor, D. (1882).   *Reign of Christ on Earth.* S. Bagster & Sons, London.

Taylor, J. B. (2009).   *Ezekiel. Tyndale Old Testament Prophecies* (Vol. 22). Inter-Varsity Press, Nottingham, England.

Taylor, V. (1966).   *The Gospel According to Mark.* Palgrave Macmillan. London.

Tenney, M. C. (1954).   "The Importance and Exegesis of Revelation 20:1-8," *Bibliotheca Sacra,* April, pp. 137-148.

Thayer, J. H. (1973).   *Thayer's Greek English Lexicon.* Zondervan, Grand Rapids, MI. (original published 1896)

Unger, M. (2002).   *Unger's Commentary on the Old Testament.* AMG Publishers, Chattanooga, TN.

Vlach, M. (2020).   *Revelation 19:15 and the Coming Reign of Jesus over the Nations*, https://sharperiron.org/ 30 Sept.

Ward, H. D. (1841).   *History and Doctrine of the Millennium. A discourse delivered in the conference on the Second Advent near.* Boston, MA.

Webb, B. (2016).   *The Message of Zechariah. Bible Speaks Today*, IVP Academic, Downers Grove, IL.

Webb, R. L. (2006).   *John the Baptizer and Prophet: A Socio-Political Study.* Wipf & Stocke Publishers, Eugene, OR.

Werner, H. (2004-17).   *Werner Bible Commentary.* www.wernerbiblecommentary.org/

West, N. (1889).   *The Thousand Years in Both Testaments.* Scripture Truth Book Company, Fincastle, VA.

Whedon, D. (1907).   *Whedon's Commentary.* Eaton & Mains, New York, NY.

Whitcomb, J. C. (1985).   "Christ's Atonement and Animal Sacrifices in Israel," *Grace Theological Journal*, Vol. 6, No. 2, pp. 201-217.

Whitcomb, J. C. (1994).   "The Millennial Temple of Ezekiel 40-48," *The Diligent Workman Journal*, May, pp. 21-25.

White, C. M. (2010).   *Animals in the World Tomorrow* (PPT presentation). Sydney, Australia.

White, C. M. (2013).   *Cities in the World Tomorrow* (PPT presentation). Sydney, Australia.

White, C. M. (2015).   *Days of the Lord.* Sydney, Australia. Sydney, Australia.

White, C. M. (2018).   *A Note on the Melchizedek Priesthood.* Sydney, Australia.

White, C. M. (2021).   *The Invisible Rulers over the Nations.* Sydney, Australia.

White, C. M. (2021).   *The Lake of Fire in History and Prophecy.* Sydney, Australia.

White, C. M. (2021).   *The Sanctity of Nationhood in the Bible (Bible study).* Sydney, Australia.

Wilderberger, H. (1991).   *Isaiah 1-12. A Commentary* (Translated by Thomas H. Trapp). Fortress Press, Minneapolis, MN.

Wilson, G. H. (2002).   *Psalms Vol. 1, NIV Application Commentary.* Zondervan, Grand Rapids, MI.

Wiseman, D. J. (1973).   *Peoples of Old Testament Times.* Oxford University Press, Oxford, England.

Worldwide Church of God. (1965).   *Ambassador College Correspondence Course.* Pasadena, CA.

Worldwide Church of God. (1976).   *Systematic Theology Project.* Worldwide Church of God, Pasadena, CA.

Worldwide Church of God. (1985).   *Ambassador College Bible Correspondence Course*, Lesson 23, "What is God's Purpose for Mankind?" Worldwide Church of God, Pasadena, CA.

Worldwide Church of God. (1987).   *In the Beginning. Answers to Questions from Genesis.* Worldwide Church of God, Pasadena, CA.

Worldwide Church of God. (1987).   *Russia and China in Prophecy.* Worldwide Church of God, Pasadena, CA.

Wright, C. J. H. (2003).   *Deuteronomy, New International Bible Commentary*, Hendrickson Publishers, Peabody, MA.

Wright, C. J. H. (2004).   *Old Testament Ethics for the People of God.* Inter-Varsity Press, Leicester.

Wright, C. J. H. (2006).   *The Mission of God. Unlocking the Bible's Grand Narrative.* Inter-Varsity Press, Nottingham.

Zimmerli, W. (1983).   *Ezekiel 2 - A Commentary on the Book of the Prophet Ezekiel Chapters 25-48.* (Translated by James D. Martin). Fortress Press, Philadelphia, PA.

ABOUT THE AUTHOR

Craig Martin White has spent decades studying, researching and analysing the many Scriptures on the 1,000 year reign of the Messiah. To this end, he wrote a number of articles and Bible studies on the subject with the long-term goal of producing a comprehensive book – a sort of manual that can be used for research, study and in sermons. This book is the synthesis of those writings and more.

There have been many who have written on the subject, producing articles, booklets and books. These include many conservative scholars and commentators, Churches of God, Jehovah's Witnesses, Sunday Adventists and Christadelphians. Some Protestant scholars who hold similar views on His reign include: John Nelson Darby, John Walvoord, Charles Ryrie, Norman Geisler, Chuck Missler, Walter Martin, Rousas Rushdoony, Greg Bahnsen, Gary North, John Bright, Herman Ridderbos, George Beasley-Murray and Gregory Beale.

They understood much about the Millennium, but not necessarily all the details. In other aspects they have insights that we should take note of.

He has lived in several countries and travelled to a number of others, noting how they possess both positives and negatives. Some are in dreadful condition from corruption, oppressive regimes and poverty. While others enjoy relative peace, prosperity and reasonable governments.

All of these need replacing by the Messiah and for a new order to be ushered in under His rule.

He possesses qualifications in a number of areas: include a Bachelor of Arts, Graduate Diploma and Master of Arts from several universities in addition to numerous other studies including certificates and units in law, librarianship, computer studies, policy development, project management and financial markets.

He has a keen interest in Biblical studies and doctrines, prophecy, ancient Middle Eastern history, physical anthropology/human biology of human species, global politics and world trends in light of Bible prophecy.

Made in the USA
Columbia, SC
19 October 2024